THE SOCIAL WORLDS
OF NINETEENTH-CENTURY
CHAMBER MUSIC

The Social Worlds of Nineteenth-Century Chamber Music

Composers, Consumers, Communities

MARIE SUMNER LOTT

UNIVERSITY OF
ILLINOIS PRESS
Urbana, Chicago, and Springfield

Publication supported by the AMS 75 PAYS Endowment of the American Musicological Society, funded in part by the National Endowment for the Humanities and the Andrew W. Mellon Foundation

First Illinois paperback, 2018

1 2 3 4 5 C P 5 4 3 2 1
♾ This book is printed on acid-free paper.

Library of Congress Control Number: 2015938565
ISBN 978-0-252-03922-5 (hardcover)
ISBN 978-0-252-09727-0 (e-book)

ISBN 978-0-252-08384-6 (paperback)

CONTENTS

FIGURES AND TABLES

MUSICAL EXAMPLES

ACKNOWLEDGMENTS

This book and its author have benefited from the generosity of many scholars and professionals, including old friends, new friends, and kindly strangers. I would especially like to thank those who read some or all of the manuscript at its various stages (including as articles or proposals) and offered advice and encouragement. That list includes Martin Nedbal, Cindy L. Kim, Lara Housez, Cristina Fava, Jennifer Ronyak, Doug Shadle, Christina Bashford, Daniel Beller McKenna, Mark Evan Bonds, Carlo Caballero, David Gramit, Charles Youmans, and many others. The idea for this book began with my master's thesis, completed at the University of Northern Colorado under the guidance of Jonathan Bellman and Deborah Kauffman, and continued with my doctoral dissertation, advised by Ralph P. Locke at the Eastman School of Music. The present, expanded treatment of nineteenth-century chamber music and its audiences was made possible by research funding from the Pennsylvania State University, which provided travel support for archival research, and from Georgia State University, which provided for summer writing. I am grateful to my GSU colleague Curtis Bryant, who engraved the musical examples for chapter 4.

Laurie Matheson, editor in chief at the University of Illinois Press, has been patient and kind as she shepherded me through my first book-publishing experience. Her colleagues at the press have been a joy to work with, and I hope that I have not caused them more than the usual headaches associated with an author's first project. Dawn Durante and Marika Christofides helped me wrangle files, contracts, and other digital forms of paperwork. Mary M. Hill did a wonderful job with the copyediting. Dustin Hubbart's art team designed a beautiful cover.

I am also indebted to the libraries and archives that preserve documents and odd items for decades, just on the off chance that someone might want to see them one day. I thank the staff and librarians at the Sibley Music Library (especially Jim Farrington and Alice Carli, who spearheaded that institution's digitization project, enabling you, dear Reader, to access most of the obscure scores discussed in this book online) and the libraries of the Pennsylvania State University and the Georgia State University. Judith Picard, archivist at the Lienau-Schlesinger publishing house in Frankfurt am Main (Germany), provided guidance and access to rare business records and scores from the Schlesinger archive. Warmest thanks to her for helping me to understand the print records and to read the terrible handwriting they preserve. The Sächsisches Staatsarchiv in Leipzig (Germany) houses the other publisher's archives discussed in chapter 1; their staff was patient and accommodating in the summer of 2009, and they have graciously allowed the reproduction of images from the Peters and Hofmeister archives. For permission to reproduce paintings in the introduction, I would also like to thank the Bridgeman Images Group, Art Resource Group, and Superstock.

Portions of some chapters have been published in earlier versions. Some of the analysis in chapter 3 appeared as "Changing Audiences, Changing Styles: String Chamber Music and the Industrial Revolution" in *Instrumental Music and the Industrial Revolution* (Orpheus, 2010). Some of the discussion of Brahms's string quartets was published in "At the Intersection of Public and Private Musical Life: Brahms's op. 51 String Quartets" in the *Journal of the Royal Musical Association* (November 2012), though that article also discusses movements from these works that are not examined in this book. An earlier version of the discussion of Brahms's string sextets was published as "Domesticity in Brahms's String Sextets, Opp. 18 and 36" in *Brahms in the Home and the Concert Hall* (Cambridge University Press, 2014).

Finally, I extend thanks to several people who have shaped this book indirectly by giving me examples to live by and offering models of musicianship and scholarship. At every stage of my educational career I have been blessed with wonderful teachers. In addition to Ralph, Jonathan, and Debbie, I wish to acknowledge the profound gratitude I feel toward Marian Wilson Kimber, Wilbur Moreland, and Dana Ragsdale, all formerly of the University of Southern Mississippi.

THE SOCIAL WORLDS OF NINETEENTH-CENTURY CHAMBER MUSIC

INTRODUCTION

String Chamber Music and Its Audiences in the Nineteenth Century

On a chilly winter evening in Berlin, a group of men sits in a candle-lit room playing a string quartet. They are joined by a middle-aged woman dressed in black, who sits as close as possible to the ensemble in a comfortable upholstered armchair. She looks down and keeps her body still, leaning her cheek on her hand; she is mesmerized by the music she hears, giving it her full attention, perhaps closing her eyes to shut out distractions. The room is a large one with high ceilings, tastefully and expensively decorated with fine wallpaper, paintings, and draperies. Near the top of the walls, a series of marble busts have been installed, peering down at the room's inhabitants. At the edges of the room, tables and chairs have been placed at a respectful distance, and more onlookers and listeners sit there, also giving their full attention to the quartet.

Earlier in the day, in Frankfurt, a similar group of men gathered to play a string quartet. They, too, sat in a well-appointed room surrounded by fine fabrics, carpets, paintings, and bibelots. Their room was somewhat smaller, cozier even. At the center of the space a four-sided music stand—that particular piece of furniture that denotes that a true music lover lives here—stood at the ready with the parts opened. The four gentlemen, now seated in their places, looked to the violinist, who, with one quick motion, breathed in sharply and placed his bow on the string.

On the surface, these two scenes, common enough in the nineteenth century to be immediately recognizable from a variety of paintings, drawings, or descriptions in novels and stories, describe two iterations of the same type of occasion: a domestic performance of string chamber music in an upper-middle-class home. But upon further consideration, two very different events may be inferred from the visual cues described. In the larger room, the high-art and culture signifiers in the form of classically inspired busts and, most importantly, the presence of a select audience give the impression of a concert-like event in a private space. The image described is figure 0.1: Carl Johann Arnold's watercolor *Quartettabend bei Bettina von Arnim* from 1856, which depicts the violin virtuoso Joseph Joachim and his quartet playing at the home of Arnim (née Brentano), the respected Romantic poet and author. It exemplifies the sort of "semiprivate" performance that was common in the nineteenth century, a holdover from the previous century, when aristocrats like Arnim would hire or invite professional musicians to perform for their friends and families. In the later era, these semiprivate events served multiple purposes, including as rehearsal trials for public performances and opportunities

FIGURE 0.1 Carl Johann Arnold, *Quartettabend bei Bettina von Arnim* (1856). Bildarchiv Preussischer Kulturbesitz, Berlin / Frankfurter Goethe-Museum with Goethe-Haus, Freies deutsches Hochstift, Frankfurt am Main, Germany / Lutz Braun / Art Resource, New York.

to cultivate connections to patrons and supporters of the arts and their institutions. In many ways, this sort of semiprivate event mirrors modern fund-raisers and by-invitation performances for patrons of the arts and educational institutions. Like its modern counterpart, the event was intended to be publicized for the benefit of both the attendees, whose social status would be elevated by their increased cultural capital, and the professional musicians (and the composers whose work they played), who would likewise gain status and publicity.

The second scene, however, bears fewer resemblances to modern practice, as it depicts what I will describe as a truly private event—one that took place regularly without listeners or attendees and that may or may not have been publicly acknowledged. I have described here the scene painted by British artist Mary Ellen Best (1809–91), who married a schoolteacher and made her home in Frankfurt beginning around 1840 (see figure 0.2). In the painting *Anthony Playing String Quartets with Friends* (1842–45), Best shows her husband in what must have been a common scene in their home.[1] Several later portraits depict family scenes in which a violin or violin case is always nearby, as though casually put down and picked up again throughout the day. (Because Best brought a fairly large dowry to the marriage, Anthony gave up his teaching job and became a man of leisure.) This image represents a more common practice in the nineteenth century but one that has nearly evaporated at the beginning of the twenty-first century. In the Romantic era, accomplished amateurs, or performers and musicians with significant training who for various reasons pursued music as an avocation or

FIGURE 0.2 Mary Ellen Best, *Anthony Playing String Quartets with Friends* (1842–45). Private collection / Bridgeman Images.

hobby rather than as a profession, supported a rich and diverse ecosystem of musical activity. They attended concerts, performed in casual recreational capacities, participated in more organized groups such as community choirs and orchestras, and apparently bought sheet music in astounding quantities, as we shall see.

Music played an important role in the social life of the nineteenth century, and music in the home provided a particularly convenient way to entertain and communicate among friends and colleagues. String chamber music, especially, fostered a variety of social interactions that helped to build communities within communities. The basic question at the heart of this study is: What music was available to musical consumers in the nineteenth century, and what does that music tell us about their musical tastes, priorities, and activities? In the course of studying surviving examples from the period by both well-known and virtually unknown composers and comparing those works with available information about the distribution of sheet music and performances, several distinctive subgenres of string chamber music emerge, and they seem intimately connected to particular social uses of music. Thus, an examination of the compositional aspect of music production—the choices made by composers and arrangers—leads to a more nuanced understanding of the social aspects of music consumption, and vice versa.

Why Music for Strings?

String chamber music has long been neglected in studies of the Romantic era, which have tended to focus on the piano and the orchestra, in part because these fields feature innovative works by the most familiar and revered composers of the age. The heroes of nineteenth-century compositional history wrote relatively few string chamber works, and these do not in the main offer up radical innovations or create new genres. They do not appear at first glance to represent a lively area of ongoing activity. For instance, if we combine the string quartet outputs of the canonic figures associated with Romantic instrumental music—Schumann, Mendelssohn, Brahms, and Dvořák—we can count only twenty-six works over a seventy-year period, and more than half of those (fourteen quartets) are by Dvořák alone. Thus it would seem that string chamber music production died out after the 1820s, notably after the deaths of Beethoven and Schubert, who had both been prolific string quartet composers. Carl Dahlhaus noted and dismissed this lacuna in his *Nineteenth-Century Music* in 1989: "Not until the modern music of our century was the history of the string quartet, *which virtually seeped away in the nineteenth century*, resumed in representative bodies of works by Schoenberg, Bartók, and Hindemith. . . . Thus, we have little cause to speak of a continuous history of the string quartet after Beethoven and under his influence."[2]

The present study, however, is not concerned primarily with creating a single continuous history of chamber music after Beethoven. Certainly Beethoven's influence on the chamber music of some later composers is significant, but this is merely one of many threads worthy of exploration. Without a clear understanding of the other options available to composers and performers of string quartets, any connections we discern between later composers' works and Beethoven's seem almost perfunctory, rather than meaningful and communicative. Rather, I shall focus on the relationship between the large and varied body of string chamber works published in the nineteenth century and the communities they served.[3] These communities differed in significant ways from those that chamber music with piano addressed, and the composers of these works faced different sorts of challenges and enjoyed different sorts of opportunities. Naturally, there is some overlap between music lovers who performed string quartets or quintets and those who participated in piano trios, quartets, and quintets, but I intend to show that when a composer or a publisher created a string chamber work for the marketplace, he (nearly always he) addressed a social setting and group of participants different from those he imagined when writing a piano trio or a wind quintet.

In the received standard history of the nineteenth century, the piano and its proponents provide the neat framework for a narrative of musical developments centered on technological progress and compositional innovation. The most acclaimed composers of the first Romantic generation—Robert Schumann, Felix Mendelssohn, Frederick Chopin, and Franz Liszt—began their careers as virtuoso pianists, creating new genres and musical styles that partook of the technical and expressive advantages of the developing instrument in the 1820s and 1830s. These composers moved to other musical pursuits in subsequent decades, including composing and conducting symphonies and large choral works; creating new genres such as the tone poem; and promoting the work of other composers, such as Mendelssohn's "Bach revival" and Liszt's advocacy for Wagner's music dramas. The standard narrative splits at this point in history. The history of compositional developments follows the Romantic generation into the public arena, while the history of musical life becomes concerned with the piano's role in everyday music making, especially with the musical activities of women in the home.[4]

Chamber music for strings resists easy incorporation into this dominant narrative for two reasons. First, chamber music's association with musical conservativism and orthodoxy has colored its reception since at least the 1840s. Already in the mid-nineteenth century, composer and critic Robert Schumann detected a stagnation in the string quartet style of his day, fearing that if innovation did not arrive soon, the genre would wither and die.[5] One reason for string music's apparent orthodoxy lies in the fact that stringed instruments themselves experienced only subtle organological changes in the nineteenth century in comparison to the piano or to wind instruments, which radically changed the timbre of the orchestra in symphonic and operatic works. The instruments of the violin family achieved a nearly perfected state of design in the mid- to late eighteenth century, with only slight modifications after the 1790s. Although performers such as Niccolò Paganini created new playing techniques and opened new avenues of expression, few composers responded to these developments with new genres, and the vehicles for string-instrument virtuosity remained the familiar variation set, sonata, and concerto. The stability or stasis of stringed-instrument design and manufacture is reflected in compositional styles and generic conventions that did not stray far from their Classical origins until the last decades of the nineteenth century.

Observations that string chamber music remained essentially conservative in its treatment of genre, form, harmony, and the like, however, also betray modern historiography's obsession with innovation. In creating a history focused solely on radical changes by a few composers, we risk ignoring the elements of nineteenth-century musical life that made the period distinctive in favor of creating a linear narrative of progress that ends in the present day. Lost in the process is the original context and meaning of the few works that remain after historical "pruning." We regain some of that context and uncover new layers of meaning by focusing instead on the music and musical activities that shaped everyday life for professional and amateur musicians, sometimes highlighting compositional breakthroughs that address particular social uses of chamber music, sometimes exploring the qualities of seemingly "trivial" or conservative works that engaged listeners and performers from a variety of backgrounds throughout the century.

Second, inasmuch as it is possible to construct a linear history of chamber music in the nineteenth century, that history actually reverses the historiography of piano music described above. In other words, the first half of the century saw a flowering of social uses for chamber music that had not existed before or were less common in earlier decades (including performance of transcriptions and arrangements of larger works, such as those explored in chapter 2), and the major innovations in musical style and new genres of chamber music appeared later in the century. Although the instruments and genres of string chamber music did not change much after the 1790s, their roles in musical life expanded rapidly around the turn of the century and in its first three decades, encompassing a larger percentage of the public. Composers made subtle adjustments to musical style within those conventional genres to suit the tastes and social situations in which chamber music played an integral part. A more nuanced understanding of chamber music's dissemination in print and its use in social settings throughout the period leads to a new image of the musical consumer and listener of the later nineteenth century.

In writing about musical consumers and their use of chamber music, it is important to note what we can and cannot know and what we must infer from a variety of incomplete, sometimes contradictory, sources. Unlike public concerts and theater performances, private gatherings of musical friends did not usually produce a paper trail of tickets, subscription lists, programs, advertisements, or concert reviews for modern-day historians to follow.[6] Thus, the participants in these gatherings have remained "invisible" to modern researchers, hidden from posterity despite the powerful effect they had on musical life and thereby on the more public forms of music making that flourished in the second half of the century. The producers and consumers of chamber music did leave some traces of their activities, however, in the form of published sheet music and business records, which are explored in detail in chapter 1, as well as diaries, letters, autobiographical anecdotes, and public musings on chamber music in journals and newspaper reports.

Despite the challenges it poses to the modern scholar, the privacy of chamber music performance actually is one of the reasons that a clearer understanding of it is so vital to nineteenth-century studies at large. The chamber genres provide a unique opportunity to examine the music and ideas that the middle classes chose to bring into their homes, the prized "private" space that played a much more important role in self-expression during the nineteenth century than in previous eras. Furthermore, because chamber music—especially string chamber music—engaged multiple players in a conversational style or styles, it encouraged interaction within and outside the familial unit. Unlike solo piano music or song, both of which privilege a single performer as the star, chamber music such as string quartets and quintets allowed consumers to come together in leisurely pursuits that spoke to their shared interests. The various styles explored by composers for distinct audiences are differentiated first and foremost by the nature of the relationships between parts in the ensemble. For this reason, I have chosen to focus on works for three to eight players in the present study, eschewing duos and sonatas and favoring the string quartet and related genres (quintets, occasionally sextets) in order to get to the heart of social music making. In some instances, works with piano are brought into the discussion as a useful point of comparison, but the focus here is on string music and what it tells us about musical life in the nineteenth century.

Throughout the book, I have drawn upon the evidence of actual communities where possible, such as documented meetings of performers who gathered for weekly or occasional quartet parties. These are most common when dealing with the activities of professional musicians who played chamber music in casual get-togethers at home or while traveling in addition to performances they might give as part of their professional obligations. Such accounts of recreational music making frequently describe a mixture of professional and amateur players and of upper-class and middle-class musicians. Although many of the gatherings described involve professional musicians (i.e., men who made their living through paid musical activities, including performance, teaching, and composition), they demonstrate the importance of amateur music lovers to the sustained development of music and musical life. They also confirm that string chamber music was largely a male-exclusive activity. For example, chamber music parties hosted by composer and cellist George Onslow (1784–1853), based in Paris during the social season and at his country estate just outside the metropolis during the summer, included professional and amateur players, generally men. Onslow represents members of the wealthy upper middle class who frequently mixed with the minor aristocracy and with more obviously "middling" professionals such as violinist Pierre Baillot and bassist Domenico Dragonetti, who visited the Onslow estate for chamber music evenings. Onslow's English father had immigrated to France in 1781 and married a wealthy French woman, thereby gaining a life of leisure and wealth through her dowry. George Onslow inherited their estate, which allowed him to pursue music as an avocation, though he did publish with French and German firms, and his works were performed in public concerts and in private gatherings. Similarly, but at a lower socioeconomic level, Prague composer and violinist Václav Veit (1806–64) held a professional position as president judge in the city's judicial system, but he published several popular string quartets and quintets that reflect his own after-hours musical recreations, as we shall see in chapter 1.

Louis Spohr's, Felix Mendelssohn's, and Robert Schumann's chamber music evenings feature in their correspondence and memoirs, and these evenings served different purposes depending on the image each composer sought to project. In Spohr's case, the account in his autobiography (discussed in detail in chapter 3) emphasizes the cozy country house that he purchased outside Kassel and the music room he remodeled there; he and a few "friends of music" gathered to play quartets and enjoy "a frugal supper." His emphasis on the intimacy of the gathering, the inclusion of families, and the informality of the event reinforces the image of a bourgeois or middle-class lifestyle that Spohr promotes throughout his book. On the other hand, Schumann's descriptions of his gatherings (discussed in chapter 4), descriptions that were published in the *Neue Zeitschrift für Musik* as a series of music reviews, emphasize the restriction of their quartet parties to similarly progressive or radical male musicians for the purpose of exploring the current state of the genre. In Mendelssohn's case, correspondence about quartets and quartet playing in his early years emphasizes his fascination with Beethoven's late quartets and his interest in following the revered master's example in his own works (most notably in his first two quartets, opp. 12 and 13). Later references involve more clearly casual or recreational performances with visiting musicians at home and on his travels in Italy and elsewhere. The change in focus evident in his performance activities is similarly reflected in his published works, such as the sometimes maligned op. 44 quartets, with their "Classical" or conservative orientation.

Throughout much of this book, analysis of the music that survives and critical responses to it allows modern scholars to infer the type of audience for whom it might be intended, based on evidence of activities that appear to have been widespread, if underdocumented, such as in proposing the sorts of music that Anthony Best and his friends might have played. Where evidence of specific gatherings is available and where it is not, the work of Benedict Anderson offers a new way to consider the importance of print in developing a network of musicians from a variety of backgrounds throughout much of central Europe and Britain and the different ways in which these intertwined communities used chamber music to solidify their individual and group identities. He coined the term *imagined community* to describe a network of dispersed individuals who connect to each other through a variety of media without necessarily meeting in person.[7] We might call them virtual communities or social networks in recognition of the similarity of this concept to modern-day practices, in which readers and consumers connect to like-minded colleagues, friends, and even celebrities whom they might never or rarely meet face-to-face. In the nineteenth century, those virtual communities included not just nations and nation-states, the focus of Anderson's work, but also social classes, schools of artistic thought and philosophy, and political parties that transcended national and regional identities. Derek Scott's book *Sounds of the Metropolis* emphasizes that many characteristic features of nineteenth-century popular music allowed it to be "exported" successfully to metropolitan and urban centers throughout Europe and North America in part because the urban experience of life in Paris, London, Vienna, and New York, for instance, was very similar.[8] Despite regional and national differences, the middle-class or working-class musical consumer based in one of these cities would naturally have shared much in common with his or her counterpart in any of the other cities, and therefore each participated in a virtual or imagined community of city dwellers. The same is true of genres that we label "art music" today, including instrumental chamber music. Far from merely producing and purchasing a consumable product, middle-class musicians used their leisure time to participate in the musical public sphere through their private activities—including the composition, performance, and publication of chamber music—much as they participated in the public sphere of ideas through reading, writing, and conversation.[9]

The Middle Class Defined

The communities of musicians studied or proposed in this book share a variety of characteristics despite the differences in taste, experience, or goals that their musical activities sometimes addressed. All of the works considered here appear to address members of the middle classes, who made up the larger proportion of musical consumers and producers in this period. Professional composers, performers, conductors, and music teachers of this era mostly came from some segment of the middle classes or rose to that social status as adults. Likewise, the music that they produced was primarily directed at middle-class (or upper-middle-class) consumers with the resources to purchase sheet music, take music lessons and buy instruments, perform in various capacities, and attend concerts. Thus, it behooves us to consider just whom or what we mean when we say "middle class(es)" and how they did and did not differ from the aristocratic patrons who facilitated musical life in earlier eras.[10]

Professional affiliations provide one useful way to circumscribe the middle classes in the nineteenth century. In the wake of the Enlightenment's ideological reforms and the gradual spread of the Industrial Revolution, individual and group identities became more closely connected to professional identities, and economic or working concerns increasingly colored other cultural values. For the purposes of this study, the term *middle class* denotes families or individuals without hereditary aristocratic titles who earned their livings through intellectual or creative endeavors rather than through physical labor. This group includes the upper echelon of the middle classes, the bourgeoisie, who, in their leisure pursuits and everyday lives, did not differ very much from their aristocratic neighbors; in fact, the bourgeoisie frequently interacted with titled nobility in the first half of the century in some locales and came to replace them as a ruling class despised by lower-class activists in the later decades of the period. This group frequently owned or rented large homes and properties, where they might host musical gatherings of various kinds. One example would be the factory owner or landowner who might maintain a townhome in the city where much of his business was done, such as Birmingham or Leipzig or Marseilles, and a "country home" in a suburban community nearby.

At the other end of the middle-class spectrum lie those individuals and families whom we might separate from the working class by profession but who did not fully "belong" to the well-heeled middle classes in other ways. For instance, though schoolteachers in most of central Europe certainly earned a living through their intellect and did not, for the most part, labor with their own hands, this profession did not pay well enough or provide one with enough cultural cachet to partake of all the benefits of middle-class life. School teaching served as a common "gateway profession" between working-class and middle-class status. The son of a shopkeeper or laborer might be sent to school and educated in hopes of raising the family fortunes, and within two or three generations, that family's descendants might rise from laborer or servant to governess or schoolteacher to civil servant or bureaucrat. Between the landed bourgeoisie and schoolteachers, the core of the nineteenth-century middle classes includes Europe's wealthy merchants and entrepreneurs, civil servants, university professors, bankers, factory and office managers, doctors, and lawyers.[11] These professions required and rewarded education, rational thinking, emotional control, and hard work—traits that became the guiding values of middle-class culture in the nineteenth century throughout most of the Western world and its spheres of influence and that characterize chamber music connoisseurship.

The European middle class established itself first and most firmly in urban and suburban environments that supported the economic and working conditions of their professions and provided cultural outlets for entertainment and civic engagement. Not coincidentally, these metropolitan centers also fostered the institutions of the growing music industry from the mid- to late eighteenth century throughout the twentieth century. Cities such as London, Vienna, Paris, and New York were the first places to maintain major publishing houses, opera companies and music theaters, conservatories and professional music schools, professional ensembles, and public concert series. Small towns and agricultural areas did not support the associations and clubs or the social outings and cultural events—including music industry—that made up the bulk of middle-class leisure pursuits. They also could not support multiple manufacturing facilities, universities, government offices, and retail and banking centers that employed middle-class and bourgeois men. Whether in the great metropolises of London, Paris, Berlin, and Vienna or in smaller cities such as Lyon, Marseille, Leipzig, Dresden, Birmingham, and Edinburgh, middle-class life revolved around sociability, active participation in public and private affairs, and commerce.

The rise of the middle classes and a distinctive middle-class culture cannot be separated from the rise and fall of political and philosophical liberalism in Europe in the late eighteenth and early nineteenth centuries.[12] Middle-class individuals sometimes defined themselves in opposition to the aristocrats who governed them, creating a culture that stressed "the principles of achievement and education, work and self-reliance" to support "the emerging vision of a modern, secularized, postcorporate, self-regulating, enlightened 'civil society.'"[13] But those middle-class individuals also frequently sought to emulate those same aristocrats, especially in cultural life outside of any political activity in which they might engage. In the earlier decades of the nineteenth century, members of what German scholars call the *Bildungsbürgertum*, or the "cultivated bourgeoisie," to use David Gramit's term, often interacted with the aristocracy in social gatherings.[14] When the populations of the working class and the poor increased toward the midcentury both in the countryside and in urban centers as peasants moved from the land into factory work, members of the upper middle class came under criticism for their role in what some critics saw as the hoarding of wealth and the abuse of power.[15] After the revolutions of 1848, constitutional monarchies and empires took or maintained control of central Europe, partly by establishing a compromise with the middle classes. The establishment of unified, nationalist-leaning governments created a wide swath of bureaucratic appointments and opportunities for upward expansion, placing members of the upper middle class in positions of power without displacing monarchs and dignitaries, who retained ultimate control of their states. The expansion of empires across eastern Europe, Africa, and Asia meant more government offices and oversight, creating more administrative positions and jobs for educated white male members of the middle classes—and opening social and cultural opportunities to the servants and women who depended on them. Middle-class culture flourished in the second half of the century throughout Europe, espousing the ideals of education, self-reliance, and self-regulation at the same time that many of its members worked to control and "civilize" the peoples of the rest of the world under colonial rule.

These cultural and political concerns influenced the production, consumption, and reception of music in the nineteenth century in a variety of ways. The association of some musical styles and genres with a privileged lifestyle, for instance, has an important bearing on chamber music in this period. Around the turn of the nineteenth century, chamber music allowed members of the middle classes throughout Europe to engage in musical activities previously accessible only to the aristocracy or to the very wealthy. Through arrangements and cheaper publications, those of more modest means could experience the latest trends in musical fashion and, at the same time, become acquainted with the most respected works from music's recent past (such as the quartets of Haydn and Mozart). On the other hand, such musical activities were only accessible to members of the middle classes who had the time and resources to pursue them, not to the working class (such as household servants, laborers in various industries, factory workers, clerks, etc.), who worked longer and harder for lower pay. The exclusivity of chamber music and its inappropriateness for the concert hall (or for the larger halls that encouraged lower ticket prices) led some commentators later in the century to associate it with the oppression of the lower class by those with political and cultural power.

In the earlier stages of the middle class's emergence, two main cultural features distinguished it from the lower class (allying the middle class with the upper class) and made its members recognizable to each other: education and leisure. Education defined as cultural literacy—a familiarity with art, music, and literature—formed the foundation of "respectable" society in the late eighteenth and early nineteenth centuries and continues to influence cosmopolitan culture in the twenty-first century. A thorough background in what we now term the liberal arts or humanities was favored by the middle classes because it supported their goals of public engagement and employment in the intellectual arena. It served the double purpose of fostering academic and moral development on a personal level and providing the knowledge and skills necessary in business at the professional level. A common educational background also smoothed social interactions between casual acquaintances. Classical references or the discussion of important or new artworks and inventions featured prominently in conversations and correspondence. This emphasis on education also contributed to the canonization of certain texts and artworks as the most significant and representative examples of genres, styles, and artists. The canon of works that continues to dominate modern conceptions of sophistication in cultural life (in music, painting, literature, and architecture) jelled in the nineteenth century in response to the variety of influences and interests that guided middle-class life at that time. Members of the middle classes frequently gathered for music making with new friends and acquaintances both at home and abroad or in the countryside. The ability to contribute to a musical evening or to converse about music intelligently was, like dancing, a required social skill.

This educational paradigm supported the professional aspirations of the middle classes, but it also highlights the other main signifier of their status, which is the availability of time and resources to pursue leisure activities. A classical education separate from specific technical or vocational training included philosophy, literature, painting and art appreciation, musical tutelage including some composition, mathematics, architecture, and science—largely "impractical" areas of inquiry. It allowed members of the upper middle class to demonstrate their worldly detachment from the stuff of everyday necessity. Education and educational pursuits—including, for the young man whose family could afford it, the Grand Tour—represented a necessary luxury of the leisured class, which flaunted its achievements through participating in clubs and scientific associations, attending and participating in performances, and collecting artifacts and artworks.[16] Middle-class culture outwardly scorned ostentatious spending and the accumulation of wealth for its own sake, but educational and self-improvement pursuits, including music, provided an acceptable means to demonstrate status.

The outward separation of work and leisure resulted in a new emphasis on domesticity and domestic life centered on the nuclear family, with clearly defined roles for men, women, and children.[17] Organization of life into public and private worlds emerged when the economic and educational or civil professions became profitable enough to free certain individuals and their families from creating the materials of survival such as growing, preparing, and preserving food; building, cleaning, and maintaining the home; and spinning thread, weaving cloth, and sewing clothes. Members of the middle classes purchased these goods and services from retailers and servants, leaving those who had done these tasks in the past to supervise from a social and literal distance. This development has often been portrayed as affecting mainly women, whose "accomplishments" (arts and crafts, music) filled otherwise idle hours, facilitated courtship and sociability, and improved marriage prospects. But men, whose work usually only required them to be in or near the office during the daytime hours—often between 9:00 and 6:00, with several breaks for meals, walks, coffee, reading, and other leisure activities—also found themselves in need of occupation at home, where little or no work awaited them at the end of the day.

Masculine Leisure in the Private Sphere

The late eighteenth and nineteenth centuries witnessed a "separation of spheres" into a gender-coded binary system of public life involving active male participants in government and commerce, and private life built by and around the female observers and beneficiaries who provided a sanctuary for publicly active men.[18] This model, however, fails to consider the role and venue of masculine leisure activities in this period. Increasingly throughout the century, men required opportunities to gather outside work without attracting pressure from the authorities, especially during periods when censorship restricted men's ability to gather in public due to the perceived potential for political uprisings. During these times—for instance, during the July Monarchy in France (1830–48), in Biedermeier Vienna (1815–48), and in the contemporaneous "Vormärz" period in Prussia—men's associations and clubs were monitored by the local authorities, and impromptu political and philosophical discussions in coffeehouses or other public venues were discouraged when not banned outright. During these decades, domestic music making and other activities primarily engaged the nuclear family because larger gatherings of more diverse groups aroused suspicions from the police. As scholar Carol Harrison has shown with particular reference to the French citizens of smaller cities like Besançon and Mulhouse, middle-class and upper-middle-class men of nineteenth-century Europe needed spaces in which they could socialize together without compromising their social standing. With the emphasis on leisure as a sign of status and independence, men required recreational activities that filled a variety of "requirements," including sociability, self-improvement, learning, and masculinity. Such pursuits could not be satisfactorily developed at home, in the smallish spaces of middle-class townhouses, which in accordance with middle-class values of modesty and self-control could not be grandiose. These pursuits also required distance from the feminine and feminizing domestic environment. Thus, middle-class men formed associations and clubs (*cercles*) for entertainment and leisure in semiprivate, semipublic settings, such as the private salons and upper rooms of taverns and restaurants, the rented spaces of civic buildings, and the specially built lodges and headquarters for leisure associations. This tradition of the male club had been an important aspect of cultural life for the leisured classes in the eighteenth century, and it expanded in the nineteenth century. In German-speaking realms, the need for class segregation and semiprivate male sociability resulted in an increase in Masonic and other lodge cultures and "secret societies."[19] In the upper middle class's larger homes or country estates, separate rooms and suites accommodated men and their activities so that they, too, could achieve this distance. In the musical world, this sort of activity is best represented by the proliferation of associations for music, including both the Gewandhaus orchestra and concert hall in Leipzig and the Gesellschaft der Musikfreunde in Vienna. Both institutions began with the support of amateur music lovers from the wealthy middle classes in the late eighteenth century and gradually moved toward professionalism after the mid-nineteenth century.[20]

Particularly in relation to domestic musical activities, private music making has tended to remain associated with women performing in their own homes, especially with women playing keyboard instruments and singing. Countless manuals and journal articles from the nineteenth century outline the specific duties of the domestic woman regarding music, dictating that she should play music to soothe her husband and family, to entertain guests, and to teach her children the art. Men's participation in domestic music has usually been portrayed in fiction and in scholarship as a part of courtship, with four-hand piano music providing an especially convenient way for the sexes to interact in a chaperoned environment. When men performed music in their own leisure time outside the structure of courtship, though, they generally eschewed the keyboard, favoring instead those instruments that were taboo to women for much of the period, the string and wind instruments. Thus, chamber music for strings provided the leisurely outlet that middle-class men needed, allowing them to engage in nonprofessional activities that were at the same time associated with learning and accomplishment (and, increasingly, with a growing nationalist pride in Austro-Germany).

Anecdotal evidence of string chamber music performance indicates that it remained a clearly male-dominated activity through the nineteenth century until at least the 1870s, possibly as late as the 1890s. Despite a few noteworthy exceptions, women musicians typically participated in chamber performances as pianists, as singers, or as listeners.[21] Christina Bashford, using evidence from diary entries, memoirs, published advertisements, journal articles, and domestic fiction, has demonstrated that the overwhelming majority of amateur string chamber music performances in nineteenth-century Britain involved only men. Bashford points out that music making was portrayed or understood in eighteenth-century and Victorian England as an effeminizing endeavor, in contrast to the more obviously virile male pursuits (hunting and riding, sports such as rugby and rowing, etc.). Thus, upper-class and middle-class men in Britain frequently downplayed their chamber music pursuits in their public representations of themselves (i.e., in letters and memoirs that would be read by later generations) while continuing to play music in private and semiprivate scenarios.[22] Richard Leppert's landmark study of music and imagery in England also notes that portraits of English gentlemen feature stringed instruments more often than others (though, oddly, never in performances of string quartets or other chamber genres) and that these portraits often provide other visual clues to contradict the possible feminizing effect of music, such as ceremonial swords, military uniforms or other insignia, and paintings in the portrait's setting of horses and the hunt.[23]

Throughout Europe, male musicians worked to ensure that their activities were understood as cerebral and worth male attention and constructed their activities as distinctive from female musicking, helping to create (or exacerbate) the division between serious chamber music and trivial salon or parlor music.[24] Harrison notes the same tendency in France: "The music of a gentlemen's association could not have been confused with feminine, domestic performance. Most societies of the first half of the century stressed instrumental music. . . . Musical associations generally disdained simple piano accompaniment: they aspired to performing symphonic or opera scores."[25] Notably, anxiety about music's possible effeminizing effect is less apparent in the Austro-German and eastern European regions, where music was a natural part of the education of boys and young men. University life often included casual and organized musical performances, where students were encouraged to play instruments and sing together, as well as to attend concerts and performances of music in domestic and public spaces.[26] For the upper-class and middle-class men of central Europe, at least, this engagement with music in their formative years continued as they matured and took on leading roles in industry, politics, and culture as adults.

Iconography of the late eighteenth and nineteenth centuries corroborates the notion that middle-class and upper-middle-class men were especially associated with string chamber music, or vice versa. I have already described what is perhaps the most famous image of string chamber music in action from this period (Carl Johann Arnold's *Quartettabend bei Bettina von Arnim*, from 1856). A similar portrayal of the Saint Petersburg composer and violinist Alexei Lvov (1799–1870), who also composed the Russian imperial anthem adopted in 1833, depicts the male quartet seated around a table in a small residential room with three visible listeners (see figure 0.3). Lvov, a military officer and later aide-de-camp to Tsar Nicholas I, provides another example of the porous boundaries inherent in the study of middle-class musical life and of chamber music in the nineteenth century. His father was a professional musician, and Lvov had lessons in violin and composition from an early age, but he attended the Institute of Communications as a young man and pursued a career as a civil engineer while also sometimes performing on international tours with his string quartet. Lvov hosted private concerts at his home in Saint Petersburg that featured visiting artists and his own performances. Although he enjoyed an elevated status in Russian social and political life, Lvov belongs to the broadly defined "upper middle class" rather than the aristocracy because of the nature of his professional life outside of music, and an important aspect of his day-to-day experience was the recreational and semiprofessional performance of string chamber music.

Nancy November has explored string quartet iconography and the insights it can give us about nineteenth-century listening practices, especially regarding the dominant forms of "serious" music and listening practices.[27] She suggests that French and German musicians present two very different modes of listening and promote somewhat opposing roles for the quartet in musical culture. The French appear more concerned with individual performances and the effect made on the listener by the visual, theatrical display of the players, while the Germans seem more interested from an early stage in propagating a distinctly intellectual, "deep listening" approach based on "the work itself." As November notes, the German approach has become pervasive in modern assessments of chamber music and its composers, rendering alternative listening and performing practices—and the compositional styles associated with them—to be dubbed lesser by comparison, beginning, perhaps, with the most famous account of male quartet playing from the nineteenth century, by Richard Wagner.

FIGURE 0.3 Paul Rohrbach, *Alexei Lvov's String Quartet* (1817–after 1862). Fine Art Images / SuperStock.

Though not associated with the composition or performance of chamber music himself, Wagner made a singularly influential contribution to the male encoding of string chamber music in the nineteenth century. The opera composer's well-known indictment of French musical understanding, "On German Music," published in the Parisian *Gazette musicale* in 1840, featured an imagined or idealized domestic performance of string quartets as its centerpiece. This passage is often quoted as an example of the ideal German domestic scene occurring in every household on the other side of the Rhine, and it probably does describe a common family ritual in Germany and elsewhere at the time. In the context of Wagner's morality tale, though, it serves a very different purpose, focusing on capable amateur *composers* rather than performers. The passage in question follows a lengthy description of "the lot of hundreds" of underappreciated musicians in Germany, who die unknown with their talent unacknowledged by the public. This being the case, Wagner claims, thousands of capable musicians did not bother to take on such a burden of professionalism.

> They rather choose a handicraft to earn their living, and give themselves with all the greater zest to music in their leisure hours; to refresh themselves, grow nobler by it, but not to shine. And do you suppose they make nothing but handicraft-music? No, no! Go and listen one winter-night in that little cabin:

> there sit a father and his three sons, at a small round table; two play the violin, a third the viola, the father the 'cello. What you hear so lovingly and deeply played, is a quartet composed by that little man who is beating time. But he is the schoolmaster from the neighboring hamlet, and the quartet he has composed is a lovely work of art and feeling.—Again I say, go to that spot, and hear that author's music played, and you will be dissolved to tears; for it will search your heart, and you will know what German Music is, will feel what is the German spirit.[28]

Note that this passage does not focus on the performance of the work, though it is "lovingly and deeply played," but on the fact that the quartet was composed by the local schoolmaster and that his amateur creation is "a lovely work of art and feeling" rather than mere "handicraft-music." In this and later passages, Wagner portrays the true German spirit embodied in middle-class cultural values: modest, devout (though, for Wagner, devotion belongs to Music rather than any other deity), law-abiding and eager to please, learned and engaged in an intellectual pastime. The genre that best exemplified these qualities for Wagner and, perhaps, for his readers in France and elsewhere was the string quartet.

Chamber Music at the Intersection of Public and Private Life

As suggested in the previous sections, chamber music existed at the intersection of professional and amateur performance and of serious and recreational music making. This was part of its appeal to various consumers and producers in this era, but it complicates the convenient binaries used by modern scholars to understand the Romantic era. Perhaps the most vexing of those is the notion of a clearly delineated private and public life. The gendered "separation of spheres" into a feminine private or domestic space and the inherently masculine public space has been critiqued in a variety of disciplines in the past ten years or more, but it remains stubbornly pervasive in music history because of the specialized circumstances that live music performance creates. Music scholars have tended to rely solely on the venues for performance to characterize music and musical activities as "public" and "private."[29] But as I've already suggested, opportunities for masculine leisure (and thus for string chamber music) tended to include events in what I will call "semiprivate" and "semipublic" spaces. These include recreational playing outside of the home but in a highly regulated space, such as an exclusive club or fraternity or a rented space. Frequently, house parties or house concerts and gatherings of friends and colleagues to play or hear chamber music fall into the semiprivate category because they involve listeners other than the performers and required an invitation. As opposed to truly private performances, intended for the pleasure of the performers alone, these semiprivate events might also take place as practice runs for an upcoming performance or tryouts of a new work, in addition to performances "merely" for entertainment.

Thus, semiprivate events, as described in this study, include performances where a few listeners are invited, but tickets and press coverage are not involved. In other instances, a "concert" or a "reading" at the home of a well-to-do patron (aristocratic or upper middle class) would attract more listeners, and it might even be written about in the local press, with some indication of the program. Although these events were not "public" in terms of open access to all, they also were not "private," as they formed an important part of the public presentation of music and had a strong effect on the public images of the participants. Thus, I refer to them here as "semipublic." We might also place subscription concerts in this category, as events that required tickets and were publicly known but highly exclusive and inaccessible to those without a significant connection to the organizers or performers. Finally, when the word "domestic" comes into play in this study, it will mean primarily music happening in the home of at least one of the participants—in a private context, usually without listeners.

The "public sphere," though, also embraces a variety of activities beyond public concert hall attendance. It includes not just the visible activities that middle-class participants created en masse but also the public dissemination of ideas, especially via print media. The explosion of print during the late eighteenth and early nineteenth centuries allowed the formation of public life in ways that have been both celebrated and decried. The "reading mania" that hit Europe's middle-class consumers at this time has been lauded as a sign of increased literacy and engagement in some quarters at the same time that the novel was then (and is now) described as a trivial genre, filled with trite moral messages and allegories of conformity. Print media, in the form of journals and newspapers, broadsides, pamphlets, books, and other reading materials, created the public forum in which ideas could be shared and debated over a growing geographical sweep.[30]

In the musical world, printed music and printed reviews in journals and newspaper feuilletons served the same purpose, allowing composers and performers (both amateur and professional) to share ideas and to communicate in an open public forum from their posts throughout Europe.[31] Publishers of music, like their counterparts in the book trade, recognized that the public sphere included a variety of individuals with disparate but overlapping needs and tastes. The music they produced reflects those tastes in the choice and treatment of genres, as evidenced by the "easy" or "light" piano trios and violin duos that proliferated in this period. More subtle manipulations of musical style within genres likewise demonstrates attention to the needs of consumers; performer- and casual listener–friendly quartets and quintets feature repetition and predictable harmonic patterns, for instance, whereas composer- or critic-oriented quartets flirt with the boundaries of musical convention. The chapters that follow demonstrate several examples of these different subgenres within the world of string chamber music.

The circulation of printed materials was particularly important for the development of chamber music because newly composed chamber works were rarely performed in public venues. String quartets and other chamber genres did occasionally appear on public concert programs beginning early in the nineteenth century, but orchestral and solo virtuoso works made up the bulk of the public concert repertoire. Concert series devoted to the performance of chamber music in Paris have been chronicled by Joël-Marie Fauquet, Jeffrey Cooper, and others, and chamber concerts began to make a foothold in the middle of the century, but these series focused on the masterpieces of the late eighteenth century, particularly Haydn, Mozart, and Beethoven, with only the occasional inclusion of a newly composed work.[32] They provide at best a partial picture of the chamber music world of this time, demonstrating a growing connoisseurship for late eighteenth-century music throughout the nineteenth century and representing a concert hall ideal that would eventually come to dominate concert life by the turn of the twentieth century.[33] Similar developments governed chamber music concerts in London, where series organized by John Ella and the Musical Union or the Beethoven Quartet Society promoted quasi-religious contemplation of music in quiet settings aided by extensive program notes.[34]

The complex of expectations that have attended the rise of the "modern" concert hall ritual has caused modern musicians to overlook a wealth of material from the nineteenth century that indicates a vibrant, engaged public for string chamber music. By holding all works and events to the same standard of contemplative listening, learned displays of musical logic or counterpoint, and seriousness, we reduce the string quartet and related genres to a highly selective group of works that, as the following chapters show, do not represent the whole of nineteenth-century musical experience and that, perhaps more importantly, do not address the many aspects of this music that made it inviting to amateurs, professionals, and listeners in the first place.

Although the public concert became a dominating force in musical life during the nineteenth century, the primary "audience" for whom many composers wrote in the first three quarters of the period was not a listening audience gathered at a professional performance. Rather, composers' public consisted of the critics and music lovers who would purchase and review (and play) their works throughout Europe. Nineteenth-century music lovers sometimes used chamber music as a pleasant diversion, as a learning and teaching tool, and as a social ladder. Printed music, like the printed word, connected them to each other and to the wider world, creating and supporting a diverse collection of communities within communities, a plethora of options that allowed musicians of all sorts to find their personal niche in the musical world of their time.

CHAPTER 1

Publishing Chamber Music

Archival Evidence for Chamber Music Production and Consumption

Printed music played an integral role in the musical lives of the middle classes, who consumed printed media in increasingly large quantities throughout the nineteenth century as literacy of all kinds gradually extended into much of the social fabric of Europe and North America. Social and cultural historians write of a "reading craze" or reading mania in this period, and literary scholars have tracked the increase in literacy and in consumption of the written word in order to understand better the reception of all kinds of literature, from monumental histories and collections of poetry or prose to less obviously "highbrow" writings in journals, magazines, and broadsides or pamphlets. Even ephemeral printed material intended to be read and discarded or redistributed until it fell apart—items such as greeting and visiting cards, flip-books, and paper dolls—can offer insight into the consciousness of nineteenth-century society. Like these other printed forms (including items related to the visual arts, such as posters and photo albums or picture books), sheet music in the nineteenth century moved from a precious rarity to a valued commodity and gradually into the realm of ephemera, with cheap publications not intended for long keeping and use; all three categories and the various gradations in between coexisted in the nineteenth century, contributing to a vibrant musical environment. Although some editions of music were clearly intended as luxury goods—the musical monuments and special editions that were fast becoming an important part of the publisher's and musician's musical life—much printed music was produced and consumed as part of a daily, weekly, or monthly diet of consumable art. New production technologies allowed new modes of consumption, and these in turn began to influence the methods producers used to wring as much profit as possible from the trading of intellectual and artistic materials.

Chamber music in this era was typically printed and sold in sets of parts rather than in full scores. This practice reinforces the notion, now somewhat lost, that the publication of a piece of new music was intended to facilitate performance of the work, not study. In order to engage the music at all, some performance skill was necessary, unless a piano arrangement was also available. Printed music addressed an audience of instrumental performers at various levels of ability. Publication of chamber music scores in the nineteenth century tended to favor works by "Classical" composers, however the publisher construed that notion. For example, Ignaz Pleyel's series of pocket scores (his Bibliothèque Musicale, begun in 1802) included quartets and symphonies by Haydn and works by Mozart, Beethoven, Johann Nepomuk Hummel, and George Onslow. A similar series of smallish-format scores issued by C. F. Kistner's firm in the early 1840s included quartets and quintets by Haydn, Mozart, Beethoven, and Onslow.[1] Thus, already in the 1810s, we see the canonization process at work and the special role that publishing played in creating and reinforcing the canonic status of works by the "Classical Masters."

This chapter investigates the institution of chamber music publishing by looking closely at three internationally significant publishers whose archives are now available to researchers looking for a clearer understanding of mid-nineteenth-century life. In all three cases, we shall see that publishers sought to balance their production of "monumental" and "ephemeral" products to establish and maintain a reliable source of income and new musical material for themselves and, by extension, the musicians who relied upon them. The publishers examined here were based in northern Germany—in Leipzig and Berlin—but distributed music throughout Europe and North America. Individually, the three firms represent different models with diverse priorities and business strategies: a small business established by a chamber music lover and copyright activist (Hofmeister); a larger firm that grew with the musical marketplace, changing hands at several points and evolving to address the needs of a growing public (Peters); and a midsize firm that specialized in practical music for private and public use (Schlesinger, later Lienau-Schlesinger). Together, these three companies give us a snapshot of the music business as it developed throughout the Romantic era. In France, England, and Austria, music firms operated on similar principles, adopting the same strategies for success and falling prey to the same misjudgments and market pressures. These three German businesses interacted with their counterparts elsewhere, operating separate branches in Paris or Vienna, for example, and employing representatives there to report back on what was popular, to acquire new works by local composers and musicians, and to nurture business relations with the various other producers of music—booksellers, performers, concert promoters, and so on.

The two Leipzig-based firms have several features in common from their shared roots in the early decades of the century, but after the midcentury mark, they adopted different business models in response to changes in musical and cultural life. Both firms specialized from their founding days in instrumental and small-ensemble music, printing few operatic works and a large number of chamber works, songs, and orchestral works. They both began as retail businesses founded by individuals ("Peters" by F. A. Hoffmeister in 1800 and "Hofmeister" by Friedrich Hofmeister in 1807) and grew into corporations with an international scope by the 1840s.

Friedrich Hofmeister established himself as a leader in the field of music publishing early in his career. He made it his life's work to organize music publishers and sellers in the German lands in order to secure fair trading practices, to serve consumers better and more efficiently, and to raise the prestige of his profession. In 1817 he began collaborating with Carl Friedrich Whistling to publish monthly or bimonthly installments of the *Handbuch der musikalischen Literatur*, today often referred to as the Hofmeister-Whistling catalogs.[2] These catalogs record what music was published by whom and at what cost to the consumer, providing an invaluable tool for modern-day researchers. In the nineteenth century, they allowed music sellers and publishers to advertise their music (and music by foreign publishers distributed in German lands) and to acquire new works for their shops, promoting collegial distribution and greater variety for the consumer.[3] Hofmeister also established the Verein der Deutschen Musikalienhändler (Society of German Music Sellers) in order to promote ethical and collegial business relationships among competitors and to lobby for copyright and other legislation to protect publishers and artists from piracy. Hofmeister's firm remained a family business until its demise after World War II, at the death of the founder's great-grandson, C. W. Günther.

The firm we know today as Peters was cofounded by composer Franz Anton Hoffmeister and organist Ambrosius Kuhnel as the Bureau de Musique in Leipzig in 1800 and sold fourteen years later to C. F. Peters, who ran the business under his own name. Over the next seventy-five years, the firm changed hands several times as owners retired or died, but it retained the name Peters, which by midcentury functioned as a brand, revered throughout the German-speaking musical world (and beyond).[4] This "branding" became even more important after the launch of the Peters Edition in 1867; works with its distinctive cover design were produced with a new speed-printing process pioneered by the firm's owners, Julius Friedländer and Max Abraham, in collaboration with engraver and inventor Carl Gottlieb Röder. The Peters Edition specialized in works the firm could produce in large quantities and emphasized items in the public domain—that is, works not subject to the new copyright laws. The firm continued to acquire works by young up-and-coming composers, buffering the investment risk of acquisitions by producing works that cost very little and brought in a large profit.

By contrast, Adolph Martin Schlesinger's firm, which he founded in Berlin in 1810, specialized in opera and opera-derived works in the first half of the century, producing full scores and arrangements of works by Weber (with whom Schlesinger negotiated exclusive publishing rights in 1814), Gaspare Spontini, Gaetano Donizetti, Fromental Halévy, and Giacomo Meyerbeer. In its early decades, the firm published music in many forms, including original chamber works, songs, piano works, and orchestral music, but it soon began to specialize in practical dance music and arrangements. For instance, a contract with the Prussian Crown prompted the publication of a collection of army marches for use by regimental bands in the 1820s. When Robert Lienau took over the firm in 1864, he introduced a focus on pedagogical works and works by younger composers, then bought several smaller publishing firms to expand his catalog, including the Viennese firm Haslinger, which published popular waltzes by Lanner and Strauss and a large collection of quadrilles and other parlor dances. Schlesinger's chamber music catalog included a large number of transcriptions created to disseminate operas and other works for larger forces in manageable formats for amateur musicians (discussed in chapter 3). In the later decades of the nineteenth century, under Lienau's leadership, opera arrangements for chamber ensembles gave way to folk songs and other folk-inspired recreational pieces for string quartet, piano trio, and other combinations. Schlesinger was only one of many firms who published such works, and the shifts in his catalog's offerings demonstrate trends noticeable in the output of other firms from the nineteenth century.

The various types of evidence these firms have left for modern historians point toward a vibrant, if volatile, market for chamber music throughout the nineteenth century. In particular, their print records (*Druckbücher*, or catalogs of published works, and *Auflagebücher*, or catalogs of impressions, including reprints) contain much information that sheds new light on the distribution and popularity of music in all its forms during the period in question. Balance sheets (*Calculationsbücher*) offer a glimpse at the economics of publishing music at this time and demonstrate the difficulties composers and publishers faced in making music available to a sometimes fickle public.[5]

Druckbücher and *Auflagebücher*: What Did Peters and Hofmeister Print?

Information drawn from sources like the Hofmeister-Whistling catalogs suggests a rapid decline in chamber music production beginning around 1830. Publishers appear to have stopped producing new works in string chamber genres or produced fewer of them in the following decades, and music in piano solo and song forms increased significantly. Music histories have tended to take this information at face value, drawing the logical conclusion that the public's interest in performing string chamber music waned during or after the Napoleonic Wars with the decline of the aristocracy. Because chamber music (especially the string quartet) had long been associated with princes and their courts, the dissolution of resources for court appointments and the like seems to have resulted in less chamber music and more widespread dissemination of songs and piano works

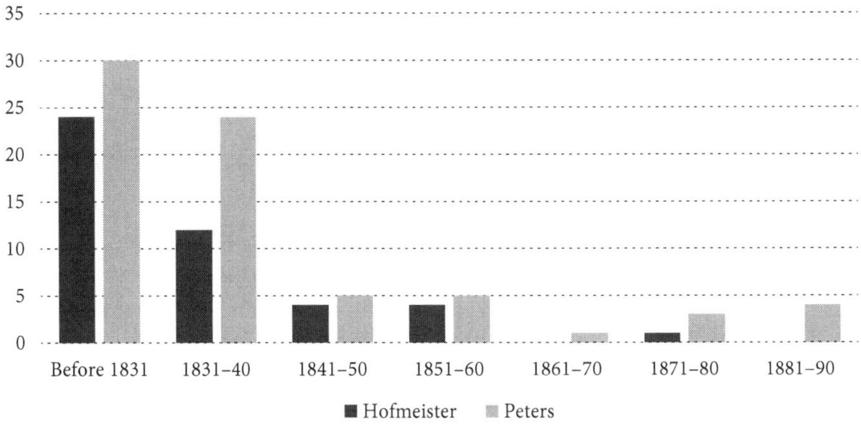

FIGURE 1.1 New works for string chamber ensemble published between 1800 and 1890 by the Hofmeister and Peters firms.

that were accessible to a broader audience with less leisure time. The print-run catalogs of Hofmeister, Peters, and Schlesinger likewise indicate that fewer new works were published in later decades, with a precipitous drop in production in the decade between 1840 and 1850 (see figure 1.1).

That overall impression of decline and uninterest, though, is refuted in part by the *Auflagebücher* kept by Peters and Hofmeister, which scrupulously list each reprint of every work published by the firms beginning with the first impression and continuing into the twentieth century. Figure 1.2 shows a page from the Hofmeister *Auflagebuch*. This document shows the date of each impression and the number of copies made in the right-hand column, with text running perpendicular to the other entries, which indicate from left to right the publisher's number (unique to the work or edition), the composer and title, the number of music plates created for the work, and information about the title-page engraving: "Stein" indicates a lithographed (*Steingedruckt*) title page, and the name or initial underneath indicates who engraved it. The Peters *Auflagebuch* gives similar information, though in a slightly different format, with entries ordered alphabetically by the composer's last name rather than in the order of publication. As figure 1.2 shows, some works were printed and reprinted as often as every other year, some were reprinted multiple times within the same year, and others were printed only once or twice and then abandoned. Chamber works were frequently printed in small initial print runs of fifty to one hundred copies and then reprinted in increments of twenty-five, fifty, or one hundred depending on demand. In some cases, a work was reprinted in increasingly larger print runs, presumably because the public liked it and new consumers wanted to acquire their own copies.

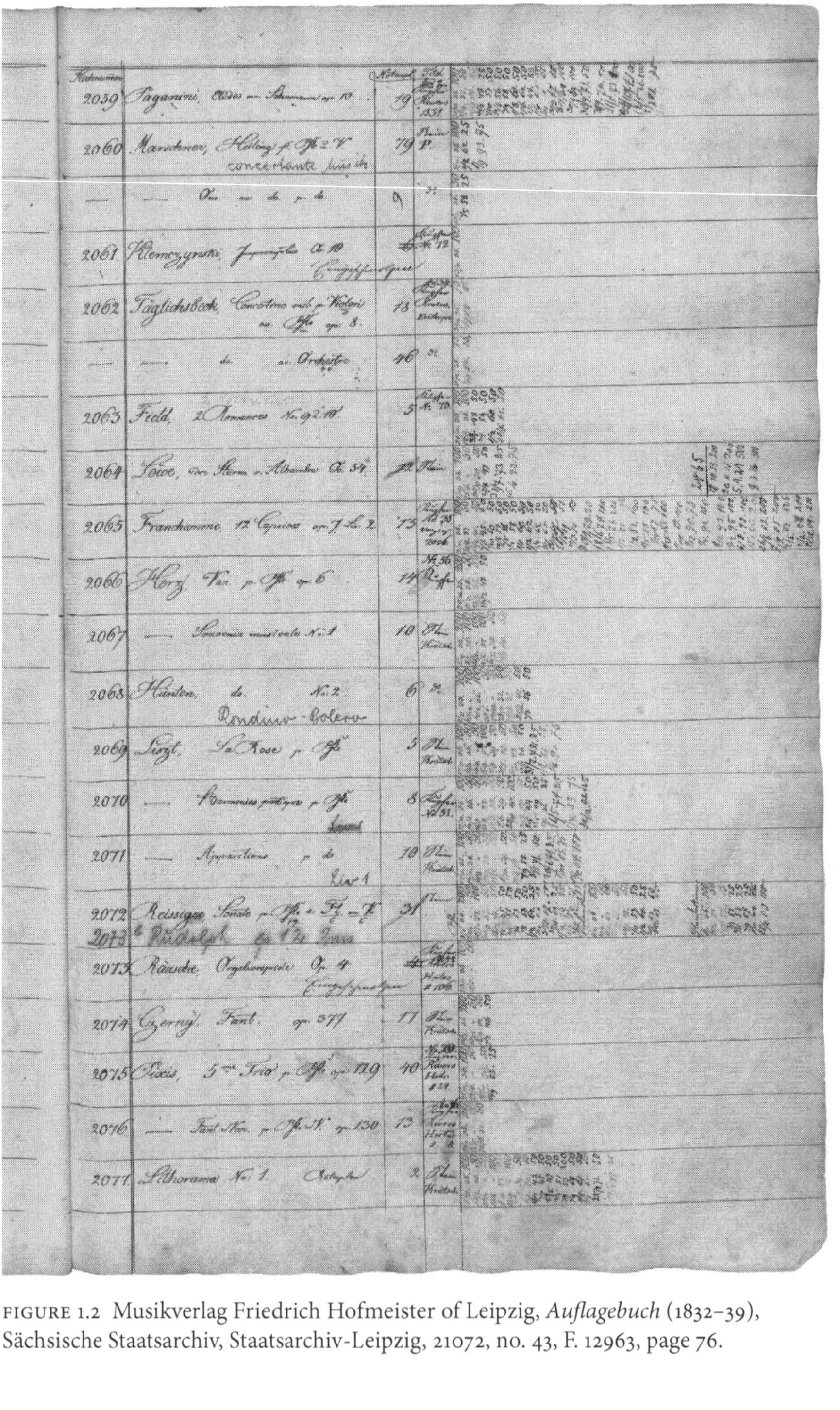

FIGURE 1.2 Musikverlag Friedrich Hofmeister of Leipzig, *Auflagebuch* (1832–39), Sächsische Staatsarchiv, Staatsarchiv-Leipzig, 21072, no. 43, F. 12963, page 76.

When we add the number of reprinted works produced in any given decade to the number of new works published at the same time, a more complex picture of the chamber music marketplace emerges (see figure 1.3). Certainly the number of new works and the number of overall works produced both declined over the course of the century, but that decline is less drastic and less straightforward

FIGURE 1.3 Total number of works printed for string chamber ensembles between 1800 and 1900 by the Hofmeister and Peters firms, including reprints.

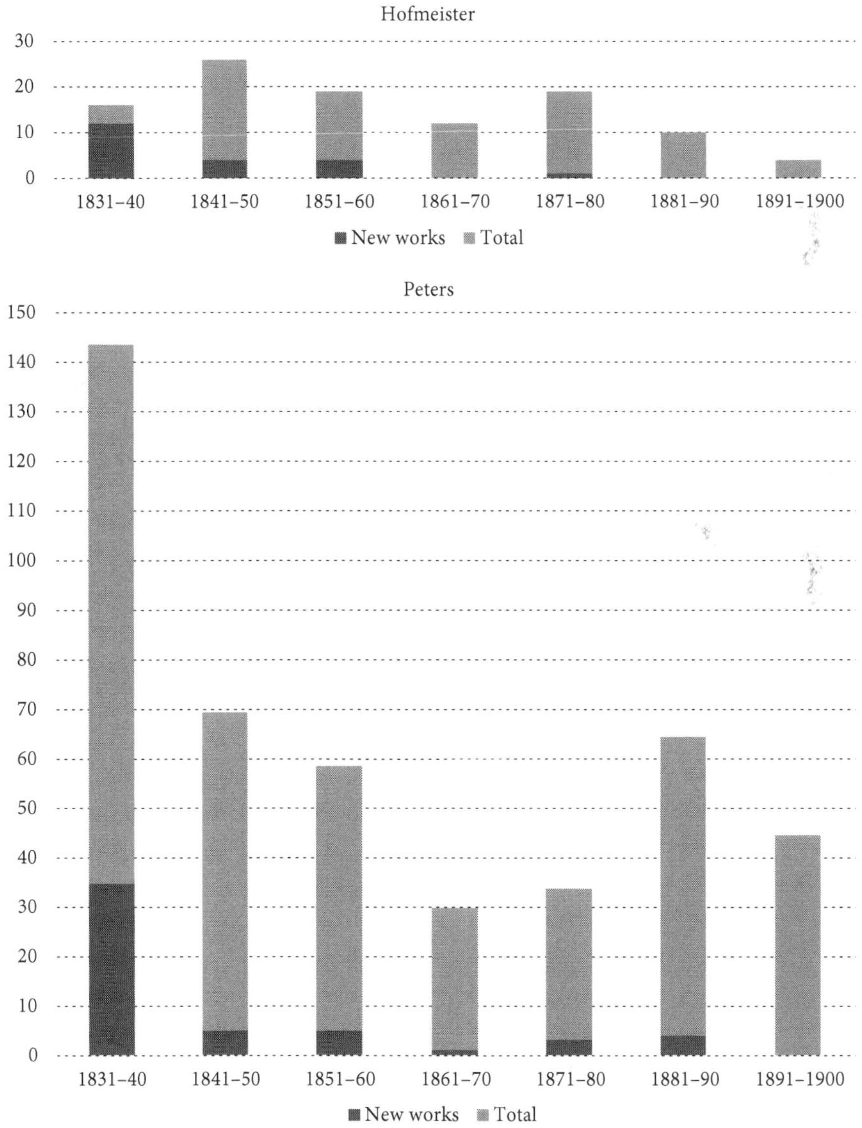

than the number of new publications alone indicates. These data suggest a continuing demand for chamber music throughout the nineteenth century, though that demand seems to have shifted to older works, with new works less highly sought-after than reprints of favorite pieces and works by familiar composers.

These familiar older works do not, in the main, include music by today's revered masters of the eighteenth and early nineteenth centuries. Though works by Haydn, Mozart, and Beethoven were reprinted and distributed in the nineteenth century, they did not represent a significant area of commercial activity until fairly late in the period. Table 1.1 shows the number of works printed by Peters and Hofmeister, organized by genre, and it indicates which composers' works they published. Note that Peters published nearly twice as many string quartets and quintets as any other chamber genre in the firm's catalog and that Hofmeister published half again as many quartets as works with piano. Although modern discussions of Romantic chamber music frequently highlight the development of the piano quartet and quintet as significant innovations by composers such as Robert Schumann and Johannes Brahms, these genres did not make up a large percentage of the firms' chamber music outputs. They were far outnumbered by

TABLE 1.1 String chamber works printed by Hofmeister and Peters

Hofmeister			Peters		
Genre	**No. of works**	**Composers**	**Genre**	**No. of works**	**Composers**
String quartets	49	Dotzauer (6)	String quartets	54	Spohr (14)
		Becker (3)			Reissiger (6)
		Molique (3)			B. Romberg (6)
		Praeger (3)			A. Romberg (6)
		Schneider (3)			Onslow (3)
		Spring (3)			Ries (3)
		Verhulst (3)			Rode (3)
		Veit (3)			Berlyn
		Voigt (3)			Dotzauer
		Hiller (2)			Fesca
		Mendelssohn (2)			Grund
		Nicola (2)			Grützmacher
		Braun			Jansa
		Burgmüller			Kalliwoda
		Femy			Kuhlau
		Fesca			Leibmann
		Gerke			Lindpainter
		Gross			Kunstmann
		Haydn			Nohr
		Müller			Taubert
		Pape			
		Reinecke			
		Rossini			
		Strauss			
		Thomas			

Hofmeister			Peters		
Genre	**No. of works**	**Composers**	**Genre**	**No. of works**	**Composers**
String quintets	9	Veit (4) Fesca (2) Dobrzynski Dotzauer Vogel	String quintets	6	Fesca (2) Spohr (2) Ries Reissiger
Piano trios	15	Pixis (3) Praeger (3) Marschner (2) Czerny Gouvy Hunten Kulenkanpe Lowe Reissiger Thomas	Piano trios	25	Reissiger (12) Hummel (3) Kalliwoda (2) Skraiye (2) A. W. Bach Jansa Kiel Kullak Nottebohm Reichel
Piano quartets and quintets	16	Czerny (3) Blahetka (2) Wilms (2) Dezczyrski Farrenc Kalkbrenner Krogulski Lubin Marschner Mendelssohn Müller Schloesser	Piano quartets and quintets	14	Reissiger (5) Ries (3) Czerny Grund Kuhlau Leonhard Nottebohm Spohr

Note: A number in parentheses following a composer's name indicates the number of distinct works composed by that composer and published by the firm if more than one. For example, Hofmeister published six distinct string quartets by Dotzauer and only one by Fesca.

works for strings alone and for piano trio, both of which were reprinted regularly and therefore retained a strong position in the musical life of the age. In this way, music history has distorted the relationship between "new" and "old" genres in the nineteenth century and given special prominence to two exceptional works.[6] Tables 1.2 and 1.3 show the most reprinted works by genre for both firms—their "best sellers" list, as determined by the number of copies printed over time. In both cases, a firm's most popular composers in a given genre were also the most prolific, suggesting that these composers and their publishers had hit upon a formula for success that benefited both.

Peters's most successful and popular composer of string chamber music for most of the nineteenth century was the violin virtuoso Louis Spohr (1784–1859), the *Kapellmeister* in Kassel (then the seat of power for the electorate of Hesse) from 1822 to his death. Spohr's string quartets generated many thousands of copies of

TABLE 1.2 Peters's "best-selling" works (works that the firm reprinted in large quantities throughout the century)

Composer	Work	No. of printings	How late was it reprinted?
String works			
Romberg, B.	Trios for Cello, Viola, & Bass (1823–24)	16	to 1866
Spohr	Quatuor brillant, op. 43 (1818)	14	to 1867
Spohr	Quartets, op. 4 (1806)	12	to 1900*
Spohr	Quartets, op. 74 Quartets, op. 58 Quartets, op. 45	8–9	to 1866/67
Kalliwoda	Quartet, op. 61 (1835) Quartet, op. 62 (1836)	6	to 1859
Piano works			
Reissiger	Piano Trio, op. 25 (ca. 1824)	35 (1833–66)	to 1900*
Hummel	Grand Piano Trio, op. 83 (1819)	24 (1830–66)	to 1900*
Reissiger	Piano Trio, op. 77 (1832)	19+	to 1900*
Reissiger	Piano Trio, op. 85 (1834) and all subsequent Piano Trios	Almost every year after the first print	to 1900*
Hummel	Piano Trio, op. 96 (1822)	17 (1830–66)	to 1900*

* Peters reprinted Spohr's quartets, Hummel's piano trios, and Reissiger's trios in the Peters Edition collection after 1867.

music. Peters published nine sets of quartets by Spohr, totaling eighteen works, between 1830 and 1856. The firm reprinted many of these pieces into the 1860s and reissued the op. 4 quartets in a Peters Edition volume. The total number of copies printed rivals that of Carl Reissiger's very popular piano trios, despite the smaller print runs of twenty-five to forty copies instead of fifty to seventy-five. Peters printed almost fourteen thousand copies of string quartets by Spohr between 1830 and the mid-1860s and then printed another eleven hundred copies of his op. 4 set of three quartets. With the exception of op. 4, though, Spohr's string quartets appear to have lost their market value more quickly than Reissiger's piano trios; Spohr's reputation declined after his death in 1859, despite the high esteem in which musicians such as Hans von Bülow and Johannes Brahms held him.

A slightly younger contemporary of Spohr, the Czech composer and jurist Wenzel Heinrich (or Václav Jindřich) Veit (1806–64), based in Prague, met with similar success as a composer of popular string chamber music. Although he was not as prolific as Spohr (Veit published only seven works for strings in his lifetime), his works outlasted those of the more famous composer. Hofmeister steadily printed his string quintets and quartets into the twentieth century, including Veit's String Quartet op. 3, which was printed twenty-four times between its introduction in 1836 and 1906. Thus, it averaged a new impression almost every three years for

TABLE 1.3 Hofmeister's "best-selling" works (works that the firm reprinted in large quantities throughout the century)

Composer	Work	No. of printings	How late was it reprinted?
String works			
W. H. Veit	Premiere Quintet (1835)	11	1890
	Quintet No. 2, op. 2 (1837)	8	1885
	Premiere Quartet, op. 3 (1836)	24	1906
	Quartet No. 2, op. 5 (1838)	13	1885
	Quintet No. 3, op. 4 (1838)	Similar to op. 5 above	
	Quartet No. [3], op. 16 (1840)	11	
	Quintet No. 4, op. 20 (1843)	9	1889
Reinecke	Quartet, op. 16 (1848)	6	1893
Verhulst	Quartets, op. 6 (1839)	4	1884
	Quartet, op. 21 (1845)	3	1873
Piano works			
Reissiger	Piano Trio, op. 40 (1826)	28	1885
Marschner	Piano Trio, op. 111 (1841)	16	1896
Marschner	Piano Quartet, op. 36 (1826)	11	1884

seven decades. A total of 1,225 copies circulated over the course of the century, slightly fewer copies than Spohr's most successful work—his op. 43 *quatuors brillants*, which were reprinted fourteen times, creating 1,380 copies. On average, each printing of a Veit quartet or quintet created fifty new copies, ensuring that this work was always available to the music-purchasing public, though never in large quantities. Veit's subsequent works were not quite as popular, but their numbers remain impressive for the period: the two quintets, opp. 1 and 2, were reprinted ten times, resulting in five hundred copies of each, and the second and third quartets, opp. 5 and 16 (1838 and 1840), were each reprinted more than ten times, leading to over six hundred copies of each. Whereas Spohr's works appear to have met with resounding success in his lifetime and then fallen quickly out of favor, Veit's works were more modestly distributed but lasted longer in the public consciousness (or, at least, in music shops). As one of the first Czech composers to adopt Romantic musical innovations developing in Austro-German culture, Veit holds an important place in the history of Czech music, but his works remain largely unknown today.[7] These popular works share a musical style based on comfortable figuration and repetition, which we will explore in greater detail in chapter 3. (Although we will not deal with piano chamber works, it bears mentioning that the most popular piano trios of the Peters catalog, works by Carl G. Reissiger, also bear some striking similarities in terms of their use of repetition and the overall treatment of form and genre.)

Veit's quartets and quintets utilize what had become standard multimovement structures in the late eighteenth century. They contain four movements with the expected procession of sonata form, slow movement (often a ternary or theme-and-variations form), dance (minuet or scherzo), and rondo or sonata form finale. By adhering to generic conventions, Veit ensured that sheet music purchasers would know what to expect, but the varied details within movements and within the Classical forms made each work a unique performance experience. For example, in op. 3, Veit incorporated Alexei Lvov's 1833 hymn "God Save the Tsar!" which won the competition for a new imperial anthem that year. The movement's structure recalls Haydn's "Emperor" Quartet, but a few significant departures remind us that Veit's work belongs to the later Biedermeier tradition, including gestures that make the work more accessible and pleasurable for players and features that hint at a more Romantic musical language despite the conservative form.

Veit's string quartets and quintets, like similarly popular works by other composers, employ seductively simple melodies and frequently venture into unexpected harmonic territories during transitional and developmental passages. These pleasurable surprises take place in the context of a generally Classical formal style that takes advantage of gestures and textures designed to make the work readable and enjoyable for the players. In informal readings of his works, performers have said to this author, "they play themselves, right off the page."

In fact, that sense of "playability" distinguishes many of these popular works from the more revered pieces of the same period—works by Beethoven, Schubert, Schumann, and Brahms—which often feel more difficult for both the player and the listener. The popular works of the nineteenth century employ an accessible style that lies well under the hand and brings pleasure to the performer without requiring much study or practicing. At the same time, the works remain repeatable because the tunes and figuration are simply fun to play; the parts fit together well and easily, providing hours of enjoyment to the players. The works of Veit and Spohr, for example, utilize common figurations in the violin lines and accompanimental textures that allow the melody-carrying soloist to "sing" without fighting to overcome the volume and bustle of a polyphonic texture in the other three voices. The first violin dominates these works, though the cello or viola sometimes also exposes a theme or repeats one already played by the violinist. Hummel's and Reissiger's piano works privilege a similar comfortable style for the pianist—frequently "brilliant" without being difficult—and for the stringed instruments. The works of Johann Wenzel (or Jan Křtitel Václav) Kalliwoda, Reissiger, and Spohr follow predictable and acceptable patterns of form and technique that allow casual performers to enjoy new works with a leisurely approach—once a group has played one Spohr quartet, the next work and the next feel comfortable and familiar enough to sight-read.

Encountering familiar gestures in new combinations and tried-and-true forms filled with exciting new themes kept these works fresh and engaging for new consumers, prompting them to purchase work after work by the same author. Historian Karin Wurst has noted a similar trend in leisure consumption in many different activities of the nineteenth-century middle class. For instance, novelists, poets, and producers of almanacs and magazines capitalized on the public's eagerness for a novel but comfortable new experience. Wurst notes that "the reading craze [of the late eighteenth century] was propelled by this desire to repeat the sensation of pleasure. . . . Readers selected reading materials that displayed the same basic structures with only slight variations."[8] Elisabeth Le Guin has noted the same "pleasure of repetition" in the earlier works of Luigi Boccherini.[9] Significantly, Boccherini's main achievement is in string chamber music, which accounts for the bulk of his output; he wrote over three hundred chamber works, of which over one hundred are string quintets with two cellos and nearly one hundred are string quartets.

These characteristics made the popular string chamber works of the early Romantic era perfectly suited for their consumers and for those consumers' specific uses of chamber music, but these works also led to the style's decline in the last decades of the nineteenth century and its near absence from twentieth-century musical consciousness as represented by performances and histories of music. Modern concert hall listeners tend to find these works repetitive, boring, or uneventful because they often lack rigorous developmental procedures or surprising formal and harmonic innovations. In short, works designed to appeal to an audience of active, if amateur, performers do not always appeal to concert hall listeners. But just because composers and publishers of this music had found a successful formula to sustain the interest of their target audiences did not guarantee immediate financial success for every work. Especially in comparison to the lighter works of the era, chamber music with strings involved a considerable long-term commitment in order to make a profit. Printing new chamber music was expensive, time-consuming, and risky, as business records from the period show.

Calculationsbücher: How Did These Firms Make Money?

Peters and Hofmeister published a fairly large quantity of chamber music in the nineteenth century—or, at least, a surprisingly large quantity compared to expectations based on modern generalizations about chamber music in this period. They capitalized on consumers' desire for novelty, and they used a "print-on-demand" system for much of the period. This model was actually held over from the music-copying business model of earlier eras, in which a music shop would acquire one or more copies of a new work and create handwritten copies for

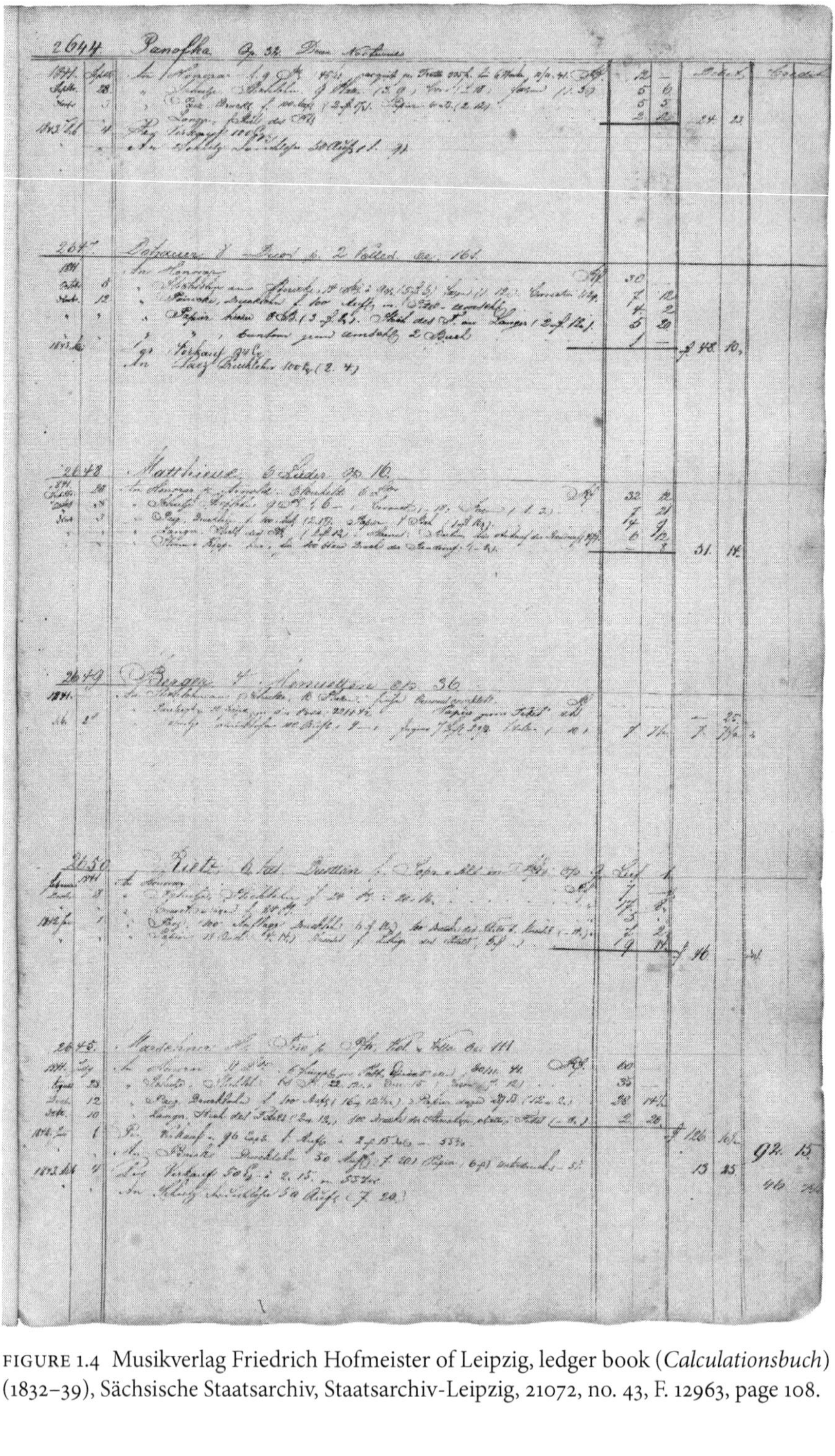

FIGURE 1.4 Musikverlag Friedrich Hofmeister of Leipzig, ledger book (*Calculationsbuch*) (1832–39), Sächsische Staatsarchiv, Staatsarchiv-Leipzig, 21072, no. 43, F. 12963, page 108.

patrons, which cost considerably less than preparing movable type for a large print run or than creating engraved plates. Commercial manuscript copying continued in most of continental Europe through at least the 1780s.[10] In theory, the print-on-demand system allowed firms to invest in new musical works "up front" and then reap the rewards of a good investment for decades thereafter. In most cases, however, and especially regarding chamber music, these reprints were absolutely necessary in order for the firm to make any profit at all on a musical work. Even for the most popular works in a chamber music publisher's catalog, initial printings of string quartets, piano trios, and other works for multiple players represented a significant expense.

For both Peters and Hofmeister, surviving *Calculationsbücher* provide some evidence of the costs involved in printing music. Figure 1.4 shows a page from Hofmeister's ledger book for 1841. It lists five works: two nocturnes by Heinrich Panofka, a set of duos for cello by Friedrich Dotzauer, a collection of *Lieder* by Johanna Mathieux, a set of minuets for piano solo by Ludwig Berger, a collection of favorite vocal duets for soprano and alto by Julius Rietz, and a piano trio by Heinrich Marschner.[11] Table 1.4 gives a transcription of the Marschner entry, which includes the following expenses: (1) the honorarium paid to the composer; (2) the engraving (*Stichlohn*) of the parts; (3) the printing (*Drucklohn*) of one hundred copies of the set of parts (*Aufl.*) and the cost of the paper; and (4) the engraving of the title page (*Stich des Titels*) and printing of one hundred copies.[12] These investments added up to 126 talers and 10.5 groschen. A year after the honorarium was paid, ninety-six copies were sold at the customary wholesale price, bringing in 92 talers and 15 groschen but leaving the work in the red. A reprint in 1842 cost 13 talers and 25 neugroschen for fifty copies, and the sale of

TABLE 1.4 Transcription of Hofmeister's *Calculationsbuch* entry for Marschner's piano trio

				Debit	Credit
26	**45**	**Marschner, H. Trio p. Pfte, Viol, & Vcelle, Oe 111**			
1841	July	An Honorar jj Lor , 6 [??] 30/11. 44. Pt	60		
August	28	" Schulze, Stichlohn 60 Pt (22.12. Corr (5—) Laçon (7.12)	35		
Decb	12	" Paez, Drucklohn f. 100 Aufl. (16 . 12½), Papier dazu 29 B. (12, 2)	28 14½		
Oct	10	" Langer, Stich des Titels (2 , 12,) 100 Drucke der Stereotyplatten Titel	2 20		
				126 10½	
1842 Juli	1	Per Verkauf v. 96 Expl. Aufl. à 2 gr. 15 ? 55%			92 15
		An Ponicke Drucklohn 50 Aufl. (7. 20.) Papier (6)		13 25	
1843 [?]	4	Per Verkauf 50 Exp. à 2.15 m. 55%			46
		An Schultz Drucklohn 50 Aufl. (7. 20.)			

these brought in a little more than 46 talers. At this point, the firm had still not made a net profit on the work. Thus, Hofmeister only began making money on Marschner's trio with the third printing in 1843, which generated another fifty copies at the same price, though the ledger does not show the sale of this batch. The firm's *Auflagebuch* shows many subsequent printings of this work—fourteen in all, from 1846 to 1896, totaling 675 copies. Thus, Marschner's trio was popular enough to be reprinted thirty-five years after his death, but the total circulation of this work in the nineteenth century consisted of fewer than one thousand copies.

To contrast the relative long-term value of this work with a more immediately profitable example, we turn to Hofmeister's light or practical works for piano, which cost less to print and sold at a higher profit. For example, in 1843 the firm printed twelve hundred copies of *Leinates Klänge*, a set of waltzes for piano solo by Joseph Labitzky (1802–81), at a cost of 153 talers and 6.5 groschen (see table 1.5). The firm sold 1,155 of these that year for 231 talers, netting a profit of 78 talers. The ledger shows seven subsequent printings in the next two years, each one for two hundred copies of the work, costing just over 10 talers and selling at a profit for 40 talers.

TABLE 1.5 Transcription of the *Calculationsbuch* entry for Labitzky waltzes

			Debit	Credit
2916	**Labitzky, Leinates Klänge. Waltzer, op. 92 à 2 ms.**			
1843	An Honorar Pt 125	84 22½		
Mai 1.	Paez auflagen—9 Ps (3 22½) 12%	5 20		
	—für die übungkauf auf Stich			
Juni 21	Druck 1200 Auflagen	21		
	für d. Titel, 4—, Drucker 4. 5.	8 5		
	—73½ —f. Arrang. (3—)	30 19	153 6½	
1843 15/9.	Per Verkauf <855 Ex. m 60%			231 —
	An Ponicke Drucklohn 200 Aufl. (4.15) Papier cot. (6—)		10 15	
1844 Feb. 2	Per Verkauf 200 Ex. m. 60%			40 —
	An Paez Drucklohn 200 Aufl. (4. 24) Papier cot. (6—)		10 15	
" Apr. 20	Per Verkauf 200 Ex. m. 60%			40 —
	An Paez Drucklohn 200 Aufl. (4. 24) Papier cot. (6—)		10 15	
" Aug 10	Per Verkauf 200 Aufl.			40 —
	An Paez Drucklohn 200 Aufl. (4. 24) Papier cot. (6—)		10 15	
Dec 6	Per Verkauf 200 Ex			40 —
	An Ponicke Drucklohn 200 Aufl. (4.15) Papier cot. (6—)		10 15	
1845 [??]	Per Verkauf 200 Ex			40 —
	An Ponicke Drucklohn 200 Aufl. (4.15) Papier cot. (6—)		10 15	
2 Juli	Per Verkauf 200 Ex			40 —
	An Paez Drucklohn 200 Aufl. (4. 24) Papier cot.		10 15	

Even with the increased circulation of reprinted copies and the inclusion of the dozens of works that have heretofore gone unacknowledged in musicological accounts, the overall quantity of chamber music in the marketplace was small. Of 8,500 individual plate numbers in the Hofmeister catalog (indicating distinct works in some cases or collections such as "three string quartets" in others), only 76 correspond to chamber works for three to eight players, including works with and without the piano but not with winds. Thus, about 1 percent of Hofmeister's output was chamber music by my definition. At Peters, the situation is slightly better: of 4,172 plates between 1832 and 1865 (the year that the Peters Edition began, with a new plate numbering system), 106 works were chamber music, or about 2.5 percent. Clearly, chamber music was an exclusive endeavor indeed.

These rather bleak proportions, however, require some contextualization. Regarding production, several issues come into play. Like other multiplayer instrumental works, chamber music of the nineteenth century tended to employ several movements, resulting in long works that required many plates to produce. The sheer quantity of sheet music produced—in terms of number of pages—for an individual chamber work dwarfed most of the smaller-scale works for piano and song that formed the rest of the firm's catalog, which could be printed on two or four pages and required considerably fewer plates to engrave and print. Returning to figure 1.2, which shows a single page from Hofmeister's *Auflagebuch*, we see that works such as a collection of nocturnes by Czerny, three piano pieces by Krollmann, four *Lieder* by Dorn, and the "Air varié" by Beriot required between ten and fourteen plates to print. The string quintet by Veit required forty plates, and the quartet arrangement of Hesse's Third Symphony required thirty-five. In general, the much more numerous works in small genres (especially songs and piano genres) required fewer than twenty plates, whereas chamber and orchestral works used between thirty and eighty. In performance (whether in concerts or in casual domestic settings), these multimovement works take more time to play, with one or two works possibly providing an entire afternoon's entertainment, as opposed to the miscellany of songs, duets, and shorter works that might make up an evening's entertainment at the keyboard.

Regarding consumption, we must consider the entire ecology of chamber music's circulation. The much smaller print runs and low number of published works for chamber music might indicate less interest in these works than in solo piano works and songs, but at least two factors affected the number of copies needed. First, the number of players using a single copy of a chamber piece reduces the number of potential purchasers for any work considerably. Although four players will use and enjoy a string quartet, only one copy is needed—unlike solo works or songs, which require individual players or households to acquire a copy for their own use (or to borrow one) and will only be used by one or two performers at a time. If I were a cellist, for example, participating in a friendly string quartet meeting once or twice a week, I might never purchase chamber music for my group's use if the violinist has a particular fondness for finding and acquiring music for us. If my ensemble were to handle music acquisition very democratically, I might be expected to purchase a fourth of the music we would play. Of course, I might borrow or trade a set of parts with friends or family members who play in other regular ensembles, and I might also inherit a library of music from previous generations of music lovers. This situation is amplified by the second factor: the proliferation of music lending libraries throughout Europe in the early nineteenth century.[13] Scholar Tobias Widmaier has examined the development of circulating libraries in German-speaking lands and their role in musical society.[14] Many of the major publishers of the nineteenth century operated lending libraries in addition to selling their wares to music shops and directly to patrons. Book and music sellers also operated lending services that allowed patrons to try out new works before purchasing them. In these cases, patrons agreed to purchase a certain amount of music in a given year or quarter, and then they could take out and bring back any piece they wanted during that period. Private music lenders—that is, lenders not connected to a publisher or shop—established themselves in most of Europe's large and small cities as early as the 1770s, but they proliferated in most locales in the second third of the nineteenth century. (One early nineteenth-century commentator noted that lending institutions sprang up "wie Pilzen aus dem Boden," or "like mushrooms from the ground.") Between 1850 and 1880, the number of documented lending libraries in German lands alone rose steadily from seventy-six in 1850 to nearly four hundred by 1880.[15] Such lending services obviously competed with sellers of sheet music because they allowed music lovers to enjoy a work without purchasing it. On the other hand, music publishers established lending services because having and maintaining an avid "readership" for printed music was good for business. With hundreds of subscribers demanding that libraries stock multiple copies of the most popular piano works, songs, and chamber pieces, the lending services helped to ensure that copies of newly printed works would be distributed and tried out by musical amateurs. Furthermore, circulating libraries made music available to a demographic that would not have been able to purchase it because of the high cost of printed music, which remained a luxury product throughout the nineteenth century, especially before the technological innovations of the 1860s. When new printing processes brought down production costs, Peters introduced a new model for publishing and distributing music that reflects new ways of thinking about music's role in cultural and social life in the later Romantic era.

The Peters Edition

Around 1867, Peters introduced a new speed-printing process for music, and the firm's partnership took full advantage of the technology to change the orientation of its business. The Peters Edition (or Edition Peters) represents not only a new mode of presentation and distribution for music but also an important development in the mentality of music producers, with far-reaching consequences for music consumers and for music historiography. Max Abraham (1831–1900), who would later become the sole owner and proprietor of the firm, spearheaded the initiative for the new edition using technology originally developed by his business partner, Julius Friedländer. Carl Gottlieb Röder, who had long been one of Leipzig's most important music printers, also played an important role. He developed the new lithographic techniques that made print runs of ten thousand or more copies possible in 1863.[16] The Peters Edition used this new process to create a catalog of publications that celebrated the compositional heroes of the eighteenth and nineteenth centuries, including new editions of Classical texts annotated by contemporary performers and scholars. In essence, the Peters Edition solidified the then-developing canon of great works and facilitated development of critical music editing and musicology in the mid-nineteenth century. The first works to bear the Edition Peters imprint were the two volumes of J. S. Bach's *Well-Tempered Clavier* in 1867. Subsequent volumes included new editions of works by Handel, Mozart, Beethoven, Schubert, Haydn, and Mendelssohn.

Peters was not the first firm to enter this field, though it did so with a motivation rather different from that of its predecessors. Peters's main business rival in Leipzig and in the world of music distribution, Breitkopf und Härtel, had begun to print the first complete works editions of Classical masters in 1806. These included the collected works of Haydn, Mozart, Muzio Clementi, Jan Ladislav Dussek, and Johann Baptist Cramer, produced using an early lithographic process that did not employ mechanical presses. In the 1820s, the firm printed works by Handel and Bach, including some works that had not been printed since these composers' deaths more than half a century before. Breitkopf und Härtel also printed the *Allgemeine musikalische Zeitung* beginning in 1798; this journal was the first and, for the first half of the nineteenth century, the most important outlet for the relatively new field of music criticism and music-historical research. Perhaps the firm's greatest legacy, and one characteristic of the Romantic turn toward historicism, is the Bach Edition, published in collaboration with the Bach Gesellschaft from 1851 to 1900. For this and similar complete works projects, Breitkopf und Härtel's business model focused on the creation of high-quality luxury editions that documented the masterworks of the past and the present for the future. The firm's collected works editions were produced and distributed via subscription, making these collections the privilege of organizations and individuals with a significant disposable income. The Peters Edition model, on the other hand, sought to make these same works accessible to a wider public through inexpensive editions that were, nevertheless, high quality, a balance made possible by the speed-printing process's faster production time and ability to use lighter, cheaper paper.

Chamber music (in parts and in score format) was an important element of the Peters Edition project, and new editions of the complete string quartets of

Beethoven and Mozart, for instance, formed a cornerstone of the catalog. The main focus of this project was, from its outset, to create a collection of accessible editions for culturally or historically significant works, including music for keyboard, many volumes of songs, some orchestral scores, operas, and choral works. For the larger pieces such as symphonies and stage works, the Peters Edition included two-hand and four-hand piano versions more often than full scores, though the scores of all of Beethoven's symphonies were published around 1872 as nos. 1020a through 1020i. Arrangements of Schubert's and Beethoven's other works were published in this series, too, such as selections from Beethoven's string quartets for piano and arrangements of his and Mendelssohn's piano concerti for two pianos.

Later in its history, the Peters Edition included these "classics" and newer works by young composers, such as Edvard Grieg, Ethyl Smyth, and Louise Heritte-Viardot. The firm's *Auflagebuch* records the print history for all the Peters Edition works. For many of them, print run numbers tend to be in the thousands rather than the hundreds as in earlier logs. The firm printed ten thousand copies of Bach's *Well-Tempered Clavier* between 1868 and 1873, then reprinted it twelve times before 1891, resulting in over fifty thousand circulating copies of this work. The print runs for chamber music are considerably smaller, though still much larger than in previous decades. For example, earlier printing of Spohr's quartets began with print runs as low as forty or as high as eight hundred in the 1830s; reprints averaged around fifty copies through the 1860s. The firm rereleased Spohr's three quartets, op. 4, in 1889 and printed five hundred copies of each work initially. It then reprinted each one in 1894 or 1895 and around 1900, each time reprinting two hundred copies. The company printed another two hundred copies of Quartet No. 1 in 1904.

Peters printed works by Classical composers (Haydn, Mozart, Hummel, and Beethoven) and by popular authors from later decades (Reissiger) in larger quantities than its newly acquired works by living composers. Table 1.6 shows some representative print statistics for both well-known and less familiar chamber works included in the Peters Edition catalog. As with works by revered but less popular Classical and early Romantic composers (Luigi Cherubini, Carl Ditters von Dittersdorf, Spohr), those by relatively unknown living composers were printed in more modest numbers. The larger runs of canonic works provided the necessary ballast that allowed Peters to take risks on composers such as Grieg and Smyth, as well as Strauss, Mahler, and other innovative composers in the later decades of the century.

Max Abraham's business decisions reflect the ongoing development of a middle-class culture in northern Germany after the mid-nineteenth century. Disseminating these examples of great works supported the notion of *Bildung*, or self-cultivation, through education and intellectually stimulating activities.[17] (Abraham's other contributions to Leipzig and to the firm's role in that city include the establishment of a musical reference library open to the public.) By making these works available in affordable, well-produced editions, Abraham associated his firm with the *Bildungsbürgertum*, or the educated upper-middle-class citizens

TABLE 1.6 Print-run information for selected works published in the Peters Edition series

Genre	No. of works	Composers	No. of copies, 1867–1900
String quartets	24	Beethoven (parts)	8,020
		Beethoven (score, 4 vols.)	ca. 1,800 per volume
		Mozart	8,650
		Haydn	2,980
		Schubert (score, 3 vols.)	500; 500; 900
		Mendelssohn (score and parts)	900; 4,450
		Spohr, op. 4 (3 quartets, parts)	ca. 1,000 per work
		Grieg, op. 27 (score and parts)	300 and 2,150
		Dittersdorf	1,150
		Cherubini	1,100
		Scholz, op. 46	800
		Lux, op. 58	700
		Schumann, op. 41 (3 quartets, score)	600
String quintets	7	Mozart	3,650
		Mendelssohn	1,750
		Beethoven, op. 29	1,125
		Boccherini	900
		Smyth (score and parts)	150 and 250
		Heinrich XXIV, op. 4	125
Piano trios	6	Beethoven	18,000
		Mendelssohn	11,100
		Reissiger	9,300
		Hummel	5,350
		Schubert, Nocturno	3,150
Piano quartets	7	Mozart	8,800
		Beethoven	8,500
		Mendelssohn	4,200
		Schubert, Adagio and Rondo	3,200
		Weber, op. 8	2,100
		Heritte-Viardot, Spanish Quartet	800
		Becker, op. 19 (piano/score)	600
		Becker, op. 19 (parts)	200
Piano quintets	2	Hummel, op. 87	2,750
		Bungert, op. 18	1,400
Arrangements for piano trio	3	Beethoven horn sonata, op. 17	4,200
		Schubert quintet	1,450
		Schubert octet	1,400

and patrons who sought to enrich their knowledge of music and its role in a shared artistic heritage by studying scores and participating in performances of high-quality musical works. This elite segment of the population had always been involved in private and semiprivate musical activities, including chamber music performances (as discussed in the introduction), but the Peters Edition project took that participation and intellectual interest in music to a new level of institutionalization. The nationalist canon-building element of the project is significant for historiography: Peters and its contemporary publishing colleagues played a leading role in creating a modern repertoire of masterworks that reinforced the reification of Bach, Haydn, Mozart, and Beethoven that had been under way since the early decades of the century.

The cheap production and wide dissemination of these works allowed the firm to make a profit and to participate in shaping the German cultural heritage and consciousness that influenced nationalist politics and middle-class identification. More importantly, Peters's business model in the new era turned former models on their heads. Beginning with this collection, Peters used prints and reprints of important *highbrow* music by accepted masters from the past to create a solid financial foundation that allowed it to make riskier investments in new music by young composers. Breitkopf und Härtel used a similar approach, exemplified by its publication of collected works editions and other musical monuments, which generated revenue and prestige for the press at a relatively low acquisitions cost. Hofmeister and, as we will see, Schlesinger tended to produce what modern critics and historians call *lowbrow*, or "trivial," music in addition to pedagogical works to generate revenue that could be used to produce less lucrative music. In both models, music for small ensembles such as string quartets and quintets played a central role in creating or maintaining a catalog of works that would appeal to music buyers throughout Europe.

A Different Kind of Chamber Music: The *Auflagebücher* of A. M. Schlesinger

Adolph Martin Schlesinger (1769–1838) founded his publishing house in Berlin in 1810 and quickly became one of the most important music distributors in Prussia. Like Peters, Schlesinger published inexpensive editions of familiar works and newly acquired works, most famously establishing a contract with Carl Maria von Weber in 1814. Unlike both Peters and Hofmeister, though, Schlesinger did not focus on producing original works for domestic performing ensembles or parlor pianists (i.e., works composed for string quartet or piano trio). Rather, Schlesinger's emphasis on opera and operatic works led the firm to produce dozens of arrangements and transcriptions of these larger works for domestic performance, and these arrangements also reveal several trends in chamber music consumption throughout the period 1800–1900 that have not been explored in previous musicological treatments of this era.[18]

According to the firm's *Auflagebuch*, original works for strings or for piano and strings account for about 60 percent of the firm's ninety-six chamber music publications between the firm's founding in 1810 and the end of the century, but these are concentrated in the early decades of Schlesinger's history.[19] The firm published the first edition of Beethoven's two string quartets, opp. 132 and 135, in 1827 and Mendelssohn's first two piano quartets, opp. 1 and 2, in 1823 and 1825, respectively. During this earlier period, it also published works by Spohr, Pierre Rode, Carl Czerny, and Reissiger, as well as less familiar composers whose works have not left an impression on music history (M. G. Damm, G. A. Schneider, W. Lenss, Johann Benjamin Gross, Léon de Saint-Lubin). Schlesinger did not focus on producing multiple chamber works by the same author, as Peters or Hofmeister did. Schlesinger reserved this practice for opera composers such as Weber or for arrangers such as Heinrich Panofka, C. W. Henning, and Moritz Kässmayer.[20]

The remaining 40 percent of the firm's chamber music output consists of arrangements for chamber ensembles, such as operas and overtures arranged for string quartet or quintet and collections of folk songs and other works. The firm published thirty-seven of these between 1810 and 1900, concentrating on different types of repertoire to suit the changing demands of its audience (see table 1.7 for a chronological listing of these works). Between 1810 and 1850, the

TABLE 1.7 List of chamber-music arrangements published by Schlesinger, ca. 1810–1900 (according to the firm's *Lagerbuch*, or print log)

1810–50	14	Fioravanti	Dorfsängerinnen
		Spontini	Overture to *Cortez*
			Overture to *Olympia*
		Boieldieu	Johann von Paris
		Weber	Der Freischütz
			Oberon
			Preciosa
		Meyerbeer	Robert le Diable
			Struensee (for Quintet)
		Halevy	La juive
			L'éclair—Der Blitz
			Der Guitarrenspieler
		Donizetti	La Favorite
		Weber	Overture *Oberon* (new edition)
1851–70	6	Meyerbeer	Festmarsch—Schillerfeier
		Weber	Overture to *Euryanthe*
			Jubel-Ouverture
			Aufforderung zum Tanz
			Polacca, op. 72
1871–90	6	Kässmayer	Volkslieder (12 vols.)
			Himmelstrachlüssel für Streichquartett
			"Musikalische Miscellianen" für Streichquartett
		Suk	Böhmischen Volkslieder
		Wilhelmj	(Schubert) Duo op. 162

firm published arrangements of contemporaneous Romantic operas from the French, Italian, and German traditions, with the Germans represented by Weber alone. Adolph Schlesinger's son Maurice was vital to this aspect of the business. He established himself in Paris in 1816 by working for another Parisian publisher before setting up his own business at the rue Richelieu in 1822. From that post, he seems to have collaborated with his father and then his younger brother Heinrich, who ran the Berlin firm after 1831. (The Schlesinger records housed in Frankfurt include printing information and correspondence dealing with works clearly acquired by Maurice in Paris, such as Richard Wagner's string quartet arrangements of operas by Donizetti and Halévy.)

In the first half of the nineteenth century, Schlesinger's publications provided German and French audiences a way to experience new works and to become familiar with the operatic events of the season. More particularly, these arrangements for string quartet allowed middle-class and bourgeois men to educate themselves about such works. Certainly some men played the two- and four-hand arrangements of these works for piano that circulated at the same time, but the string quartet versions made such pieces accessible to groups of amateur string players and could have fostered conversation about the relative merits of new musical gestures and compositional or dramatic approaches in the works. Performances of these arrangements for a private or semipublic gathering in provincial towns or larger cities allowed a wider public to experience the works then gracing stages in faraway metropolises, thus ensuring that they would remain well informed and conversant in the cultural news of their day (see chapter 2).

After about 1850, Schlesinger's focus turned from these contemporary, mostly foreign, operas toward works derived from folk materials. In a transitional period between 1851 and 1870, the firm printed arrangements of large orchestral works by Meyerbeer and Weber—operatic and concert overtures, as well as quasi-programmatic instrumental works—for string quartet or quintet. After 1870 (under the leadership of Robert Lienau, who purchased the firm in 1864), the transcriptions and arrangements fall into two basic categories: folk song and folk song–like works, which were the specialty of Moritz Kässmayer (1831–84), and canonic repertoire arranged for new ensembles, such as Schubert's Duo for Violin and Piano, op. 162, arranged for string quartet.[21] Like the Peters Edition published in the 1860s through the end of the century, Lienau-Schlesinger's new focus reflects the wider cultural and social interests of these decades. The folk song–like works concentrate on music in the Austro-German tradition and reinforce the public interest in this music as an original source for German culture.[22] Kässmayer's several volumes of folk songs are organized according to geographical or ethnic groupings. These collections do not, in the main, present "exotic" folk songs from outside central Europe—none of the volumes collects songs from the British Isles, the Americas, or Spain, for instance. The collections emphasize German-speaking and Austro-Hungarian regions such as Styria (vol. 3), Bohemia (vol. 2), Hungary (vol. 5), Austria (vol. 7), Vienna (vols. 10 and 11), and Germany (vols. 1, 4, 6, 12, and 13). One volume of Norwegian songs rounds out the collection of ancient Germanic lands.

Because print-run information for these works has not survived for posterity, we cannot know how popular these works were in their time or at what point in the century Schlesinger stopped reprinting the earlier operatic arrangements. The stark change in focus for newly produced music after the midcentury, though, suggests that audiences for string chamber music rather suddenly lost interest in opera. The coincidence of this shift at the same time that Europe was erupting in revolutionary fervor around 1848 and the decades that followed feels significant. That the catalog turns suddenly to folk-derived materials emphasizing a pan-Germanic culture after the Franco-Prussian War surely also reflects the political and social climate of the 1870s and 1880s and a newfound or newly emphasized interest in celebrating ancient Germanic culture in artworks designed for every level of music lover and consumer. Such musical expressions of nationalist pride and solidarity have long been recognized in large-scale works—choral works, orchestral pieces including overtures and tone poems, operas and music drama—and in programming practices, with the rise of concerts promoting Austro-German music and didactic programs that served to educate the listening public about the history of "good music." These publications, which seek to bring such nation-building activities into the private sphere of domestic string chamber music performance, bear further consideration as an important avenue for middle-class and bourgeois musicians to explore their own changing social, political, and cultural identities in the turbulent nineteenth century.

CHAPTER 2

"Domesticating" the Foreign in Arrangements of Operas, Folk Songs, and Other Works for Chamber Ensembles

Of the several chamber music styles and genres that flourished in the early nineteenth century, the most surprising for modern-day scholars and musicians may be the chamber arrangement. Although most students and scholars of nineteenth-century music are aware of two- and four-hand piano arrangements of string quartets and other works, the arrangement of an opera or a piano trio *for* string quartet is uncommon in today's music history narrative. Yet, as we have already seen, music publishers throughout Europe produced operas and stage works, as well as other orchestral pieces and folk song collections, *en quatuor* (arranged for string quartet) during the long nineteenth century (ca. 1789–ca. 1914), just as they produced operas and other works in two- and four-hand piano reductions, in vocal scores, and in several other unfamiliar formats, such as arrangements for two flutes or two violins. Arrangements allowed publishers to capitalize on the popularity of stage works and the virtuoso singers who brought them to life, but arrangements also played a significant role in the education of the public. Because it could be difficult for music lovers to attend premieres of important or daring new orchestral, choral, and theatrical works in the cities where they occurred and nearly impossible for those who lived elsewhere to attend these performances, transcriptions and arrangements brought the latest musical developments to audiences who otherwise might not encounter them. Arrangements and transcriptions served as one of the most efficient modes of transmission for new or newly discovered works in this period. They also allowed amateur and professional performers to re-create a performance that they had heard in a public concert or at a theater, to study and analyze a new work, and to learn the important pieces in a canonic repertoire that was becoming standardized. Like any artifact associated with the everyday lives of a previous era, the main value of these works for modern scholars lies in the subtle ways they transmit the musical and cultural values of the musicians who produced and consumed them.

As the type of transcription most familiar to modern-day readers, the transcription for piano provides a convenient starting point for considering the different functions of transcriptions in musical life. Nineteenth-century piano transcriptions fall into two categories: virtuosic showpieces and pedagogical or practical arrangements. The virtuoso transcriptions of operatic works by pianists such as Franz Liszt, Louis Moreau Gottschalk, and Sigismund Thalberg re-created the grandeur of the opera stage in seemingly impossible solo performances filled with brilliant displays of the musicians' technical abilities at the keyboard. These transcriptions, really fantasias or variation sets, frequently dealt with a small selection of familiar or popular musical themes from the opera, and much of the musical material in the "transcription" was newly composed by the pianist-composer. Although the best examples of these transcriptions provide intriguing interpretations of the original works upon which they are based, they are (in general) intended to showcase the skill of the performer, not the content of the original work.[1] On the other hand, the arrangement of a work for piano to facilitate study or rehearsal (as in vocal scores of operatic and choral works) sought to provide as much of the original as possible, though some content was inevitably lost in translation. Liszt's two- and four-hand arrangements of Beethoven's symphonies, to take one famous example, were intended in part to make these monumental works accessible to the average music lover with a piano at home.

The string quartet transcriptions and arrangements discussed in this chapter fall mostly into the latter category, though we shall see that the arrangers of these pieces made pointed decisions regarding the content and the form of the music they published. The resulting arrangements differ from their piano-oriented counterparts in significant ways, and they reflect the changing role of chamber music—and that of opera and folk song—in musical life over the course of the nineteenth century. In translating an opera or other work for string quartet, arrangers combined seemingly opposed genres and social settings, bringing the opera house into the parlor in some cases and the countryside into the city in others.

Berlin-based publisher Adolph Martin Schlesinger provides an excellent case study; the firm produced dozens of opera transcriptions, collections of folk songs, and arrangements of Classical works for amateur chamber musicians between 1800 and 1900, as discussed in chapter 1. Robert Lienau bought the Berlin branch of the firm with full rights to its catalog in 1864, and the archive of the still-active publishing firm in Frankfurt am Main has preserved most or all of these arrangements. This cache of scores allows modern scholars to study aspects of the arrangements that indicate changes in the social and political uses of music and the changing tastes of musical consumers, at least in Berlin and Paris and probably in many more cities where Schlesinger's and Lienau's businesses distributed printed music.[2]

In the first few decades of the nineteenth century, Schlesinger (like his colleagues in Leipzig and elsewhere) focused on French- and Italian-language works, especially French grand operas by Gaspare Spontini, Fromental Halévy, and

Giacomo Meyerbeer. This focus on foreign-language works reflects the repertoire of most European opera houses at that time, but for Berlin-based Schlesinger, the influence of Prussian king Frederick Wilhelm III was especially important. The king appointed Italian composer Gaspare Spontini (1774–1851), whose French and Italian operas had been popular in Paris, as leader of the Hofoper (the Royal Opera Company) in 1820. The appointment created friction between supporters of the mostly French and Italian repertoire favored by the aristocracy and supporters of the Nationaltheater, which produced German-language operas. Though the two theaters had merged officially in 1807, tensions between them continued to color reception of new works throughout the first half of the nineteenth century. For example, when Carl Maria von Weber's *Der Freischütz* was premiered under the direction of Karl von Brühl at the Nationaltheater in 1821, it played to an audience primarily made up of Romantic critics and artists and wealthy citizens who attended a public performance. Just the previous month, Spontini's *Olimpie* was performed in German translation at the Royal Opera House to an audience mostly consisting of the royal court and members of the nobility in a more exclusive by-invitation performance.

Schlesinger prospered despite these tensions by making friends on both sides of the debate. He secured exclusive rights to print Weber's music in 1814, and he entered into agreements with Meyerbeer and Halévy and other composers of grand opera via his son Maurice's Paris branch of the business. During the 1830s and 1840s, he also published arrangements of works by Gaetano Donizetti and Vincenzo Bellini. (Some of these arrangements were made by Richard Wagner, including the string quartet arrangement of Donizetti's *La favorite*.) By maximizing his connections to both musical camps and to both "foreign" and native operatic talents, Schlesinger ensured that no matter what opera was most popular in a given season or with a certain demographic, he would be able to supply the demand for socially respectable entertainment that arrangements provided.

Transcriptions of Complete Operas, ca. 1810–1850

Like the vocal scores and piano versions of operas with which modern musicians are more familiar, string quartet transcriptions provide a scaled-down version of the opera for performance in the middle-class parlor. In most cases, they retain the original keys of the individual numbers and translate the titles or text incipits, rendering a linguistic and a musical "translation" of foreign-language works such as the French grand operas popular in the first half of the century. In this way, the arrangers working for Schlesinger created a version of the opera that would be accessible to German string-playing amateurs. In the case of operas that were presented in German translation in Berlin and elsewhere, the string quartet transcriptions may also reflect the version of the opera that audiences encountered in the theater or read about in the press.

The transcriptions considered here rearrange the contents of the opera to achieve a desired musical organization and recompose some numbers, but a large proportion of the opera itself remains, as opposed to later chamber arrangements that treat only a few of the opera's most memorable tunes or dramatic moments. (For this reason, I use the term *transcription* to describe these quartet versions of nearly complete operas and the term *arrangement* or *medley* to describe the more fantasia-like publications common in later decades.) In each of the four works considered here, though, the arranger made a series of compositional choices that had a profound effect on the presentation of the opera being transcribed, and the changes in content and order of movements frequently go well beyond the addition or omission of individual arias or scenes common in vocal scores and four-hand arrangements of the same period. Such changes to the work may be interpreted in light of its new intended audience of sheet music purchasers. The three French transcriptions considered here all treat works composed and premiered in the first three decades of the nineteenth century: François-Adrien Boieldieu's *Jean de Paris* (1812), Meyerbeer's *Robert le Diable* (1831), and Halévy's *La juive* (1835). These three works demonstrate the breadth of approaches to opera transcriptions for string quartet, and they show the various reactions arrangers and audiences had to grand opera's greatest talents when their works were brought to German stages. A brief comparison to transcriptions of German Romantic operas by Carl Maria von Weber provides a useful point of reference for the differences in transcription practice and what they may suggest about the relationship between transcription and reception of operatic innovations.

Johann von Paris, as it was known in German, premiered in Paris in 1812 and was performed in translation during the next decade in Prague, Vienna, and Berlin. Friedrich Starke's transcription of the comic opera offers a series of vignettes that "Germanize" the plot and musical style.[3] For each number in the transcription, a German title or incipit at the beginning of the first violin part provides some context and clarifies the action of the scene.[4] Here as in other chamber transcriptions, Starke has removed ensemble numbers and finales so that the remaining movements feature the main characters' most important numbers from the opera. In *Johann von Paris*, only three of the seven numbers from the first act appear in the transcription, resulting in a more streamlined first "half" consisting of an overture, an aria, and a duet. The second act retains every number except the second overture and the opera's finale. The transcription ends with a climactic duet in which the two protagonists reveal their love and their true identities to each other rather than with the perfunctory choral affirmation of this event.

As table 2.1 shows, Starke's omissions create a quartet version that emphasizes the most tuneful and memorable numbers of the original and capitalizes on the numbers that fit musical topics or types popular in other recreational genres, especially genres associated with male leisure, such as songs for male choruses.

TABLE 2.1 Summary of contents for Boieldieu, *Jean de Paris* (operatic version) and Starke's quartet transcription as *Johann von Paris*

	Vocal score (1812)		Quartet version
	Ouverture	1	Ouverture (Andante–Allegro con moto)
1	Introduction et Choeur		
2	Trio		
3	**Air**	2	Duetto [*sic*]: Begiebt mein Herr sich auf die Reise (Allegro moderato)
4	Air et Choeur		
5	**Duo**	3	Duetto: Der Ruhm über alles zu lieben (Tempo di Marcia)
6	Air		
7	Final		
Act 2			
8	Ouverture		
9	**Duo**		
10	**Air**	4	Aria: Der Ritterschaft Zierde u. Glanz (Allegro moderato)
		5	Duetto: In einer schmachtenden Romance (Andantino)
11	**Choeur**	6	Chor: Last zu dem Fest (Allegro maestoso)
12	**Romance** et Choeur	7	Romance: Der Troubadour (Allegretto)
13	**Duo**	8	Duetto: Der Man den ich erwähle (Grazioso)
14	Choeur Final		

Note: Items in **bold** indicate movements transcribed in the quartet version.

For instance, the only aria that remains in the first act of the quartet version ("My lord embarks on the journey") is the comic patter-filled number that Johann's page, Olivier, sings at an inn. Note that the name of the secondary, nonnoble character Olivier remains French, but the opera's hero, Jean, is Germanized to Johann. The duet that Starke retains ("Duty above all") is a martial number about knights and their duties to honor and love noble ladies. This fun romp is followed by Johann's act 2 aria that also extols chivalric duties and benefits ("The brave and gallant knight"). Thus, the quartet version emphasizes musical numbers filled with archaic local color that evoke images of noble men engaged in gender- and class-appropriate activities.

Starke removed most of the opera's choruses and the more "chatty" ensemble numbers that advance the plot in the original stage version, thereby creating a chamber version that is more appropriate for the quartet environment because it privileges repetitions of longer melodies and carefully controlled dialogue among the ensemble members. Unlike fast-paced comic opera finales, where four to six members of the cast sing at the same time in an artful frenzy, the exchange of melodies in the duets and arias emulates a more leisurely, even genteel conversational style. Omission of the choral numbers makes sense for different reasons: in these operas, choruses employ a fairly consistent homorhythmic or homophonic texture rather than a polyphonic one, and the thick four-voice texture of the chorus combined with the orchestra parts would require the arranger to make several compromises to bring off both the accompaniment and the vocal parts in a suitable arrangement. In the solo and ensemble numbers retained in the quartet versions, by contrast, the orchestral parts are easily condensed into two or three of the quartet parts while one or two players act as the solo singer(s).

The relatively small scale of the two-act comic opera allowed Schlesinger to publish the string quartet version of *Johann von Paris* in a single "book"; actually, the publication includes one book per player, as these works were issued in parts only. For longer and more complicated works such as the grand operas of the 1830s, however, the firm frequently published transcriptions in multiple volumes, providing one or two acts in each book and spacing out the publication by a few months in a serialized distribution plan. For Meyerbeer's *Robert le Diable* (Robert the Devil), Jacques Strunz created a four-book transcription that combines the final two acts into a hefty book 4 containing twice as many individual numbers as each of the previous books.

Strunz's quartet version of Meyerbeer's massive 1831 hit capitalized on the recent success of *Robert le Diable* in Paris and its 1832 performance in Berlin.[5] (Karl von Brühl, the same music director who had led the premiere of Weber's *Der Freischütz* to critical acclaim in 1821, produced the German *Robert der Teufel*.) Strunz's transcription goes further than Starke's *Johann von Paris* in adjusting the work for German chamber enthusiasts. The quartet version of *Robert* rearranges and omits several of the opera's components; in some movements, Strunz created completely new musical works from operatic materials rather than providing straightforward transcriptions. Strunz retained almost all of the solo, duet, and dance numbers but removed the longer recitative-filled scenes and several of the choral numbers.[6] Table 2.2 compares the contents of the original opera (as published in full score by Schlesinger in 1831) and the quartet transcription, published in 1832. The omissions reduce the length of the opera somewhat, but, more importantly, they remove portions of the work that do not work well for stringed instruments or that are not pleasurable to play. Grand opera's lengthy accompanied recitatives create a continuous stream of dramatic music in the stage work, but in the string quartet version, they would be superfluous. Without the text, they do not further the plot or the musical argument, and they quickly become tedious in a quartet setting. (I will return to the difficulty of playing operatic recitative in string quartets below.) Thus, in the transcription, they are removed to make way for the arias and ensemble numbers that present a more enjoyable experience for the string players.

In the stage version of the opera, ten separate choral numbers bring Meyerbeer's medieval fantasy to life in demonic drinking songs, tales of traveling knights, dances by spectral nuns called forth from the grave, chivalric tournaments, and vivid banquet halls filled with courtiers. The quartet version omits all but four of

TABLE 2.2 Summary of contents for Meyerbeer, *Robert le Diable* (operatic version) and Strunz's quartet transcription as *Robert der Teufel*

	Full score (1831)		Quartet version
Acte I	1. A. **Ouverture** & Introduction	Livr. 1	1. Ouverture
	B. Choeur des Buveurs		
	C. **Ballade**		2. Ballade
	D. Suite & Fin de Introduction		
	2. **Romance**		3. Romance
	3. Finale: A. **Sicilienne**		4. Sicilienne
	B. Scène du Jeu		
Acte II	4. Entr'acte et **Air**	Livr. 2	5. Air
	5. **Duo**		6. Couplets
	6. **Choeur dansé**		7. Choeur Dansé
	7. **Pas de cinq**		8. Pas de cinq
	8. Recitatif & Final		
Acte III	9. Entr'acte recitatif & **Duo bouffe**	Livr. 3	9. Duo
	10. La valse infernae (choeur)		
	11. Couplets et Scène		
	12. **Duo** et Scène		10. Duo
	13. Trio (sans accompagenment)		
	14. Duo		
	15. Final A. Recitatif & Évocation		
	B. **Bacchanale**		
	C. Recitatif		
	D. **1er Air de Danse**		11. Pas de Taglione
	E. 2me Air de Danse		
	F. **3me Air de Danse**		12. Air de Ballet (incl. music from Bacchanale)
	G. Choeur dansé		
Acte IV	16. **Entr'acte & Choeur de Femmes Recitatif**	Livr. 4	13. Andantino-Allegro
			14. Allegro moderato
	17. Choeur		
	18. Final A. Scène & Cavatine		
	B. **Duo**		16. Poco Andante
	C. **Cavatine**		15. Poco Andantino
	D. **Choeur & Stretta**		17. Poco Andantino
Acte V	19. Entr'acte & Choeur des moines		
	20. **Choeur (Prière)**		18. Prière
	21. Scène & Duo avec Choeur		
	22. Air		
	23. **Grand Trio**		19. Allegretto molto moderato
	24. Choeur Final		

Note: Items in **bold** indicate movements transcribed in the quartet version.

these choral scenes, keeping the "Chœur dansé" that accompanies the court wedding in act 2, portions of the two choruses of attendants from the beginning and end of act 4, and the cathedral prayer that permeates the final act. In each of these cases, Strunz modifies the choral music to suit his own purposes. For instance, he recomposed the choral prayer from the opera's final act (no. 18 in the quartet transcription) to create an impressive instrumental translation of this dramatic moment in the opera. Although the published full score indicates that the hymn could be omitted in theaters without an organ or to shorten the production, Strunz put in an extraordinary effort to make it work in the string quartet version. The opera's short scene opens and closes with a hymn performed on the organ to characterize the church interior. In the central section of the number, a priest intones the hymn in four-measure phrases as a chorus of the people responds to each phrase in harmony. Strunz's arrangement uses these raw materials to create an effective ensemble number (see the complete movement in appendix 1). The quartet version opens with the closing chorale from the operatic number (the triplet motif in the quartet's cello adds some rhythmic vibrancy in an otherwise static number), followed by a free contrapuntal arrangement of the chorale's main motives (section A, mm. 1–31). Then the viola and cello intone the priest's line in loud octaves, alternating with the soft choral response interspersed in four-bar phrases (section B, mm. 32–67). The second half of the movement modulates to B♭ major for another treatment of the chorale tune (section C, mm. 68–85), then returns to the tonic, F major, to revisit the B section's alternating phrases. The final twenty-three measures (marked "Coda") close the quartet movement with new material based on the chorale's rhythmic profile and melodic contours; the newly composed section reinforces the serene mood of the scene.

In the staged opera, the hymn tune of this "prayer" permeates the final act. It is reprised in each of the choral numbers that follow, including the work's finale, when the celestial choir celebrates Robert's redemption. It provides the sonic backdrop against which the culminating drama of the work unfolds. Strunz's additions and reworking of the scene's original materials allowed him to create a longer ensemble piece that features the quartet's potential for a homogeneous sound, emphasizing its choir-like qualities in contrast to the soloistic orientation of much of the rest of the work. By drawing out this number, he creates an atmospheric piece that can ring in the minds and ears of the players as they move on to the final trio and the end of their operatic adventure, but in a quartet-appropriate style that removes the original stage trappings and places the music in a pure instrumental context.

The emphasis on instrumentally satisfying style in these transcriptions—that is, on passages that work well for the players, regardless of their importance in the texture of the original—continues in the transcription's final movement, the Grand Trio, in which Alice works to convince Robert to repent his wicked ways rather than joining Bertram as a servant of hell. Her last trump card is a letter from Robert's mother begging him to repent and revealing that she had been seduced and deceived by Bertram and that he, Robert's true father, had abandoned her. At the moment in the opera when Robert reads this letter, a pair of keyed trumpets introduce a new B-minor melody with this instruction: "The keyed trumpets should be placed outside of the orchestra: they should produce an effect as though they come from afar, from another world." Strunz's transcription of this moment in the opera is exact; the first violin plays the trumpet melody over dry, staccato chords in the lower instruments (see example 2.1).

In m. 205, though, Strunz omits Robert's monotonous vocal line (he intones the letter's text in fits and starts to convey the character's horror and bewilderment) and transcribes instead the trumpet and the flute melodies in euphonious parallel thirds played by the quartet's two violins. The opera's woodwind and horn interjections are represented in the quartet version in the violins (mm. 214–19), and when Alice's vocal line enters to repeat the letter's words, the two violins play her melody in parallel octaves. Robert is effectively silenced in this passage in favor of an inviting and memorable instrumental number for the quartet's enjoyment.

Strunz's treatment of another emblematic scene from the opera perfectly demonstrates the possibility for a transcription to soften the effect of a potentially scandalous work by "domesticating" it for the home.[7] At the end of the third act of *Robert*, a fantastical ballet scene portrays a group of reanimated nuns as they rise from the grave and dance a bacchanal in praise of life's carnal pleasures. The "Ballet of the Nuns" was calculated to provoke and intrigue audiences in its conception and execution. Both the Parisian and Berlin productions of the opera featured the dancer Marie Taglioni; it was her first famous use of dancing *en pointe*, or dancing on the tip of the toes to suggest weightlessness.[8] Strunz disassembled the act 3 finale to create two self-sufficient numbers at the end of his book 3 and to create a dramatically and musically climactic ending for this book. His no. 11, titled "Pas de Taglione [*sic*]," uses parts of the orchestral music from the ballet but does not transcribe the music as it appears in published scores. No. 12 ("Air de ballet") incorporates more orchestral music from the finale's dance scene in an Andantino that features the cello in a cantabile theme, then a fast "Bacchanale" section borrowed from the opening of the finale. This newly created pair of movements allowed Strunz to bring to the quartet members' minds the famous scene of Taglioni dancing *en pointe*, which they may or may not have seen but about which they certainly would have read in the press. Separating the finale into two distinct numbers separates Taglioni's performance from the ensemble bacchanal, rendering her scene more singular and noteworthy and (perhaps) protecting her name and reputation from the unsavory implications of the bacchanal. Musically, this recomposition ends the book with an effective slow-fast binary form. Thus, Strunz's version places this music in the context of a conventional instrumental work for strings, borrowing some of the quartet genre's respectability to clean up the potentially offensive nature of the scene.

One final example from the *Robert* transcription shows Strunz treading much more lightly on the original work. In the act 1 romance "Va dit-elle mon enfant" (Go, my child, she said), Alice tells Robert of his mother's death. The operatic song is a binary form in E major; a homophonic texture reigns throughout, as the orchestra sympathetically accompanies Alice's tale with instrumental color

EXAMPLE 2.1 Strunz, string quartet transcription of no. 19 Grand Trio, from Meyerbeer's *Robert le Diable*, mm. 196–227.

EXAMPLE 2.2 Strunz, string quartet transcription of no. 3 Romance, "Va, dit-elle, mon enfant" (Go, tell my child), from Meyerbeer's *Robert le Diable*, mm. 1–35.

provided by the winds in the introduction, interlude, and closing sections. Strunz's arrangement adheres to Meyerbeer's original, transcribing the entire work with practically no changes (see example 2.2). The first violin most often serves as vocal soloist, and the wind solos from the original are provided here by the quartet's second violin and viola, playing as a horn duo in mm. 3–10 and 56–58, for example, or by the first violin if Alice is silent, as in mm. 21–27, where the woodwind punctuations of Meyerbeer's score are played by the first violin in Strunz's transcription. The entire number takes just 125 measures, and the simple style of the song lends itself well to arrangement in a "violin with strings" style.

EXAMPLE 2.2 (continued)

The movement emulates the simple French art songs (called "romances") popular at this time, and Strunz's arrangement provides a fitting quartet analogue to those recreational domestic works. In other words, because this operatic number already utilizes a style appropriate to the salon or parlor, no significant changes are needed.

As Romantic opera became increasingly "grand," or filled with more daring displays of expense and excess, string quartet arrangers made more radical adjustments to the opera's content and style to fit them into the austere chamber format. Halévy's 1835 work *La juive* (The Jewess, published as *Die Jüdin* in Berlin) created a sensation at its premiere with a spectacular procession of the principal characters riding live horses onstage and a lavish fifteenth-century festival. Critics singled out the authenticity of the armor, the sets, and the props as especially effective in transporting the audience to a sixteenth-century city. Its plot features forbidden love between a Jewess and a Christian, along with the more or less usual operatic tropes: adultery, disguises and mistaken identities, religious fanaticism, and lifelong vendettas. When Heinrich Panofka created his transcription of *Die Jüdin*, he employed tactics used by Strunz and other arrangers to make the work more manageable for domestic audiences, and he took greater license with the original material in service of his audience.

The first sign of Panofka's intervention in the work is the overall shape and scope of the transcription itself. He divided the original five-act opera into three separate volumes, or "suites," each with six movements (see table 2.3). Each suite contains an assortment of solo, ensemble, and instrumental numbers. These movements seem to be arranged to maximize the potential for instrumentally satisfying music and to achieve a balanced variety of ensemble interactions and musical textures within the suites. Because of this shuffling, the arrangement of *La juive* is the least straightforward of the works studied here and the most disconnected from its original dramatic context. Items are moved and rearranged, even dismembered and reassembled throughout the three suites. Suite 1 contains most of the opera's first act but receives two noteworthy revisions, both showing Panofka's preferences for a "quartet-ized" work here. The opera's first act is fairly chorus- and recitative-heavy, a necessary feature that allowed Halévy to explain the complicated setting and backstory of the work for the operatic audience.[9] Panofka removed the opening "Cavatina" following the introduction, presumably because it features three characters singing in a recitative-like style with choral interjections (thus, it is not a cavatina in the Italian sense of the word, a short lyrical song). The character Leopold's "Serenade" remains in the transcription, but this work is quite short, leaving the first book without a strong solo aria.

To remedy this problem, perhaps, Rachel's romance from act 2 ("He will come") is moved into suite 1, preceding the instrumental waltz (no. 6) that ends the first suite. Suite 2 begins with the last item from the opera's act 2 and includes a variety of items excerpted from acts 2, 3, and 4 in no particular order (as far as the stage action is concerned), ending with the opera's most famous number, the tenor aria for Eleazar in act 4 ("Rachel, when the Lord's saving grace," discussed below). Suite 3 begins with the "People's Chorus" of the opera's final act but then "backs up" dramatically to revisit items and portions of items from previous acts. This decision allowed Panofka to incorporate several important duo and trio numbers from the opera without concentrating them all in the middle book of the three-suite transcription. The final movement of the transcription returns to the act 1 procession on horseback, which made a strong impression on audiences and critics of the time. Thus, Panofka ends each of the three suites of his transcription with a famous moment in the opera, even reserving the act 1 finale's music to end the transcription in a grand style.

Most unusually, the act 3 "Pantomime and ballet," which featured the entrance and interactions of the victorious knights in the original opera, appears throughout the arrangement, with individual sections of the ballet scene excerpted from

TABLE 2.3 Summary of contents for Halévy, *La juive* (operatic version) and Panofka's quartet transcription as *Die Jüdin*

Vocal score		Quartet version	
Acte I	1. **Introduction et Chœur**	Suite 1	1. Introduction et Choeur
	2. Cavatine		
	3. **Serenade**		2. Serenade
	4. **Chœur**		3. Choeur
	5. **Chœur des Buveurs**		4. Choeur des Buveurs
	[from Acte II: 10. Romance]		5. Romance
	6. **Valse**		6. Valse
	7. **Final [partial below]**		
Acte II	8. Entracte et Prière		
	9. **Trio [below]**		
	10. **Romance [above]**		
	11. **Duo [below]**		
	12. **Trio** "Je vois son front"	Suite 2	7. Grand Trio
	[from Acte IV: 21. Duo]		8. Duo
	[from Acte III: 17. Pantomime et Ballet]		9. Air de Ballet [Moderato]
Acte III	13. **Air***		10. Scene et Duo
	14. **Duo***		
	15. Bolero*		
	16. Recitative et Chœur		
	17. **Pantomime et Ballet**		11. Air de Ballet [Allegro—Con grazia]
	18. Finale		
	A. Chœur		
	B. Sextuor & Chœur		
	C. Malediction		
	D. Morceau d'ensemble		
Acte IV	19. Scene & Duo		
	20. Duettino [full score: Scene]		
	21. **Duo [above]**		
	22. **Air**		12. Air: Rachel quand du Seigneur
Acte V	23. **Chœur**	Suite 3	13. Choeur du people (Chor des Volkes)
	24. Marche funèbre		
	25. Finale		
	[from Acte II: 9. Trio "Tu possedes dit-on"]		14. Trio: Tu possedes diton (Du verwahrst, hörte ich)
	[from Acte III: 17. Pantomime et Ballet]		15. Air de ballet [Moderato]
	[from Acte II: 11. Duo "Lorsquà toi je me suis données"]		16. Duo: Lorsquà toi je me suis données (Als mein Herz dir sich hingegeben)
	[from Acte III: 17. Pantomime et Ballet]		17. Air de ballet [Allegro non troppo]
	[from Acte I finale 7. Finale]		18. Marche de cortège

* Vocal score nos. 13 (Air), 14 (Duo), and 15 (Bolero) do not appear in the full score reprinted as no. 36 in the *Early Romantic Opera* edition.

their original context to serve as short interludes between arias, duos, and trios (see nos. 9, 11, 15, and 17 in the string quartet version). The pure orchestral music from the ballet provides a welcome ensemble opportunity for quartetists, breaking the potential monotony of a long series of duets and solo numbers featuring the first violin as the star "singer." In this instance, Panofka's dismantling of the ballet is similar in theory to Strunz's recomposition of the "Pas de Taglione" in his *Robert* transcription, though more radical. Whereas Strunz created two stand-alone movements and placed them at the end of his third book in an analogous position to the music's original context at the end of *Robert*'s act 3, Panofka abandons the pretext of presenting the opera in its original form in favor of creating a balanced, chamber-appropriate version of the work for amateur string quartetists.

Just as the overall rearrangement of operatic components demonstrates Panofka's concern for balance and musical interest in a chamber-appropriate style, his approach in individual numbers is calculated to increase players' enjoyment of the work and to emphasize (what Panofka must have considered) its most important scenes. Eleazar's aria from act 4 ("Rachel, quand du Seigneur," or "Rachel, when the Lord's saving grace") is the cornerstone of the drama, as it brings together the most important themes of the plot and features the original work's true star, the tenor Adolphe Nourrit (1802–39). Nourrit's request for an opera that would challenge him as a musician and as an actor—a leading character who could not easily be described as a villain or a hero—prompted Halévy to compose the work. Nourrit collaborated in shaping the work, even composing the text for this lengthy aria, which depicts the character wrestling with his emotions: his love for Rachel and desire for her happiness almost overcome the anger, resentment, and pain he harbors from mistreatment by Cardinal Brogni and others in the first half of the scene. The relentless taunting of the crowd (the choral interjections), however, drives him to despair, leading to his and Rachel's death in the opera's final act. The string quartet version also allows the first violinist to embody the role of the star tenor in a musical form of playacting.

The aria in its original version is a standard four-part scene on the Rossini model, as table 2.4 shows.[10] Halévy made use of the full expressive power of the orchestra in his colorful orchestrations, and the arrangement retains many of these instrumental sections, which typically allow for engaging conversational textures. Panofka omitted sections that would be difficult for the string players and that might detract from the aria's essential components in the chamber setting, such as the recitative-filled introduction (part 1). The transcription begins with six measures based on the woodwind quartet music that introduces the slow aria section (part 2), though it omits the English horn duet that foreshadows Eleazar's melody. In the opera, this "exotic" sound helps to characterize Eleazar as a Jewish outsider; in the transcription, the duet would seem redundant, as it merely presents the melody in its entirety before the character sings it. In the transcription's m. 7, the first violin plays the tenor's melody while the lower three

TABLE 2.4 Summary of "Rachel, quand du Seigneur" from Halévy, *La juive*

Section	1 **Introduction**	2 **Slow aria**		3 **Transition**	4 **Fast aria**			**Coda**
Drama	Conversation (death sentence announced)	Aria: Eleazar laments Rachel's fate	(woodwind interlude)	"I could save her with a word . . . but no! I won't let them have her!"	Aria: "God reveals that you [Rachel] must die by my side, forgive me"	"She belongs to the God of Jacob"	Aria: "God reveals that you [Rachel] must die by my side, forgive me"	(Instrumental)
Musical form and style	Recitative	ABA		Recitative + chorus	C (aba′)	Recitative + chorus	C (aba′)	
Quartet version	**[omitted]**	**mm. 1–58** vln 1 = voice of Eleazar	**mm. 59–63**	**mm. 63–75** orchestral parts only, not vocal lines (no chorus) and **shortened**	**mm. 76–100** vln 1 = voice of Eleazar	**mm. 101–13** orchestral parts only, and **shortened**	**mm. 114–50** vln 1 = voice of Eleazar	**mm. 151–63**

instruments accompany with a reduction of the orchestral parts (see example 2.3). At the end of the original vocal line, Halévy's full woodwind interlude is included in the transcription before the aria's B melody enters in m. 25 (again, in the first violin).

Although the repetitions in the aria sections (parts 2 and 4) remain intact, the chorus-and-recitative sections (part 3 and the interruption in part 4) are significantly shortened. In fact, the quartet version omits the choral music altogether in these sections, dividing the orchestral parts among the quartet players instead. At the end of the movement, Panofka includes the full instrumental coda, again demonstrating a preference for instrumental music in the quartet version. The

EXAMPLE 2.3 Panofka, transcription of no. 12, "Rachel, quand du Seigneur" (Rachel, when the Lord's grace) from Halévy's *La juive*, mm. 1–38.

removal of the recitatives and choruses may serve an interpretive purpose in this transcription, as well as a practical one. Just as Strunz "silenced" Robert in the trio of his *Robert der Teufel* transcription, Panofka has silenced the harassing crowd and antagonists of this scene from *La juive*. What remains are the main character's most lyrical and tortured lines, accompanied by "pure" instrumental music drawn from Eleazar's only supporter in the opera, the orchestra. With this and other compositional decisions that "domesticate" the opera for German (and perhaps French) middle-class sheet music purchasers, Panofka magnifies the elements of the scene that made it an operatic success—the solo singing power of the tenor and his nuanced performance of the simple, affecting melodies—while

EXAMPLE 2.3 (continued)

removing or softening aspects that would not transfer well to the setting. Placing this solo centerpiece within the context of a reconceived version of the opera that privileges ensemble numbers—especially at the end of suite 2, which contains no other solo numbers—further enhances its importance in the new quartet version of the work.

Clearly, Heinrich Panofka, who was renowned in his lifetime as both a violinist and a singing teacher, prioritized the enjoyment of the players over unnecessary fidelity to the score in his transcription of *La juive*. In creating a quartet version of the opera, he made a variety of important decisions that hinge on the function of the new work within the social setting for which it was intended. In the works of fellow opera arranger and violinist C. W. Henning, we do not see the same effort to adjust the work or to domesticate it for the home. Henning's transcriptions deal with the music of German Romantic icon Carl Maria von Weber (1786–1826), in particular *Der Freischütz*, which was the source of much recreational music after the composer's untimely death. Perhaps because the composer had died, Henning felt a certain respectful fidelity was required in translating Weber's works for the domestic sphere.

Henning's Weber transcriptions differ from the French opera ones in that they transmit the entire work from beginning to end without omissions (with one notable exception) and without changes to the musical content of individual numbers. Henning's transcriptions retain the original keys, include as much of the orchestral parts as possible, and transcribe all of the accompanied recitative in addition to the more tuneful aria portions. Whereas Panofka altered Halévy's music to suit the needs of his audience and create a playable piece, and Strunz extended Meyerbeer's music to enhance the effect of individual numbers, Henning treated the materials of *Der Freischütz* with extreme caution. The transcription of Agathe's act 2 scene, which contains the folk-like "Gently, gently, pious words" in a four-section number similar to Halévy's "Rachel, when the Lord's saving grace," provides a good example. Table 2.5 shows the form of this aria, and appendix 2 provides the complete quartet movement.

TABLE 2.5 Summary of "Leise, leise, fromme Weise" from Weber, *Der Freischütz*

Section	1 **Introduction**	2 **Slow aria**		3 **Transition**	4 **Fast aria**
Drama	"How could I possibly sleep?"	"Waft softly, gentle song"		[horn calls] "What's that? It's him!"	"My pulse is racing, my heart is beating"
Musical form and style	recitative	A (aab) aria (Adagio) with recitative	B (Andante)	recitative/arioso	C aria (Vivace)
Quartet version	**mm. 1–16**	**mm. 17–60** vln 1 = Agathe	**mm. 61–73**	**mm. 74–106** vla = horns	**mm. 107–198**

In the stage version, Agathe's aria is continually interrupted by accompanied recitative, a characteristic of Weber's free-flowing operatic style. Agathe observes the world around her and worries about her beloved Max between strains of the main aria melody. Henning dutifully transcribed all of this material into the printed parts, where the players must differentiate recitative from aria (or unmetered music from metered passages) for themselves. In the lower three parts, this difference is not immediately obvious in most cases because the recitative and aria frequently begin and end within measures. This publication requires a skilled quartet leader to help the other players navigate the frequent changes of meter and tempo. Particularly for players unaccustomed to playing in this operatic style, the fluidity required to bring off this sort of music is difficult to achieve without practice. This transcription of operatic recitative differs markedly from the approximation or evocation of recitative in original string quartets of the time, such as those by Beethoven (opp. 131 and 132) and Mendelssohn (opp. 12 and 13). The key, E major, is also a difficult one for string players, requiring left-hand acrobatics and barring access to open strings. Thus, in his enthusiasm to present Weber in as transparent and uncompromised a way as possible, Henning created a quartet version that makes what may be considered unreasonable demands of the players.

Henning's string quartet version of *Der Freischütz* reproduces Weber's music exactly, with one glaring exception: the finale to act 2, the famous Wolf's Glen scene, which forms most modern musicians' lasting or only impression of the opera, is missing. Act 2 ends with the trio "How? What? Horror!" (also a measure-for-measure transcription of that number in the opera) and a note to the players ("Ende des zweiten Actes") at the bottom of each part. Act 3 begins in the next book with its entr'acte. In other words, the parts do not indicate that perhaps the most memorable and important scene of the opera, in which the cursed bullets are cast through demonic magic, has been omitted.

Henning may have removed this number for pragmatic reasons; the operatic scene would have been outrageously difficult to transcribe well due to its complicated musical structure. It is also possible, though, that he cut this scene because it contains the most potentially offensive and outlandish material of the opera's plot. Without it, the opera might be read as the tale of an ordinary but well-meaning young man overcoming more powerful rivals to win the heart and hand of an innocent young woman. Although Max is portrayed as a bumbler and a coward, he only seems a villain in the second act finale, when he agrees to take part in a satanic ritual to cast magic bullets aided by representatives of hell. Omitting this scene has the effect of eliminating the hero's moment of weakness and removing any doubt about the quality of his moral character.

Musically, the scene is easily the most spectacular and complex one of the opera, as it is filled with melodrama (i.e., spoken dialogue accompanied by the orchestra), the combination of chorus and soloists with orchestra, and highly evocative orchestral passages to depict the storms, fires, demons, and will-o'-the-wisps that accompany the casting of the bullets. The unconventional musical style and structure of this scene set it apart from the rest of the opera; it has been classified as innovative and revelatory, and for that reason, this scene more than any other in the work has been anthologized and referenced as the most important component of the opera in the nearly two centuries since the work's premiere. In the context of the rest of the work, however, this scene disrupts a seemingly natural progression of recognizable topics and styles associated with everyday music making. As previous commentators on *Der Freischütz* have noted, the opera is filled with touchstones of German musical Romanticism even without considering the Wolf's Glen scene. Multiple hunters' and foresters' choruses evoke the late eighteenth- and early nineteenth-century *Männerchor* tradition; various folk song–like numbers such as the Bridesmaids' Chorus of the last act bring to mind *Volkston*-style *Lieder* and choruses from the Biedermeier period; drinking or hunting songs and overtures filled with hunting horn motifs evoke the natural world or an idealized portrayal of rustic life in "olden times" that inspired the Romantic imagination. Finally, waltzes and polonaises in the first and second acts bring to mind the numerous collections of stylized dances and practical dance music that characterized domestic musical entertainments in this era. Despite the difficulty of performing the exact transcriptions of the other numbers, the quartet version of *Der Freischütz*, without the Wolf's Glen scene, provides a chamber-appropriate version of the opera purged of its most salacious content and centered on domestic entertainment styles that would have been immediately familiar to upper-middle-class music lovers. (Notably, a contemporaneous quartet transcription published by Weigl in Vienna also leaves out this one vital number.)

Although Panofka, Strunz, and Henning clearly had different notions of what was and was not vital to the performance of these works, their transcriptions show signs of a shared interest in transmitting as much of the opera as possible within the confines of acceptable domestic musical practices. These works and the other complete opera transcriptions of the first half of the nineteenth century served as a vehicle to gain familiarity with the latest trends and the most important works on Europe's opera stages, much like the two- and four-hand versions for piano and piano-vocal scores that circulated at the same time. The string quartet versions differ from piano-centric transcriptions, though, in that they would have addressed an audience of male domestic amateur musicians and (possibly) their listeners. Certainly piano transcriptions were available to both men and women, but the string quartet transcriptions would have been accessible primarily to men, who were the main practitioners of string quartet playing. This fact of social setting and audience may explain why the quartet versions of the operas studied here—especially the French operas—contain so many changes and intercessions by the arrangers. Much more than arrangements or transcriptions for piano, these quartet versions present a work that has been adjusted to suit the needs of its consumers, with the arranger making interpretive decisions on their behalf. Portions of the work that would be unappealing have been removed, new instrumental versions of key moments in the work have been created to emphasize their importance, and some music has been rewritten to conform to the string quartet (and masculine) ideal of intellectual rigor and formal balance or cohesion. These intercessions are evident in all of the transcriptions discussed here, but they are most evident—most invasive, we might say—in the work that would likely have been most "foreign" to North German string players, *La juive*, a French work set in the distant past and centered on Jewish characters in the predominantly Catholic society of the fifteenth century. Tellingly, these intercessions are least evident in the transcription of *Der Freischütz*, which depicts identifiably German characters in a nearly everyday situation (despite its chronological setting in the seventeenth century) made even more commonplace by the omission of the fantastical scene at the end of act 2. The transcriptions of these operas allowed them to be incorporated into German domestic musical life by highlighting musical styles and interactions that would be familiar to sheet music consumers of the 1830s and 1840s and by removing or reconfiguring aspects that would not be.

Schlesinger stopped producing new chamber arrangements of operas after the midcentury. The firm printed a few arrangements of orchestral works by Meyerbeer and Weber in the 1860s, but by the early 1870s, folk song–based works in a light and popular style virtually took over the firm's string chamber music output. This change in direction likely reflects new owner Robert Lienau's decision to focus on more directly appealing, practical works that addressed the music-purchasing audiences that he saw emerging in the second half of the century. For example, he also acquired the Haslinger firm, which was based in Vienna at this time, including its full catalog of waltzes and popular songs. While the bulk of Lienau-Schlesinger's string chamber music turned to folk materials, the firm also suddenly began producing works for piano trio, an ensemble for which it had published no arrangements in earlier decades. The piano trio arrangements differ in significant ways from the earlier string quartet opera transcriptions; thus, a brief discussion of them here provides a useful point of comparison.

Establishing a Musical Canon through Chamber Arrangements, ca. 1870–1910

Complete transcriptions of operatic or symphonic works were rarely produced for piano trio (I have not encountered any among the archives of Peters, Hofmeister, Schlesinger, or Breitkopf und Härtel), but suddenly in the 1870s, Lienau-Schlesinger and other publishers started producing opera-based works for this genre. The firm published two separate collections of piano trios in this style, one titled *Trios for the Pianoforte, Violin, and Violoncello after Melodies of the*

Most Beautiful Operas, and the other titled *Trios . . . after Melodies of the Most Famous Operas of the Classical Masters*. J. N. Rauch's trio based on Mozart's *Don Giovanni* (translated to *Don Juan*, as in other arrangements from the era) was the first and only work published in the series based on "beautiful operas." Although the title page indicates that Halévy's *Die Jüdin* would be included in addition to eight other (unnamed) works, only the *Don Juan* trio was advertised in the Hofmeister-Whistling catalogs, suggesting perhaps that the series of "beautiful" operas was canceled or replaced by the collection of trios based on "Classical" ones.[11] Lienau may have been attempting to compete with rival collections of arrangements based on Italian and French works by emphasizing the "Classical," or Austro-German, contents of his series. For instance, the Ricordi firm in Milan published string quartet and piano trio arrangements and fantasies based on the Italian operas to which it owned the rights, and Litolff, a publishing firm based in Braunschweig, issued a similar set of "Trios dramatiques" that included the trio on themes from *Der Freischütz* discussed below.[12] Both of these firms published arrangements of Italian and French operas from the midcentury in addition to standard or canonic eighteenth-century offerings. Mozart's operas were the most frequently arranged works (note that Lienau-Schlesinger published two separate arrangements of *Don Giovanni* for piano trio, one in each series), but Beethoven and Weber were well represented in collections and individual works produced throughout Europe.

The differences between these opera-based trios and the earlier opera transcriptions point to changes in musical practice and possibly in musical literacy during the last quarter of the nineteenth century. The most important difference regards the proportion of the original opera that these arrangements present: the piano trio arrangements extract a few of the opera's most popular melodies and use them as raw materials to create a multimovement work in a more clearly instrumental style than the transcriptions of the first half of the century. J. N. Rauch's three-movement trio on themes from Mozart's *Don Juan*, for instance, uses one main aria or ensemble melody per movement, labeled for the performer. The first movement treats Zerlina's playful aria "Batti, batti, o bel Masetto," the second is based on Giovanni's duet with her, "La ci darem la mano," and the third features Giovanni's serenade "Deh vieni alla finestra." None of these movements is especially flashy for any of the players, and the structure of each one is straightforward. The trio provides a very easy, simple way for domestic musicians to enjoy three of the most common moments from the opera. J. Hopfe's somewhat more advanced trio on themes from the same opera incorporates a similar selection of popular excerpts in its three movements, though they are not labeled for the performers.[13] The trio begins with a short sonata-form movement that uses Don Ottavio's act 2 aria "Il mio tesoro intanto" as the primary theme and a fragment of Donna Anna's act 3 aria "Non mi dir" as the secondary theme (see example 2.4). The finale juxtaposes Giovanni's "Champagne aria" ("Fin ch'han dal vino") with the duet "La ci darem la mano," which served as the basis for many operatic variations in the period. Both works emphasize important excerpts from the opera that surface again and again in nineteenth- and twentieth-century anthologies and fantasies.

A contemporaneous single-movement trio based on themes from *Der Freischütz* excerpts the opera's most memorable moments to create a musically unified work based on the opera's most popular tunes and scenes.[14] Composed by French organist Charles Renaud de Vilbac (1829–84) and violinist Augustin Lefort (1852–1925) and published by Litolff in 1870, the trio scatters the operatic excerpts

EXAMPLE 2.4A Hopfe, trio based on Mozart's *Don Giovanni*, movt. 1, mm. 13–34 (Don Ottavio: "Il mio tesoro" paraphrase).

EXAMPLE 2.4B Hopfe, trio based on Mozart's *Don Giovanni*, movt. 1, mm. 45–51 (Donna Anna reference).

almost haphazardly, with no apparent regard for the original work's plotline (see table 2.6). It begins with the atmospheric, ominous music of the Wolf's Glen scene from the end of act 2, with tremolos and long tones in a low tessitura; the rising sixth in the piano's right hand and the violin transcribe the chorus's "Uhui!" The trio then moves backward (dramatically) to Max's arioso "Through the Woods" from act 1's third scene. After a short transition, a brief snatch of the act 2 duet between Aennchen and Agathe leads to the thematically related Bridesmaids' Chorus from the end of act 3. Finally, the act 1 waltz music leads to Agathe's affecting, folk-like aria "Gently, gently, pious words," and the *Allegro vivace* music of the opera's finale closes the trio in a lively fashion. Although the movement back and forth in the plot's timeline feels incongruent, the succession of aria, duet, chorus, dance, and hymn-like aria gives the trio a compelling musical assortment, and it transmits the most recognizable and characteristic music of the opera.

Clearly, the goal of these works is not to learn the music or style of the opera as a whole but to play with the themes and create a new musical experience for performers who either already know the opera well or who might want to know its most important or "iconic" themes. In addition to canonizing the opera as a work worthy of its continued place in the pantheon of Classical masterpieces, trios like these canonize specific moments within those operas, reflecting a shared conception of the work that reduces it to the most relevant sound bites that would come to represent the characters and dramatic themes of the whole. The two *Don Juan* works, tellingly, reproduce a collection of musical moments similar to those excerpted in other fantasies of the era—Chopin's op. 2 variations on "La ci darem la mano," of course, but also Liszt's "Don Juan Fantasy," which similarly provides a set of variations on "La ci darem" and a bravura treatment of Giovanni's "Fin ch'han dal vino." Notably, music associated with the noble Don Ottavio—the cool-tempered fiancé of fiery Donna Anna—appears less frequently in solo piano virtuoso potpourris, whereas the respectful love and support between him and

TABLE 2.6 Summary of the "Trio dramatique" based on themes from *Der Freischütz*

Measures	Character	Melody text or title	Location in opera
1–26	Orchestra and chorus	Wolf's Glen scene	No. 10, act 2
27–34			
35–66	Max	"Durch die Wälder"	No. 3, act 1
67–78	Aennchen and Agathe	"Schelm, halt fest!"	No. 6, act 2
79–125	Chorus	"Wir winden dir den Jungfernkranz"	No. 14, act 3
126–38			
139–88	Orchestra	Waltz	No. 3, act 1
189–204			
205–38	Agathe	"Leise, leise, fromme Weise"	No. 8, act 2
239–329			
330–71	Ensemble	Finale	No. 16, act 3

Donna Anna is showcased in Hopfe's chamber-appropriate fantasy, which would fit well into a domestic performance dominated by a husband and wife gathered with their children and friends.[15]

At the same time that these arrangements or medleys became popular for the piano trio, arrangements of a different sort began to appear for string quartet. Table 2.7 gives a transcription of the inside cover of Vasa Suk's arrangement of Bohemian folk songs, published in 1888, which advertises Schlesinger's *Collection of Especially Pretty Music Pieces in Small Settings for String Instruments.* It

TABLE 2.7 Transcription/translation of works listed in the Schlesinger *Collection of Especially Pretty Music Pieces in Small Settings for String Instruments* (1888)

Composer	**Title**	**Instrumentation**	**Arranger**
Beethoven	Favorite Andante in F Major	Quartet	Dont
Boccherini	Famous Minuet	Quintet (2 cellos)	
[Boccherini]	Famous Minuet	Quartet	Rehbaum
Prume	Melancholy, op. 1	Violin with quartet	Grünwald
[Prume]	[the same]	[violin] with quintet (bass)*	
Chopin	3 Mazurkas	Quartet	Rehfeld
Ernst	Andante spianato, op. 8 no. 1	violin with quartet	Heermann
[Ernst]	Andante cantabile, op. 8 no. 2	[violin with quartet]	[Heermann]
[Ernst]	Elegie, op. 10	[violin with quartet]	[Heermann]
[Ernst]	La Romanesca	[violin with quartet]	Grünwald
Lipinski	Adagio elegiac	violin with quartet	
Paganini	Carnaval of Venice	violin with quartet	Ghys
Jansa	Variations, op. 31	Quartet	
Rank	Ave Maria, op. 15	viola with quartet	
Ressel	Oberländler	3 violins, viola, cello, bass (Clarinet ad lib.)	
Vollweiler	Variations on a Russian Folk-Hymn, op. 14, quartet		
Kässmayer	Folksongs, humorously and contrapuntally worked-out for quartet, 13 vols.		
[Kässmayer]	4 small pieces for 3 violins, op. 39		
[Kässmayer]	Trio on Folksongs, humorously and contrapuntally worked-out, op. 40		
Suk	Bohemian Folksongs, op. 9, for quartet		
Jántsy from Lotz	Authentic Hungarian National Dances, for quartet, books 1 & 2		
Panowitz	Serenade on folksongs, op. 1 for quartet		
[Panowitz]	Serenade in a Russian Style, op. 2, for quartet		

* Quintets for two violins, viola, cello, and double bass were more common in the nineteenth century than the now-standard two violins, viola, and two cellos.

includes several chamber works or works for piano arranged for string quartet or for violin with string quartet—in particular, several Classical chamber works are arranged for new chamber ensembles for the late Romantic amateur player. The list includes works by canonic composers of the past, including "Favorite Andante[s]" by Beethoven and Luigi Boccherini, Paganini's *Carnival of Venice*, and selected mazurkas by Chopin. It also includes works by violinist-composers whose names have mostly fallen out of the modern (twenty-first-century) concert repertoire but whose works were still popular in the late nineteenth century, such as Karol Józef Lipinski (1790–1861), Leopold Jansa (1795–1875), and Heinrich Wilhelm Ernst (1814–65).

Arrangements of chamber works for different chamber ensembles were fairly straightforward in terms of their translation of the original into a new format. For instance, violin virtuoso August Wilhelmj (1845–1908) arranged Schubert's Grand Duo in A Major for Piano and Violin (D. 574, published posthumously as op. 162) as a string quartet in the 1880s.[16] The first movement generally gives the bass line to the cello, divides the inner voices of the piano accompaniment between the second violin and viola, and gives the treble melody from Schubert's violin line or piano right hand to the new quartet's first violin. Longer lines in the duo's violin or right-hand piano part are sometimes divided between the quartet's two violins or between the second violin and viola. In the first movement's exposition, the closing materials in the duo's mm. 57–63 are replaced with more thickly scored cadential figuration than Schubert's original; the new passage-work takes advantage of the full quartet texture in this closing section to create a more energetic announcement of the completed modulation to E major (V). Nonetheless, Wilhelmj's translation of Schubert's duo into a string quartet makes minimal intrusions into the score—his "fingerprints" as arranger are less evident here than in the contemporaneous works for piano trio or in the earlier quartet transcriptions of grand operas.

Celebrating a Pan-German Cultural Tradition, ca. 1870–1910

In the last quarter of the nineteenth century, arrangements and variation sets based on folk songs and exotic or national materials for string quartet, which constitute a final category of "light" works for this ensemble, flourished alongside arrangements of "serious" music by Classical and post-Classical composers. As the contents of Schlesinger's advertisement cited above suggest, these two types of string chamber entertainments existed side by side and served the same audience of amateur players. Such *Volkstümliche* works, or works in the folk song style, formed a significant portion of Lienau-Schlesinger's string quartet output in the last decades of the nineteenth century, and they reflect contemporaneous trends in musical life toward the exploration of national and "exotic" materials.[17] Like the earlier works that helped to domesticate and canonize opera for middle-class audiences, these folk song arrangements allowed domestic music consumers in an expanding "Germany" to synthesize a variety of musical styles and influences, thereby creating or celebrating a unified "German" musical language at the same time that proponents of a cultivated tradition sought to clarify the important differences between art and folk musics. The unification of territories into a German Empire in 1871 following the Franco-Prussian War fulfilled a long-held wish for the political realization of a culturally defined German nation with a shared cultural and genetic heritage rooted in the rural cultures of the peasantry (the *Volk*). Folk song and folk-related materials had represented ethnic or national identity for artists and scholars since at least Johann Gottfried Herder's *Volkslieder* collections of the late eighteenth century. By the 1870s and 1880s, when the string quartet arrangements discussed here were composed, published, and purchased for performance in leisurely private environments and in public concerts or recitals, the notion of a pan-Germanic folk encompassed people and traditions from the North Sea to the Alps and from the Rhineland to imperial Russia. By assimilating the constituent territories' musics into a style that could be readily digested and understood by middle-class sheet music purchasers, Lienau and his contemporaries created a means to communicate the shared values and ideals of this newly defined empire, in addition to making a profit in an increasingly difficult music-economic climate. Although the evidence of string quartet publications and reprints, combined with the scattered reports of musical activity in "ephemeral" sources, problematizes fatalistic claims of a decline in musical literacy over the nineteenth century, the changing social role for chamber music certainly meant that publishers had to diversify their offerings to keep their establishments in business.[18] One way they diversified was by offering works at a variety of difficulty levels, and folk song arrangements provided a light, easy chamber medium for string players (including, probably, younger students and beginners).

Schlesinger's main arranger or collector of folk song–based works for strings was Moritz Kässmayer (1831–84), who composed thirteen volumes of folk songs "humorously and contrapuntally worked out" for string quartet in addition to other light recreational works.[19] The collection includes Slavic and German works representing different regions and identities that had a long history of German or Austrian political connections, except for the Norwegian songs of vol. 9. Notably absent is representative folk music from the British Isles, France, and Italy and more exotic folk music from the Orient and the New World.[20] As a whole, this collection deals primarily with musical materials that could be connected to a Germanic cultural heritage.

The folk song settings are far simpler in style and performance demands than the operatic works from the first half of the century. Kässmayer's arrangements privilege the sort of pleasurable, collegial playability that Panofka's and Strunz's opera transcriptions demonstrated—as did much newly composed domestic string music from the first half of the century, discussed in chapter 3. By the

1860s and 1870s, however, the threshold of accessibility appears to have been lower than in earlier decades. Each volume contains four short movements, each a presentation of a single folk song, with the title and a text incipit at the top of the page in each part. The formal style of these works eschews the instrumental forms of the Viennese Classical tradition (sonata-allegro form and its variants, rondo form, etc.) in favor of a simpler theme-and-variations structure for each of the movements, and all of the movements follow the same basic procedure. For example, in the first volume of *Deutsche Lieder*, op. 14, three of the four songs or movements open with the original tune in the first violin, lightly accompanied with block chords or reiterated tonic pitches in the lower three parts (see, e.g., the first presentation of the tune "Der Zimmergesell" in no. 2, example 2.5).

In all four movements, the first presentation of the tune in the violin(s) is followed by several renditions of the theme, arranged so that each instrument plays the complete tune once while the other players accompany. Kässmayer varied the accompaniment patterns and textures rather than the tune itself, ensuring that the original folk song is always audible. At the end of each movement, a fifth or sixth variation brings the ensemble together in a finale-like manner. Here, the tune may be varied for a rousing effect to close the movement. The freestanding structure of the work allows each movement to be performed independently,

EXAMPLE 2.5 Kässmayer, *Deutsche Lieder*, op. 14, no. 2, "Der Zimmergesell," mm. 1–12 (theme presented by the first violin over a simple accompaniment).

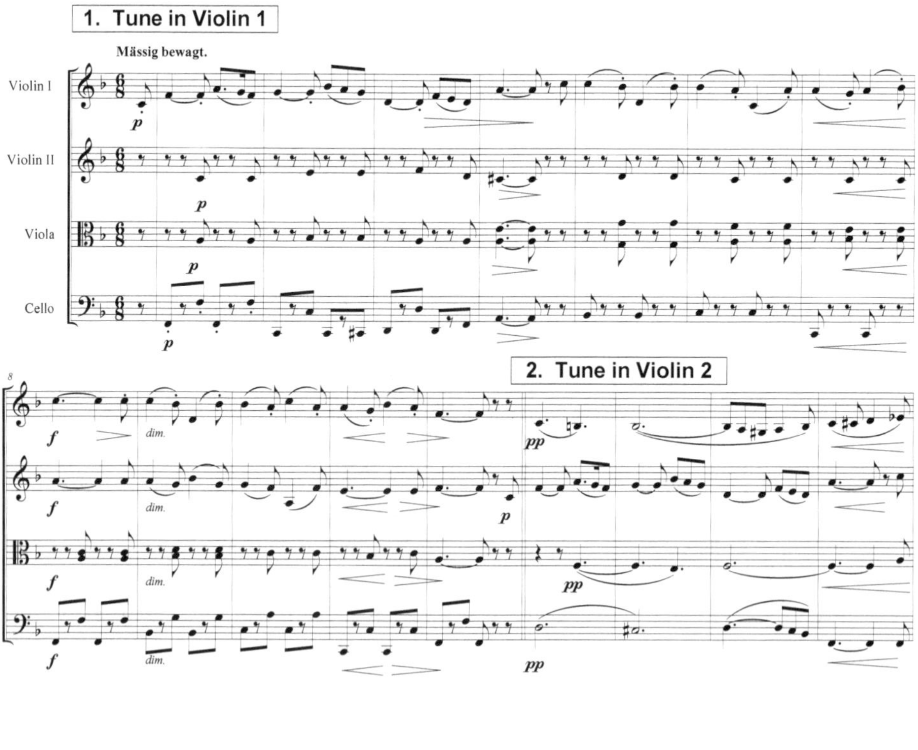

possibly by a string orchestra with multiple players per part. For example, "Der Zimmergesell" ends with a Presto section in which Kässmayer provides a gigue-like (or, more appropriately, jig-like) interpretation of the original siciliana tune (example 2.6).

This first volume includes an interesting anomaly that connects Kässmayer's work to the wider culture of folk song collection and dissemination during the nineteenth century. No. 4, "Mein Herz ist im Hochland," is actually based on a text, "My Heart Is in the Highlands," by eighteenth-century lyric poet Robert Burns, a Scotsman.[21] Kässmayer did not designate it as such in the score, but he used the German translation of the poem's opening line and a traditional German tune associated with it.[22] His brief arrangement follows the procedures

EXAMPLE 2.6 Kässmayer, *Deutsche Lieder*, op. 14, no. 2, "Der Zimmergesell," mm. 61–80 (final variation).

outlined above: it presents the complete tune four times, played by each ensemble member in turn, starting with the first violin (see the full movement in appendix 3, with annotations). He then added a colorful "finale" variation to end the movement and the volume. After the second violin plays its B-minor version of the tune (originally in D major) in mm. 49–63, Kässmayer indicates harmonics and instructs the players to create a flute-like sound that evokes the pipes of the Highlands (see mm. 69–85). The printed parts indicate "Flglt.," or "Flageolet," to clarify the desired effect.

German music lovers had a long history of appreciation for Highlands music and Scottish traditional folk imagery, which formed an important foundation for their own Romantic reimagining of the origins of German cultural traditions in painting, poetry, philosophy, and music. Perhaps nowhere was the poetry of the fictional Gaelic warrior-hero Ossian more heartily embraced, for instance, than in the artistic and musical responses to it by German (and German-educated) composers and songwriters.[23] Early German writers on folk song, notably Herder, based their studies on Scottish and Ossianic materials, or they began there before moving to studies of more local sources. By the 1870s, Burns, who frequently "borrowed" from the folk materials of his surroundings to create his popular poetry, had been accepted as a model for folk and folk-like traditions. In 1877, for instance, the publisher Rieter-Biedermann in Leipzig published a four-volume *Burns-Album*, consisting of "one hundred songs and ballads by Burns, with their Scottish national melodies for singer with Piano accompaniment." The edition reproduced the texts in "Scottish" (presumably Gaelic) and German. Kässmayer's arrangement of "Mein Herz ist im Hochland" in his own collection of *German* songs demonstrates the importance of Scottish traditions as a model for German nationalism in the nineteenth century and the speedy cultural construction of a shared folk "tradition" in the hundred years that followed Herder's coining of the term *Volkslieder*. At the same time, the blatant appropriation of that Scottish material as German is echoed in the collection of folk songs as a whole, with their tendency to present the music of various ethnicities and cultures as one body of material, implying that the Norwegian, Hungarian, Czech, Styrian, Austrian, and Viennese materials belong together in one German collective. In creating these *Volkstümliche* works for string quartet—or for amateur string quartet players and their listeners—Kässmayer and Lienau provided an instrumental analogue to the collections of folk songs and folk-inspired parlor pieces produced at the same time for singers and pianists. The string quartet versions of these works adhere to what were by then the standard conventions of recreational string chamber music for the domestic atmosphere: each player gets an opportunity to play the tune, and the work as a whole facilitates an exploration of folk traditions from throughout the German-speaking lands or areas with strong political and cultural ties to Austro-Germany. Like other works considered in this and subsequent chapters, these "light" string quartets supported the activities of a select community of (primarily male) music lovers in the home.

* * *

Whereas the earlier string quartet arrangements of contemporary operas served multiple practical functions in the musical life of the 1830s and 1840s, including the subtle canonization of some works and styles, these later arrangements more obviously engage an ideological and political purpose related to nation building and canon formation, in addition to their value as recreational works for amateur musicians. Musicologist James Parakilas has explored the implications of arranging or transcribing large public works for private consumption in smaller forms, in particular as piano arrangements. Drawing on several connotations of the word "domesticate," he notes that these new formats gave opera new meaning as a "timeless" or "universal" artwork appropriate for the genteel environment of the home: "Music cannot be canonized without being taken away from its original situation, its original context, and given new surroundings, new homes. The new surroundings are in part musical surroundings: a work becomes canonical when it is no longer found or heard or spoken of most often in the company of other works from the same time and place, but in the company of its fellow canonic works, from whatever times and places. But canonization also means making new social settings for music."[24] Through transcription, operas, symphonies, oratorios, and church music could be brought into the home, a safe space for exploration and contemplation, and in that way they also were absorbed into the fabric of the consumers' lives. In other words, they became ordinary rather than extraordinary; they were tamed and made familiar rather than exotic or foreign. Producing and consuming arrangements allowed musicians to appropriate new musical styles and to incorporate them into a shared language of cultural literacy.

Throughout the nineteenth century, string quartet arrangements also participated in the canonization and domestication of exotic or innovative musical styles by reassigning them a desired cultural value that they lacked in their original contexts. Operas originally designed for lavish theaters filled with glittering costumes and props onstage and (in some cases) aristocratic patrons in the audience acquired a more "learned" and austere musical style by drawing upon the association between the string quartet and intellectual rigor. Converting sensuous, even scandalous scenes from French or Italian operatic works into "pure" instrumental music may also have "sanitized" them for conservative audiences. Thus, a Meyerbeer or Spontini opera could be made more Germanic for Berlin- or Vienna-based audiences, and when arrangers shuffled the scenes from the original opera to create a more unified and balanced whole from its disparate parts, they remade the work in the image of familiar models. Likewise, by incorporating musical traditions and folk songs of cultural groups spread throughout the central and eastern European regions into string quartet collections and suites, later arrangers brought folk traditions from foreign lands into the homes of metropolitan middle-class consumers. Whether as enticing postcards from far-off locales or as an appropriation of musical materials belonging to a marginalized "Other," these folk-based arrangements relocated the music they borrowed from rustic villages to cities and towns, giving them a home in new social and musical surroundings and expanding the musical and, perhaps, the cultural experiences of the sheet music purchasers who played them.

Chapter 3 explores original string quartets and quintets that seem specifically designed for the same sheet music purchasers who might enjoy these transcriptions and arrangements. In fact, the evidence concerning reprints revealed in chapter 1 suggests that the works studied in chapter 3, which were mostly composed in the 1830s and 1840s but were frequently reprinted in later decades, most likely were sold and played alongside the folk song collections created in the 1870s and 1880s.

CHAPTER 3

Music for Men of Leisure

An Examination of the Domestic String Style

In addition to works such as arrangements of operas and dances for string chamber groups, which were clearly designed with at-home use in mind, the early nineteenth century produced a wealth of chamber works that lacked obvious markers of their "lowbrow" social usefulness but apparently catered to a similar audience of recreational musicians—amateurs and professionals playing music for fun, presumably in private or semiprivate spaces. Like works in other social and practical genres that characterized the nineteenth century, these works were widely acclaimed in their time but are forgotten or ignored today because they were closely tied to an everyday social practice—in this case, the casual performance of string chamber music—that has largely disappeared. Recovering some understanding of these works and the social practice they facilitated, though, allows us to add much-needed nuance to our understanding of the string quartet and quintet genres as they developed in the Romantic era. These genres, in particular, suited the needs of masculine leisure, and, as we shall see, a distinct subgenre with its own stylistic conventions developed within them to address this audience.

In this chapter I first demonstrate some of the ways that the musical style of string quartets and quintets from the 1830s and 1840s reflects specific social uses of music in middle-class life by examining works of three composers clearly linked to this cultural milieu: Louis Spohr, George Onslow, and Friedrich Kuhlau. These composers belonged to the middle classes, and their music appealed to their neighbors and friends, as well as to a broad audience of sheet music purchasers throughout Europe who shared the composers' middle-class identity. In addition to their professional activities as composers, performers, conductors, and teachers, these three men also engaged in private, recreational music making during their "off-duty" hours that mirrored the activities of their patrons and other consumers of music. Their musical creations for this audience reflect the practice of their social peers—members of the *Bildungsbürgertum*, or the upper middle classes. An analysis of representative works establishes a stylistic norm against which we can compare other works, such as Franz Schubert's contemporaneous string quartets and quintet. In these works, Schubert reveals a familiarity with the domestic style of his peers and uses that style to create a provocative musical portrait of his own domestic circle.

Three "Unremarkable" Composers

The three composers discussed here represent three related but distinct options for musical careers in the nineteenth century. They occupied three separate tiers within the broadly defined middle class, and they belong to different national traditions, but the similarities in their activities and relationships with friends and patrons throughout central Europe support the notion of a shared cosmopolitan identity and culture. George Onslow (1784–1853), a wealthy upper-middle-class landowner, had no need of commissions and therefore composed for his own pleasure; he resided on his family's estate outside Paris, where he frequently hosted private and semiprivate musical gatherings.[1] His works were published in France and Germany in addition to being performed in Paris's chamber concerts by that city's leading musicians.[2] Ludwig (Louis) Spohr (1784–1859) was famous throughout Europe as a virtuoso violinist and composer of musical fireworks for his own concertizing. He also composed operas, oratorios, and symphonies. For over thirty years, he was the music director at the court of the elector of Hesse in Kassel, where he was a well-respected middle-class artist of international stature. Friedrich Kuhlau (1786–1832) came from a lower-middle-class family; his father and grandfather were military musicians in Saxony, but Friedrich moved to Copenhagen to avoid conscription in Napoleon's army in 1810. He held a court appointment as a chamber musician but without pay, requiring him to perform a variety of other jobs as a theater chorus master and music teacher. Kuhlau supported himself, his parents, and his siblings by writing large quantities of student-level works for piano and for flute in addition to operas and other works.[3]

The lives and careers of these composers do not parallel the typical composer-genius biography associated with masters such as Haydn, Mozart, and Beethoven, but each one represents the mundane side of musical life in the first half of the nineteenth century. They might be labeled "unremarkable," to use Philip Bohlman's phrase, or "ordinary," in the sense that they provided the everyday musical experience that formed the backdrop for the more "remarkable" or extraordinary achievements of their better-known contemporaries and successors.[4] During their lifetimes and for several decades afterward, all three composers enjoyed a good reputation across Europe. Kuhlau met several times with Beethoven during his second trip to Vienna in 1825. The publisher Adolph Martin Schlesinger included Kuhlau in festivities he organized to celebrate the publication of Beethoven's latest string quartet in A minor (his op. 132).[5] The Schuppanzigh quartet performed the work at these private parties, and it may have been influential for Kuhlau's own quartet begun six years later, discussed below. Onslow was highly praised in print by Robert Schumann, whose personal library contained many of the older composer's works.[6] Finally, Spohr's reputation as a great wielder of both bow and pen was secured in the first half of the 1820s during his concert tour of London, Paris, and Dresden and during his first years in Kassel, when his most successful opera, *Jessonda*, was introduced. (C. F. Peters published the opera in a string quartet arrangement, in fact.) Spohr's reputation as an operatic composer waned in the 1830s, but his *Violinschule* of 1832 and the oratorio *Die letzten Dinge* cemented his renown as a performer and composer of the highest order.[7] All three composers published simultaneously with German and French firms (and Danish ones, in Kuhlau's case), demonstrating their music's wide appeal to audiences throughout Europe, not just in their own countries or regions. They were, in fact, only expunged from the annals of music history in the last decades of the nineteenth century.

Like dozens of composers in similar circumstances, their music appealed to middle-class audiences in part because it reflected their own musical activities as members of that class. Chamber music parties were a regular feature of life at Onslow's country estate in Clermont-Ferrand. A well-respected pianist who studied with Hummel and Cramer in his youth, Onslow played the cello as an accomplished amateur later in life. He turned to this instrument after resigning from public concert appearances early in his career because it gave him an opportunity to make music with other members of his social peer group. While in the country during the summer months, he and his neighbors played his own works alongside those of Haydn, Mozart, and Boccherini. Spohr likewise played chamber music domestically with his fellow musicians, and these private quartet parties were quite separate from the more formal musical evenings that he provided for his patrons. He describes them in his autobiography as an institution related to the purchase of a particularly pleasing country house, an association that serves to further strengthen the relationship between leisurely music and comfortable domestic surroundings, as the following passage from his autobiography demonstrates: "The only thing I missed in the new house was a spacious music room. I therefore had a partition wall removed that separated two rooms on the first floor. . . . I established here also a quartet circle, at which, in turn with some other families who were lovers of music, we gave three quartets every week, and concluded the evenings with a frugal supper."[8] The inclusion of the performers' families and of a "frugal supper" at the end of the evening depicts a cozy environment of entertainment and friendship. Spohr tells the reader, too, that the quartet parties occurred only in the winter months and that they continued from their establishment in 1824 through 1858, when, at the age of seventy-four, the composer ceased playing in them regularly.[9] Spohr describes similar quartet parties that took place during his family's vacations in Marienbad. There the quartet included an unnamed local linen weaver "who was a good violin player."[10]

Kuhlau's correspondence suggests that the casual performance of string quartets had a significant effect on his own compositional choices as well. In an 1829 letter to Carl Böhme, then owner and operator of the Peters publishing firm in Leipzig, Kuhlau thanks the publisher for his hospitality during a recent trip and for his patronage, as they had established a business relationship at that time. Kuhlau continues, "When I can return to Leipzig, I will bring along for you my first three quartets for string instruments, which we can try out at your charming country house."[11] That the Peters firm sought to establish a relationship with Kuhlau to publish his very marketable music and that it was apparently interested in his string quartets suggests that this genre, like the flute and piano fantasias, medleys, and variation sets, appealed to the firm's targeted audience of sheet music purchasers. Unfortunately, no string quartets from this projected set survive.[12]

Two years later, in 1831, Kuhlau wrote from Copenhagen to his French publisher, Aristide Farrenc, about his latest projects. After business regarding dedications and opus numbers for several works in press at that time, Kuhlau continues:

> But then I must write a composition of a most ambitious sort, which may well last the entirety of next winter, and these are the circumstances: a rich local businessman and great friend of music has asked me to compose for him 6 quartets for string instruments. He will provide a very generous commission for this work, and will make arrangements for its publication himself. Because I have long wished to try my hand in this genre of composition, I have taken on this order with pleasure. As soon as I have finished this work, I will let you know how things are going for me, and will again diligently compose . . . for you.[13]

Kuhlau describes his patron as a *Kaufman*, or businessman, and a music lover, clearly placing him in the cultivated bourgeoisie.[14] The patron probably either wanted works for his own performance or saw commissioning a set of quartets as a way to achieve greater status within Copenhagen society. Either way, these works—of which only one, the op. 122 quartet in A minor, was completed before Kuhlau's untimely death—certainly belong to the body of "middle-class" works that address an audience of amateur music lovers and performers.

That these composers (and many like them) wrote for a large audience of sheet music purchasers and amateur performers seems clear, but the question remains, How did they address that audience differently from composers writing for the elite circle of music critics or professional musicians? And how does string chamber music differ in this sense from music for piano or for the voice? A large part of the appeal and marketability of these composers' works comes from the use of musical gestures and styles designed with the pleasure of the performer as their primary goal, focusing on the experience of actively playing music, as opposed to the cerebral contemplation of it. Onslow's, Spohr's, and Kuhlau's chamber works provided an outlet for communal performance within a small circle of friends rather than for an attentive listening audience, and the musical style they developed in these works was particularly suited to that aim.

The Difference between Five and Four: Quintets versus Quartets

Well before the composition of the works under consideration here, which date from the 1830s, the string quartet had accrued a certain mystique that lent it an elevated quality, particularly for younger composers. Compositional treatises and guides available in the early to mid-nineteenth century exhibit a reverence for the string quartet as a genre that would deflect many an intrepid innovator. But as we have already seen, the same combination of string instruments prompted many firms to publish an abundance of string quartet arrangements of orchestral and stage works for use in the home or salon. Though these works arranged for string quartet obviously enjoyed popularity with middle-class consumers, the string quartet as a self-sufficient genre continued to garner almost religious devotion and fear among connoisseurs and composers, creating a widening gap between the music later categorized as "art" and that labeled "popular."

The string *quintet* suffered none of this angst, however, as it had not yet accumulated a genre-specific set of characteristic features or requirements.[15] In fact, commentators at the time point with surprise to the ease with which a composer could try new ideas in the quintet as opposed to the quartet. Carl Czerny, for instance, described the string quartet as,

> in many respects, the *most refined, as well as the most difficult* of all kinds of composition; as it presents all means for the creation of noble and original ideas, strictly regular and skillful working and development, aesthetic beauty, and grand conception; but it denies, on the contrary, whatever, in other kinds of composition, supplies the place of these requisites and conceals their want . . . and hence, *the quartet remains the most hazardous, but at the same time also, the most honorable touchstone for a composer*, both as regards his creative powers and his scientific acquirements.[16]

Regarding the string quintet, though, he writes:

> The structure of the quintet is, in all its parts, exactly similar to that of the quartet; but the reflecting composer will be astonished to find what an influence this accession of a single instrument has upon the invention of ideas, melodies, chords and figures. We possess a greater freedom of movement in the extended sphere; have increased means for filling up the chords; and can, in the accompaniment, combine several different progressions and effects. The imitations and passages acquire greater consistency when we form two concerted harmonies; &c. &c.[17]

Though Czerny does not put it this way, the quintet—with its greater variety of textures—seems to have become the perfect vehicle for composers writing in a new, light style rooted in congenial *participatory* music making. It seems to have been viewed as a more flexible, even relaxed genre. Composers who wrote both quartets and quintets, such as Spohr and Onslow, tended to approach the two genres with different expectations. For example, most of Spohr's string quartets reside very clearly in the *quatuor brillant* tradition, meaning that they emphasize brilliant or virtuosic playing by the first violin with punctuation or support from the other three instruments.[18] Spohr frequently referred in letters to hiring a quartet to accompany him either in small, salon-sized versions of his (or others') concertos or in his own quartets. Even those works that the composer did not designate as *brillant* strike today's listeners as saturated with virtuosity for the leader of the group only.

Spohr's quintets, however, present a very different visage. Here, though virtuosic passagework plays a role, the brilliant style of the writing is more evenly distributed to the five players. In some ways, these works evoke the *quatuor dialogué*, a relatively short-lived genre that emphasized the passing of lines or motives from one member of the ensemble to another with carefully calculated (some might say stilted) equality between parts. This approach differs somewhat from late eighteenth-century ones (employed by Haydn and Beethoven in particular) that favored motivic development, often in a learned fugal or contrapuntal style. Domestic works from the early nineteenth century emphasize the presentation of a full lyrical melody by several members of the group in turn, rather than the melody's constituent parts, as we shall see.[19] In his string quintets, Spohr allows each member of the group a turn at the melody while affecting an air of spontaneous development from one musical thought to the next. His single string sextet (op. 140, published in 1850) utilizes a similar style, filled with repetitions and sequences that allow most of the players a turn with the work's melodic components.[20]

With thirty-four string quartets and thirty-seven string quintets surviving in his output, Onslow was one of the most prolific string chamber music composers of the nineteenth century, and his works have been lauded as the first representatives of the Romantic string quintet.[21] Onslow's decision to compose quintets seems related to his choice to write music primarily for casual use at home rather than public works for the concert or theater stage. Though successful in their time, Onslow's four symphonies and two operas represent a small proportion of his time and energy, and there is no indication that the composer sought out unfulfilled opportunities to compose and perform more of these for the public arena (as opposed to, for example, Schubert, who wrote a series of unsuccessful, unstaged operas, attempting to build a more public career). A comparison of his compositional style in the two string chamber genres shows significant differences in approach.[22] The quartets are compact, serious, and generally minor mode oriented. They reveal a composer very much aware of his models, with prominent Haydnesque gestures, including the placement of minuets and scherzos as second rather than third movements. Even in major-mode works such as op. 47 in C major, Onslow shows a predilection for minor inflections in both melodic gestures and in harmonic procedures. His first movements readily conform to conventional descriptions of sonata form: secondary theme and key areas represent short detours on the path to the development sections, which, though not very lengthy in proportion to the movements, display extra heft because they often incorporate fugato textures. Inner movements likewise present weighty musical materials such as the Adagio religioso of op. 46, no. 3 in G minor, or further explore minor-major color shifts, as in the minuet of op. 46, no. 1. The quintets, on the other hand, evince a leisurely approach and a lighthearted character; in general, they strike the listener as less studied, though not unschooled. Like Spohr's quintets, Onslow's works in this genre share melodic materials freely around the ensemble and emphasize euphony and brilliance in a style that aims to bring pleasure to musicians playing in the home with or without an audience to hear them.

Domesticity in Music: Form, Technique, Texture

In the interest of presenting an analysis that illustrates the principles of composing for Europe's middle-class domestic audience, the following discussion is limited to three representative works composed within a few years of each other: the single string quartet by Kuhlau, his op. 122 in A minor (1831), Onslow's String Quintet in E Major, op. 39 (1831), and Spohr's String Quintet in A Minor, op. 91 (1834).[23] These works follow sonata procedures that are recognizably distinct from the intensely motive- and development-driven ones of so many Haydn and Beethoven movements. They consistently emphasize the presentation and repetition of long lyrical melodies by as many members of the group as possible, a feature that is especially common in secondary key areas. Throughout each work, we hear less motivic work in general, even in transitions and closing sections. Rather, the three composers utilize harmonic and melodic sequences of longer phrases to effect a transition from one formal section to the next. Composers emphasize this large-scale repetition through their choices of voicing and through smaller-scale repetitions such as brilliant passagework and symmetrical melodic forms with clear antecedent-consequent phrases. The resulting sonata forms consist, then, of lengthy expositions and recapitulations with brief developments. All three works also consistently deploy pastoral- and rustic-style topoi, which are characterized by repetitive gestures (e.g., ostinatos, drones, and repeated accompanimental figures in inner voices).[24]

Secondary key areas provide the most tellingly similar treatment of musical materials in these works. In the first movement of Spohr's op. 91 quintet, for instance, the first violin introduces the secondary theme in mm. 57–79 (example 3.1). After a short transition, we hear the theme again in mm. 87–99, virtually unaltered, but played by the second violin. Kuhlau uses the same device for the secondary theme of his quartet op. 122, as shown in example 3.2. Onslow creates a similar effect in his first movement by having the first violin present the secondary theme and then immediately repeat it with slight ornamentation. In all three cases, the composer presents a sweet, singing theme (the marking *dolce* is common), usually placed in the high register of the instrument.

Onslow begins his quintet with lyrical repetition in the primary theme/key area as well. After a slow introduction, the first cello presents the primary theme in the high "tenor" register of the instrument, indicated by the "false" treble clef in the

EXAMPLE 3.1 Spohr, String Quintet in A Minor, op. 91, movt. 1, mm. 57–93.

score (example 3.3).[25] The first violin then picks up the melody and repeats it with a brilliant-style extension, highlighting the fact that this movement showcases at least two highly capable performers, a trait common to all three works. In each work, the texture throughout the first movement remains busy, sparkling with passagework in two or three parts for long stretches.

The prevalence of brilliant-style passagework in this quintet prompts a further observation about the audience for these pieces. Although these works seem designed for leisurely playing in a domestic environment, they require a level of technical skill we are unaccustomed to associate with amateurs today due to changes in the use of that term. In the nineteenth century, "amateur" retained its literal meaning; in the case of music, it denoted a lover of music and musical practice, or someone who might be highly accomplished and capable but who did not pursue music as a vocation. Thus, the designations "amateur" and "professional" indicate merely whether a person earned a living as a musician, with few if any implications regarding his or her technical and expressive ability. In many cases, one's social class and family obligations (or gender) might preclude the possibility of a career in music or in certain kinds of music, meaning that many highly capable performers from the upper class or middle classes played only in private gatherings.

EXAMPLE 3.1 (continued)

EXAMPLE 3.2 Kuhlau, String Quartet in A Minor, op. 122, movt. 1, mm. 125–55.

EXAMPLE 3.3 Onslow, String Quintet in E Major, op. 39, movt. 1, mm. 21–41.

The singing tenor line for cello seems to be another characteristic of this style, aiding the composer in presenting lyrical themes that project out of the thick texture of the Romantic string style's frequent tremolos and double-stops. It is especially common in string quintets with two cellos, a scoring that allows the first cellist to sing while the second cellist provides a harmonic foundation, but quartets also make use of it. For instance, in the middle of the recapitulation of Kuhlau's second movement, the cello repeats the movement's main theme in the ultra-high register to a filigree-like accompaniment in the first violin. The appearance of this technique has been described as an ongoing and distinctively cellistic tradition with origins in the virtuosic cello playing of Boccherini. By the 1830s, though, this feature had become a gesture used in chamber music by composers of a variety of backgrounds (i.e., not just cellists). For example, Beethoven uses this range in much of his op. 132 quartet in A minor, and Schubert does so in his two-cello quintet in C major. The high range must have seemed especially appropriate for these lyrical moments because the unusual tessitura soars above the quartet or quintet texture more audibly than a similar passage in the violin or viola or in the normal, lower cello range.

The short development sections of these works explore melodic materials from the exposition less earnestly and rigorously than we might expect for works composed in the post-Beethovenian 1830s. In place of a heroic struggle to regain the tonic, we hear a leisurely reinterpretation of the melodies, often in a sequential manner. In the Spohr quintet, for example, the development section begins by presenting segments of the primary and secondary themes layered atop one another, such as in m. 125 (see example 3.4, where the primary theme in the second violin and secondary theme in the cello are marked). The exposition had taken us to the relative major (C major), but the development begins anew on the tonic A, quickly altered to a dominant with the addition of a seventh. This procedure

EXAMPLE 3.4 Spohr, String Quintet in A Minor, op. 91, movt. 1, mm. 123–45.

is repeated several times in mm. 125–81, as the music travels around the circle of fifths in a clear, uncomplicated progression.

Already in m. 181, we find ourselves securely in A minor once again, confirmed by the first violin's restatement of the primary theme, which begins the recapitulation. This development, with its brevity and straightforwardness, fulfills the requirements of a standard sonata form first movement without becoming too self-consciously serious; it spins out some of the most enjoyable moments of the exposition and returns to those materials in the recapitulation as quickly as possible. Kuhlau uses a similar procedure in his string quartet first movement, whose development emphasizes thematic repetitions.

The tendency to present and restate themes and musical ideas persists in the finales of these works, all three of which employ modified sonata forms. As in the opening movements, repetition provides lightness and gaiety in both large-scale and small-scale gestures. Onslow's finale ventures the farthest from what we might call normative sonata-allegro procedure. By combining elements of theme-and-variations and sonatina structures, the composer creates an innovative and fun finale in keeping with the casual entertainment style of this subgenre. Proceeding from the opening of the movement, we encounter exposition procedures that have by now become familiar. The primary theme is presented by the first violin and restated by the first cello. After a short transition based on motives of the first theme, the secondary theme is presented in the dominant (B major) by the first violin and then modified in a second statement with minor-key inflections. The exposition closes with brilliant flourishes and a cadenza-like passage for the first violin. At this point (m. 87), we might expect some sort of developmental section, but instead the primary theme returns in the tonic (E major). Omitting the development from what has seemed up to now a sonata-allegro movement would normally result in a sonatina form, a light form that would not be out of place in a finale. In m. 111, though, the music suddenly turns from E major to E minor, and the primary theme is reinterpreted in a dark, foreboding style. This change is prepared in the most careful and notable way in the printed parts and score (see example 3.5).

Marked with a double bar line and key change and with the indication "Minore," this section looks like a common minor-key variation from a set of variations, the likes of which formed the core of the domestic music repertoire (e.g., variations for piano or string duo on opera tunes or popular song themes). The eight-measure theme is bracketed by repeat signs and characterized with a sudden *fortissimo* dynamic and staccato and marcato indications. The minor mode is short-lived, though, and in m. 119 the music quickly turns to G major and begins to develop the primary theme in a quasi-learned style. M. 133 returns to the minor mode for a reprise of the development section's eight-bar theme, creating a short, self-contained ABA' section within the movement's development section. A double bar and key change (back to the original four sharps) with the word "Maggiore"

EXAMPLE 3.5 Onslow, String Quintet in E Major, op. 39, movt. 4, mm. 109–38.

EXAMPLE 3.5 (continued)

at the top of the score signal that we have returned to the sonata-like finale and that the minor-mode episode was simply a brief detour. The recapitulation picks up where it left off, bringing back the secondary theme and its repetition in the tonic.

Onslow's introduction of a brief but memorable episode in the midst of a sonatina-like form serves a few purposes. First, it links this last movement with its predecessor, the third-movement minuet marked "La Melinconia," which also uses the courtesy markers "Maggiore" and "Minore" at important key changes. It is tempting to draw connections here between this work and the last movement of Beethoven's string quartet op. 18, no. 6, which Onslow almost certainly knew. Though it is impossible to rule out Beethoven's influence on Onslow, the movements each attest to their respective composer's own proclivities: Beethoven placed his "La Malinconia" movement at the beginning of the finale of his quartet and recalls it in a dramatic and climactic way at the end of the work, as he had done in similarly iconoclastic pieces such as the "Pathétique" piano sonata. Onslow, on the other hand, had a penchant for the programmatic. His "Bullet" quintet, which depicts his injury in a hunting accident and subsequent delirium and convalescence, was composed in 1829 and published as his op. 38 just prior to the quintet discussed here.[26] Onslow places his "La Melinconia" as the third movement of the work and labels it "Menuetto." It evinces a decidedly lighter, tongue-in-cheek style than Beethoven's depiction of intense emotion.

Second, and perhaps more importantly, the finale's interpolated theme and variations continue the noticeable trend in these domestic works toward repetition. The finale allows a further opportunity for performers and listeners to enjoy the theme of the movement by presenting it in a different light. Given in the minor mode with an altered character, the theme is fresh and exciting yet familiar—comfortable without being worn thin. This variation segment takes the place of the development section, expanding the use of materials without introducing new elements or breaking the existing themes into motives and putting them back together.

Taken as a whole, these works by geographically dispersed composers represent the homogeneity of middle-class musical life in central Europe during the early nineteenth century. The frequent repetitions, brilliant string style, lyrical singing melodies, and formal procedures emphasizing complete themes rather than motivic splicing make this music especially pleasurable for performers. The equitable division of themes and repetitions also gives these works a distinct style. The composers seem to have made a noticeable effort here to ensure that as many players as possible have the opportunity to expose or repeat a structurally important theme. Rather than reduce the ensemble to one homogeneous unit or a solo with accompanying voices, these works privilege a texture that emphasizes the group's makeup as a collection of individual voices interacting with one another and retaining their unique personalities. This relationship among the individual players distinguishes these works from the more developmentally driven works of Haydn and Mozart, for instance, and from contemporaneous works for piano and strings. In piano trios by Reissiger and Hummel, for instance, the relationships among the players are frequently less "equitable," partly because of the nature of the ensemble and possibly because of social factors. These works often place the main melodies of the work (the primary and secondary themes in a sonata form first movement, for example) in the string parts, while the pianist's role is to accompany and support the strings in those passages, then to effect modulations and transitions via sparkling passagework.[27]

The same characteristics that made domestic string chamber music so attractive to recreational players may also have made such works more enjoyable to casual listeners in domestic or semiprivate environments than to listeners in more formal venues. In settings where a variety of activities might be taking place simultaneously with musical performance—such as family gatherings and vacations abroad as guests of local friends and acquaintances—the casual listener might also find this style appealing. Unlike works that require the listener to follow a complex musical argument from beginning to end or that experiment with new timbres and styles, juxtaposing unfamiliar harmonies, works in a domestic style allow the listener to attend to sections or melodies that come and go with regularity in a predictable fashion. For this reason, perhaps, works by Onslow, Spohr, Kuhlau, and other composers in this tradition are making a gradual comeback in the realm of recorded music, especially on budget labels such as Naxos and in online music-streaming services. In the twenty-first century, domestic music is heard again in casual settings as families and friends perform a variety of mundane activities, attending to music sporadically while cooking, reading, driving, and so forth.

The retention of "Classical" elements, such as the use of a four-movement sonata structure, ensures that these works maintain a connection to the learned tradition. Unlike more obviously "frivolous" works designed for the parlor, these string quartets and quintets belong to what could easily be coded as a respectable (manly) avocation appropriate for members of the cultivated bourgeoisie or the *Bildungsbürgertum*. The association between this style and performance in conventional middle-class homes, moreover, provides an interpretive opening when we note the domestic style's use within other works, such as the "late" chamber music of another seeming outsider to the Haydn and Beethoven motivic school of composition: Franz Schubert.

A "Remarkable" Composer's Use of the Domestic Style

Born in 1797, Franz Schubert was a slightly younger contemporary of Spohr, Kuhlau, and Onslow. Certain of his chamber works share many of the common characteristics of the two quintets and quartet discussed above, including—as generations of critics and scholars have at times complained, at times hailed—a predilection for repeating long lyrical themes rather than fragmented melodic cells.[28] For example, the celebrated C-minor quartet movement (Quartettsatz, D. 703) of 1820, the young composer's manifesto of musical maturity, includes repetitions of themes in its two secondary key areas (this being the first famous example of Schubert's three-key expositions), as well as several other features common in the three works discussed above.

The first secondary key area features the violin in a soloistic lyrical style that explores the submediant. After barely establishing C minor as the tonic, the movement arrives at A♭ major (VI) at m. 27. The first violin presents the song-style theme (marked *dolce* in this and later iterations) to an ostinato accompaniment in the inner voices and cadential punctuations in the cello (example 3.6). The theme is repeated in mm. 39–60 in the higher octave and with a more sustained bass line. Schubert's already expansive twelve-measure theme is extended in its repetition, creating an illusion of suspended time in this section that contrasts beautifully with the frenetic tremolos and rocketing scalar figures of the primary and transitional materials.

The second secondary key—G major (V), the "correct" key in typical sonata form procedure—is characterized by a short *Ländler*-like theme that is also

EXAMPLE 3.6 Schubert, Movement for String Quartet in C Minor, D. 703, mm. 27–49.

presented by the first violin. The eighth-note anacrusis emphasizes the theme's accented downbeats, and the lilting quarter-and-eighth-note rhythm provides the rustic quality typical of this triple-meter dance common in the German and Austrian countryside (example 3.7). As in the A♭-major passage, this theme is repeated an octave higher in mm. 100–104. In the recapitulation, Schubert uses these repetitions to "correct" the omission of the relative major in the exposition. He presents the first secondary theme in B♭ major (V of III) and E♭ major (III), then recapitulates the second secondary theme in C major (I). Thus the repetition of the theme set up in the exposition allows Schubert to explore three keys with this theme alone and a plethora of more and less distantly related keys throughout the movement.

Taking prominent repetitions one step further, the secondary key area of the first movement of Schubert's G-major string quartet (D. 887) includes no fewer than four separate iterations of the secondary theme, a song-like tune first presented in mm. 64–77 by the first violin with a homophonic accompaniment (example 3.8).

The theme is immediately repeated by the second violin, followed by an unsettled ***fff*** tremolando transition that ratchets up the tension of this movement. The

EXAMPLE 3.7 Schubert, Movement for String Quartet in C Minor, D. 703, mm. 93–106.

EXAMPLE 3.8 Schubert, String Quartet in G Major (D. 887), movt. 1, mm. 64–83.

theme reappears in m. 110 in the cello, where it is presented in the singing tenor range, as we might expect after becoming familiar with this style in the contemporaneous works of Onslow, Kuhlau, and Spohr.[29] The viola gives the exposition's final statement of the theme in mm. 142–53. Thus the theme is paraded through the ensemble and given an airing by each constituent in turn. Schubert emphasizes the communal nature of this section by setting the theme apart in every instance of its repetition. Each statement of this melody is preceded by a pause in all activity; the solo instrument holds a syncopated pitch that leads to the first note of the theme as the other instruments rest and then pick up their accompanimental figures at the downbeat. Schubert literally stops musical time at the introduction of this haunting melody, a feat that seems extraordinary amidst the raw energy of the surrounding materials. That Schubert calls such attention to these repetitions of the melody increases the impression that each instrumentalist in this quartet is a soloist, controlling the musical texture and leading the ensemble for at least this thirteen-measure period. As the other instruments pause, the new leader takes up his or her position, and the soloistic nature of the introductory measure allows for a wide range of interpretive decisions and subtle manipulations of tempo and dynamic.

Attempts to explain the rampant use of large-scale repetition in Schubert's music tend to take on an apologetic tone, defending Schubert against accusations of long-windedness and lack of developmental capacity.[30] If we view passages like these, though, as an opportunity for each ensemble member to shine soloistically in the tradition of domestic music making, the quartet becomes a model of topical and hermeneutic subtlety, as well as a powerful expressive outlet. Schubert contrasts the unstable opening gesture's dramatic intensity with the secondary theme's artistic leisure to create a work that presents despair and rupture alongside comfort, even nostalgia. This juxtaposition, a feature of several chamber works from the composer's last five years, bears further reflection in light of his particular relationship to the domestic sphere.

More than any of the other canonic composers of the Classical and Romantic eras, Schubert is associated today with the Biedermeier tranquility of early nineteenth-century musical life. The famous Schubertiade gatherings have received considerable attention in biographies and studies of the composer's life and times. Musicologist Ruth Solie has suggested that the specific group of friends who made up the normal cast of characters for these events constituted a surrogate family for Schubert in his adulthood, as his relationships with his father and brothers became more strained and remote after his adolescence.[31] Descriptions and drawings of these gatherings always portray Schubert at the center of the group (literally and figuratively), always seated at the piano. In accounts of Schubert's musicianship written during his lifetime in diaries and letters, as well as in later reminiscences by his friends and family, the composer is portrayed as an avid pianist and singer who accompanied his friends and played sonatas, duets, and dances for their listening pleasure.[32] String chamber music never features in these descriptions of the composer and his friends at play, despite the centrality of string music in his formative years.

In contrast to the mostly later accounts of domestic music making around the piano, discussions of Schubert's early years feature string music for small orchestra and chamber ensembles almost exclusively. Schubert spent his youth playing violin and viola in quartets at home with his father and brothers. During his years of study at the Kaiserlich-königliches Stadtkonvikt (Imperial and Royal City College), Schubert played violin in the school's recreational orchestra, where he met several of the male friends with whom he would remain intimate throughout his lifetime. During the holidays, he made music with his family at his father's home. After leaving school and passing the teacher's exam, Schubert continued to participate in domestic music as a string player. His friend Leopold Sonnleithner, whom Schubert met in 1816, would later recount that the Schubert family music parties added players on string and wind instruments—all men—during the years 1814 through 1820.[33] As the ensemble at these weekly gatherings grew, the men began to perform symphonies, choral works, and concertos for assembled listeners. Sonnleithner notes that by the autumn of 1820, "the enterprise had now reached its zenith and in fact had already passed it, as its original purpose had been abandoned, the practices had been turned into productions and pure orchestral playing had been mingled with music of the oratorio."[34] Thus he confirms that the original design of these gatherings had been recreational rather than professional and that such activities originally centered on instrumental music making, especially string music, rather than keyboard works or singing. Sonnleithner also takes care to document the middle-class status of the participants. After a listing of regular players on the various orchestral instruments he notes, "Apart from a few professional musicians, most of the gentlemen belonged to the merchant-tradesman or minor official class."[35]

In other words, these get-togethers exemplified just the sort of masculine musical entertainments described earlier, and they bear many resemblances to similar gatherings held by Spohr and Onslow, as well as by countless other musically inclined bourgeois men at this time. The addition of vocal and concerted works along with a sizable listening audience signaled the dissolution of the group's original role as an outlet for masculine domestic entertainment for two reasons. First, the introduction of piano soloists and singers added women to the usual company of performers; female pianists and singers began to participate in the "practices" (*Übungen*), as Sonnleithner calls them, after about 1818 at the request of listeners whose students and daughters desired an opportunity to play with an ensemble. Second, the increased number of performers and listeners pushed the performances into the semiprofessional, semipublic realm of the hosted salon rather than private or semiprivate recreational music among (male) friends.

Leopold Sonnleithner's article describes a similar trajectory for the domestic performances that his father hosted (and in which Leopold and Schubert participated).[36] The Sonnleithners began with weekly readings of quartets and symphonies arranged for quartet on Friday evenings, but they soon graduated to biweekly "practices" that included larger ensembles playing more difficult repertoire, including choral music and concerted works performed by virtuosos traveling through Vienna. Listening audiences of up to 120 people became common after the group moved to a larger venue with salons that could accommodate such a crowd. Both groups (the Sonnleithners and the Schuberts) ceased their activities around 1820, and afterward such regular gatherings for string music disappear from the record of Schubert's life.

The year 1820 also had special significance for Schubert, as this year marks the beginning of his independence. Having decisively separated himself from his father and his father's school a year earlier, Schubert committed himself to a musical life and career, which likely meant that he would never marry under Vienna's marriage consent laws because of his low and unstable income. In 1821 he was admitted to the Gesellschaft der Musikfreunde, which confirmed his rising fame in the city; later that year he moved into the home of Franz von Schober, with whom he would live (when healthy) for the rest of his short life. Not long after he and his friends stopped participating in domestic and semiprivate string music performances, the first recorded Schubertiade performance occurred in early 1821, marking the beginning of a tradition of piano-centric musical gatherings that more frequently included women participants in readings, dancing, and other "trivial" entertainments, as well as performances of Schubert's songs. Coincidentally or not, the Quartettsatz discussed above (composed in December 1820), with its startling juxtaposition of violent passion in the primary theme area and Biedermeier domesticity in the second, marks a sudden change in Schubert's musical style at the same time that we note a sudden change in his musical and social activities.

The occasional string music rehearsals and performances that have been documented in Schubert's life after 1820 appear to have been "one-off" or ad hoc assemblies related to the promotion of individual new works. They are concentrated in the period following 1824, when Schubert composed several ambitious masterworks for string chamber ensemble, including the A-minor "Rosamunde" quartet (D. 804), the D-minor "Death and the Maiden" quartet (D. 810), and the G-major quartet discussed above (D. 887, his last work for string quartet, completed in 1826). These works received performances in both private and semiprivate spaces at the time of their composition. Schubert's final chamber composition, the monumental C-major string quintet (D. 956) discussed below, was not played in a documented performance (public, private, or otherwise), as far as the available sources indicate. The A- and D-minor quartets bear few signs of the domestic style discussed in this chapter, but the G-major quartet, with its four extravagant repetitions of the opening movement's secondary theme, and the C-major quintet connect to that tradition in significant ways at important moments in Schubert's personal and professional life.

The "Rosamunde" quartet in A minor is the most self-consciously "public" of Schubert's later string chamber pieces. It was the only one to appear in print during his lifetime, and it was performed by violinist Ignaz Schuppanzigh (also the premier performer of Beethoven's late string quartets) in his subscription concert on 14 March 1824. This presentation took place as a semipublic event (as a subscription concert, it was advertised and reviewed in the press) that was supervised and performed by professional players and intended for an exclusive listening audience. Moritz von Schwind wrote to his and Schubert's longtime friend Franz Ritter von Schober that "[Schuppanzigh] is quite enthusiastic and is said to have rehearsed particularly well."[37] Schubert dedicated the work to the famous violinist and quartet leader when it was published as op. 29, no. 1. Other than a postperformance report from Schwind to Schober, the quartet is not mentioned again in correspondence.[38] No record survives of Schubert and/or his friends playing this quartet in private.

The D-minor and G-major quartets, however, were both performed in clearly private settings and in semiprivate scenarios among Schubert's friends, but they are less copiously documented than the frequent gatherings for keyboard- and voice-centered recreations. They appear to have occurred *outside* the usual circle of the Schubertiades and to represent an alternative musical gathering or activity that somehow did not belong to that sphere and its participants. In January 1826 the D-minor quartet was rehearsed at the home of musical amateurs Karl and Franz Hacker, brothers who played the first violin and viola parts. A mutual friend of the brothers and Schubert, the doctor Josef Hauer, played second violin, and the Court Opera cellist was the only professional player engaged for the performance. Apparently this group read through the work on 29 January and again the next day before performing it at the home of another friend, Josef Barth, on 1 February.[39] Schubert biographer Otto Deutsch differentiates between rehearsals (*Proben*) at the Hacker residence, during which Schubert made revisions to the score, and the 1 February performance (*Aufführung*), though it is not clear whether the latter was a concert in today's sense or a "by-invitation" affair. The D-minor quartet was performed again at Franz Lachner's home on 26 February. Lachner, unlike Barth, was a professional musician; his first post was as conductor at the Theater am Kärntnertor, and he later served as general musical director in Munich. (He and Schubert met when he moved to Vienna in 1822.) This performance, too, must have been a semiprivate presentation of the work among friends. A year later, in March 1827, the G-major quartet was apparently rehearsed at Lachner's lodging, but no record of a performance surfaces until plans for Schubert's solo concert got under way.[40] The first movement of this work was performed as the first item on the subscription concert's all-Schubert program on 28 March 1828.[41]

Perhaps because these gatherings and the works associated with them contradict the nineteenth-century image of Schubert as a *Mädchencharakter* (a girlish character), they have been suppressed and deemphasized in the modern musicological literature.[42] More detailed accounts of them may have been destroyed or overlooked in the collection and transmission of documents related to Schubert's life. It is also possible that these gatherings were construed by Schubert and his friends as a more professional or "work-related" activity because of their connection to the active promotion of Schubert's work in the public arena of publishing and concertizing. Certainly such performances (so far as they are documented for modern critics) do not represent a significant area of ongoing activity and enjoyment. Schubert and his friends, though engaged musically in other genres and styles, do not appear to have sought out sustained opportunities for string performance in the way that other typical male middle-class and bourgeois musicians did at this time. After Schubert left his father's home for good in 1818, his private musical recreations focused on the feminine domestic genres of song and piano pieces.

As a free-spirited artist and Romantic tone poet, as a political liberal, and, by some accounts, as a libertine, Schubert characterized himself as an outsider to mainstream Viennese or Austrian society and to the normal trappings of mundane nineteenth-century life. In his staunchly middle-class and religiously conservative family, he felt out of step with paternal expectations. His intimate friendships with men, his apparent but unsubstantiated homosexuality, surely also contributed to his anxieties.[43] More pertinently, Schubert's refusal or inability to marry and set up house placed him outside accepted social norms for middle-class men of his day and led to feelings of isolation and persecution. His contraction of syphilis in 1822–23 amplified his desolation, and it led him to a swift downward spiral into bouts of depression and mania as he struggled to come to terms with his own mortality.[44] The "late" style of his chamber works composed after 1823 reflects this struggle in part through its use of stylistic markers to create a musical topic that clearly evokes the domestic coziness that he would never experience as an independent adult.

Schubert's now-famous letter to his friend Leopold Kupelwieser dated 31 March 1824 echoes complaints and regrets voiced in earlier letters and diary entries with greater candor:

> In a word, I feel myself to be the most unhappy and wretched creature in the world. Imagine a man whose health will never be right again, and who in sheer despair over this ever makes things worse and worse, instead of better; imagine a man, I say, whose most brilliant hopes have perished, to whom the felicity of love and friendship have nothing to offer but pain, at best, whom enthusiasm for all things beautiful threatens to forsake, and I ask you, is he not a miserable, unhappy being?—"My peace is gone, my heart is sore, I shall find it never and nevermore" [a line from Goethe's *Faust* and from Schubert's own "Gretchen

> am Spinnrade"], I may well sing [that line] every day now, for each night, on retiring to bed, I hope I may not wake again, and each morning but recalls yesterday's grief. Thus, joyless and friendless, I should pass my days, did not [Moritz von] Schwind visit me now and again and turn on me a ray of those sweet days of the past.[45]

This letter also connects Schubert's deepening depression or melancholy to his composition of chamber music. After noting that he had written only a few new songs, Schubert continues, "But I have tried my hand at several instrumental works, for I wrote two Quartets for violins, viola, and violoncello and an Octet, and I want to write another quartet, in fact I intend to pave my way towards [a] grand symphony in that manner."[46] The two quartets of 1824, the A-minor "Rosamunde" quartet and its D-minor "Death and the Maiden" counterpart, remain essentially public works, works not composed with the domestic market or his own domestic performances as the primary audience. They evince no clear connections to the style of Spohr or Onslow, and Schubert may have designed them (as the Schuppanzigh performance and dedication suggest) as demonstrations of his musical potential, his compositional prowess, hence Schubert's suggestion that in these works he might "pave [his] way towards [a] grand symphony." The G-major quartet Schubert completed two years later, though, makes clear references to the domestic style in its secondary theme area, as discussed above. Here, the domestic style functions as a topic or musical sign that would resonate with potential listeners and amateurs like the members of the Gesellschaft der Musikfreunde and (perhaps) Schubert's own family members and longtime acquaintances.

In a similar way, the composer's last completed chamber work, the C-major string quintet (D. 956), composed four years later in September and October 1828, uses the domestic style to express Schubert's intense feelings of loss and nostalgia. He wrote the work just after moving into his brother Ferdinand's house in a Vienna suburb, a move suggested by his doctor because of his failing health. As in the G-major string quartet, the first movement of the string quintet cordons off the secondary key area as a realm of repose and pleasure. Moving to flat-side keys harmonically, suspending time by drawing attention to a transitional gesture, and reveling in the pleasant sounds of parallel thirds and sixths signal a respite from the barreling pace of the preceding sections. The movement opens with a tentative presentation of the primary theme that eventually (in m. 33) grows into a *fortissimo* statement surrounded by angular leaping motives that drive the theme toward the dominant. An accented repeated-note passage with sforzandos and a long crescendo climbs into the high register in all five instruments in mm. 49–56, reinforcing the tense, running effect. In mm. 57–58, though, we hear a strong arrival on G major (V) followed by a G dotted quarter note in the two cellos (naturally, in the tenor range), bringing the modulatory processes to a sudden halt. When the second cello slides downward by half steps to E flat, the harmony instantly shifts to ♭III, and the secondary theme is introduced by the two cellos in parallel thirds to an accompaniment of pizzicato and staccato punctuations in the upper strings (example 3.9). A gentle Biedermeier-like song blossoms here, complete with euphonious parallel motion, a plucked accompaniment and off-beat punctuations in the upper strings that evoke a guitar or harp, and a singable melody in a narrow range.[47] All thoughts of the rigor and strife of the earlier transition are abandoned. The theme moves in m. 71 to C major and cadences on G in m. 79, but once again the held dominant pitch is led downward to E♭, and we are treated to another statement of the lengthy twenty-two-measure tune in its entirety in the same key, this time in the two violins; note that four of the five players engage this pleasant tune in the exposition.

This significant interlude in the midst of the movement provides the performers an opportunity to display a sensitive interpretation of a theme designed to sound well on the instruments. It also suggests an acknowledgment or remembrance of quiet evenings spent performing congenial music with friends and family, a sonic depiction of domesticity upset by a return to the roiling activity of the opening (when the exposition is repeated) and then the development section (when moving to the second half of the work).

* * *

Both producers and consumers of music benefited from the wealth of possible opportunities for private and public music making. Domestic musicians received a steady diet of well-written works designed specifically to bring them pleasure, and composers and publishers enjoyed the satisfaction and financial gains associated with having a large body of consumers ready to support their work by buying sheet music. This foundation of support allowed the producers of music to engage in other musical activities that might prove less lucrative because they addressed a smaller audience. Spohr, Onslow, and Kuhlau provide excellent examples of composers who addressed different audiences in different works. These three composers wrote some works clearly designed for public consumption in large venues (operas and symphonies), works for their own professional use (violin concertos and *quatuors brillants* in Spohr's case, piano quartets and sonatas in Kuhlau's), and works to be enjoyed privately with friends, which, via publication, they shared with a wider community of music lovers (chamber music such as the works discussed above). In chamber music, this relationship resulted in a style that addressed middle-class consumers, including players but perhaps also casual listeners, through repetition, long lyrical themes, and the use of characteristic textures and developmental procedures.

In addition to addressing a particular marketplace niche, this style communicated an entire way of life that would soon be idealized and become the subject of nostalgia. In fact, we already see this process in Spohr's idyllic description of

EXAMPLE 3.9 Schubert, String Quintet in C Major, D. 956, movt. 1, mm. 55–86.

his own quartet parties surrounded by family members in the warmth and comfort of his cherished music room on a cold winter afternoon. The association of domestic string playing with domestic bliss is as explicit in the autobiography of one of Europe's most accomplished violin virtuosos as it is implicit in Schubert's late chamber music. Later composers, most notably Johannes Brahms, would reminisce about this period and this style in both writings and works, as we shall see in chapter 6.

CHAPTER 4

Redefining the "Progressive" Style in Responses to Beethoven's Late Quartets

Throughout the nineteenth century, some composers struggled to find an appropriate answer to the enormity and profundity of Beethoven's works, particularly in those forms and genres most closely linked with his legacy: the sonata, the symphony, and the string quartet. Composers writing in these genres could expect inevitable comparisons not only to Beethoven but also to his predecessors Haydn and Mozart. Some composers embraced this comparison by entering into a dialogue with their artistic forebears, creating new pieces rich in allusions to the best-known works of Beethoven and others.[1] These allusions sometimes also suggest a critique of previous composers' works and their innovations.[2]

Nineteenth-century string quartets also show signs of this dialogue, but in the intimate quartet genre the conversation is often more personal and introspective than in larger concert hall genres such as the symphony. In this and subsequent chapters, I will show that composers who considered themselves progressive in different ways shared a single goal of fostering musical progress in the string quartet genre and how they communicated that goal to fellow composers and musicians in a musical dialogue that continued throughout the long nineteenth century. Their works often demonstrate a response to Beethoven and to more recent composers, representing a private conversation not just among the four members of the performing quartet (as in many works discussed in the previous chapters) but also among the composers of the past, present, and future.

In music history of the twentieth century, it has been customary to refer to musicians who composed in Classical genres like the sonata, string quartet, and symphony as "conservative," following the precedent set by late nineteenth-century polemicists. Critics who adhered to the New German School ideas espoused by Wagner and Liszt in their writings and their musical activities—Franz Brendel after he took over the *Neue Zeitschrift für Musik* from Robert Schumann, Hans von Bülow in the earlier portion of his career, Richard Pohl and others in the later decades of the century—insisted that the only appropriate response to Beethoven's iconoclastic works was to dissolve the old forms and replace them with new ones.

They implied that any attempt to create new music in the old forms was a waste of time and talent. By portraying composers such as Mendelssohn, Schumann, and Brahms as conservative composers working in dead forms, Brendel and Pohl established a tradition of criticism that has pervaded discussions of Romanticism from the second half of the nineteenth century into the twenty-first century.[3]

Musicians who created new modes of expression through innovative forms and compositional procedures in "traditional" genres such as the string quartet and symphony, however, considered themselves progressive in ways different from those of their contemporaries writing symphonic poems and the like. Whereas Liszt, Wagner, and their successors avoided addressing Beethoven head on in genres associated with his achievements, composers in the Mendelssohn-Schumann circle responded directly to the innovations of Beethoven and his predecessors on their own terms and in the genres where those innovations were introduced. The musicians considered in this chapter took up the challenge that Beethoven issued in his late works by responding with music that invites direct comparison to Beethoven, Mozart, and others. By entering into dialogue with earlier works, the composers considered here created an exclusive community of musical insiders, all interested in fostering "progress" in the genre of chamber music and by extension in musical style overall. In chapter 5, we will encounter several composers who wrote programmatic chamber works for various reasons. Some of these composers were connected to the New German School via their relationships with Liszt and others, while others belonged to the Leipzig School represented by Mendelssohn and Schumann; some belonged to neither school but pursued programmatic composition for personal reasons rather than political ones. In every case, programmatic chamber music offered a unique opportunity to engage with the most pressing issues of their day: the definition and advancement—the "progress"—of musical Romanticism.

In the musical discussions that follow, formal analysis is the primary means of describing how composers engaged in an ongoing dialogue with previous and later musicians. By adhering to certain formal and generic conventions while eschewing or varying others, musicians communicate their own values and priorities in a shared musical language. The combination of certain forms and formal types, harmonic progressions and relationships, motivic and melodic allusions or quotations, and other "signs" conveys a musical "narrative" that other musicians follow upon exploring the work in performance or study. Most of the analysis here is of an "overview" type that compares the overall structure of the movement or work being studied to previous examples, rather than a painstaking dissection of phrase structures and motivic relationships or detailed voice-leading graphs.

Formal types and generic conventions governed the main compositional pedagogy of the nineteenth century, as represented by texts such as the Czerny composition treatise cited in chapter 3, Anton Reicha's composition treatises (published in French and translated into German by Czerny), and Adolf Bernhard Marx's more famous texts on composition and musical form, as well as nineteenth-century analyses of works by Mozart and Beethoven.[4] For that reason, I have embraced a "dialogic" method of formal analysis and design that is loosely related to the sonata theory of James Hepokoski and Warren Darcy but always infused with analytical tools drawn from other methods.[5] Most prominent among those other methods is topical analysis, which draws upon work by Leonard Ratner and his students.

Beethoven's Influence on String Quartet Culture

From a certain point of view, it is not an exaggeration to say that Beethoven single-handedly changed music culture's approach to and understanding of the string quartet. At least, for a certain type of listener, musician, or consumer, his works introduced a new mode of participation and meaning in the string quartet genre. This segment of the chamber music–loving population differed in significant ways from the mostly more casual consumers and producers proposed in previous chapters. The composers, critics, and musical activists who commented on Beethoven's late works, in particular, shared an earnest desire to see "progress" in musical culture in terms of both musical style and musical perception by the public.

Nineteenth-century reactions to Beethoven's late string quartets reflected shifting priorities among the press and more broadly in musical life, as scholar K. M. Knittel has shown. In early reception of the quartets, baffled critics struggled to understand the new language of Beethoven's late-period style. Almost at a loss for words, critics of performances and publications continually advised readers to hear the works multiple times, to study the scores or four-hand arrangements, and to keep in mind that Beethoven's deafness and his illness had led him to create these works.[6] At least two reviewers noted that the works, though difficult, repay the effort to get to know them. An anonymous review of the E♭ quartet, op. 127, for the *Allgemeine Musikzeitung* of 1827–28 states, "He who hears it for the first time cannot usually find his way around, much less pass judgment. Therefore, one must necessarily hear it many times and examine it closely. For that purpose, however, it is extremely inviting and one returns again gladly to it."[7] Beethoven's amanuensis and early biographer, Anton Schindler, noted that, like many of the initial critics and even later commentators, he was confused by the works at first, though some "unconditional believer[s]" saw the beauty in them almost immediately. One such enthusiast was Count Franz von Brunsvik of Budapest, "who could truly call himself Beethoven's pupil." Schindler went on to say, "We spent two whole winters together studying these quartets with the help of his excellent fellow-students. Our study revealed the harmonic and technical beauties of the music, but, as for recognizing a logical sequence of ideas, our efforts here and elsewhere remained fruitless."[8]

This notion that the consumer of the quartets, whether performer, listener, or student, was obliged to study the works with great care in order to achieve understanding would become a guiding principle of musical aesthetics in the Romantic age. The simultaneous development of a *Kunstreligion* (art-religion) philosophy and the increased interest in metaphysical and philosophical matters evident in various writings of the period led to new modes of criticism and a sharper divide between "art" and "popular" or "entertainment" music. The metaphors used to describe the string quartet changed at this time, reflecting a shift in attitudes that Beethoven's works brought to the foreground.

Reviewers and music lovers had used the now familiar metaphor of "friendly conversation" to describe chamber music, especially string quartet playing, since at least the 1770s, and this notion remained common into the first decades of the nineteenth century, as Dörte Schmidt has shown.[9] In addition to Goethe's oft-repeated description of listening to quartets as hearing "a few intelligent people conversing with one another," reviews by Friedrich Reichardt (1773), at least two anonymous reviewers for the *Allgemeine musikalische Zeitung* (1800 and 1810), and Giuseppi Carpani (1812) employed similar language. In 1828, though, in his first review of Beethoven's quartets in A minor and F major (opp. 132 and 135), Marx noted a change in the composer's style of address that required a different level of participation on the part of the players: "It is no more four cheerful brothers in art [amateur music lovers] who make music for their and our own joy; it is four deeply moved creative spirits who in noble freedom and wonderful sympathy linger in a tangled, fourfold brotherly embrace. If the executants do not build one uniform alliance of noble, equal, free, brotherly spirits, then a complete realization of the artwork is not possible; besides, there's no hope for full of satisfaction of the players."[10] Schmidt emphasizes that Marx's reading of the quartets places them in a particular political context—one with which Beethoven has long been associated—of liberalism and democratic government. She also notes that rhetoric by Marx and others expresses independence and universal freedoms as inherently male characteristics; they describe a "brotherhood" of free men, for instance. Thus, here again, the string quartet serves as a useful metaphor for upper-middle-class cultural ideals because of its association with masculine private-public activities. On the other hand, and more importantly for the present discussion, the passage specifically notes that Beethoven's latest quartets do *not* engage the typical quartet audience of their time: amateur musicians playing for their own pleasure. In trying to describe the differences between this work and earlier quartets, Marx notes that the musical style does not suggest four distinctive voices with opposing or complementary points of view, as in clearly domestic works, or a single voice supported by three friends and colleagues, as in *brillant*-style works. Rather, in these late quartets, the four individual performers must give themselves over to the singular "spirit" or vision of the composer, creating a unified ensemble or conduit through which the music flows while (paradoxically) maintaining their own individuality.[11]

Although Beethoven's late quartets and works like them clearly engaged male players, both professional and amateur, in private and semiprivate environments as contemporaneous domestic works did, the nature of that engagement is different. The relationships between the parts and the whole changed in these works so that unity and what would soon be called "organicism" in the work became the highest ideal. In these self-consciously progressive works, the individuals came together for a single effect rather than soloistic shining moments. Hence, we see in these works a musical style that emphasizes motivic development, formal subtlety, and novelty of musical language.

The Nineteenth Century's "A-Minor Mood"

In the mid- to late nineteenth century, A minor proved to be an important key for string quartets, despite its odd absence from the repertoire during the eighteenth century. Joseph Haydn, Ignaz Pleyel, Franz Xaver Richter, and Wolfgang Amadeus Mozart (four of the most influential quartet composers of the Classical era) did not publish a single A-minor quartet, and Beethoven published only one, but nearly every composer of string quartets in the nineteenth century composed a work in this key. Oftentimes, a young composer set his first string quartet in this key, as in the cases of Felix Mendelssohn and Robert Schumann. In other instances, a composer's return to the quartet genre after a long hiatus is marked by an A-minor work, as demonstrated by the works of Norbert Burgmüller and Franz Berwald discussed below.[12] Many of these A-minor works display a preoccupation with Beethoven's A-minor quartet, op. 132, of 1825. The special approach and reverence that Romantic composers adopted in this tonality is similar to the exceptional stance that Beethoven took toward his favorite key for self-consciously important works, C minor.[13]

The musical characteristics of these works and their composers' comments about them suggest an elite and informed audience, and they demonstrate an interest in composing to continue a train of thought begun by another (in this case, previous composers of string quartets). Although the dialogue is exclusive and in some ways private, these published works also reflect their composers' strong desire to be understood as heirs to Beethoven's legacy. The privacy in these works is dramatically "performed" in the sense that they demonstrate a composer's individual membership in a highly selective group of musical innovators. Like an "inside joke" or a special handshake, the suggestive, allusive traits in these quartets mark the composer and the listener as special, linked in an intimate and important way.

This group of composers and connoisseurs was especially interested in advancing musical "progress," or revitalizing musical life by building on the achievements of earlier innovative composers. For these young musical revolutionaries in the nineteenth century, the best model was Beethoven. They took as their starting point a poignantly personal work of Beethoven's late style, one closely connected to the maestro's personal aura of genius and divinity. Beethoven's String Quartet in A Minor, op. 132, contains one of the most memorable movements in the composer's instrumental output, the "Heiliger Dankgesang eines Genesenen an die Gottheit, in der lydischen Tonart" (Holy song of thanksgiving of a convalescent to the Deity, in the Lydian mode). Beethoven composed this movement in response to a severe illness (a stomach ailment) from which he recovered in early 1825. The movement alternates reprises of reverent, chorale-like music in a modally inflected quasi-religious style with sections that express the recovery of strength and renewed sense of vigor marked "Neue Kraft fühlend" (Feeling new strength). Few works in the composer's oeuvre exhibit the vulnerability and candor of this quartet.[14]

In addition to this overtly extramusical element and the tantalizing connection it provides between the work, the composer, and potential performers and listeners, op. 132 offers a wealth of irregularities that have fascinated musicians and scholars since its first performances. The formal innovations and disruptions, melodic and harmonic ambiguities, and interrelationships between movements and between this work and its fellow late quartets elicited a continual stream of commentary throughout the nineteenth and twentieth centuries.[15] The first movement's unusual sonata form has proven particularly alluring for commentators, and composers of late nineteenth-century quartets adopted several of its peculiarities, which suggests they should be examined here in some detail.

Beethoven presents his primary and secondary materials three times, not counting developmental extension and working out in transitional sections. Thus, borrowing the language of James Hepokoski and Warren Darcy, we could describe the movement as containing three rotations of primary and secondary theme/key materials, as opposed to the more usual two rotations in a sonata-allegro form (exposition and recapitulation).[16] Some analysts describe these rotations as two expositions plus one recapitulation, while others prefer two recapitulations. The form has no proper development section but deploys developmental techniques throughout the three rotations and the transitional areas between the main theme/key groups. The ambiguity in the structure prompted string quartet composers in the decades immediately following Beethoven's death to embrace a fluid approach to sonata form, leading to a variety of experiments, as discussed below.

The work opens with an introductory fugal section that grows out of a four-note motive common to the three quartets commissioned by Prince Nicholas Galitzin, opp. 127, 132, and 130 (example 4.1).[17] This motto returns throughout the quartet and is associated with the primary theme materials, but, more importantly, it signals formal seams in the first movement. At m. 103, for instance, it introduces the second rotation of exposition materials, this time beginning in E minor (v) and modulating to C major (III), the "correct" secondary key for a minor-mode sonata form. At m. 193 the motto introduces the recapitulatory third rotation, which

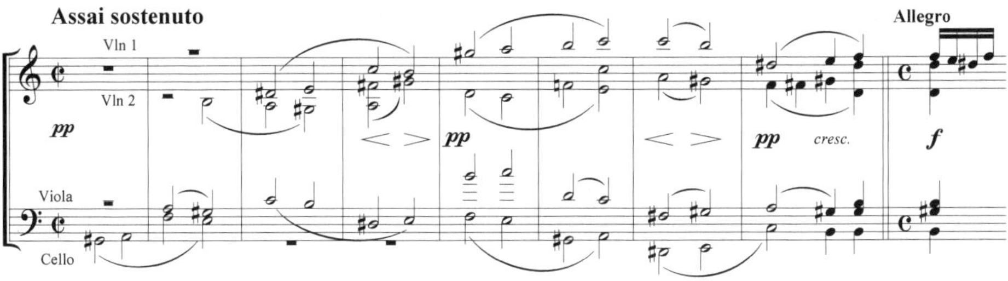

EXAMPLE 4.1 Beethoven, String Quartet in A Minor, op. 132, movt. 1, mm. 1–9.

presents the primary and secondary materials in A minor, seemingly resolving the movement's harmonic conflict. Later composers sometimes also used a three- or four-note gesture to herald thematic returns or significant junctures in their own formal designs.

The movement's secondary theme presents an unusual harmonic riddle that would resurface in later A-minor string quartets. The theme first appears in F major (VI) in mm. 48–59. Whereas the first theme seems unsteady, ill formed, and even indecisive, the secondary theme is self-assured, grounded, and comfortably rustic (example 4.2). With the support of a repetitive accompaniment from the viola and cello, the two violins present a singing tune in two four-measure phrases. F major, therefore, is presented as a stable rival to the unstable tonic, A minor. This unusual choice of key helps to unite the movements of the quartet. The second movement, a waltz-based scherzo, begins in A major and modulates to F major (♭VI) for its secondary material. The third movement's prayer of thanksgiving is set in the Lydian mode, based on F.

Strong connections to the music of the past are prevalent throughout the quartet, even beyond the borrowed modality of the "Heiliger Dankgesang," and those connections resurface in later works throughout the nineteenth century. The short fourth "movement" of Beethoven's quartet, really an intermezzo labeled *Alla Marcia*, disperses the calm of the preceding movement's close with processional dotted rhythms marked *forte*. The first half of the movement forms an independent rounded binary dance in the eighteenth-century style in A major, but it leads suddenly (*attacca subito*) into a more "modern"-sounding section of instrumental recitative. This nod toward opera increases the work's dramatic effect by juxtaposing a purely instrumental dance form with the instrumental affectation of sung speech. The recitative section ends with a lengthy cadenza-like passage for the first violin and a strong authentic cadence resolving on the downbeat of the next movement, linking this intermezzo to the rondo finale.

Beethoven's finale (Allegro appassionato) employs a frantic waltz topic throughout. Here, the notion of F major as a stable alternative to the A-minor tonic is abolished, but the rondo explores a variety of keys: i, V, v, iii, III, and ♭VII. The

EXAMPLE 4.2 Beethoven, String Quartet in A Minor, op. 132, movt. 1, mm. 48–60.

coda, with a sudden presto version of the refrain that borders on manic, turns unexpectedly to A major in m. 298. The key change is preceded by four measures of musette-like material based on the refrain's main motive (example 4.3). This musette passage recalls the musette trio of the second movement, creating an intermovement connection that was not lost on later composers, as we shall see. With three of the four instruments holding drone-like sonorities, the sudden stasis after the movement's frenetic pace stands out dramatically and emphasizes the almost nonsensical modal switch.

Beethoven's enigmatic late style is on display in this quartet in all its troublesome glory. The tightly woven motivic connections, the intriguing tonal relationships and idiosyncratic keys, the combination of instrumental and vocal styles, and the continuing renewal of inherited forms all sparked Beethoven's successors to take up the arguments proposed in this quartet and to pursue them to different ends. Each composer responded to Beethoven's challenge in his own way, and as the years progressed, later composers took up the arguments of their more

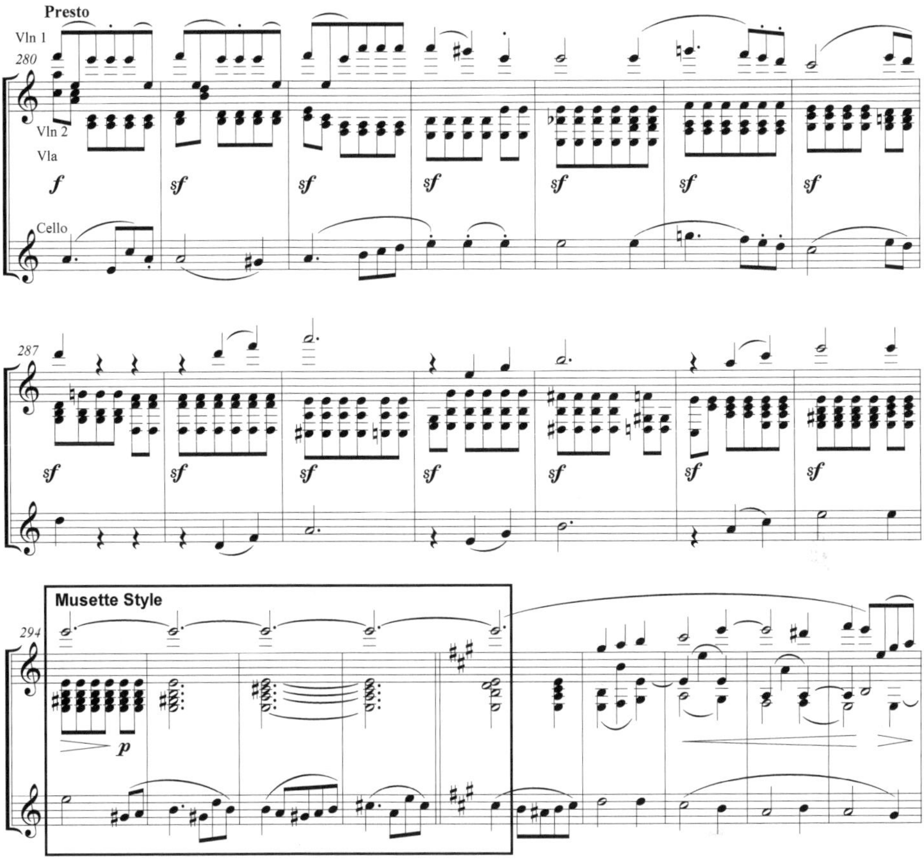

EXAMPLE 4.3 Beethoven, String Quartet in A Minor, op. 132, finale, mm. 280–302.

immediate predecessors in addition to the Classical masters, creating a web of allusion and commentary. These works represent the concrete expression in music of the abstract ideological debate raging through the century in music journals and letters. In subsequent decades, enterprising composers took up the banner of musical progress on manuscript paper rather than in newsprint.

Felix Mendelssohn-Bartholdy and Norbert Burgmüller

Felix Mendelssohn and his contemporary Norbert Burgmüller (1810–36) were the first to respond to Beethoven in the quartet genre. Mendelssohn did so in his first published quartets: an A-minor quartet, op. 13, composed in 1827, and an E♭-major quartet, op. 12, composed later in 1829; both works were published in 1830.[18] Burgmüller took up the challenge in his fourth quartet, op. 14 in A minor, composed in 1835. Both men were inspired to compose an A-minor quartet by encounters with fellow composers and a desire to prove their own musical mettle in works that represent the most cutting-edge techniques of their day. Mendelssohn's letters to fellow composer and Zelter composition student Adolf Lindblåd indicate that Mendelssohn's first exploration of Beethoven's late quartets in 1827, when they were brand new, provided a strong catalyst for his conception of the genre—he singled out elements from opp. 127, 130, and 132.[19] These comments also show us that the young composer was interested in responding to Beethoven's works with similarly radical musical creations and that he hoped his friend and colleague would join him in this effort. Eight years later, Burgmüller would respond to the stimulus provided by evenings in Mendelssohn's company, during which the two composers and their friends explored the quartet repertoire and discussed musical matters. It was probably at this time that Burgmüller was introduced to the late quartets of Beethoven, and he may well have gotten to know Mendelssohn's two published quartets then, too. Thus, Burgmüller's A-minor quartet probably also reflects a reckoning with or critique of Mendelssohn's musical experiments.

Mendelssohn's op. 13 quartet in A minor is widely acknowledged to be one of the composer's early masterworks. The first of his completed and published string quartets, it was written at the young age of eighteen during the summer and autumn of 1827, just months after Beethoven's death the previous March. Mendelssohn's correspondence with Lindblåd describes the composer's first reactions to Beethoven's last works. In 1828 he wrote:

> Have you seen his new quartet in B flat major? And that in C sharp minor? Get to know them, please! The piece in B flat contains a cavatina in E flat where the first violin sings the whole time, and the world sings along. . . . The piece in C sharp has another one of these transitions, the introduction is a fugue!! It closes very scarily in C sharp major, all instruments play C sharp; and the next entry (the next movement, that is) is in such a sweet D major, and such little ornamentation! You see, this is one of my points! The relationship of all 4 or 3 or 2 or 1 movements of one sonata to another and their respective parts, so that from the bare beginning throughout the entire existence of such a piece one already knows the mystery that must be in music. Help me put it there![20]

As R. Larry Todd has noted, Mendelssohn seems particularly impressed with the "relationship of the parts to the whole" in Beethoven's works.[21] But Mendelssohn also ecstatically notes the presence of vocal forms and styles (e.g., the cavatina) and the unusual use of counterpoint (the fugal introduction of op. 131). Op. 132 in A minor is conspicuously absent from Mendelssohn's comments, although it was published at the same time as opp. 130 and 131, thus Mendelssohn would have undoubtedly studied it alongside these works. The omission at first suggests that the A-minor work made a less intense impression on the young composer than its B♭-major and C♯-minor counterparts, a suggestion immediately discounted by Mendelssohn's enclosure with the letter of his recently completed string quartet in A minor, along with commentary on its construction and meaning. The A-minor quartet is filled with allusions and references to Beethoven's late works that Charles Rosen describes as "intended to be noticed, to produce the satisfied glow that comes from being in on the secret."[22] Mendelssohn sent the work to his composer friend and provided him with some verbal cues as to its meaning and its relationship to Beethoven's innovations, but he left much of the detective work to Lindblåd, presuming that he would understand the work's message.

Later published as op. 13, the quartet demonstrates two structural features that clearly constitute a response to Beethoven's late quartet style. First, Mendelssohn created a cyclical structure in which the finale recalls music from the first movement, linking the four movements of the work through motivic and harmonic recollection. Second, he based the string quartet on a preexisting texted work of his own, providing an "extramusical" expressive dimension to his quartet similar to Beethoven's "Heiliger Dankgesang." As he described the work to Lindblåd, "The song that I append to the quartet is the theme of the same. You will hear its notes resound in the first and last movements, and sense its feeling in all four."[23] Additionally, fine details refer to op. 132, especially the use of instrumental recitative and the triumphant ending in A major.

Mendelssohn composed the song "Frage" in 1827 and published it as part of his op. 9 collection of twelve songs in 1830. The song opens with a question, "Ist es wahr?" (Is it true?), followed by an expectant silence (example 4.4). When the

EXAMPLE 4.4 Mendelssohn, "Frage" for voice and piano, op. 9, no. 1, mm. 1–13.

question is repeated in the third measure, the rhythmic and harmonic profile becomes a motto that Mendelssohn used throughout the quartet.[24] The song functions as an expressive catalyst and as a formal reference point. The first movement opens with an eighteen-measure adagio introduction that recalls the song in a chorale style and includes a direct quotation of the question motto in mm. 13–15 (example 4.5a). This introduction is recapitulated in the finale's coda section, which returns dramatically to A major from the quartet's overriding A-minor tonality in a section marked *Adagio come I°* (example 4.5b). The question motto takes pride of place here, with its rhythm shaping the second half of the section.[25]

The cyclical structure of the work connects it to Mendelssohn's understanding of Beethoven's late quartet style (as described in the letter to Lindblåd), but the specific technique of thematic recall used by Mendelssohn also connects the quartet to Beethoven's ninth symphony and other cyclical works, including *An*

EXAMPLE 4.5A Mendelssohn, String Quartet in A Minor, op. 13, movt. 1, mm. 1–17.

EXAMPLE 4.5B Mendelssohn, String Quartet in A Minor, op. 13, movt. 4, mm. 365–88.

die ferne Geliebte, which made an indelible impression on later generations of musicians and critics. The finale opens with a section of instrumental recitative for the first violin. As does the finale in Beethoven's last symphony, Mendelssohn's finale recalls and rejects themes from earlier movements of the quartet, though Mendelssohn's recollections are spaced over the entire movement rather than paraded through at the beginning. The thematic idea that eventually takes over the work is not a new theme but the song-based introduction in A major from the first movement. Although the first movement—after the introduction—had been in A minor and the finale begins in that key, some commentators have called this an A-major quartet for this reason.

The brief song form in the second movement utilizes motives and an overall style related to "Frage," but the opening melody's cantabile theme suggests a hymn or chorale topic as well. The nearly homorhythmic texture, four-bar phrases separated with rests, and narrow ranges combine to create a hushed, reverent quality not unlike the style of Beethoven's "Heiliger Dankgesang." The use of F major (VI) for this movement surely alludes to op. 132's key scheme and use of the Lydian mode. The middle section of the movement begins with a fugato section, another reference, perhaps, to the prevalence of contrapuntal display in Beethoven's late works. Indeed, the fugato theme bears a striking resemblance to the fugato section of Beethoven's op. 95 "Serioso" string quartet. Mendelssohn recalls his fugato in the finale, where it is melded with the movement's opening recitative and the slow movement's theme. His use of contrapuntal artifice throughout op. 13 connects him to the long history of German music that he revered, especially the work of J. S. Bach, a figure who hovers over Beethoven's late style as well. This tendency toward technical—that is, compositional—display is especially appropriate in this quartet, which pointedly combines reverence for the past with innovative designs associated with a progressive style.

Rosen describes the structure of Mendelssohn's quartet as "laid out with a kind of precocious virtuosity, a facile display that Beethoven, I think, would have disdained."[26] The overt, showy compositional style of the work, though, points us toward Mendelssohn's intended audience of fellow composers—best exemplified by Lindblåd, the lucky recipient of the work in manuscript, but also present throughout Europe. A small body of composers seeking a new musical style, attempting to figure out the next step in the music-historical process (those who were "in on the secret"), was scattered across the Continent, representing one of many "imagined communities" held together by music journalism and printed sheet music.[27] Newly published works like this one allowed them to communicate with each other about their ideas as to what that next step might be.

Mendelssohn's first string quartet embraces many of the most innovative elements of Beethoven's late style, but clearly the strongest impression created by the late quartets was the older master's attention to the overall effect of the work. Thus Mendelssohn responded with a work whose most striking characteristic is an approach to form and effect that connects the individual movements into an integrated whole. His contemporary Norbert Burgmüller would take the opposite approach, responding to individual elements of Beethoven's and Mendelssohn's style and innovating within movements.

Born in 1810, Norbert Burgmüller belonged to the generation of young Romantic composers that included Mendelssohn, Chopin, Schumann, and Liszt. Like Mendelssohn, Burgmüller demonstrated remarkable talent at an early age, and he was sponsored by Count Franz von Nesselrode-Ehreshaven, who brought the young man from his hometown of Düsseldorf to Kassel to study with Moritz Hauptmann and Louis Spohr.[28] During his first years there, Burgmüller completed three quartets, later published as his opp. 4, 7, and 9. These works display a Romantic sensibility in their chromaticism, their lyrical tendencies, and their reconsideration of established forms. They also demonstrate the influence of

Burgmüller's teacher Spohr in their obvious affinity with the latter's brilliant style of violin playing and writing, especially as evidenced in his *quatuors brillants*. Burgmüller's A-minor quartet, op. 14, composed in 1835—ten years later and after his return to Düsseldorf—reflects a very different set of influences, and its style represents a significant departure from his earlier musical style.

Upon his return to Düsseldorf from his studies in Kassel, Burgmüller found Mendelssohn installed as the city's new music director, the position left vacant after Burgmüller's father's death in 1824 and the one that Norbert had hoped to fill. In his professional capacity, Mendelssohn worked hard to increase the cosmopolitanism of Düsseldorf's musical and artistic life, bringing new repertoire and rehearsal methods, increasing the variety and breadth of musical performance opportunities, and altering the proportion and relationship of dilettante performers and professional musicians in civic ensembles.[29] His personal relationships with the artists and musicians of the city, moreover, brought further recognition of the musical world beyond the city's boundaries. Mendelssohn and Burgmüller, along with a few other friends, spent many happy evenings exploring the musical literature together. Wilhelm Müller von Konigswinter, a poet and amateur musician who wrote the first biography of Burgmüller, remembered evenings filled with readings at the keyboard by various members of the group, dominated by Mendelssohn and Burgmüller; the former treated them to vocal works by Bach, Handel, Gluck, Haydn, Mozart, and Beethoven, while the latter brought scores of symphonies, operas, and oratorios. In the winter of 1833–34 they formed a casual string quartet in which Burgmüller presumably played the violin and Mendelssohn the viola. Müller writes, "And so we soon added Haydn's, Mozart's, and Beethoven's quartets, and henceforth other efforts to many a lovely and pleasant evening."[30] In Mendelssohn, Burgmüller found a kindred spirit, and his creative achievements of the period between 1833 and his early death in May 1836 bear witness to the influence of the conversations and musical evenings they shared.[31] In particular, the fourth string quartet, published posthumously as his op. 14, demonstrates a recognition of Beethoven's late style (and Mendelssohn's early style) and his response to it.

Whereas Mendelssohn looked to cyclical construction and inspiration from poetic and vocal sources to respond to Beethoven's formal innovations, Burgmüller's quartet focuses on the recasting of sonata form as a fluid and dramatic movement type. By embracing thematic and harmonic ambiguity, Burgmüller created suspense in a first movement that constantly requires the listener (or analyst) to reevaluate the relationships between the parts and the whole. Although his alterations of sonata form are not as drastic as Beethoven's and do not incorporate cyclical design like Mendelssohn's, they nonetheless serve to reorient the form, moving the climactic denouement—the "double return" of thematic material and tonic simultaneously—from the beginning of the recapitulation to the beginning of the coda. The quartet begins with a theatrical, recitative-like introduction followed by a primary theme group without a strong articulation of key or character (see example 4.6a). The theme lacks cadential motion and periodicity that

EXAMPLE 4.6A Burgmüller, String Quartet in A Minor, op. 14, movt. 1, mm. 1–25.

would make a determination of key clear-cut, and the presentation of the head motive over first D minor, then A minor (m. 13), and C major (m. 21) harmonies increases the modal ambiguity. Mm. 39–46, however, present a quintessential second theme and topic in C major (example 4.6b), with two four-bar phrases, a plucked accompaniment that suggests a rustic style, and a lyrical theme in the two violins that emphasizes parallel sixths and tenths. As in the first movement of Beethoven's op. 132, this theme is not allowed to cadence onto its tonic but is extended through melodic sequences that serve as transitional materials before the introduction's opening gesture returns in m. 56.

As though to connect this ambiguity to his models, Burgmüller uses a four-note motto throughout the first movement to draw attention to his formal innovations. It is not connected to programmatic gestures, as Mendelssohn's had been. We hear it first in unison at m. 79: $\hat{5}$–$\flat\hat{6}$–$\hat{4}$–$\hat{5}$ in the key of C major (example 4.7). The motto resembles Beethoven's op. 132 motto just closely enough to recognize the homage, but the younger composer's use of the gesture differs wildly. Both mottos consist of an upward half step, a skip (a sixth in Beethoven, a third in Burgmüller), and stepwise motion in the opposite direction. Beethoven's motto, used in his introduction, suspends harmonic and metric ambiguity with chromaticism and overlapping contrapuntal entrances that create a mysterious atmosphere at the beginning of the work. Burgmüller, however, saves the motto for use as a

EXAMPLE 4.6B Burgmüller, String Quartet in A Minor, op. 14, movt. 1, mm. 38–46.

EXAMPLE 4.7 Burgmüller, String Quartet in A Minor, op. 14, movt. 1, mm. 74–81.

confirmation of arrival at the dominant, and his use of homorhythm and sforzandos helps this theme to dispel ambiguity rather than sustain it. The motto's function as a closing, confirming gesture here heightens its effect as a disruptive, surprising feature later in the movement.

The second half of the movement combines developmental and recapitulatory functions, using the four-note motto to guide listeners (and performers) and to provide dramatic revelatory moments at significant junctures along the way. Here, too, Burgmüller's careful attention to formal strategies allows a subtle narrative to unfold without the aid of text or vocal suggestions. The "development" begins with a reprise of the introductory material in the tonic (A minor). A sinister, minor-key version of the secondary theme appears in m. 107 on the minor dominant (v), hinting that the music may already be on its way toward the retransition, which seems to begin in earnest at m. 114. When the four-note motto returns in E major (B–C–A–B), it confirms arrival at the dominant. A "recapitulation" begins with the hesitant primary theme in A minor, but after just four measures the cello revolts, boldly turning the quartet away from A minor toward D♭ and further sequential development. By m. 145, the music has arrived once again at E major (V), and quiet, tentative dominant chords lead to A major and a reprise of the secondary theme/key materials. When the ensemble sounds a unison E in m. 193, we might expect—based on previous unison statements of the motto—that the four-note motto will confirm A major and usher in final closing materials in that key, but the final pitch is a surprising G♮ ($\flat\hat{7}$), notated in double-stops in three of the four parts (see example 4.8). The key signature changes to A minor, and a coda based on the minor-mode version of the secondary theme begins.

Like his Beethovenian model, Burgmüller's end-oriented form suspends the movement's tensions until the last possible moment and even then does not fully resolve them. Although the last four measures contain A-major chords, the last tones die away without any indication of the mode, leaving open the possibility of resolution in either minor or major at the end of the quartet. The young composer's rearrangement of sonata form elements treats the form as a malleable process, responding specifically to Beethoven's own recasting of the form. Whereas Mendelssohn's response addresses the large-scale concern of unity with an innovative programmatic solution (the inclusion of a song), Burgmüller rejects the intrusion of the word into the quartet genre and offers a different solution, engaging both composers (Mendelssohn and Beethoven) in a dialogue about the appropriate boundaries between genres.

Subsequent movements continue to engage Beethoven and Mendelssohn through significant use of the submediant (VI) and other gestures. Burgmüller's Andante draws on the quasi-sacred style of Beethoven's op. 132 and Mendelssohn's chorale- or hymn-like second movement. An F-major ternary form, the

EXAMPLE 4.8 Burgmüller, String Quartet in A Minor, op. 14, movt. 1, mm. 191–97.

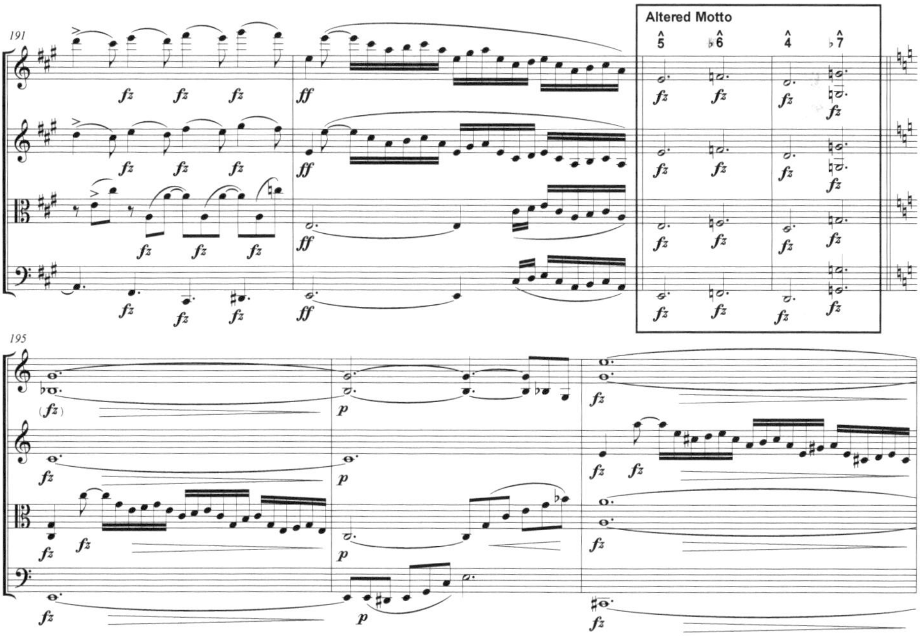

Andante, too, makes reference to the i–VI relationship explored in the Beethovenian model, and the movement ends with a characteristic faux-modal gesture that seems to engage both the "Heiliger Dankgesang" and Mendelssohn's op. 13. As the movement draws to a close, the first violin floats into the high register over a very quiet (***ppp***) tonic chord in the lower strings. After its arrival on F in m. 154, the viola unexpectedly descends by step: F–E♭–D♭–C, suggesting with these lowered scale degrees an Aeolian modal inflection. This small detail in the viola's line introduces an oddly discomfiting element at the end of an otherwise clear-cut movement.

Burgmüller's fourth-movement finale is left to settle some of the arguments raised by the first two movements.[32] Like Beethoven's op. 132 (and unlike Mendelssohn's A-minor quartet), Burgmüller's quartet closes with a rondo. The long sonata-rondo movement visits I, V, VI, and ♭III. Thus F major and C major—both prominent keys in earlier movements and significant keys in Beethoven's op. 132—are explored in the developmental middle section of the form. Burgmüller's incorporation of keys that had figured in earlier movements resolves the harmonic conflicts of the work as a whole without the aid of thematic recall, possibly signaling to Mendelssohn that in a unified work, all four parts of the sonata cycle can relate to one another without such overt compositional means.

Mendelssohn and Burgmüller, the first composers to take up the challenge of Beethoven's late quartets in their own works, did so to mark themselves as members of a self-consciously experimental and exclusive circle of composers and musicians. Responding to works that few understood and fewer championed, they formed a "club" of musical insiders within the already connoisseur-heavy chamber music establishment. While the critics of their day lacked words to describe Beethoven's musical innovations but sensed that something had changed in the nature of quartet composition and performance, Mendelssohn and Burgmüller demonstrated that change in tone and embraced a new mode of participation. Burgmüller's quartet may be read as an acceptance of the new professionalism that Mendelssohn brought to the genre and to musical life in Düsseldorf, and it marks him as a worthy compatriot of the new progressive group of composers, effectively severing his ties to Spohr. Little did he know that in a few short years Mendelssohn and his fellows would be labeled conservative by a new group of self-styled progressives. But at this early point, in the 1830s and 1840s, the definers of a progressive musical style included Mendelssohn, Burgmüller, and the next composer to take up the Beethovenian challenge, Robert Schumann.

Robert Schumann and the String Quartet

In 1838 the *Neue Zeitschrift für Musik* ran a series of articles by Robert Schumann titled Quartett-Morgen (Quartet mornings). The first of these begins with the author musing about the formation of an amateur group of quartetists gathering to read through new works in the genre and assess their worth:

> "There was the Schuppanzigh, there is the David Quartet, why not also—," I thought as I picked up my trifolium. "It wasn't that long ago," I thought to myself, "that Haydn, Mozart, and one other [a wry reference to Beethoven] lived and wrote quartets: How could such forefathers produce so few worthy grandchildren, who have learned practically nothing from them? And isn't it possible that a new genius is lying just under one's nose, waiting for contact? With one word, Most Honored Ones, the instruments [could] stand ready, and several new things could be played at our first matinee." And without further thought, as it seems musicians [are] always hanging around, there they sat at the music stands. I happily report on the works that fascinated us that morning—if not in a critic's succinct style, rather in lighter ways—the first impressions as they took hold of me, of each [subsequent impression] on me, together with [my] perceptions of them, [and] the impressions they made on the quartet players themselves. For I often attach more value to a simple curse of the musicians than to entire aesthetic systems.[33]

Several aspects of this introduction deserve emphasis here. Schumann's insistence in the final phrase that the musicians' opinions about the works would bear more weight than an aesthetic system (*ganze Aesthetiken*), or a theoretical model based on philosophical musing, allies him with practical musicians and composers, demonstrating his close connection to the act of making music, even in his journalistic enterprises. This attitude would be even more apparent a few years later by contrast with his successor Franz Brendel, whose university training and musical amateurism made his journalistic work much more "academic" and philosophical than Schumann's music-centric discussions, which he frequently illustrated with printed musical examples. It also highlights the fact that Schumann himself was no string player and that he would rely on the opinions of more experienced performers to determine the quartets' (and quintets') value as chamber music. The importance of "playability" and accessibility to performers clearly mattered to Schumann, and they played a role in his (and his contemporaries') conception of the genre—probably more so than for piano sonatas and other works. In a similar vein, Schumann notes that he would not write his reports in his usual critical style (in "succinct" or efficient style) but in a more chatty, friendly way. Thus the Quartett-Morgen reports would emulate letters or conversations among musicians with similar interests, reflecting and perhaps serving as a model for similar gatherings within the newspaper's virtual community of readers and followers. These gatherings and the reports they facilitated affect a light-hearted, collegial style despite their serious purpose—to explore the current state of the repertoire and support the continued progress of the genre since the efforts of the Classical masters.

Six Quartett-Morgen reports were published, though numbers 4 and 5 were combined into one report that dealt with the works of a single composer, Hermann Hirschbach.[34] The series of articles covers sixteen works by ten composers (see table 4.1) and chronicles Schumann's own feelings about the current state of the genre well before he began composing his own quartets. Notably, Schumann and his group read several works from manuscript copies that were, apparently, sent to him by their composers.

Some of these represent works by up-and-coming students at the Leipzig Conservatory, such as J. J. H. Verhulst, a Dutch composer who arrived in Leipzig early in 1838. In other cases, the reports serve as reviews of recently published works, as in the case of Louis Spohr's *quatuor brillant* and the quartets by C. Decker, Carl Gottlieb Reissiger, and Luigi Cherubini. The works reviewed in the series included music by composers we have encountered already in chapters 1 and 3, composers who wrote specifically, it would seem, for an amateur audience whose uses of music differed from Schumann's aims here in marked ways. Whereas the domestic amateurs addressed by Wenzel Heinrich Veit, Reissiger, and Johann Wenzel Kalliwoda would play this music for fun, Schumann's aim was to elevate and advance the genre (and, thereby, musical style overall). He describes Reissiger's work as derivative and unoriginal; too much of the music reminds him of Spohr, Onslow, Beethoven, and Mozart. Schumann concludes that Reissiger's A-major quartet, op. 111, no. 1, "is a quartet for the entertainment of good Dilettantes, who have enough to do, where the artist of skill with an overview has already read the

TABLE 4.1 Listing of works discussed in Robert Schumann's Quartett-Morgen reports published in 1838

Report no.	Publication information	Works reviewed (quartets for two violins, viola, and cello, unless otherwise stated)
1	8, no. 46 (8 Juni 1838): 181–82	J. J. H. Verhulst, Streichquartett [manuscript]
		Louis Spohr, Quatuor brillant, op. 97
		Leopold Fuchs, Quatuor . . . avec une Fantaisie sur un Chant russe national, op. 10
2	8, no. 49 (19 Juni 1838): 193–94	C. Decker, Premier Quatuor . . . C-moll, op. 14
		Reissiger, 3 Quatuors . . . , op. 111, no. 1 (A-Dur)
		Cherubini, 3 Quatuors . . . , no. 1 (Es-Dur)
3	9, no. 10 (3 August 1838): 41–42	W. H. Veit, 2tes Quartett . . . (E-Dur), op. 5
		J. F. E. Sobolewski, Trio für Piano forte, Violine u. Violoncello (As-Dur) [manuscript]
		Leopold Fuchs, Quintett f. 2 Violinen, 2 Bratschen und Violoncello (Es-Dur), op. 11
4 and 5	9, no. 13 (14 August 1838): 51–52	Hermann Hirschbach, 3 Quartets and 1 Quintet [manuscripts]
6	9, no. 20 (7 September 1838): 79–80	Leon de St. Lübin, 1stes grosses Quintett für 2 Violinen, 2 Bratschen und Violon cell. (Es-Dur), op. 38
		L. Cherubini, Quartett . . . Nr. II (C-Dur)

entire page; a quartet to hear near pretty girls under soft candlelight, while true Beethovenians close the door to suckle and feast on each individual measure."[35] Schumann singles out the comfortable, pleasant, entertaining qualities of Veit's, Spohr's, and Reissiger's works, noting that Spohr's op. 97 feels immediately familiar to those acquainted with the composer's earlier works, if a bit "unquartet-like" due to the lack of conversational texture or rigorous counterpoint.

Reading through the articles gives a good sense of the composer-critic's concern that the string quartet not fall into decline. Schumann feared that the quartet genre would fail to thrive and eventually find itself extinct, but he clearly abhorred attempts at quartet writing that resulted in mere copies of late eighteenth-century techniques. (He elaborated on this position in a later essay on a prize-winning quartet by Julius Schapler in 1842.)[36] The works that received his greatest invective in this and other genres were those by composers who ignored contemporary innovations, such as Léon de Saint-Lubin and Leopold Fuchs. What, then, did Schumann want from quartet composers? What traits did he long to see in these works that disappointed him, as is increasingly apparent in the successive reports? His answer came in a group of three string quartets written within four months of each other in 1842 and published together as Schumann's own op. 41 in early 1843.[37]

Like the Quartett-Morgen reports, the op. 41 quartets strike a didactic or pedagogical tone. These three quartets, taken together, constitute one large work that responds to the challenge of creating progressive chamber music for the nineteenth century, or what Schumann would call the "new poetic age," and I posit that they represent Schumann's attempt to show the way for future progressive composers.[38] Several important choices indicate that Schumann, like his idol and the dedicatee of the quartets, Mendelssohn, responded to Beethoven's op. 132 quartet specifically and to his late style generally in these works. The opus as a whole replicates the A minor–F major–A major trajectory of Beethoven's work. No. 1, the quartet in A minor, contains many gestures that indicate a familiarity both with op. 132 and with Mendelssohn's op. 13, perhaps also with Burgmüller's quartet. The innovative approach to sonata form that the composer developed in the piano works of the 1830s, called "parallel form" by scholar Linda Correll Roesner, reappears in his first string quartet.[39] Here, Schumann's presentation of thematic material and its immediate repetition with variations (rather than a clearly delineated exposition, development, and recapitulation) seem directly connected to Beethoven's use of three theme/key rotations in the first movement of op. 132. Schumann's return to a formal design that juxtaposes two rotations of theme/key material without a long or distinctive development section between them in this work may have been prompted by Beethoven's model.

The relationship between Schumann's quartets and Beethoven's is further underscored by the later composer's harmonic procedures within individual movements. The first movement of the A-minor quartet begins with a thirty-three-measure Introduzione that closes in A minor (see example 4.9). The main body of the movement is a sonata-allegro form in F major (VI) complete with exposition, development, and recapitulation sections that never engage A minor as a significant tonal center (the first movement ends in F major). The dual tonality of this movement is never satisfactorily resolved in the first quartet. As Julie Hedges Brown and Roesner have noted, the real resolution to these harmonic ambiguities does not occur until the finale of the third quartet in A major (op. 41, no. 3), a rondo in the *style hongrois* (the stylized form of "Hungarian" Gypsy music). Schumann's altered rondo form finale in the A-major quartet clearly engages the rondo finale of Beethoven's op. 132. Both movements expand the normal boundaries of related tonalities by exploring distantly related keys visited in earlier movements. Brown furthermore demonstrates that Schumann's

EXAMPLE 4.9 Schumann, String Quartet in A Minor, op. 41, no. 1, movt. 1, mm. 1–44.

use of the *style hongrois* in both quartet finales and in similar finales in his other chamber works supports the experimental, almost transgressive, formal procedures he employs; by harnessing both positive and negative stereotypes associated with Gypsies in his lifetime, Schumann uses this musical topic to highlight the Romantic, "progressive" formal designs in his quartets.[40]

The finale of the A-minor quartet sets up a cyclical reference that evokes Beethoven and Mendelssohn simultaneously, incorporating a musical gesture that will return in the A-major quartet's finale. At the end of the A-minor finale, Schumann introduces a sudden stop and change of texture (example 4.10). At m. 258 we encounter an unexpected change of key and scoring from the full-ensemble busy-ness that had dominated the movement to static drones in the cello and first violin, while a musette-like theme emerges in octaves in the middle

EXAMPLE 4.9 (continued)

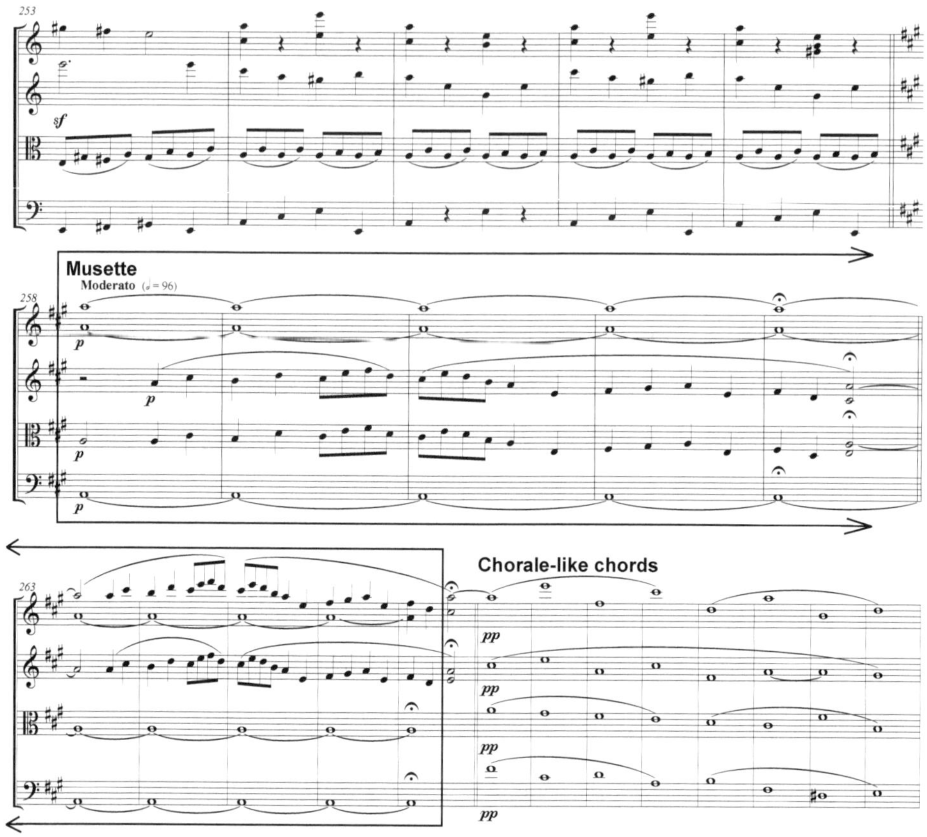

EXAMPLE 4.10 Schumann, String Quartet in A Minor, op. 41, no. 1, movt. 4, mm. 253–75.

voices. This arresting moment at the end of the quartet is followed by an even stranger passage of chorale-like chords similar to the calm, quasi-religious tone of Beethoven's op. 132 and Mendelssohn's op. 13 in mm. 268–89 before the music returns to its original tempo and style for a rousing finish in the final thirty-four measures. The musette passage comes out of nowhere in this quartet; it has not been prepared in any way, and the tempo and texture changes are jarring in a movement with so much forward momentum. That Schumann draws such attention to this passage lends it extra significance. In fact, the passage is strikingly reminiscent of the musette passage from Beethoven's op. 132 quartet; this gesture is then repeated, albeit very briefly, in a cyclical allusion in the A-major quartet's finale (mm. 101–5). This musette moment is the most conspicuous allusion to Beethoven in these works, and Schumann saves it for the end as though he wished to make perfectly clear the relationship between his quartets and the quartet legacy that he inherited.

Even Schumann's F-major quartet, op. 41, no. 2, can be read as a response to Beethoven. Like the "Serioso" quartet, op. 95, Schumann's terse, tightly woven quartet makes the most of its thematic and tonal materials in an economical form. No note is wasted in this short work. Unlike Beethoven's grim F-minor quartet, though, Schumann's work embraces the bucolic, pastoral qualities of this key, and it seems to represent for him a long-drawn breath of fresh air after the high energy of the first quartet and before the serious business of resolving the opus's conflicts in the A-major quartet. Schumann draws a parallel with Beethoven in this work, but his quartet's character is the polar opposite of its model.

Schumann's quartets deploy the same progressive features of Beethoven's op. 132 quartet that Mendelssohn and Burgmüller had a few years earlier. The dedication of this set of three quartets to Mendelssohn solidifies the link to that older composer's efforts in this field. Although the dedication would seem to point us to Mendelssohn's op. 44 quartets (also a group of three; published in parts in 1839, in score in 1840), it seems more likely that Schumann was thinking of Mendelssohn's earlier quartets when he dedicated these works. The full score of op. 13 was published by Breitkopf und Härtel in 1842, at the same time that Schumann was studying quartets by the Classical masters and noting "quartet thoughts" in his and Clara's joint household diary (the "Haushaltbücher"). Schumann also knew Burgmüller's works well, and he appreciated their novelty and ingenuity, as Mendelssohn had. Eulogizing the young composer in the *Neue Zeitschrift*, Schumann exclaimed, "Since Franz Schubert's early death, none has been more painful to us than that of Burgmüller. Fate, instead of thinning the mediocre multitude which surrounds us, has taken from us one of our greatest artists."[41] Although his obituary does not include Burgmüller's string quartets in its list of compositions, Schumann may have learned of them from Mendelssohn, or Schumann may have gained access to them after 1839.

Finally, the publication history of Schumann's quartets sheds some light on his audience as well. Schumann was adamant that a full score should also be printed, though his publisher, Raimond Härtel, balked at the expense. Schumann pleaded and cajoled, arguing that the parts would sell better if performers also had a score to show them how the various pieces of the works fit together and pointing out that his music was more complex than many contemporary works in the genre.[42] Härtel finally obliged with a score, but it did not become available until 1848.

Schumann's desire to see the works in score format is telling. Naturally, his suggestion that a score would improve performances and thereby sales of the work rings true, but another probable consideration is Schumann's intended audience. I noted above that the didactic or pedagogical tone of the quartets mirrors that of the Quartett-Morgen reports. Clearly the audience for the quartets themselves was similar to the intended reading audience for the reports: musical or artistic insiders and experimenters looking for guidance in the critique and creation of a new poetic art. As a pianist himself, Schumann most often studied music in score format at his desk or at the piano. During the spring of 1842, he and Clara read through many quartets by Haydn, Mozart, and Beethoven together at the piano, and we may assume that this was his primary means of connecting to unfamiliar or new works.[43] Thus, perhaps because Schumann composed the quartets with fellow composers, critics, and students of music in mind, he saw the printed score as the greatest tool in disseminating his musical ideas to the wider world.

The String Quartets of Franz Berwald

In 1849, at the age of fifty-five, Swedish composer Franz Berwald (1796–1868) completed two string quartets. Although he had composed quartets earlier in his career, the two later works prove somewhat mystifying partly because they were left unpublished.[44] Contrary to Schumann's goal of sending his musical works out to as many recipients as possible, Berwald withheld these works from public consumption, reserving them instead for a small circle of trusted musical acquaintances. An examination of their musical style shows that, despite their private use and carefully controlled reception, Berwald's 1849 quartets exhibit the same engagement with the genre's history that the works discussed above display. The circumstances of Berwald's career suggest that the quartets likewise present one composer's suggestions for the continuation of the string quartet genre's progress in the nineteenth century and beyond.

Berwald's career in music began early and continued in fits and starts throughout his life.[45] A native of Stockholm, he left Sweden to seek greater fame and understanding on several occasions: he moved to Berlin in 1829, then to Vienna in 1841, back to Stockholm the following year, to Paris and then Vienna again in 1846, and finally home to Stockholm permanently in 1849. During his itinerant youth in the 1820s through 1840s, Berwald focused on large forms such as symphonies, tone poems, oratorios, and operas.[46] Despite several attempts to support himself and his family with composition alone, Berwald never secured a stable position in German musical life. Performances of his works fell flat because their wild harmonic language and revised approach to form did not please listening audiences or performers. Apparently his waspish personality and enormous ego also won him more enemies than friends, resulting in few useful contacts in the cities he visited. Without steady musical employment, Berwald relied on his keen business sense and managerial skills to make his living, spending the last two decades of his life as the manager of a factory, a successful (if frustrated) member of the middle classes and of Stockholm's vibrant social scene.

When Berwald settled in Stockholm in 1849, he turned his compositional efforts almost exclusively to chamber music, creating a pair of string quartets, four piano trios, two piano quintets, and two sonatas for violin and piano. Though he composed one piano concerto for a particularly talented student in 1855, Berwald eschewed the larger genres during this decade.[47] His newfound position as the director of a glassworks owned by an amateur violinist allowed him the time and leisure to compose, and his association with the city's professional and nonprofessional musicians offered the opportunity to hear his works in private settings. The products of this cozy atmosphere, however, differ markedly from the domestic style discussed in relation to Spohr, Kuhlau, and Onslow in chapter 3. Rather, true to Berwald's compositional nature, they share several similarities with the progressive works of Mendelssohn, Burgmüller, and Schumann, as well as with contemporaneous (nonchamber) works by Franz Liszt, with whom Berwald later corresponded and to whom he dedicated his A-major piano quintet.[48] It would seem that, having finally found a small receptive audience among Stockholm's chamber music connoisseurs, the composer took this opportunity to experiment, creating works that test the boundary between the innovative and the truly bizarre.

The quartets engage the two dominant music-political positions of the later 1840s. Berwald's A-minor quartet shares many of the mannerisms associated with quartets in that key, and it establishes a dialogue with the "conservative" composers of the Leipzig tradition represented by Mendelssohn, Schumann, and others. The E♭-major string quartet, on the other hand, clearly responds to developments in the Lisztian approach to "progressive" music. Both groups, we should remember, thought of their works as Romantic and progressive, but they disagreed on the musical nature of those terms. Berwald used the string quartet genre to test out both options.

One of the most striking characteristics of both quartets is their attention to large-scale unity. In the A-minor quartet, Berwald connects the four separate movements to each other by indicating that they are to be played without pause and by composing passages at the beginnings and endings of movements that smooth transitions melodically and harmonically. These connections create a work that flows continually from beginning to end. For instance, after the first movement fulfills its recapitulatory obligations in mm. 186–201 with closing materials in the tonic, Berwald introduces the head motive of the secondary theme in F major (VI, a recurring key in this work as in other nineteenth-century A-minor string quartets) in m. 206 (see example 4.11). Over the next twenty measures, the music vacillates between A minor and F major harmonies, finally ending with an F^7 chord followed by a long pause. The second movement's main theme begins immediately in B♭ major.

The transitions between the second and third movements and between the third and fourth movements create even smoother junctures by overlapping melodic and harmonic transitional passages at the end of one movement and the beginning of the next. For example, the final four measures of the Adagio (the second movement) decorate tonic harmony (B♭) with turns and mordents that resemble the circular melodic motion introduced by the cello in the opening measures of the Scherzo. This turn-like figure is present in one or more voices throughout much of the third movement and gives the Scherzo its gigue-like

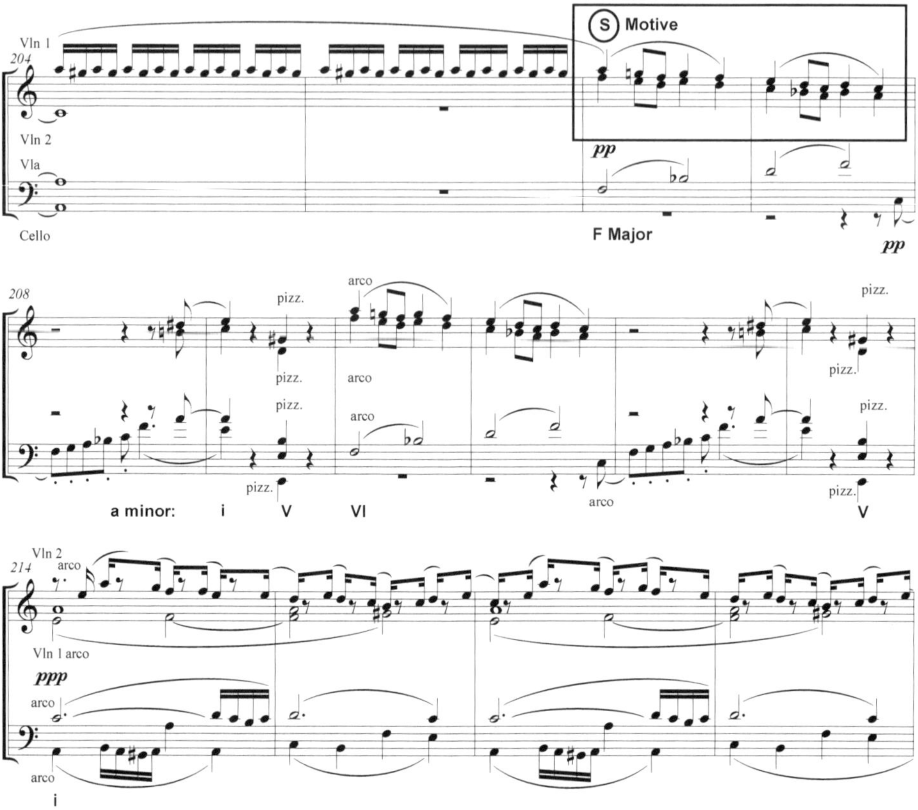

EXAMPLE 4.11 Berwald, String Quartet in A Minor, movt. 1, m. 204, through movt. 2, m. 5.

character. Harmonically, the Adagio leads directly into the Scherzo (resolving vii°7 to I in B♭ on the downbeat of the new movement), and the first twelve measures of the Scherzo gradually move the harmony from the second movement's tonic (B♭) to F major, the new tonic key. The third and fourth movements are similarly connected by a codetta at the end of the Scherzo that introduces elements of the finale's themes and prepares the new key, A major (see example 4.12). This transition ends with a two-measure tag that recalls the neighbor motive at the end of the first movement's Introduzione section (compare example 4.12 to 4.13). This brief recollection gives the quartet a vestige of cyclicity.

The first movement of the A-minor quartet opens with an Introduzione that functions in some ways like the quartet-inspiring song of Mendelssohn's op. 13 quartet, creating thematic and harmonic unity through recurring features and musical gestures (see example 4.13). The first four measures create an unsettled atmosphere rather than present a theme, with a slightly learned pose in mm. 1–12 and a recitative-like passage in the first violin in mm. 3–4. Mm. 5–9, however,

EXAMPLE 4.11 (continued)

introduce a song-like theme in the top line with clearly accompanimental writing in the other three instruments. This song is rejected by the group: it fails to cadence and is followed by silence and a return to the atmospheric music of the opening measures. This opening tactic seems to allude to Beethovenian drama in the style of the Ninth Symphony and the late string quartets. Significantly, the rejected song's first iteration begins in F major, the now-familiar tonal rival to A minor in these quartets. A second iteration of the song-like theme in C major occurs in mm. 15–18, followed by the dominant-emphasizing neighbor-note gesture mentioned above.

As in earlier A-minor quartets, the proposal and rejection of both the F major tonality and the song theme recur as primary features of this work as the A minor–F major–C major triangle struggles for harmonic resolution. The Scherzo movement is set in F major, and the three keys vie for attention in the outer sonata form movements (the first and fourth movements). The song theme's rejection in the Introduzione is expanded and explored in the second movement, the

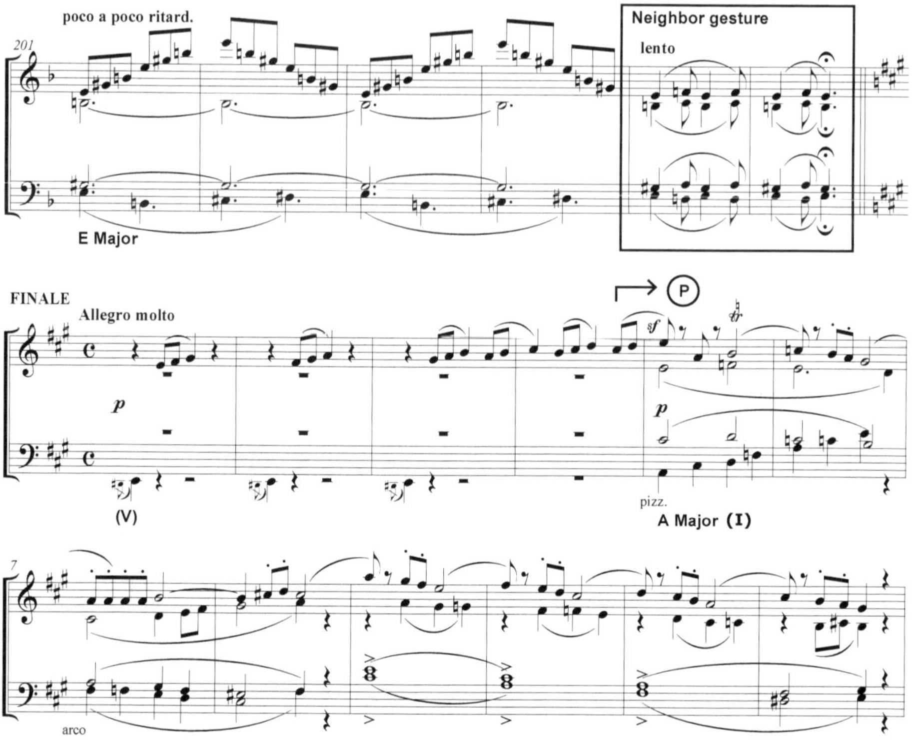

EXAMPLE 4.12 Berwald, String Quartet in A Minor, movt. 3, m. 201, through movt. 4, m. 12.

Adagio, as a proposed second theme with a sweet, pastoral topic set in F major, or V in the movement's B♭ tonality, is stymied by the cello not once but twice in the movement.

Whereas the A-minor quartet clearly displays a rapprochement with previous progressive works in the genre, the E♭-major quartet demonstrates a new approach to cyclicity that seems almost to caricature earlier examples. Like its A-minor counterpart, the E♭ quartet's movements proceed smoothly from one to the next with no breaks. The individual movements are titled for clarity, but no double bar-lines disrupt the flow. This work seems, upon first hearing or glance, to conform to the four-movement model: an introduction is followed by a slightly strange sonata form movement, a ternary slow movement, and a scherzo. But in place of the expected finale at the conclusion of this Scherzo, Berwald inserts a recapitulation of the first two sections of the slow movement. This reprise leads straight into a recapitulation of the primary- and secondary-key materials from the first movement. Thus, Berwald has created a nested form or palindrome, in which the Scherzo forms a dramatic centerpiece surrounded by the conventional elements of a four-movement form (see table 4.2). This is cyclicity taken almost to the extreme.

EXAMPLE 4.13 Berwald, String Quartet in A Minor, movt. 1, mm. 1–20.

In addition to this unconventional large-scale formal scheme, the individual components of the work hold several formal innovations, some seemingly related to previous examples from the quartet literature, and others apparently of Berwald's own design. Berwald's alterations of formal ideas unify the individual components of the quartet and create a fully integrated work in which each part contributes to the effect of the whole. The first movement's sonata form sets up these connections with a three-key scheme whose ramifications play out in subsequent movements.[49] The movement opens with a waltz-like primary theme in the

TABLE 4.2 Formal analysis of Franz Berwald, String Quartet in E♭ Major

Movement information	Observations on form	Observations on style
I. Allegro con brio—Allegro di molto (B♭–E♭)	Sonata form with big introduction Strong presence of P in exposition, but not in recapitulation Two S areas: C minor (vi) and A♭ major (IV)	In dialogue with Beethoven (337 mm.)
II. Adagio quasi Andante (A♭)	Ternary A B C A♭ G D♭ → G	A = almost hymn-like or song B = dialogue between vln 1 and vc C = fugato (49 mm.)
III. Scherzo Allegro assai (C minor, E♭ major)	Rondo: refrain is S, not P!	Centerpiece of the movement Like a development for the whole work (390 mm.)
IV. Adagio (A♭)	A and B of movt. 2	(26 mm.)
V. Allegro di molto (E♭)	P and S1 of movt. 1 + Coda	(100 mm.)

tonic (example 4.14); the first secondary theme is introduced in C minor (vi, or the relative minor) at m. 79. With its stormy character, it seems like the opposite of a standard secondary theme (labeled S1 in example 4.15). At m. 138 a second secondary theme (labeled S2 in example 4.16) appears in A♭ major (IV), and this candidate conforms to normative expectations for a euphonious, lyrical theme with a slightly rustic character and a subdued homophonic accompaniment.

EXAMPLE 4.14 Berwald, String Quartet in E♭ major, movt. 1, mm. 29–37.

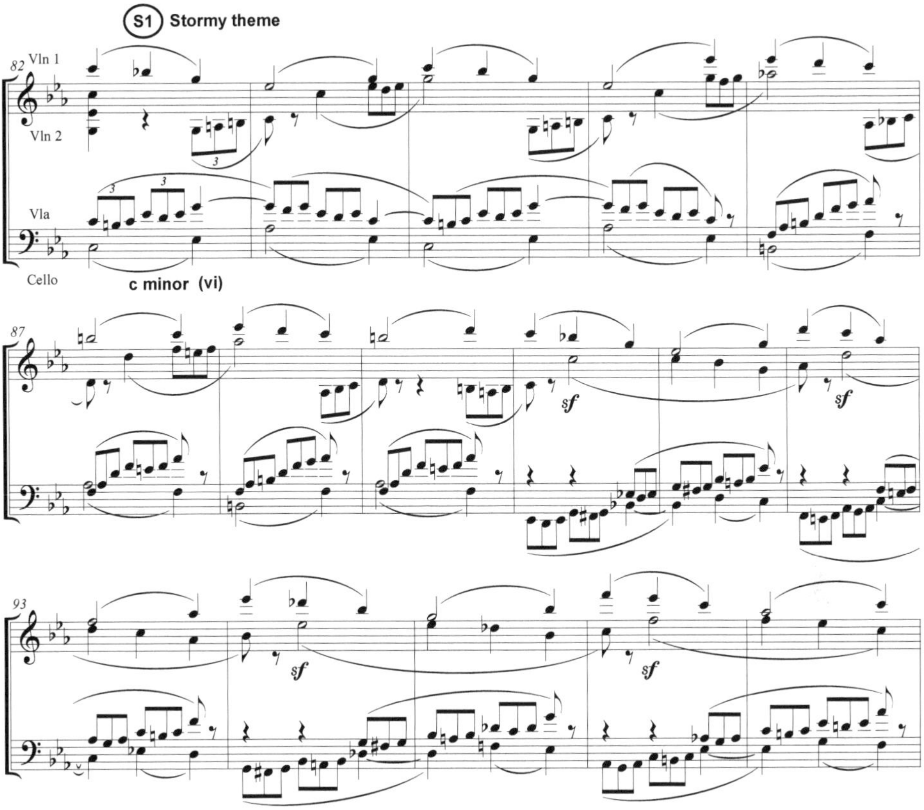

EXAMPLE 4.15 Berwald, String Quartet in E♭ major, movt. 1, mm. 82–97.

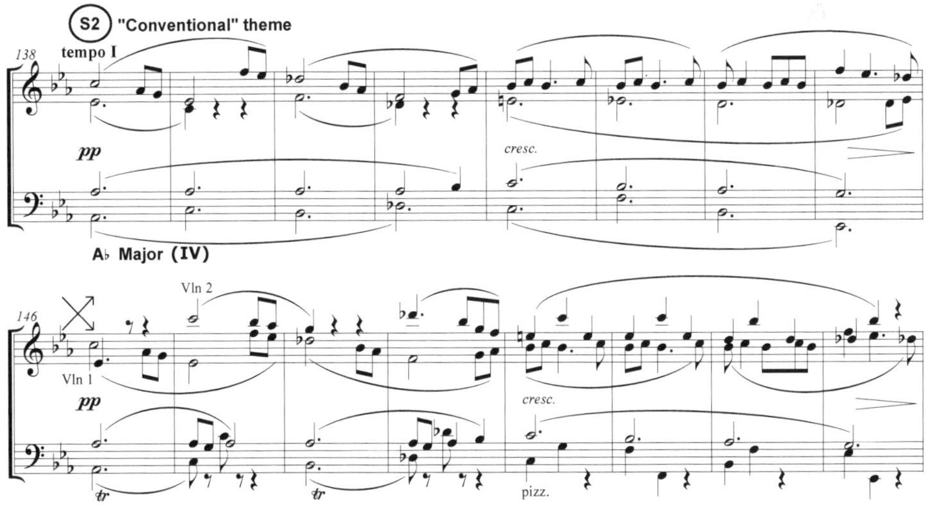

EXAMPLE 4.16 Berwald, String Quartet in E♭ major, movt. 1, mm. 138–53.

As in Schubert's three-key expositions, the presentation of two distinct secondary theme/key complexes allows Berwald to explore a wider variety of more distantly related keys than would ordinarily be found in a sonata-allegro movement. Berwald fulfills the promise of the two secondary key areas by setting the second-movement Adagio in A♭ (IV, the key of S2) and the Scherzo in C minor (vi, the key of S1). Thus the smaller details of Berwald's approach within the first movement's form appear to generate large-scale features of tonal and formal unity for the work as a whole.

In that vein, the nature of the first movement's recapitulation also affects the cyclical form of the quartet. Berwald saves a reprise of the primary theme for the final cyclical recall at the end of the quartet rather than recapitulating it within the sonata form movement.[50] Thus the cyclical element is not just a superfluous gimmick or programmatic device; rather, it completes a musical process left unresolved at the end of the first movement. Likewise, the eventual return of the second-movement materials, in their original key of A♭, fulfills the expected repetition of A-section materials in a ternary form. Berwald staves off fulfillment of normal generic or formal resolution in each of these movements until the end of the work, essentially leaving the movements open-ended until the final cyclical reprise.

The cyclical nature of this work on every level—from the construction of individual themes to the organization of movements to the overall scheme of enfolding the movements within one another—marks it as an experimental work that tests the bounds of progressiveness in string quartet writing. It also links Berwald to the most forward-thinking artists of his day, no matter how one defines or limits "progressive" composition. Most notably, it links Berwald to Franz Liszt, whose B-minor piano sonata and E♭-major piano concerto both feature a multisection, one-movement form that reevaluates the multimovement sonata paradigm. Liszt's E♭ concerto, moreover, shares with Berwald's quartet a formal design that favors cyclicity, in addition to sharing the same tonic key.

With the two 1849 string quartets, Berwald retreated into a musical community that allowed him to explore new ideas and present them to an appreciative audience. Composed with his inner circle of colleagues and friends in mind, the quartets demonstrate an experimental freedom that we also see in Berwald's more public works (such as the *Symphonie singulière*) but that never found an audience in the wider musical world. Although the quartets remained unpublished in the composer's lifetime, they were not unknown in Stockholm, where they made a strong impression on those musicians interested in a new musical style.

* * *

Throughout the nineteenth century, but particularly at its volatile midpoint, some composers, artists, and authors sought new ways to improve upon the achievements of the past. By picking up the thread of a conversation (or an argument) where Beethoven had left off in 1827, the composers considered here created a progressive music for their time that differed from the musical styles and ideals we have come to associate with that term. An examination of their music in the context that they intended, as opposed to the context created for them by later journalists and agitators, introduces much-needed nuance into the narrative of musical style in the Romantic era. Mendelssohn, Burgmüller, Schumann, and Berwald (along with many others) redefined the conventions of the string quartet to suit their own needs. The style they established or maintained—focused on motivic integration, formal innovation and experimentation, and harmonic daring—has come to represent good chamber music style in the twentieth and twenty-first centuries. We should note here that this style is also a composer-centered one in which the driving force of the composition is the musical argument made in the conception and working out of the piece. These progressive composers purposely sought to distance themselves from the more conversational and leisurely performer-centered style being developed at the same time by their contemporaries, as Schumann's criticism and Mendelssohn's correspondence clearly show. Meanwhile, some contemporaneous composers sought to distance themselves from earlier traditions by introducing overt programmatic elements into the string chamber genres.

CHAPTER 5

Creating "Progressive" Communities through Programmatic Chamber Music

We have already seen how composers and publishers used musical style to harness chamber music's ability to reinforce or create bonds of community among domestic sheet music purchasers and self-consciously avant-garde or "serious" composers following the model of Beethoven's late works. Composers interested in new modes of musical narrative in the nineteenth century also recognized the chamber genres as a unique opportunity to explore techniques that would bring together performers and listeners. The development of programmaticism in the nineteenth century allowed composers to draw on an audience's shared experiences and knowledge beyond music and musical history. This may be one reason why the composers most commonly associated with programmatic composition in this era tend to be those who used music to promulgate political or artistic views and created musical works responding to a shared cause, such as the nationalist schools of eastern Europe or the New German School, centered in Weimar. Considerations of programmatic music have tended to ignore chamber genres, but a reexamination of selected programmatic string quartets and quintets reveals the many ways that progressive composers of diverse compositional schools utilized musical narrative to celebrate or create ties within social and political groups. Here, as in chapter 4, my definition of "progressive" composition includes works and composers associated with the New German School and those related to other traditions, such as the Leipzig School, based on the ideals of Mendelssohn and Schumann, so long as the intention is to advance musical style by drawing upon specific innovations of earlier generations.

Nineteenth-century programmatic chamber works contradict the notion of chamber music as a last bastion of "pure" or "absolute" music, and they demonstrate the common themes that unite members of ostensibly divided schools of thought. Table 5.1 gives a listing (certainly not exhaustive) of programmatic string chamber music published in the nineteenth century. Although programmatic works made up a small percentage of the music published for string chamber ensembles, the presence of more than three dozen works by a wide-ranging group

TABLE 5.1 Selection of string chamber works with extramusical content indicated

Composer	Title	Date
Boccherini, Luigi	Musica notturna delle strade di Madrid (string quintet)	1780
Danzi, Franz	String quartets, op. 5, no. 2 (descriptive movement titles)	1790?
Danzi, Franz	String quartet "aus (Mozart's) Figaro" (op. 6, no. 2)	1801
Beethoven	String quartet in B♭ major (op. 18, no. 6) (fourth movement, "La Malinconia")	
Neukomm, Sigismund	L'amante abandonée, Quintetto dramatique	1810
Romberg, Andreas	Fantasie (for string quartet) Componirt im Hamburg 1814 wahrend der Belagerung	1814
Saint-Lubin	Introduction et Variations sur un thème russe favori, op. 6 (for solo violin with violin, viola, and cello)	1819
Neukomm, Sigismund	Une fête de village en Suisse, Quintetto dramatique	1820
Arriaga	Variations for String Quartet	1820
Turbri	"Hommage a Beethoven" (op. 15) (string quartet)	1820
Arriaga	Variations on the theme "La Húngara" (string quartet)	1822
Beethoven	"Heiliger Dankgesang eines Genesenen an die Gottheit" (third movement of A Minor String Quartet, op. 132)	1825
Cherubini	Souvenir pour son cher Baillot (string quartet)	1828
Loewe, Carl	Quatuor spirituel (op. 26)	1830
Onslow, George	String Quintet in C Minor, "La Balle" (op. 38)	1831
Onslow, George	String Quintet in E Major (op. 39) (third movement, "La melinconia")	1831
Veit, Vaclav	Premier Quatuor . . . , op. 3 (second movement, variations on a "Hymne russe")	
Fuchs, Leopold	Quatuor . . . avec une Fantaisie sur un Chant russe national, op. 10	1838
Hirschbach, Herrmann	3 string quartets: "Lebensbilder in einem Cyclus von Quartetten"	1841
Saint-Lubin	La jota aragonesa (op. 45) (for solo violin with violin, viola, and cello)	1843
David, Felicien	Les quatre saisons (twenty-four string quintets)	1845–46
Hirschbach, Herrmann	String Quartet no. 4: "Des Künsterler's einsame stunde"	1847
Hirschbach, Herrmann	String Quartet no. 13 (first movement, setting of Lenau poem in violin 1 part, notated as a vocal line with text underlay)	1859
Schuberth, Carl	String Quartet "Meine Reise in den Kirgisen Steppen"	1862
Kiel, F.	3 Waltzes for String Quartet (op. 73)	1872
Broustet, E.	Air vanié dans le style ancient (string quintet)	1870s?
Raff, Joseph Joachim	String Quartet "Schöne Müllerin" (op. 192, no. 2)	1874/76
Raff, Joseph Joachim	String Quartet "Suite alterer Form" (op. 192, no. 1)	1874/77
Raff, Joseph Joachim	String Quartet "Suite in Canonenform" (op. 192, no. 3)	1874/78
Rimsky-Korsakov	At the Monastery (string quartet)	1878–9
Sechter, Simon	Die vier Temperamente. Ein musikalischen Scherz für Streich-Quartett (op. 6)	

(continued on next page)

TABLE 5.1 (continued)

Composer	Title	Date
Romberg, B.	Divertimento on Westphalian National Themes (op. 65) (for cello and string quartet)	1880
Kiel, F.	Waltzer für Streichquartett, Neue Folge (op. 78)	1880
Liszt, Franz	Am Grabe Richard Wagners (S. 135) (for string quartet and harp)	1883
Jonas, Ernst	Liebeslied (op. 58) (string quartet)	1884
Reckzeh, Adolf	Der Mutter Wiegenlied (op. 254) (string quintet)	1885
Glazunov, A.	5 Novelettes (op. 15) (string quartet)	1886
Wolf, Hugo	Italian Serenade (string quartet)	1887
(Russian collaboration)	Jour de fête (string quartet)	1888
Wolfrum, P.	"Im Fruhjahr" (op. 13) (string quartet)	1888
Rosenhein, J.	Am Abend (op. 99) (string quartet)	1888
Rachmaninoff	Romanze & Scherzo (string quartet)	1889
Sinigaglia, L.	Hora mystica (string quartet)	1890
Puccini	Crisantemi (string quartet)	1890
Coleridge-Taylor	5 Fantasiestücke (op. 5) Prelude, Serenade, Humoresque, Minuet & Trio, Dance (string quartet)	1895
Kalinnikov, V.	2 Miniatures (string quartet, or quintet with contrabass ad libitum)	1896

of composers from different traditions suggests that combining extramusical content with the string quartet was not so unusual or taboo as previous treatments of either programmaticism or chamber music would lead us to believe. In this chapter, we will examine three programmatic works for strings, each with a different relationship to the cultural and political scene of its day: George Onslow's string quintet "The Bullet" deals with a hunting accident; Niels Gade's string quartet "Willkommen und Abschied" (Welcome and departure) interprets a Goethe poem; and Bedřich Smetana's string quartet "From My Life" provides a politically charged autobiography in tones. In all three cases, the composer has addressed a particular group of performers or listeners by using musical style and the written word to create a narrative that would resonate with a shared experience or identity. These three works demonstrate the range of possibilities for programmaticism throughout the nineteenth century, as well as different points along the spectrum of depiction, from "characteristic" works that narrate a series of events with mimetic devices to more abstract works that attempt to translate a poetic ideal into musical sounds.[1]

Before moving to the analyses, two important differences between programmatic chamber music and its more public cousins, the tone poem and programmatic symphony, need acknowledgment. First, chamber ensembles such as the string quartet and quintet prompted composers to write works based on more personal or intimate stories than larger-scaled works for orchestra. Thus programmatic chamber music tends toward autobiography, as some of the titles in table 5.1 demonstrate. Indeed, the nineteenth century's penchant for musical programmaticism was closely allied with the impulse to confess or reveal oneself in art, sometimes in response to external stimuli, or to respond personally to another artist's creation.[2] Berlioz's searing portrait of unrequited love and obsession, the *Symphonie fantastique* (1831), stems from his uncannily imaginative perspective on certain of his own life experiences. Liszt's tone poems and poetic symphonies provide a subjective "reading" of the poems, characters, and literary works he presents. When writing for chamber ensembles, though, composers often took this self-reflection even further. Smetana, for instance, composed *Má vlast* to express his love of the Czech countryside and his solidarity with the Czech people, but he turned to the piano trio or to the string quartet when he experienced a personal tragedy, such as the death of his daughter or his own loss of hearing.

Second, when writing programmatic pieces for string quartet or quintet, composers tended to follow the generic conventions of those ensembles more closely than they did in other programmatic works. These works typically adhere to the four-movement sonata cycle common in nonprogrammatic works, and they often retain the "normative" movement order and structures (sonata form, slow movement, scherzo or dance, and sonata or rondo finale). In Liszt's conception of the tone poem, the poetic inspiration for the work dictated its program and its musical shape. His symphonic poems often adopt a continuous or one-movement form in which musical materials and their development evoke or narrate the program with seemingly little consideration of Classical forms. When writing in more traditional forms such as sonata or rondo, composers of program music manipulated preexisting formal principles to create meaningful deviations that communicated the work's narrative at a structural level, in addition to evoking the events of the chosen program on the musical surface through imitative and topical gestures.[3] These works occupy a middle ground between the most daring examples of nineteenth-century "new music" and the conservative works of less innovative artists. As we shall see, this middle ground provided enough room for composers from both groups to try out new means of expression in a variety of genres, including the string quartet and quintet.

Onslow's "Bullet" Quintet

One of the earliest Romantic composers to explore programmatic techniques in chamber genres was George Onslow (1784–1853), the creator of cozy domestic music for his own use and for sharing via publication with presumably middle-class audiences, as described in chapter 3. Onslow's chamber works already create or reinforce the bonds of community and friendship in their close adherence to a domestic style appropriate for collegial playing, but in his C-minor quintet, op. 38, Onslow used that genre to further emphasize the importance of chamber playing in his life. This quintet also situates Onslow's musical activities within a thoroughly masculine life of leisure (exemplified by the boar hunt that the work evokes), and this topic may reflect a commonly held concern about music's supposed effeminizing qualities. The quintet, today referred to as "La balle," or "The Bullet," presents a conversational retelling of an exciting and horrific event in Onslow's life—the composer was accidentally shot by a friend during a hunt in the countryside, but he survived to tell the tale. Onslow's friend and fellow opera composer Fromental Halévy provided a colorful account of the incident in his 1855 remembrance of the composer:

> In 1829, a hunt was organized in [Onslow's] honor in the neighborhood of Nevers. This was to be a serious undertaking, fraught with danger, for the quarry was an old wild boar which had been unsuccessfully pursued for several days. On the day of the hunt, Onslow, dressed in complete hunting outfit, joined his friends. (He did not altogether leave behind his composition, however, for he carried with him at all times a small blank book of music paper in which to jot down themes whenever they might strike his imagination—even in the midst of a hunt. Onslow had, in fact, already begun to outline his latest quintet in this notebook.) He took up his assigned post and waited for the boar to be driven towards him, but soon, in the wondrous quiet of the forest, his thoughts turned to his composition. Forgetting his fellow hunters, he wandered off deeper into the woods, found an overturned tree stump, sat down on it, and began to write. Suddenly a shot rang out, and Onslow fell, bleeding, to the ground.[4]

Halévy goes on to describe in glowing detail Onslow's long suffering and his resolve to complete the quintet: "Onslow threw himself at the task of finishing his new quintet, composing while the fever seized him, and writing the notes down during moments of calm." The resulting string quintet was published in 1829, just months after Onslow's recovery.

In a review of the publication published in 1831 in the *Allgemeine musikalische Zeitung*, critic Gottfried Wilhelm Fink noted that the quintet is "the first product from one of the best of this art, who has received a new lease on life," and went on to remind readers that an earlier issue of the journal had announced the news that Onslow's life was in danger due to a terrible accident. He tells the story of Onslow's hunting accident more briefly than Halévy, who seems to have embellished his tale to create a more gripping story. These details may have come from firsthand accounts by Onslow and his friends, or they may be extrapolated from the work, which serves the same theatrical storytelling purpose.[5]

Onslow's quintet retains some elements from earlier and contemporaneous characteristic works, such as Sigismund Neukomm's two "dramatic quintets" and Felicien David's set of quintets "The Seasons." Onslow used the standard four-movement form with expected movement types, and the work generally depicts or evokes, via surface gestures in the melody and harmonies, the events of the program. The personal nature of the program, though, suggests a more clearly Romantic approach that moves beyond the characteristic style of earlier works. Onslow's aim seems to be a summary of his experience and its effect on him that would resonate with the community of chamber music aficionados that formed his core audience.

The quintet contains four movements: (1) a fairly straightforward sonata form, (2) an eccentric minuet with sections marked "Dolore" (Pain) and "Febbre e delirio" (Fever and delirium), (3) a short slow movement marked "Convalescenza," connected to (4) the finale, marked "Guarigione" (Recovery). As Halévy noted, the opening movement predates Onslow's accident. Several features of this movement, though, set it apart from Onslow's usual quintet practice; in fact, in some ways this movement closely resembles contemporaneous string *quartets* by the composer. Perhaps the already unusual, more serious nature of these materials suggested the idea to Onslow of portraying this momentous event in it rather than, for instance, beginning a new work for that purpose.

This quintet may well be Onslow's best-known work since the rediscovery of his music in the past two to three decades because it engages modern-day listeners with its novelty. In C minor and with a tendency toward stormy accompaniment patterns, the movement eschews the comforting sensibility of Onslow's op. 39 quintet (discussed in chapter 3). It lacks, for instance, the emphatic repetitions that Onslow typically favored in establishing thematic materials. The opening measures of the work present a hesitant, mysterious theme that might serve either as introductory material or as a primary theme presented by the second cello (example 5.1a). The quasi-learned theme that emerges in imitative entrances in m. 21 effects an almost march-like or military rigor.

The song-like secondary theme presents a strong contrast in the relative major (E♭). The symmetrical eight-measure tune is presented by the first cello in the tenor range, as is common in Onslow's style (example 5.1b), but the melody is not repeated, as we might expect in one of Onslow's more "normative" works. Rather, mm. 53–74 contain two sections of closing material, primarily in the brilliant style, for the first violin. The first cello, the "protagonist" or star of so many of Onslow's quintets because it was the part he wrote for himself to play, does not really participate in the closing materials here, contrary to his usual practice. The final measures of the exposition contain a last reminiscence of motives from the learned-style C-minor theme, bringing a somber quality back into the minds and ears of performers and listeners. This theme returns at the end of the coda to close the movement as well.

This movement, unlike Onslow's usual practice in first movements, adheres to present-day understandings of sonata form (as later codified by figures such as Adolf Bernhard Marx), but it provides many welcome surprises and innovations for the listener.[6] These features, which make this movement an accessible work for modern-day concert audiences and CD purchasers, make it atypical of

EXAMPLE 5.1A Onslow, String Quintet in C Minor, op. 38 ("La balle"), movt. 1, mm. 1–29 (P theme).

Onslow's usual style, as nineteenth-century fans or patrons of his music would certainly have noticed. In that way, the first movement could be heard as a sort of "little did they know" opening for the sensational tale that follows.

Each of the three remaining movements bears a descriptive title that explicitly ties it to individual aspects of Onslow's injury and its aftermath. In the short, evocative second movement ("Menuetto. Dolore"), Onslow uses striking harmonic juxtapositions, startling dynamic contrasts, chromatic parallel motion, and surprising articulations and rests to unsettle the listener, depicting the shooting

EXAMPLE 5.1A (continued)

incident and the confusion that followed. The movement is divided into three large sections, and the first section presents all of these tactics in quick succession (example 5.2). The movement begins in C minor, with *pianissimo* octave Cs in the lowest voice (the second cello) pierced by musical screams—a *fortissimo* F♯ diminished seventh chord in mm. 3–4 and 11–12. The music's urgency increases in mm. 17–29 as the first violin begins a chromatic ascent over a reiterated B♭ in the second cello that presses the momentum forward. Along the way the supporting harmonies emphasize diminished chords without a clear tonal goal, and the viola contributes a trill-like figure that further disquiets the texture (e.g., mm. 19–21, 23–25). In mm. 30–33 and 34–37, a series of parallel diminished seventh chords reinforce the eerie atmosphere as all four voices slide downward chromatically—the two principal players traverse a tritone here, from A♭ to D and F to B♮, respectively.

Onslow designated what would be the trio section of the movement "Febbre e delirio" (Fever and delirium, mm. 158–249). Rapid alternation between loud and soft dynamics and quick juxtaposition of sustained and more declamatory textures evoke the confusion of a feverish dream. The harmony of this section is flighty, moving from C major to E major to A♭ major and then to D♯ major in only twenty-three measures. These roaming harmonies surely present Onslow's "delirium," an evocation underlined by the anapest rhythm (two eighth notes

EXAMPLE 5.1B Onslow, String Quintet in C Minor, op. 38 ("La balle"), movt. 1, mm. 37–61 (S theme).

followed by a quarter note) that begins to assert itself here, too. The gesture, redolent of hoofbeats and drums, is commonly associated with the hunt topic and provides a motif for the recurring images or sounds of the hunt in Onslow's memory of the event.[7] The reprise of the A section does not fit easily into Onslow's program. The composer's indebtedness to tradition manifests itself here, where

EXAMPLE 5.2 Onslow, String Quintet in C Minor, op. 38 ("La balle"), movt. 2, mm. 1–49 ("Dolore" section).

the minuet must be repeated to satisfy the conventions of the genre, no matter how eccentric this particular example is.

In the third movement of "The Bullet," a short Andante sostenuto labeled "Convalescenza," Onslow again pays homage to the traditions of the chamber genre. The short movement lasts just fifty-six measures (modern performances average about four minutes), but it clearly evokes the familiar trope of convalescence best represented by Beethoven's "Heiliger Dankgesang" from the late quartet in A minor, op. 132. The instrumentalists are instructed to play "with mutes and always *sotto voce*" throughout, creating a hushed atmosphere much like that in a sickroom. Onslow evokes a four-part chorale harmonization by placing the E♭ theme (marked *dolce*) in the viola and removing the first violin temporarily, which lowers the overall tessitura (example 5.3). Mm. 9–17 effect a transition from the reverent calm of the opening idea to the somewhat more song-like secondary theme, presented in the dominant (B♭) in mm. 18–29. Although it is reminiscent of Beethoven's more familiar example of hymn-like writing for strings, Onslow's Andante movement is probably not a purposeful homage. Onslow did not approve of Beethoven's late style in general, and he pointedly distanced his music from Beethoven's in correspondence with friends and colleagues.[8] In a published assessment of Beethoven's op. 132 quartet, Onslow wrote about the exposition of the first movement only, avoiding any attempt to reconcile the work's later irregularities with his own view of proper compositional style.[9] Rather than an allusion or direct homage, I would suggest that here as elsewhere we see gifted composers using the chamber genres to express their most intimate and personal experiences. Unlike programmatic works for the concert hall, these private pieces allowed composers—even demanded them—to draw upon their own experiences to communicate with their audiences.

The quintet's finale, marked "Guarigione" (Recovery), depicts the joy of the composer's survival and rejuvenation with a sonata form movement in a brilliant style. This movement, much more so than the first, conforms to Onslow's usual practice, with abundant repetitions of flowing, running passagework, repeated themes, and a prominent role for the first cello with much interaction among the five instruments, especially between the first violin and first cello. The secondary key area bears many of Onslow's stylistic calling cards. The first cello presents a gentle theme in the high tenor range of the instrument (example 5.4). After a thematic extension in a contrasting quasi-learned topic with imitation between the two violins, the first violin repeats the entire secondary theme (mm. 97–113). The composer's use of his favorite scoring and formal processes for this passage may be interpreted programmatically within the context of "recovery." Having survived his ordeal and recovered sufficiently to resume normal daily activities, the cellist and chamber music enthusiast returns to his instrument and plays in a style that may be associated with comfort and domesticity.

EXAMPLE 5.3 Onslow, String Quintet in C Minor, op. 38 ("La balle"), movt. 3, mm. 1–25 ("Convalescenza" movt., P and S themes).

EXAMPLE 5.4 Onslow, String Quintet in C Minor, op. 38 ("La balle"), movt. 4, mm. 65–81.

Onslow's portrayal in this work of an exciting, yet horrifying, event in his life can be likened to a masterful conversational retelling. In the first movement, Onslow provides a brief snapshot of a normal day, but in the context of impending disaster and for the sake of the tale, this day displays some irregularities and foreboding, as represented by the insistence on the minor mode, the tentative style of the opening gestures, and the absence of traits typical of Onslow's quintet style. The second movement describes the harrowing event itself and its aftermath, while the third portrays a gradual recuperation. Upon making a full recovery, the composer naturally reconnects with his community—fellow music lovers and quintetists, both his personal friends and those who share his work by purchasing sheet music or attending concerts—to tell the tale of his extraordinary brush with death for their enjoyment.

Because Onslow did not publish or publicize a "program" for the work, listeners and performers relied primarily on word of mouth to receive the explanation of the movement descriptions. The set of parts printed by Probst in 1831 (the edition reviewed by Fink in the *Allgemeine musikalische Zeitung*) includes movement titles, but without the subtitle "La balle" that appeared later. Kistner published the work in a smallish format score in 1841 with movement titles but also without the work's nickname. Critics and reviewers filled in the gaps by writing about

Onslow's accident as noted above, and these reports were reprinted elsewhere (such as in *Dwight's Journal of Music* published in Boston), but surely those who enjoyed and appreciated the work best were the "insiders" of the composer's own acquaintances. Thus, like the other programmatic pieces considered in this chapter, the quintet reinforces the bonds of a geographically dispersed community.

Onslow's "Bullet" quintet does not appear to participate in a particular music-political agenda, as later programmatic works would. It is closely connected to the eighteenth-century tradition of characteristic music, but we may distinguish it from those works because of its autobiographical nature. Unlike works that retell a historical event or describe a literary work, this quintet is the product of a life-altering experience of the composer's own. As his countryman and acquaintance Hector Berlioz would do six years later (and as Beethoven had done only two years earlier), Onslow drew on his own experience to create a Romantic portrait of a moment in his own life. In this transitional work and the motivation for it, we see many of the traits that would occupy composers of programmatic chamber music in the later nineteenth century.

Gade's Early Programmatic Chamber Music

Unlike Onslow, composers of the younger Romantic generation actively participated in the musical politics of their day, rallying around the creation of avant-garde music to usher in a new stage of musical development. These composers used musical style and the emergent technologies of their day—particularly print journalism and printed music distribution networks—to build communities of like-minded musical activists, as we have already seen in the works of composers like Mendelssohn, Burgmüller, Schumann, and Berwald (chapter 4). Danish composer Niels Gade's incomplete string quartet in F major from 1840 responds specifically to the musical philosophy of Robert Schumann, whose writings Gade encountered in the *Neue Zeitschrift für Musik*. The journal circulated in Copenhagen and inspired Gade and his friends to follow Schumann's example by establishing their own Davidsbund.[10] The group included aspiring young performers and composers, dancers, actors, and writers. They gathered regularly to discuss musical, philosophical, and literary matters, to attend performances, and to visit museums; these meetings apparently also included readings from recent issues of music journals, including the *Neue Zeitschrift für Musik*. Around 1835 they formed a string quartet, in which Gade played violin.[11] Thus, very much like other self-consciously progressive composers, Gade surrounded himself with sympathetic enthusiasts who shared his interests, and his early musical works from the 1830s and 1840s were heavily influenced by these attempts to insinuate himself into Schumann's ideal vision of music's future. As Anna Harwell Celenza has noted, Gade interpreted that vision by creating programmatic music for Schumann's "new poetic age."

Gade's surviving composition diary contains literary programs for completed and projected compositions from July 1839 to October 1841. It documents the composer's plan for a string quartet in F major based on Goethe's poem "Willkommen und Abschied" (Welcome and departure; see tables 5.2 and 5.3), which he began composing in 1840.[12] Although he eventually abandoned this work, his initial attempt to create a programmatic quartet demonstrates the importance of these new compositional methods to the Romantic generation, and the two completed movements provide a welcome insight into the challenges of adjusting programmatic techniques to the string quartet genre.

TABLE 5.2 Text and translation of J. W. von Goethe, "Willkommen und Abschied"

Willkommen und Abschied	**Welcome and Departure**
Es schlug mein Herz; geschwind zu Pferde!	My pounding heart cried: To horse!
Es war gethan fast eh' gedacht;	No sooner was it thought than done.
Der Abend wiegte schon die Erde	In evening's lap lay the earth,
Und an den Bergen hing die Nacht:	And on the mountains hung the night;
Schon stand im Nebelkleid die Eiche	Already robed in mist, the oak,
Ein aufgethürmter Riese da,	A towering giant there,
Wo Finsterniß aus dem Gesträuche	Where darkness from the thicket
Mit hundert schwarzen Augen sah	With hundreds of black eyes peered out.
Der Mond von einem Wolkenhügel	The moon, from a hill of clouds
Sah kläglich aus dem Duft hervor,	Frowned out from the mists
Die Winde schwangen leise Flügel,	The winds fluttered their silent wings,
Umsaus'ten schauerlich mein Ohr;	And murmured gruesomely in my ear;
Die Nacht schuf tausend Ungeheuer;	The night made a thousand monsters,
Doch frisch und fröhlich war mein Muth:	Though fresh and joyous was my mind,
In meinen Adern welches Feuer!	In my veins, what fire!
In meinem Herzen welche Gluth!	In my heart, what glow!
Dich sah ich, und die milde Freude	I saw you, and the tender joy
Floß von dem süßen Blick auf mich;	Flowed from your sweet gaze to me;
Ganz war mein Herz an deiner Seite	Completely was my heart at your side
Und jeder Athemzug für dich.	And every breath I breathed for you.
Ein rosenfarbnes Frühlingswetter	A rose-colored spring
Umgab das liebliche Gesicht,	Wreathed your lovely face,
Und Zärtlichkeit für mich—Ihr Götter!	And tenderness for me—ye gods!
Ich hofft' es, ich verdient' es nicht!	I hoped for it, I deserved it not!
Doch ach schon mit der Morgensonne	But, alas, already with the morning sun
Verengt der Abschied mir das Herz:	Departure made my heart constrict
In deinen Küssen, welche Wonne!	In your kisses, what rapture!
In deinem Auge, welcher Schmerz!	In your eyes, what pain!
Ich ging, du standst und sahst zur Erden,	I went; you stood and gazed at the ground,
Und sahst mir nach mit nassem Blick:	And watched me with tearful eyes
Und doch, welch Glück geliebt zu werden!	And yet, what happiness to be loved!
Und lieben, Götter, welch ein Glück!	And to love, O gods, what ecstasy!

* 1827 version, from *Goethe's Werke: Vollstandige Ausgabe letzter Hand,* vol. 1, 75–76. Underlining indicates portions used in Gade's program.

** Translation modified from E. Zeydel, *Goethe the Lyricist* (1955), 34.

TABLE 5.3 Program for Niels Gade, String Quartet in F Major

1.	Es schlug mein Herz; geschwind zu Pferde! Es war gethan fast eh' gedacht;
(F)	— — — — — — — — —
	Die Nacht schuf tausend Ungeheuer; Doch frisch und fröhlich war mein Muth: In meinen Adern welches Feuer! In meinem Herzen welche Gluth!
2.	Dich sah ich, und die milde Freude Floß von dem süßen Blick auf mich; — — — — — — — — —
(B)	Ein rosenfarbnes Frühlingswetter Umgab das liebliche Gesicht, — — — — — — — — —
	welch Glück geliebt zu werden! Und lieben, Götter, welch ein Glück!
3.	Doch ach schon mit der Morgensonne Verengt der Abschied mir das Herz:
	— — — — — — — — —
	Ich ging, du standst und sahst zur Erden, Und sahst mir nach mit nassem Blick:

* As transcribed in Celenza, *Early Works of Niels W. Gade*, 71.

Goethe's poem recounts a moonlight tryst. The first two stanzas describe the nighttime journey of the speaker and the dangers and fears he encounters on the road. The third stanza conveys the relief and happiness of spying the beloved and imagining "an undeserved but hoped-for kiss." The final stanza mourns the dawn of day and separation. Gade shortened the poem and regrouped some phrases to create a three-part program around the ideas of (1) the urgency and passion of the protagonist despite obstacles in the path to the beloved, (2) a musical portrait of the object of affection and the joys of young love, and (3) the pain of departure and separation.[13] Gade moved Goethe's optimistic final lines ("And yet, what happiness to be loved! / And to love, O gods, what ecstasy!") to the second section of the program, which creates a rousing climax in this middle section and, at the same time, ensures a melancholy (quintessentially Romantic) ending for the work as a whole.[14]

Gade's programmatic works do not appear to be autobiographical, though several of his early programs treat the topic of separation and reunification. Though we cannot rule out the possibility of a love affair sparking his interest in this poem and inspiring the quartet's composition, no evidence has surfaced to suggest it. More likely, Gade encountered the poem in the course of his reading—perhaps in one of the Copenhagen Davidsbund soirées—and its intimate expression of young love's effects on the protagonist resonated with the twenty-two-year-old composer.

Celenza surmises that the two surviving movements constitute parts 1 and 2 of the program, while the unfinished third movement appears to be an unprogrammatic scherzo, as Gade frequently omitted programs for the third movements of multimovement works in his early period.[15] We might further speculate that the challenge of composing an appropriately downcast or weighty ending to close the otherwise lighthearted quartet may have caused Gade some difficulty, leading him to set aside the work.[16] His program includes parenthetical notations indicating projected keys for the first and second sections (F and B♭, respectively) but does not give a similar precompositional plan for the final section. Celenza's analysis is necessarily brief, as her goal is to explore Gade's compositional development throughout his early period. The chamber works, in her words, "do not belong among his most notable compositions. Nonetheless, they . . . represent the earliest examples of the composer's emerging romantic style."[17]

The incomplete string quartet is significant, though, because it represents an attempt to find a place for the genre within Gade's (and, more pointedly, within Schumann's) agenda for the future of music. Gade composed this work at the same time that Schumann was working on his own set of string quartets, presumably unbeknownst to Gade, and just after the publication of Schumann's Quartett-Morgen reports, published in the *Neue Zeitschrift* in 1838. Thus, both composers were struggling with the role of the quartet and of string chamber music in a new aesthetic of Romanticism. Gade used a variety of surface gestures and topics to depict the individual images and events of the poem, successfully creating a sonic interpretation of the text. His manipulation of form, on the other hand, is less successful. Like most other composers of programmatic chamber music, he seems to have felt compelled to use what we might call the generically preordained four-movement structure, and, at the same time, he attempted to create innovative approaches to those forms. The result bears all the signs of a composer struggling to reconcile contradictory impulses.

The quartet's first movement is a lengthy (531-measure) sonata form with a reversed recapitulation, in which the secondary theme is recalled before the primary theme, both in the tonic. The rushing, buoyant melody of the primary key area (marked *con fuoco*) expresses the protagonist's passion and urgency, while the sudden changes of dynamics and the colorful harmonic scheme portray the restlessness of Goethe's lines "My heart beat fast; quick, to the horse, / It was done almost before it was thought." The turn to F minor at the beginning of the development section and the scurrying, insect-like accompaniment in mm. 141–56 evoke the monsters created by night in the program's third line.

The secondary key area presents a subdued, rustic theme in C major (V) that will be highlighted in various ways throughout the work—in multiple repetitions during the development, in developmental alterations throughout, and in the recapitulation, where it supersedes the primary theme.[18] This theme finds no clear parallel in Gade's program, but it may have been inspired by the removed lines of Goethe's first stanza:

> In evening's lap the earth was lying,
> And on the peaks the night was spun . . .
> The moon, from clouded hill appeared.

These nocturnal images align with the theme's gentle rustlings and rustic character; it is unclear why Gade removed them from his program. When the development proper begins in m. 133, it moves through a series of meandering sequences based on motives from the secondary theme that culminate in an A♭-major rendition of the theme. The brief recapitulation begins at the end of this passage (m. 366) with a complete restatement of the secondary theme in the tonic, F major, followed by the primary theme, also in the tonic.

Gade's choice here to use a sonata-form first movement impedes a dramatic rendering of the poem's action, but it emphasizes the male protagonist's feelings as the main focus of the poem and of this musical treatment. The lengthy development section aptly depicts the foreboding of the moonlit ride and the protagonist's anxiety, and we might interpret the return of thematic materials at the recapitulation as expressing his resolve ("In my blood, what fire / In my heart, what glow!"). Nonetheless, the middle section of the work feels bloated with unnecessary developmental passagework, and by bringing the secondary theme back first, Gade denies the listener the cathartic resolution that traditionally makes sonata form so engaging.

The second movement, which depicts the protagonist's beloved and the couple's joy at their brief reunion, is a more successful combination of formal procedures and other musical elements in service of expressing the movement's program. Gade's handling of rounded binary form here both suits his program and feels naturally worked out rather than forced. The first section of the Adagio con espressione evokes the satisfaction and repose of having arrived at the destination so strenuously sought-after in the first movement. With its narrow melodic range (a tenth) and complementary motion (stepwise ascents answered with equivalent leaps and vice versa), this seven-measure theme traverses the same pleasurable pitch space again and again (see example 5.5). The accompaniment contributes to the idyllic quality in the first four measures with a gently throbbing F in the second violin and euphonious parallel thirds in the viola and cello. In mm. 23–27, shown in example 5.6, Gade suggests the beloved's gaze falling on the protagonist with a duet between the first violin and the cello. In the condensed reprise of this section, the duet is omitted, suggesting the poem's emphasis on the protagonist alone in those lines ("What happiness to be loved! / And to love, O gods, what ecstasy!").

The B section of this movement also emphasizes the effect of the beloved on the protagonist, rather than a portrait of the woman herself, by developing

EXAMPLE 5.5 Gade, String Quartet in F Major, movt. 2, mm. 1–7.

EXAMPLE 5.6 Gade, String Quartet in F Major, movt. 2, mm. 23–30.

the A section's theme, associated with the protagonist, instead of introducing a new theme for the object of his affection. The addition of double stops to the now-urgent reiterated pitches in the inner voices lends this passage a passionate character, while the wider range in the first violin line and the high tessitura of the cello also contribute to the increased intensity. These gestures suggest the viewer's raised heart rate, his anticipation and desire. Much like other Romantic programmatic works of this era, then, Gade's work expresses a singular subject's experiences and emotions rather than the "objective" depiction of outside stimuli common in Classical characteristic works. The return of the A section reinforces this reading by bringing the listener's (or performers') attention back again to the protagonist's happiness.

These two movements represent one composer's attempt to adapt the string quartet to his aesthetic and philosophical aims of creating a poetic musical style that would draw together and strengthen a musical community. Intended for the Copenhagen Davidsbund, the quartet exemplifies the notion of writing self-consciously "progressive" or experimental music for an audience of fellow musical radicals. Although Gade's work is not strictly autobiographical, it may have expressed his personal desire to belong to Schumann's circle. We might even read the work in a symbolic light, wherein the sought-after beloved and reunion with her in the poem represent the musical world outside Copenhagen, with Gade as the protagonist striving after acceptance into the brotherhood of musical poets represented for him by Leipzig's circle of musical luminaries—not just Schumann, but Felix Mendelssohn, Friedrich Wieck, and Clara Wieck Schumann. Inspired by the writings of Schumann, these works also demonstrate the power of print (text and music) in this period and the transnational solidarity it engendered. Gade would achieve his goal of community a few years later. He sent his first symphony to Mendelssohn, who performed it with the Gewandhaus orchestra in 1843. After that success, Gade traveled to Leipzig, where he held appointments with the orchestra and at the conservatory until 1848.

Smetana's "From My Life" Quartet

Whereas Gade's F-major quartet expressed artistic solidarity across national boundaries, the most famous of the nineteenth-century programmatic chamber works—Smetana's "From My Life" quartet, composed in 1876 and published in 1880—expresses a more narrowly nationalist communal identity. Smetana was an active promoter of Czech nationalism, and from an early age he strove to create and support a uniquely Czech musical establishment in Prague and throughout the Bohemian lands, in opposition to the German hegemony of the Austrian, then the Austro-Hungarian, Empire. Many of Smetana's works, including his operas and his programmatic orchestral works, respond to this need to support an innovative Czech musical language on Czech historical themes.[19] The string quartet also came to reflect these interests, but the chamber genre required a more subtle treatment of the nationalist topic than the operas and tone poems. Thus, Smetana's program for the quartet turns from the public histories of his people and evocations of the Czech lands common in works such as *Libuše* and *Má vlast* to an intimate portrait of his own development as a Czech composer. This portrait would then serve as a model for his contemporaries and artistic descendants, thus creating or supporting a community of outspoken nationalist artists such as Leoš Janáček, Antonín Dvořák, and Jean Sibelius. The quartet's legacy also includes programmatic chamber works by many turn-of-the-century modernists such as Arnold Schoenberg, Anton Webern, Dmitri Shostakovich, and Béla Bartók, who found in it an appropriate method for combining the personal, intimate style the genre required with the demand for works that appealed to a diverse public in the concert hall.[20]

Smetana's quartet represents the most successful chamber work of the New German School—successful in the sense that the work has retained an important place in the modern quartet repertoire, as well as in the sense that it creates a meaningful musical experience for listeners and maintains a compositional logic that, for instance, Gade's quartet lacks. Smetana, a beneficiary of Liszt's support and encouragement from his youth, considered himself an outspoken progressive and follower of the Weimar music-political aesthetic. He stated his stance outright in a letter from 1882: "My compositions do not belong in the service of *absolute music*, in which one reaches out with musical signs and the metronome."[21] Smetana turned to chamber music rarely in his more than forty years of composition; only five complete works survive. His first published work for the intimate sphere is a piano trio in G minor from 1855 that he composed in reaction to the death of his first daughter, Bedřiska, of scarlet fever.[22] The "From My Life" quartet is his next chamber piece, written after a twenty-one-year hiatus. Smetana described the composition as "almost a private one and therefore purposely written for four instruments which, as it were, are to talk to each other in a narrow circle of friends of what has so momentously affected me."[23] If it seems clear that the quartet is a deeply personal work intended for a small audience of "insiders," Smetana's active promotion of the work in the wider world appears contradictory. He sought public performances of it and was deeply hurt when the Prague Chamber Music Society rejected it for their concert series on the grounds that it was "unplayable."

Smetana's quartet comes at an important juncture in the history of nineteenth-century chamber music. It was composed with a private, exclusive group of musicians in mind, very similar to the audience of "insiders" addressed in Onslow's "Bullet" quintet and other private works, and several compositional choices suggest an affinity between these two examples. Because of the increased importance of public performances in musical and political life in the last quarter of the century, though, Smetana chose to bring the work to a wider audience, where it would have a greater effect on the current political situation. The following discussion deals first with the genesis and compositional features of the work and then turns to Smetana's change of audience, evidenced by a revised program from 1880, and the different interpretive meaning this change prompts.

In an 1878 letter to his friend and confidant Josef Srb-Debronov, Smetana explained that he "did not set out to write a quartet according to recipe or custom in the usual forms," by which he again confirmed his alliance with the progressive faction in musical life and sought to protect himself against critics whose expectations for a string quartet would surely be based on the Viennese Classical models.[24] Despite this disclaimer, Smetana's quartet contains four separate movements in a conventional sonata cycle: a first-movement sonata form, a scherzo-like polka movement, a slow movement, and a sonata form finale with the all-important coda depicting the onset of deafness and recalling themes from the first movement. Less conventional is Smetana's specific manipulation of instrumental forms to convey his program, especially in the first three movements.

In Smetana's words, the first movement "depicts my youthful leanings towards art, the Romantic atmosphere, the inexpressible yearning for something I could neither express nor define, and also a kind of warning of my future misfortune."[25] Thus, like Onslow, Smetana foreshadows doom to heighten the effect of his story. The first thirty measures of the quartet seem to present the composer himself, associated with a theme in the viola that begins with a falling fifth, suggesting a fate motive (see example 5.7).[26] Filled with large leaps and long pauses, the theme seems hesitant in this first presentation, partially concealed under the shimmering accompaniment of parallel sixths in the two violins. The theme becomes more assertive in mm. 11–16, suggesting youthful vigor as it tumbles through scalar triplets, completes two acrobatic downward leaps, and then runs up a scale, arriving at C on the downbeat of m. 17. Here, the bass line slides from E to E♭, effecting an instant tonal shift down a third to C minor—not coincidentally, the key most closely associated with Beethoven's own self-conscious explorations of fate. Smetana's second theme continues in the searching, roving vein of its predecessor to emphasize the "inexpressible yearning" of the program. Although a strong arrival at G major (III) on the downbeat of m. 69 and two measures of foundational ostinatos lead the listener to expect repose, the ensuing section flits about, alighting on one tonality and then another in quick succession. Both theme/key areas conform to the Romantic notion of a suffering artist, which points to the ambiguity or (perhaps) duplicity of Smetana's commentary on his work. Smetana paints himself here as a youth fully capable of greatness, of melancholy, and of artistic reverie. In this intimate space, which the composer says is personal and private, he nonetheless carefully portrays himself as the quintessential Romantic artist, almost on a Beethovenian model.

The second movement of the quartet, marked "Allegro moderato à la Polka," takes the place of the usual scherzo or minuet. By replacing the expected triple-meter movement with a duple polka, Smetana injects a nationalist flavor into the quartet form. The polka presents Smetana's memories of his adolescence, when (by his account) he was "known everywhere as a passionate dancer" and when, "as a composer of dance tunes, [he] lavished these upon the young world."[27] In his letter to Srb-Debronov, the composer also mentions the middle section of the movement, a trio in D♭ major in which "I paint my memories of the aristocratic

EXAMPLE 5.7 Smetana, String Quartet in E Minor ("From My Life"), movt. 1, primary theme in solo viola.

circles in which I lived for many years." Smetana's manipulation of the typical dance-movement structure might be interpreted programmatically beyond the simple portrayal of this period of the composer's life to an integration of aristocratic and peasant or folk society.

The polka section of the movement contains an introductory passage, the polka proper (example 5.8), and a short codetta. The polka tune, a simple melody of two four-measure phrases marked "Solo, quasi Tromba, sul C," exemplifies the Czech dance with its duple meter and emphasis on strong downbeats; the accompaniment's drone in the cello and ostinato in the second violin accentuate the rustic quality of this section. The ensemble passes the tune from one member to the next, but it begins in the viola, the instrument already associated with Smetana and his tragic fate in the first movement. The aristocratic trio begins in m. 85, where, after an abrupt key change to D♭ major, the music settles into an elegant style that feels almost waltz-like despite the duple meter (example 5.9).

As expected in a ternary dance form, the A section is reprised in a somewhat compressed form, but the unusual coda that follows defies convention in service of the work's extramusical narrative. A sforzando dominant chord followed by an expectant silence brings the rustic festivities to an abrupt halt. The aristocratic trio material then quietly and unexpectedly returns, effecting a deceptive cadence from V (C) to ♭VI (D♭). Beginning in m. 209, the aristocratic portrait is gradually infiltrated by elements of the polka (see example 5.10). The tempo increases ("risoluto ed animato"), and the two violins introduce tripping staccato eighth

EXAMPLE 5.8 Smetana, String Quartet in E Minor ("From My Life"), movt. 2, Polka theme.

EXAMPLE 5.9 Smetana, String Quartet in E Minor ("From My Life"), movt. 2, Aristocratic Trio theme.

EXAMPLE 5.10 Smetana, String Quartet in E Minor ("From My Life"), movt. 2, mm. 203–34.

notes, grace notes, and then syncopated rhythms, all suggesting a gradual return to the rustic style of the polka. This melodic mutation continues through m. 221, where the music cadences on F—the polka's tonic—and a sudden outburst of the introduction's sixteenth notes begins the final coda. The last four measures recall the polka's opening gestures in a slightly moody rallentando and finish the movement with an A-minor chord.

Until the surprising return of the aristocratic trio music, the form follows a predictable scherzo and trio structural plan that seems utterly appropriate to the juxtaposition of the lively polka, with its connotations of a certain Czech folkiness, and the more aristocratic waltz-like music, with its calm, staid features. The substantial repetition of the trio material suggests a commentary on the division of classes in Czech society. As though confirming the view that the German-speaking and German-acculturated aristocratic classes could benefit from an infiltrating force by way of the Czech folkish music of the polka, Smetana joins the two in the last fifty-five measures of the movement. Smetana returns to the musical expression of national fervor in the last movement of the quartet.[28]

The quartet's finale presents the most poignant aspect of Smetana's self-portrait, the onset of his deafness, in its coda. The cyclic recall in the coda of themes from the first movement depicts Smetana's reflection on his life up to that point and the promise that it held.[29] The music of the main portion of the finale falls into a short, clearly delineated sonata form. The primary theme/key area presents a rustic thick-textured passage filled with ringing double-stops and accented triplets, and the secondary theme (mm. 37–51) provides a polka-like tune similar to the theme of the second movement. The short development section concerns itself with motives related to the secondary theme, and the recapitulation restates the primary and secondary materials virtually unaltered (both now in E major) and with the transitions between them shortened. On first hearing, the coda seems to point toward a happy ending to the movement until m. 215, in which a C♯ introduced in the inner voices turns the harmony toward the minor mode (example 5.11). In m. 219, a C♮ dominant seventh chord sounds and hangs in the air unresolved for two silent measures before the piercing high E signals the onset of deafness described in the program.

The recalled themes that follow include the "Fate" motive and the secondary theme from the first movement, and the finale's main theme. The connection between a doomed fate and the onset of deafness is clear, and that initial recall here at the end of the work brings the quartet's story full circle. The remainder of the coda juxtaposes the first movement's secondary theme, associated with Romantic yearning in the original program, and the finale's theme, which expresses the joy of discovering a national musical style. In putting these two ideas together here, Smetana clarifies the notion that his life's mission has been completed: having yearned for a mode of self-expression that fit his Romantic sensibility, he found it in the pure Czech style of his most recent works. That message, first expressed

EXAMPLE 5.11 Smetana, String Quartet in E Minor ("From My Life"), movt. 4, mm. 210–65.

subtly in the finale's music alone, would become the overall message for the work when Smetana revised the program two years later.

As discussed above, Smetana originally conceived this work as belonging to the private sphere, to be performed within a small circle of musical insiders who would appreciate and understand his sorrows, despite some indications that he already hoped it would solidify his reputation for posterity (via connections to

Beethoven and other Romantic icons). A few years later, however, he changed his mind about the work's tone and redirected it to a wider public. Specifically, he recast the work to send it out into the world beyond Bohemia's borders and into the concert hall. After the Prague Chamber Music Society rejected the quartet in 1878, Smetana wrote about this slight to Srb-Debronov and explained the quartet's genesis and program. Two years later, members of the Hamburger Tonkünstlerverein planned to present the quartet in their annual concerts, and they wrote to the composer to request help with their interpretation. Smetana's response, published that year and distributed at the Hamburg concerts, contains a public "program" for the work that was intended to help the audience and the performers understand it better.[30] This new program reflects an altered position on the quartet's meaning. Table 5.4 provides a side-by-side comparison of the two programs. This change in address had at least two effects. First, it resituated the quartet, moving the work from a personal reflection on Smetana's own life to a statement about contemporary nationalist debates and politics.[31] Though in Prague the quartet could be presented as primarily an autobiographical piece, a German performance by sympathetic musicians provided an opportunity for

TABLE 5.4 Comparison of the two programs for Smetana's "From My Life" quartet

Letter to Srb-Debronov (1878)	**Letter to Hamburg Tonkünstlerverein (1880)**
As regards my Quartet I gladly leave others to judge its style, and I shall not be in the least angry if this style does not find favor or is considered contrary to what was hitherto regarded as "quartet style." I did not set out to write a quartet according to recipe or custom in the usual forms. I have already worked through the particulars of the necessary forms as a young student of music theory so that for me they are completely familiar, and I understand them well enough.—For me the form of every composition is dictated by the subject itself and thus the Quartet, too, shaped its own form. My intention was to paint a tone picture of my life.	I would wish that the title "From My Life" be printed on the program, because my quartet is no formal game with tones and with motives, that proves what the tone-poet is able [to do], rather it is truly a picture from my life that I want to present to the listeners. [The following is provided so that] one will better understand the individual movements.
The first movement depicts my youthful leanings toward art, the Romantic atmosphere, the inexpressible yearning for something I could neither express nor define and also a kind of warning of my future misfortune: [Smetana provides the opening motive from the first movement and the high E from the last.] The long insistent note in the finale owes its inspiration to this. It is the fateful ringing in my ears of the high-pitched tones which, in 1874, announced the beginning of my deafness. I permitted myself this little joke because it was so disastrous to me.	1st movement: My inclination in youth to the Romantic, to a melancholy and at the same time pathetic music style.

TABLE 5.4 (continued)

Letter to Srb-Debronov (1878)	**Letter to Hamburg Tonkünstlerverein (1880)**
The second movement, a quasi-polka, brings to my mind the joyful days of youth when I composed dance tunes and was known everywhere as a passionate lover of dancing.	2nd movement: Happy enjoyment of life, *partly on the land, partly in the salons in the higher [aristocratic] circles* (meno mosso) where I spent almost my entire childhood. *The second movement also depicts the inclination to travel; in the viola and later in the second violin described à la tromba—Posthorn!*
The third movement (the one which, in the opinion of the gentlemen who play this Quartet, is unperformable) reminds me of the happiness of my first love, the girl who later became my first wife.	3rd movement: The side of an animated heart, love, blessedness and longing after—her.
The fourth movement describes the discovery that I could treat national elements in music, and my joy in following this path until it was checked by the catastrophe of the onset of my deafness, the outlook into the sad future, the tiny rays of hope of recovery; but remembering all the promise of my early career, a feeling of painful regret.	4th movement: Recognition of the arousing national self-confidence in *our beautiful art,* joy over the already discovered way to a *national art,* happy success along this way, and then in my ear the horrible ringing, shrill tone sounded (in the quartet a high E, in real life it was A♭ major at a very high octave): the warning of my horrible fate, my impending deafness, which meant for me every happiness was lost, *to hear and to delight for myself in the beauty of our art.*
That is about the content of this composition, which, so to speak, is of a private character and therefore is deliberately written for four instruments. These [four] are to talk to each other in a narrow circle of friends of what has so momentously affected me. No more.	

Sources: The letter to Srb-Debronov (1878) is modified from the translation in Brian Large, *Smetana,* 318. The original letter to the Hamburg Tonkünstlerverein (1880) is quoted in Wiese, *Tschechische Kammermusik,* 53 (my translation).

nationalistic activism that Smetana simply could not ignore. Second, Smetana's changes to the program deemphasize its personal nature and re-create the work as a universal testament to the resilience of the human spirit, making it accessible and meaningful to a wider audience, not just to friends and supporters of the composer. The degree to which these two effects are present in the newly constituted work (taking "work" in this case to mean the combination of score and program) varies from movement to movement.

The finale, for example, takes a decidedly more public and nationalistic turn. Smetana's use of the phrase "unsere Kunst" (our art) creates a wider community of nationalist musicians, and his last sentence emphasizes the loss not of music generally but of the ability to appreciate the beauties of *Czech* music specifically.

The revised program sends a message to composers and performers that this quartet, though based on the events of Smetana's personal life, is national in scope. National music was to be cherished and supported; its loss was a tragedy unlike any other. Having found that he could incorporate folk music into his own works, Smetana hoped that others would follow in that path and that he would be the leader of a new school of Czech composers, a goal that he achieved through this quartet, his operas, and the symphonic poems. Dvořák and Janáček in particular followed his example in many of their own works.

The private program describes the first movement as a self-portrait of Smetana as a young man, but the later program shortens this description considerably to "my inclination in youth to the Romantic, to a melancholy and at the same time pathetic music style." Again, this revision serves two interpretive purposes. On the one hand, it encourages listeners to hear the music as a broader representation of youth or of Smetana's artistic development. On the other hand, it refocuses the quartet away from Smetana and toward a sort of minihistory of the emergence of a Czech musical style, which began in a cosmopolitan (more specifically, Austro-German) style ("Romantic," "melancholy") but eventually was reinvigorated with Czech folk elements. The later program for the second movement likewise removes Smetana's personal experiences from the center of the work somewhat by describing Smetana's wanderlust and his surroundings in his homeland rather than emphasizing his love of dancing. The description of life "on the land" (presumably meaning among idealized peasants singing folk tunes to pass the time) is particularly colorful. His placement of the land and the salon as two sides of the same Czech coin hints at a reconciliation, that the cultivated salons and lower-class dwellings could coexist and be equally regarded as members of the united nation. As noted earlier, Smetana's music also suggests a fruitful interaction between the two in the last section, which brings together the polka-inflected first section with the aristocratic music of the trio.

By revising his program for the string quartet, Smetana secured a place for it in the public sphere and within the then-raging debates on the future of music, demonstrating that chamber music could participate in the latest trends of nationalistic, progressive composition. Although Smetana's quartet has received considerable acclaim as the first programmatic chamber work, it is actually the beneficiary of a half-century of development in the chamber music realm. Like Onslow's "Bullet" quintet, which Smetana could easily have known from the printed score and parts or even from hearing it in performance, Smetana's work addresses a personal tragedy in his life and uses that event as the catalyst for communal music making.[32]

* * *

As composers sought to find a place for the string quartet and related private genres by cultivating their personal, exclusive nature with a specific audience niche, they laid the foundations for the future of chamber music in the fin de siècle and in the early twentieth century. Although the earlier programmatic chamber pieces have fallen out of the concert-hall repertoire (perhaps because they never belonged there), acknowledging their existence shows that the audience for private chamber music played a considerable role in the development of the genre and of nationalist and Romantic music generally throughout the nineteenth century and beyond.

CHAPTER 6

Audience and Style in Brahms's String Chamber Music

Brahms's seven chamber works for strings alone fall neatly into three categories according to chronology and genre. Like Beethoven's and Dvořák's string quartets, they reflect the gradual changes evident in their composer's style at significant stages in his compositional development: the two sextets stem from his "first maturity," the three string quartets represent what we might call a "high maturity" that flourished in Brahms's early Viennese years, and the two string quintets demonstrate a "late" style developing in the 1880s and 1890s.[1] Previous studies have not acknowledged or recognized the connections between Brahms's systematic exploration of these genres and the audiences he chose to address in them. For instance, the influence of Franz Schubert and his musical style on Brahms's first-maturity works has long been accepted in the Brahms literature, but the biographical implications of Brahms's use of that style in the 1860s have not been explored in depth. Brahms's employment at the Detmold court between 1857 and 1860 and his interactions with the Hamburg Frauenchor, or women's chorus, at that time provide some explanations for his use of a musical style closely connected to domestic music making and to works by Spohr and Onslow.

The quartets filled a very different musical and social "need" both in Brahms's personal musical life and in Viennese musical culture of the 1870s. The two string quartets of op. 51 and the single quartet published as op. 67 (1873 and 1876, respectively) confirm his commitment to the genres and forms of the Classical school and serve as a public statement of his chosen compositional path. (At the same time Brahms also began to tackle the symphony, and the 1870s saw the first performances and the publication of his Symphony No. 1 in C Minor, op. 68.) As we have seen, the string quartet provided an irresistible challenge to many nineteenth-century composers who made it their mission to bring the genre into the new age. Brahms's quartets engage the familiar themes of the genre, wrestling with the weight of tradition that continually dogged it and proposing new answers to old questions. As with other works in the vein of "progressive" string quartets (defined in chapter 4 as works that seek to advance musical style and generic approaches by building on the achievements of earlier models), Brahms's quartets address an audience of musical connoisseurs, composers, and performers for whom the works held mysteries to be teased out via repeated study, listening, and performance.

Brahms's last string chamber works, the two string quintets, summon the spirits of Mozart and Mendelssohn to very different ends. Like the contemporaneous third symphony, the F-major quintet, op. 88 (1882), responds to the New German School and its proponents—especially to Anton Bruckner's own F-major quintet performed publicly in Vienna in 1881. Conceived for the same sort of bourgeois setting populated by well-educated members of the upper middle class as his earlier chamber music but also performed in public concerts, Brahms's quintet exemplifies a synthesis of tradition and innovation in musical style and in old and new forms of musical engagement at this point in history. Eight years later, Brahms wrote what he thought would be his final work, the G-major quintet, op. 111. As a carefully controlled "farewell," the work presents Brahms as he wished the world to remember him in a collection of stylistic souvenirs from his own career and the works of his precursors. Despite its compositional sophistication and the near-virtuosic demands it makes of the players, this quintet features an accessible style for listening audiences. By this late date (1890–91), string chamber music had nearly completed its migration from the parlor to the concert hall, and Brahms's Vienna was transforming before his eyes as the end of the century approached.

Each of these groups of compositions is directed to a certain type of listener or consumer previously encountered in a different form in this book's earlier chapters, and, together, they show the evolution of performance traditions in the last four decades of the nineteenth century. Already with the sextets, Brahms's method of presentation changes between op. 18 (published in 1862) and that of op. 36 (1866) to reflect the different setting the composer encountered in Vienna when he first visited that city. The marked change in style and accessibility noticeable in contemporaneous arrangements for chamber ensemble discussed in chapter 2—not to mention the types of works arranged—speaks to the developing fissure between "serious" and "light" or "public" and "private" works. Notably, it was at this point (the 1850s and the 1860s) that publication of new chamber works for the domestic market declined sharply, as discussed in chapters 1 and 3.[2] The prevalence of reprinted editions of works by earlier generations of composers shows that chamber music continued to play an important role in musical life but that the tastes of domestic musicians turned from new works to older ones and from challenging musical styles to simpler ones at the same time that public performances of works designed for professional players became more common. In Brahms's life, though, the public and private musical realms continued to overlap until at least the 1880s. Throughout his voluminous correspondence and the recollections of him by others, Brahms's engagement in private performances of his own music and that of his heroes features regularly. Works that he composed for public presentation were given in private performance among friends, and the most intimate examples of his piano works, songs, and chamber music were frequently performed in public concerts in Vienna and elsewhere.

Unlike most of the composers considered in this book, Brahms was not a string player himself, and his participation in domestic music making always occurred at the piano. In addition to playing the piano in performances of his chamber works (the piano trios, quartets, and quintet), he frequently accompanied others such as violinists Joseph Joachim and Marie Soldat (later Soldat-Roeger) and cellist Robert Hausmann. He played four-hand piano duets and arrangements with friends with and without listeners. These private and semiprivate performances sometimes involved women as performers or as listeners, especially in his later years, when Brahms was frequently surrounded by doting ladies such as Maria Fellinger and her family. In his earlier decades, however, when Brahms cultivated the air of a disinterested bachelor in Vienna, these musical gatherings more often occurred in the music room at a friend's home, in his own workroom with his piano, in the reserved dining room of a local restaurant, or in an obliging piano manufacturer's showroom. In these situations, the assembled guests would be an intimate circle of male friends, a mixture of professional musicians, aesthetes, and members of the upper middle class (doctors, lawyers, professors, bureaucrats). As we shall see, most of Brahms's chamber music was designed to appeal to that segment of the population, with whom he himself felt most comfortable and at ease.

First-Maturity Works: The String Sextets

As other authors have noted, Brahms's string sextets are practically without precedent in the musical world.[3] Although hundreds of trios, quartets, quintets, and octets survive from the late eighteenth and nineteenth centuries, the combination of paired violins, violas, and cellos remained an unusual grouping until Brahms's works were published. The Hofmeister-Whistling catalogs list eighteen works for this combination (and four others for different combinations of six stringed instruments) published during the nineteenth century. Of these, only one precedes Brahms's op. 18: Louis Spohr's Sextet in C Major, op. 140, published in 1850.[4] Like the string quintet, whose "extra" ensemble member allows composers to revel in lyrical themes and lush harmonies without the strictures of contrapuntal conversational texture, the sextet provides infinite opportunities for a variety of soloists and accompanimental styles. With two cellos at his disposal in opp. 18 and 36, Brahms was able to take full advantage of the first cello as a soloist in passages that benefit from the warm alto tone of the instrument in its upper register. Perhaps most importantly, the sextet offered the apparent benefit of having no high-profile models in the Classical tradition. Unlike the quartet under the burdensome influence of Beethoven, the two-viola quintet pioneered by Mozart and Mendelssohn, and the two-cello quintet mastered by Schubert, the sextet was a "new" form in which Brahms could flex his own compositional muscles without much fear of comparison to earlier models.[5]

Both works come at important junctures in Brahms's personal and professional life. The first sextet, in B♭ major, composed in 1859–60 and published in 1862, is the first of several important chamber works that mark the beginning of the composer's first maturity and demonstrate many of the compositional traits that would become Brahms's trademarks. The sextet, moreover, represents his return to the field of chamber music after a six-year silence. His only chamber work in print at that point was the op. 8 piano trio (composed in 1853–54, published in 1854, and revised in 1889). Brahms composed the second sextet, op. 36 in G major, in 1864–65 just after his first visit to Vienna, and it reflects the influence of that city's musical culture, the relatively new phenomenon of public chamber music concerts in particular.[6]

The early 1850s had been a time of great productivity for Brahms. He published nine opuses of piano music and songs in 1853 and 1854, and he was heralded as the savior of modern music in Robert Schumann's "Neue Bahnen" (New paths) article for the *Neue Zeitschrift für Musik*. But in 1854 Schumann's suicide attempt, the stressful period that followed, and the high expectations the article inspired led Brahms to withdraw into the study of older music and to contemplate his role in the musical universe. The next works he completed and published represent this period of study with a strong neo-Classical aura. Scholar James Webster describes the op. 11 serenade, for instance, as "a compendium of wholesome influences."[7] After Schumann's death in 1856, Brahms separated himself from Clara Schumann and the duties as her aide and confidant that had consumed him for the previous two and a half years. He was invited to take a position at the court of Prince Leopold II in the small principality of Detmold, and he began in these first years of freedom to rediscover his own compositional voice.[8] The position was perfectly suited to the composer's needs at that time. For three months of the year he resided at the court, teaching lessons and conducting a small choir and, occasionally, the court orchestra. He spent the remaining nine months in Hamburg with his family (still drawing a generous stipend from the Detmold court), composing and finishing works for publication and touring as a performer to promote his compositions. Though the limitations of the small city's musical forces would soon push him to resign and seek a more artistically satisfying position, the three years of his Detmold tenure promoted a measure of stability and comfort that led to the two string sextets, two piano quartets (opp. 24 and 25), the piano quintet, and much vocal music.

During this time, domestic music making played an integral role in Brahms's everyday musical life. At Detmold, he gave lessons to members of the royal family and their close friends and associates, and he led them in semipublic/semiprivate performances. In Hamburg, he led the Hamburg Frauenchor, an amateur women's chorus for which Brahms wrote or arranged many works, and a smaller group of female choristers who performed vocal quartets and sextets.[9] His other compositions reflect these experiences with amateur music lovers. Like the later sets of *Liebeslieder* choruses, waltzes, and other "light" works for the domestic market, the first string sextet exudes the warm breezes and cozy environment that produced it.[10] It also demonstrates many of the musical (especially formal) traits discussed in chapter 4 in relation to works by Kuhlau, Spohr, and Onslow, as well as the late chamber works of Schubert. Writing forty years later, Brahms transcended the domestic sphere in his sextets by employing the style associated with that music to new artistic and expressive ends. Whereas Schubert's use of the domestic style was topical, perhaps symbolizing domestic happiness (as defined by mainstream

EXAMPLE 6.1 Brahms, String Sextet in B♭ Major, op. 18, movt. 1, mm. 1–42.

Biedermeier society) lost or denied via the turbulent, even violent, music of surrounding sections, Brahms's sextet is thoroughly covered in a domestic patina that suggests a nostalgic or idealized treatment of the trope.

Like many domestic quintets by Onslow or Spohr, Brahms's thematic construction in op. 18 emphasizes long, lyrical melodies made up of repeated phrases that are passed around the ensemble, creating a leisurely, calm texture (see example 6.1). The primary theme, in B♭ (I), is a remarkable forty-two measures long, with a continual forward momentum created by overlapping phrases. This momentum, though, is not a striving, goal-directed pressure to achieve closure but an airy presence that continues to renew itself well after its purpose (the establishment of the tonic) is fulfilled. The theme begins with repetition: the first cello exposes the opening idea (a) to an atmospheric accompaniment from the two violas and gently rocking foundation from the second cello; this phrase is repeated by the first violin (a') coupled with the first viola in octaves. Mm. 20–30 present an answer (b) in the violin and viola, now playing in parallel sixths and thirds, thereby increasing the effect of euphonious, domestic agreeableness. The final phrase of the first theme (c, in mm. 31–42) sustains the harmonic momentum, prolonging the dominant and suspending musical time as the performers repeat small one- and two-measure motivic ideas, toying with a variety of chromatic harmonizations of the principal theme's components. As in earlier examples, this

EXAMPLE 6.1 (continued)

primary theme group allows three of the ensemble members to assume a highlighted role. At the recapitulation of this passage in m. 234, the two violas present the primary theme, finally allowing the second viola a chance to shine. When the second violin and second cello continue the theme, this pairing creates an unusual and effective low sonority and provides sonic variety. More importantly, it closes the circle of repetitions: at the end of this theme, all six members of the ensemble will have played the movement's main melody while being accompanied by their colleagues at least once.

This opening passage displays a playful approach to the motivic work that would come to define Brahms's style. Masked in the sweet sounds of parallel sixths and thirds and deemphasized by the "heavenly length" of the thematic materials and their static accompaniments, a developing-variation approach to theme building is evident here, though always at work beneath the surface of the music. With the ear focused on the kaleidoscopic changes in texture and instrumentation, the motivic play that underscores the final section of the primary thematic and tonal area does not disturb the serene texture but enhances it by extending the thematic process. For the players, those changes in texture allow each of the members to play multiple roles in the community of the ensemble, sometimes as soloist and sometimes as accompanist, always in a new configuration that explores the relationships among the individual constituents.

The first movement's secondary theme/key area is an excellent example of the popular styles that dominate both Brahms sextets, another trait that may connect them to a domestic (rather than a learned) tradition. Following Schubert's lead, Brahms created a three-key sonata form in this movement, a procedure well suited to a style that favors large-scale repetition instead of motivic recombination. The first secondary theme (S1) evokes an elegant waltz in A major (example 6.2).[11] The pizzicato accompaniment, triple meter, and lilting dotted rhythm in the theme contribute to a dance-like atmosphere. A more song-like theme (S2, see example 6.3) is introduced in m. 85 in the dominant, F major. This theme's presentation by the first cello in the tenor range resembles similar treatments of secondary themes by Onslow, Spohr, and Schubert. As in earlier examples of domestic string music, the first violin's repetition of this theme in mm. 94–102 allows another player to enjoy a melody that she or he has already heard performed by a fellow ensemble member. The repetitions do not simply re-present material that is already familiar; rather, they provide an opportunity for each ensemble member to participate equally in the work.

Continuing in the domestic style, Brahms's development section in the first movement of op. 18 is quite short—just ninety-three measures. A new theme is introduced and developed a bit, then the secondary key area's waltz-like theme (first presented in A major) is explored in the minor mode. Rather than shorten or condense the theme, Brahms presents the entire twenty-three-measure theme in a new key. As in earlier domestic works, Brahms's approach here favors a

EXAMPLE 6.2 Brahms, String Sextet in B♭ Major, op. 18, movt. 1, mm. 61–80 (first presentation of S1 theme).

EXAMPLE 6.3 Brahms, String Sextet in B♭ Major, op. 18, movt. 1, mm. 84–102.

reiteration of the theme, cloaked in the minor mode, rather than a developmental exploration of its constituent parts.

The subsequent movements of the sextet also favor repetition in their overall forms and in rustic or popular styles. The finale, for instance, is a rondo, a form that features repetition of large sections containing relatively independent musical ideas. As we might now expect for a domestic-style piece, the refrain's primary theme begins in the first cello in the tenor range and is repeated by the first violin (see example 6.4). In this passage, the six-instrument ensemble is treated as two trios: the lower three voices present the theme in the first sixteen measures, the higher voices present it in mm. 17–32. After a brief transition in the lower voices (the first "trio"), the two groups join to present a varied form of the opening theme in the tonic before the music modulates to the dominant for the rondo's B section.

Another repetition-laden form, the theme-and-variations second movement may be connected to Brahms's own propensity toward variation sets, familiar from the many freestanding sets he composed (variations on themes by Schumann, Handel, Haydn, and Paganini, as well as sets on original themes and on a Hungarian song). The connection between variation sets and the parlor piano, though, cannot be overlooked. In his capacity as tutor and director of domestic music making, Brahms surely encountered many of the omnipresent variation sets for amateurs that formed the core of the domestic keyboard repertoire. Other musical features

EXAMPLE 6.4 Brahms, String Sextet in B♭ Major, op. 18, movt. 4, mm. 1–32.

connect the second movement to earlier chamber works familiar to Brahms's friends, admirers, and, possibly, other contemporaneous sheet music purchasers.

Each of the variations fills what we might describe as a normative role in the variation sequence, but we can also see Brahms spreading solo opportunities around the ensemble in the tradition of domestic collegiality.[12] Variations 1 and 3 feature the cellos: variation 1 resembles a cello showpiece (like the Bach cello suites), while the third variation recalls an operatic storm scene with chromatic scalar runs in the two cellos evoking wind or waves. The fourth variation highlights the two violins in a pastoral version of the theme in the major mode. The pastoral topic continues into the last variation, in which the first viola plays in a musette style. The second viola is the only instrument not featured, though it plays thematic material to "accompany" the cellos in other variations.

This variations movement connects op. 18 to Brahms's personal and professional development and to his participation in domestic music making in a topical reference to earlier styles and works. Previous commentators have noted that Brahms based the movement's theme on the archaic *folia*, a theme and harmonic progression that were often the foundation for sets of variations in the Baroque era (see example 6.5). In a nineteenth-century context, though, the Andante, ma moderato's duple meter, minor mode, and dotted rhythms also suggest a

EXAMPLE 6.5A Corelli, *folia* theme from the Violin Sonata, op. 5, no. 12.

EXAMPLE 6.5B Brahms, String Sextet in B♭ Major, op. 18, movt. 2, mm. 1–9.

funeral march. The clearest precedents for funeral marches in the chamber repertoire include the second movements of works that Brahms knew well: Schubert's E♭-major piano trio, D. 929—Andante con moto in C minor—and Schumann's E♭-major piano quintet, op. 44—In modo d'una marcia in F minor. In fact, Brahms arranged this movement alone for piano and gifted it to Clara Schumann for her forty-first birthday in 1860. The bittersweet quality of the variations must have seemed appropriate, because the day before (12 September) should have been Clara's twentieth wedding anniversary.

Brahms may have deemed the memorial air of the funeral march appropriate at the sextet's conception for another reason. In 1859, when he was composing the op. 18 sextet, Brahms wrote from Detmold to two of the members of the Hamburg Frauenchor, responding to the latest gossip from his hometown. In the middle of an otherwise playful letter, Brahms mentioned some sad news he had recently received and his reaction to it:

> Spohr is dead! He may well be the last one who still belonged to a more beautiful era of art than the one we are suffering through. In those days, one could eagerly keep a look out every week for what new and even more beautiful work had come from this or that person.
>
> Now it is different. In a month of Sundays I see hardly one volume of music that pleases me, but on the other hand many that even make me physically ill.
>
> Possibly at no other time has an art form been maltreated as badly as our dear music nowadays.
>
> I hope better things are quietly maturing, otherwise, in the history of art, our era will look like a trash heap.[13]

Brahms's choice to write a string sextet in 1860–61 may have been inspired by Spohr, a composer revered throughout German-speaking lands in his lifetime as a successor to Beethoven and a composer of "serious" music. As noted above, Spohr's C-major string sextet, op. 140, is the only known work for this instrumentation before Brahms's op. 18. It shares many of the domestic-music characteristics already noted in Spohr's string quintet, op. 91, and other works apparently designed for domestic amateur players (discussed in chapter 3).[14] With this letter in mind, perhaps the funereal quality of the second movement of op. 18 should be read as a memorial to Spohr.

In many of its features, Brahms's op. 18 sextet engages the same sort of domestic performance environment that Spohr's chamber music addressed, and it deploys gestures designed to appeal to that audience. That said, we can already see in Brahms's work the intermingling of private and public musical styles that characterized chamber music throughout the last third of the century. Documented early performances of the sextet demonstrate the middle ground that chamber music already occupied at this point in musical history: performed by professional musicians in private spaces, the sextet spoke to its domestic venue with an appropriately intimate musical style, and when performed in public venues, it evoked the exclusivity and congeniality of a private soirée. For example, Joseph Joachim performed the work publicly from the manuscript in 1860 in Hanover as part of a series of regular recitals that he established there from 1856 to 1868.[15] He also performed the work in private settings for friends and admirers, partly to promote the work and its composer, who was still a relatively unknown figure in much of Europe. Joachim wrote to Brahms in November 1860 after the premiere in Hanover, saying, "Don't be angry because I am still keeping your work! I want to take it to Leipzig and play it there on Sunday or Tuesday, at David's House or Härtel's. . . . It has not been neglected here, for last Sunday evening we played it privately, as I had arranged some music for the Ambassador in Vienna, von Stockhausen. It gave us all a lot of pleasure and went well with the same players as before."[16]

In Leipzig, Ferdinand David (1810–73), Joachim's former violin teacher and a friend of Mendelssohn and Schumann, hosted domestic chamber music evenings that included some of Europe's finest players. For instance, in an 1879 remembrance, Englishman William Rockstro describes a seemingly casual performance of a work of Spohr's in Leipzig, quite possibly at David's or Mendelssohn's home:

> As a Violinist, he [Spohr] stood unrivalled, save by one great Artist, only, whose name is now as much a "Household Word," in England as in Germany [Joachim?]. His Quartett playing was especially delightful. We well remember hearing him lead his Double Quartett in E minor, at a private party, in Leipzig, in the month of June, 1846, with a delicacy of expression, and refinement of taste, to which no verbal description could possibly do adequate justice. He was assisted, on that occasion, by Ferdinand David, and Joachim; Mendelssohn, and Gade, playing the two Viola parts.[17]

We can easily imagine a similar gathering arranged to perform Brahms's sextet fifteen years later. One potential listener or participant in such a gathering might be Hermann Härtel, whom Joachim mentioned in his letter to Brahms. Härtel was coproprietor (with his brother Hermann) of Germany's most famous and well-respected publishing house (Breitkopf und Härtel) and a friend of Mendelssohn and Schumann. Joachim may have planned a performance for him in the interest of showing off the work so that it would be published.[18] These private performances among friends and semiprivate performances like the one arranged for the visiting ambassador occurred alongside public ones with larger listening audiences such as a performance at the Leipzig Conservatory in the same month.

We might, therefore, read or hear Brahms's string sextet as a hybrid. It represents, on the one hand, the recreational domestic style of a previous era, perhaps even a nostalgic memorial to that style and its progenitors. On the other hand, it serves as a public display of the composer's skill at transforming this private style into a medium for the expression of an entire ethos. We know that Brahms was familiar with the music of Spohr and that he revered that of Schubert; he may also have been familiar with chamber works by Onslow. Just after Robert Schumann was sent to Endenich following his attempted suicide in 1854, Clara Schumann asked Brahms to sort through her husband's library of books and music, and he diligently set to work putting things in order and studying scores, books, and manuscripts that interested him.[19] Schumann's own handwritten catalog of his scores shows that he owned several volumes of chamber music by Onslow, suggesting that Brahms had access to these works during the formative years of the mid-1850s and that they may well have influenced his works composed in the early 1860s.[20]

Whereas Brahms's first sextet is clearly a late product of the performer-centered domestic tradition, the second sextet, op. 36, composed in 1864, shows a more overtly "public," or listener-centered, approach to chamber music composition, and it comes at another important juncture in the composer's professional and personal life. During his first visit to Vienna in 1862–63, Brahms met many of the city's most influential musicians, including violinist and quartet leader Joseph Hellmesberger, founder of an important series of quartet concerts, and critic Eduard Hanslick, who would remain one of Brahms's closest friends throughout their long lives.[21] (In early 1863, Brahms moved to Vienna on a semipermanent basis to conduct the Singakademie.)[22] Hellmesberger began programming Brahms's works during that first visit, beginning with the op. 18 string sextet. Wilhelm Altmann reports that this first Viennese performance failed to please audiences, which may have prompted Brahms to reconsider his approach in the next several chamber works written in and for Vienna, leading to his successful piano quartets and quintet and the second string sextet.[23]

The emphasis on repetition and on communal music making so notable in op. 18 recedes somewhat in op. 36. The rounded, lyrical themes handed off by one ensemble member to another are replaced here with slow-moving melodies theatrically revealed for listeners. For example, when an altered version of the first movement's primary theme is presented in mm. 53–74, we might first expect a straightforward repetition, but the second half of the theme is extended and intensified through the next twenty measures, prolonging the dominant harmony and ratcheting up the harmonic tension of this opening section (see example 6.6). The musical texture thickens, and unresolved dissonances pile up until the downbeat of m. 95, when the ensemble finally strikes a root-position tonic chord and the first cello bursts free with a cascade of articulated scalar eighth notes. Although in retrospect this entire section clearly belongs to the primary theme area, its function seems introductory in nature, as it gradually unfolds, preparing the listener in calculated steps for a dramatic revelation at m. 95.

The light rondo finale of op. 18 is replaced in this work with a weightier sonata form. This final movement contains almost no direct repetition, and it elides the development and recapitulation sections, creating a smooth and refined sonata style. The folk style of the themes tempers the seriousness of the form somewhat

EXAMPLE 6.6 Brahms, String Sextet in G Major, op. 36, movt. 1, mm. 67–103.

and reflects Brahms's multicultural encounters in the imperial capital. One of the main developments in Brahms's musical language attributed to his move to Vienna is the adoption of musical dialects prevalent there, such as the music of the Gypsy musicians seemingly found in every corner café. Brahms had encountered Gypsy music before, and earlier pieces incorporated this style to a certain extent, but it takes on a new prominence in works such as the op. 25 piano quartet's finale (Rondo alla Zingarese) and the op. 34 piano quintet's scherzo movement.[24]

The rustic, even exotic style employed in this and Brahms's other Viennese chamber works is one of the more palpable differences between it and its predecessor, the op. 18 sextet. Although the influence of various ethnic and cultural "others" in Vienna explains some of this compositional turn, the contemporary vogue for all things exotic can also be linked to their popularity in bourgeois salons and parlors, particularly as the subject of variation sets and collections of songs or characteristic pieces that evoke regions then broadly considered "the Orient," including the Middle East, and even sometimes eastern Europe.[25] As a young man, Brahms himself composed or arranged several of these for the Hamburg publisher A. Cranz. Using the pseudonym G. W. Marx, Brahms seems to have considered these trifles unworthy of his aspirations for high art music.[26]

Just as the second movement of op. 18 employs variations on the *folia* theme that also fit a description of contemporaneous funeral marches, the second-movement scherzo of op. 36 recycles an older dance style in a modern context. The theme of the second movement is based on a gavotte for solo piano that Brahms composed in 1854 or 1855.[27] Some aspects of this movement that suggest an archaic style, however, also make it possible to hear the theme as vaguely rustic or exotic folk music, increasing the movement's appeal for a broader spectrum of listeners or consumers. The opening theme contains frequent parallel motion between voices, a pizzicato accompaniment in the three lower voices, and short, trill-like ornaments on the second beat of mm. 1, 2, 3, and 5. The folkish quality of the materials is enhanced by Brahms's use of the natural minor scale (i.e., $\flat\hat{6}$ and $\flat\hat{7}$, or F♮ and E♭) in many melodic passages (such as mm. 6–8) and an emphasis on the minor dominant in the second half of the theme (mm. 17–32). These features give the entire theme a faux-modal sound that fits a number of "Other" cultural contexts, including exotic evocations of distant lands or suggestions of bygone eras in European history such as the Middle Ages or "primitive" folk traditions. The contextual ambiguity is part of the charm of this movement, which allows each listener (and/or group of performers) to decide which aspects of the style to emphasize in any interpretation. Perhaps the work's good reception in Vienna rested on this ability to please a diverse audience of listeners and performers.

Op. 36 was performed in both private and public settings in its first presentations, but commentators of the time suggested that it was most at home in an intermediate space, a "semiprivate, semipublic" space. The first documented performance for a listening audience featured a professional group that had grown out of casual domestic performances in Boston, Massachusetts. The Mendelssohn Quintette Club presented the sextet as part of the group's annual subscription concert series in October 1866—a semipublic event because it was publicized and formal, but available only to an exclusive audience of subscribers.[28] Like Brahms's string sextets, the group and its activities exemplify the types of works and participation that characterize the gray area between private and public in the later nineteenth century. The club began at the midcentury, as many of the period's most influential performance organizations and concert series had on both sides of the Atlantic. A group of musicians employed by Boston's theater orchestras organized regular reading sessions for their own pleasure and edification on Saturdays, when theaters in Boston were closed. Like affluent upper-middle-class music lovers in Europe, the Bostonian businessman and chamber music connoisseur John Bigelow (1802–78) hosted the earliest meetings of the club in his home. He and his family remained lifelong supporters. At Bigelow's suggestion, the group began giving semipublic, by-invitation concerts to a select audience of two hundred listeners at the Chickering Piano Company's salon in 1849. The ensemble was soon in demand beyond New England, and it began touring in 1859, making appearances throughout North America and in Australia and New Zealand over the next thirty-five years. Longtime member Thomas Ryan described the group's career in his memoirs:

> In order to appreciate the environment of the Quintette Club during our early years, we have but to remember that Boston, within a radius of one hundred miles, had a very large number of towns and cities of active working communities. . . . [T]hese towns had no theatres; their only entertainments were lectures or concerts. . . .
>
> Parlor concerts were in vogue. In Cambridge, for instance, we had for fifteen consecutive seasons a set of eight parlor concerts, given in the houses of the professors or other friends of music. The programmes were of good music only. We also had for years sets of parlor concerts in places like Milton and New Bedford.[29]

The Mendelssohn Quintette Club's success relied in part on the musicians' ability to bring a professional sophistication to otherwise private styles of musicking at home.

These performances of string chamber music in private homes by professional players mirror similar activities going on at the same time in Vienna and elsewhere among Brahms's own circle of acquaintances. A month after the publication of the op. 36 sextet in April 1866, Theodor Billroth performed the work in his home in Zurich, "partly with professionals, partly with amateurs," as he described in a letter to the composer. Billroth, who appears to have met or at least heard Brahms in 1865 when the latter was in Zürich on a concert tour, would become one of Brahms's closest friends and a great supporter of his music. (We will return to Billroth's chamber music performances a few pages hence.) Billroth's particular reaction to playing the sextet as a string player emphasizes the communal qualities and the pure sensual pleasure of participating in such a work:

> Dear Brahms!
>
> Yesterday we played your new sextette at my home, partly with professionals, partly with amateurs, and I wish to tell you what an extraordinary joy we had in the playing of it. Playing it as a four-handed arrangement for piano, I could not have any realization of the extraordinarily beneficent and happy feeling. This is due not only to the ease with which the stream of melody flows and in which one charming motif after the other associates itself, but also to the entire construction of this work of art, to the crescendo of the emotions and the harmonic entity of the whole. . . . Please accept a thousand thanks for the beautiful hours which you prepared for us.[30]

Further corroborating the semipublic, semiprivate nature of this work, Billroth wrote to Eduard Hanslick that the work "demands a small hall, better even a moderately large room" because of its intimate style.[31] The value and importance of private music making would become a frequent topic in Billroth's correspondence with both Brahms and Hanslick.

The sextets reflect an absorption of the domestic string style of a previous era mediated by Schubert and Spohr, perhaps also by Onslow. Understanding that style's role in the musical life of the early decades of the nineteenth century allows us to understand better the sextet's place in Brahms's oeuvre. Having experienced some domestic stability after a harrowing entrance onto the world stage in the mid-1850s, he was ready to move on by the late 1860s. Op. 36 marks the end of Brahms's years of searching for an individual style or voice (and audience) and the beginning of his renewed interest in creating works designed to stand next to the great works of previous epochs. In the next decade, Brahms would bring to fruition large projects that in some ways fulfilled the promises or expectations of Schumann's 1853 "Neue Bahnen" article. These include his first symphony, completed in 1877, and the three string quartets, completed in 1873 and 1876.[32]

Writing for Posterity and Fellow Composers: The Op. 51 String Quartets

Although the quartets and sextets were all intended for similarly ambiguous spaces (semiprivate, with both private and public presentations in mind), the two string quartets of op. 51 could not be more different from opp. 18 and 36. Composed just five to six years later, they reflect a completely different audience and style, even a different era in Brahms's artistic life. The public, serious compositional style meant to demonstrate Brahms's prowess and inventiveness foreshadowed in the second string sextet comes into full view in the op. 51 quartets, completed in Vienna. Some of their features, in fact, point to an almost "reader-oriented" style conceived for composers, musicians, and connoisseurs studying the works much as music scholars and students do today. It is tempting to suggest, as some authors have done, that this progression from a sensual, apparently simpler style evident in the earlier works to a more complicated and less accessible one in the later quartets reflects increased sophistication, or that Brahms's style "improved" with time and experience. Such an assessment, though, fails to acknowledge the composer's agency in actively choosing a musical style as he conceived of the work he composed, and it denies the crucial role that the intended audience played in Brahms's decision-making process.[33]

As Leon Botstein has demonstrated, Brahms's move to Vienna in 1871 prompted the composer to reevaluate his role in musical life and to reconsider the genres and styles of music that he must compose and promote.[34] Prior to the 1870s, Brahms's published music consisted primarily of private musical genres such as chamber music and song, with a heavy dose of choral works designed for performance by able amateurs like those found at the Detmold court and in Hamburg. These works were the foundation of his critical success well into the 1880s.[35] His most clearly "public" work from the pre-Vienna years is *A German Requiem* of 1868–69. Public performances (i.e., ticketed events accessible to a fairly large proportion of middle-class music lovers) and the printing and distribution of this work brought him fame throughout Europe, but especially in German-speaking lands.[36] Despite its large performance forces and public presentation, however, the requiem belongs (like string chamber music) at the intersection of private and public musical life in the nineteenth century. Its success was due in large part to its accessibility for mixed groups of amateurs and professionals and to its distribution in four-hand arrangements and other accessible formats.[37] Brahms himself noted, in a letter to the publisher Rieter-Biedermann, that the work was practical because "every movement can be done alone."[38] At the same time that the requiem garnered accolades from listeners, performers, and critics, Brahms composed one of his most financially successful works, the Liebeslieder Waltzes for vocal quartet and four-hand piano accompaniment, op. 52, a prime example of his accessible domestic style.

Not coincidentally, Brahms's composition and publication activities shifted to works for orchestra at the same time that he settled finally in Vienna. In 1871 he moved into what would be his permanent home (No. 4 Karlsgasse), and in 1877 he moved his library there from Hamburg. Though Botstein focuses on Brahms's decision to compose in the large concert hall–oriented genres of symphony and concert overture at this point in his career and the social and cultural reasons that the composer did so, the string quartet clearly also played a role in this reassessment of Brahms's musical priorities. In addition to the obvious engagement with a Beethovenian legacy and the string quartet's growing aura of profundity based in large part on Beethoven's sixteen contributions, the quartets demonstrate

Brahms's attempt to wrestle with the changing role of music in social life. In the last quarter of the nineteenth century, music became an increasingly "public" endeavor through professionalization and concert promotion and through the politicization of genres and writing about music.[39]

The two quartets of op. 51, published in 1873, present a public statement of purpose and a bold testament to Brahms's renewed self-confidence. Set in what Brahms referred to as "the famous C minor," the first quartet of op. 51 has long been associated with Brahms's anxiety about Beethoven and the influence of that "giant" on "the likes of us."[40] But as I demonstrated in chapter 4, the key of Brahms's second quartet, A minor, held a similarly charged significance for composers of string quartets in the nineteenth century, partly related to Beethoven, but more generally related to notions of continuing progress in compositional and expressive technique. In composing and publishing these two works in keys closely associated with the long tradition of quartet writing in the eighteenth and nineteenth centuries, Brahms enters into an ongoing dialogue about the fate of the genre and of music. Like Mendelssohn, Burgmüller, Schumann, and Berwald, Brahms addresses his fellow musicians (especially composers, but also performers and connoisseurs) with suggestions or musings on the state of music in his time. Filled with passages of developing variation and contrapuntal display, the quartets, much more so than the sextets of the 1860s, require a high level of concentration and a willingness to follow a complex musical argument in order to make a strong effect on either the listener or the performer. The individual movements—especially the first movements—are tightly woven studies in motivic economy. The flowing themes and repetition characteristic of the sextets are almost completely absent in the quartets. In short, this music was intended for the music-intellectual elite, which, in Brahms's case, meant the exclusive body of highly trained chamber music enthusiasts of Vienna's upper-middle-class salons and chamber music concerts.

Brahms's dedication of op. 51 to the surgeon Theodor Billroth has been discussed in the Brahms literature primarily in regard to the perceived slight this dedication meant for the composer's longtime friend and Europe's most-sought-after chamber musician, Joseph Joachim. Brahms glosses over the dedication in a letter that disparages the op. 51 quartets as unworthy of the great virtuoso: "I have just heard from Simrock that on Saturday you are playing my A-minor Quartet—in just two words I'd like to say how especially that pleases me. Actually, I didn't mean either of the two [quartets] for your violin, but waiting for something better eventually seemed useless—you must also have thought something of the sort?"[41] The dedication to Billroth, though, may tell us more about these works than previous commentators realized. Brahms's letter of dedication emphasizes Billroth's participation in chamber music performances and the supportive role he played as a host of such gatherings:

Dear friend!

I am about to publish my string quartets—not the first, but for the first time.

It is not merely the affectionate thought of you and your friendship that prompts me to put your name at the head of the first one; I just like to think of you, and with such special *plaisir*, as violinist and "sextet-player." You would doubtless accept a volume of enormously difficult piano variations more kindly and would find it more befitting your attainments? There's no help for it, you just have to put up with the dedication even with the droll little ulterior motive.[42]

As a devoted connoisseur of music with no ties to the wider world of the concert stage or virtuoso life, Billroth may represent the type of musical consumer that Brahms had in mind for these works.[43] Billroth was apparently a good pianist in addition to being an able violinist and violist. He frequently performed four-hand piano music with Brahms and other composers and pianists of their mutual acquaintance, and he performed in and hosted evenings of chamber music in his home in Zurich and Vienna throughout his adult life. In many ways, these gatherings seem to have represented Brahms's ideal musical environment, the ideal audience for whom he wrote works like op. 51.

Like the Schubertiades held a half-century before by Franz Schubert's intimate circle of friends, Billroth's music evenings featured a regular collection of participants, including Brahms, Hanslick, pianist and composer Ignaz Brüll, pianist Josef Epstein, and musicologists Gustav Nottebohm, Eusebius Mandycewski, and Max Kalbeck. Unlike those earlier gatherings, however, Brahms and Billroth surrounded themselves with professional musicians and music scholars—the proportion of professional musicians and arts leaders to dilettante or amateur performers had shifted during the half-century between Schubert's and Brahms's heydays. Note, too, that in Brahms and Billroth's gatherings, the participants tended to be all male when the music focused on chamber works or scaled-down orchestral works—that is, works appropriate to a gathering of professional men—as opposed to the vocal and piano-centric works performed at Schubert's soirées, which frequently included many women in the company. When women were invited to Billroth's music room, songs were performed (or vice versa: when new songs were on offer, the presence of women was expected).

In the 1870s and 1880s, Brahms and Billroth sent postcards and short notes back and forth weekly or daily to arrange rehearsals and performances of Brahms's new works for this casual group. The string quartets and other chamber works that Joseph Hellmesberger performed in his subscription concerts were nearly always rehearsed with a small audience of close friends at Billroth's home. For example, in April 1876, just after Brahms finished his third string quartet (published as op. 67), Billroth wrote to him, "I would be dissatisfied if your new string quartet were not played for the first time in my music room with the usual circle of friends."[44] The careful collection of appropriate listeners and participants in these evenings was key; Billroth strove to create an intellectually stimulating society within which Brahms's works could be heard and discussed. When Billroth invited Brahms to his home for an evening with singer Hermine Spies in November 1886, for instance, he wrote, "I will try to select a very appreciative audience for that evening," and he went on to suggest Hanslick, cellist Robert Hausmann, pianist Ignaz Brüll, and Richard and Maria Fellinger.[45] Similarly, in March 1888, Billroth arranged a soirée to hear Brahms's Hungarian songs, op. 103, and invited "altogether, thirty-three persons, and all enthusiasts."[46] This was a mixed group of men and women, of professional players and composers, as well as critics and historians, and of amateurs with some training. Afterward, Billroth wrote, "Minna Walter sang beautifully under Brahms' firm reins, and naturally fresh and charming. The other voices, while no longer fresh, were still musical, and Brahms so warm with it all that it was a joy. Music at home certainly has its attractions!"[47]

These gatherings frequently included some nonprofessional musicians who participated in performances and as listeners. In 1876, Brahms wrote to Billroth, "I would like to ask whether I can invite an excellent amateur and a charming person, Doctor Jurenak from Pest, and can then introduce the quartet [op. 67, no. 3] at your house." In October 1882, when they arranged a performance of the F-major string quintet, op. 88, with professionals and amateurs, Brahms wrote to Billroth: "Dr. Alois Mayer [a Viennese lawyer] is anticipating with great pleasure, since Aussee, where he played the first viola [at the work's trial performance in August 1882], that you are going to be able to be there when he can play the quintette, and invites you to hear them. . . . [I]t would be very friendly of you if you invited him." About the same evening performance, he wrote again a day or two later: "I am just thinking of Dr. Gänsbacher [a vocalist who also played the cello in chamber music], who also would like to play, but can stand it if he's just an auditor."[48]

When reading through their correspondence, it becomes clear that Billroth and Brahms both valued an evening surrounded by like-minded men of learning and culture during which they could hear and discuss music. Brahms frequently assembled a group of friends to hear a new orchestral work in his four-hand version before a public performance. He and Ignaz Brüll, for instance, read through the second piano concerto with Billroth, Hanslick, conductor Hans Richter, and Max Kalbeck in attendance. For the trial reading of his fourth symphony in October 1885, Brahms gathered the same five men plus critics C. F. Pohl and Gustav Dömpke. Whether they gathered around the piano or around a quartet or piano trio, Brahms's circle was very much a late nineteenth-century iteration of the masculine middle-class musicking that had played an important role in amateur and professional musicians' lives since at least the turn of the century.

Billroth, in particular, seems to have felt that this environment was far superior to public concert performances. ("Music at home certainly has its attractions!")

On several occasions, he commented disparagingly about the public concert audiences of his day to Brahms or Hanslick. In 1876, he wrote to Brahms about the upcoming premiere of the first symphony, saying, "I wish I could hear the symphony alone.... Think of all the stupid, ordinary people who surround one in the concert hall, of whom, in the most rare cases, fifty have brains and artistic emotion enough to feel such a work in its nucleus at first hearing; we do not even discuss understanding it."[49] In 1878, after a performance of the symphony by the Vienna Philharmonic, he wrote, "I wonder, were there twenty people in the hall who grasped the inner thought of this work? I would doubt it. The spirit that the masses grasp easily is certainly not the spirit that prevails in this work of art. I saw very many stupid faces about me."[50] The inattentive listening public was not the only reason Billroth disdained the concert hall, though. Regarding the op. 78 violin sonata, Billroth wrote to Hanslick, "As much as I would enjoy hearing it with you, I cannot, for the present, think of it as being played in a concert hall. The feelings are too fine, too true and warm, and the inner self is too full of the emotion of one's heart for publicity."[51] Billroth's observation suggests that aside from the inconvenience of having to share the work with less capable listeners, the style Brahms employed in such chamber works was in many ways inappropriate for larger spaces.

These harsh observations about public audiences and the unsuitableness of concert halls to chamber music presentation would seem to imply that Brahms's chamber works were composed solely for private enjoyment. However, Brahms's choices in the quartets and later chamber pieces demonstrate his awareness that chamber music did not belong only to the domestic realm in the 1870s and 1880s but that it lived an amphibious life in both private and public spaces. His activities in Vienna at this time, moreover, suggest that he felt a strong need to educate both professional musicians and the general public about music. His performances, his editorial work, his involvement with the Gesellschaft der Musikfreunde and other organizations to promote young musicians and provide outlets for performance all indicate that he sought to engage a public very much in need of guidance.

Thus, in publishing his string quartets with a dedication to one of Vienna's most intellectually gifted public figures, Brahms associates the genre and his works in it with a high level of learning and learnedness. Whether in private performance or study in one's home or in subscription concert presentations, these works raised the expectations placed on both listeners and performers. Like the composers of "progressive" string quartets of earlier decades, Brahms sought to sustain a lofty role for the genre as a carrier of important musical innovations and ideas.

Brahms's choice of key for the quartets further illuminates his intended audience, or at least the particular niche he expected them to fill. In his letter to Billroth announcing the dedication, Brahms wrote, "Actually, I really ought not to disclose to you that the quartet in question derives from the famous C minor, for now when of an evening you think about it and fantasize in it, you will all too readily over-fantasize, and thereafter—you will like the second one better."[52] "The famous C minor" refers to the key itself, not to a particular work; it alludes to the familiar perception that Beethoven's most profound and affecting works were composed in this key, including the "Coriolan" Overture, the fifth symphony, the third piano concerto, the Choral Fantasy, and the piano sonatas op. 10, no. 1, op. 13 ("Pathétique"), and op. 111.[53] Brahms's letter points out the special aura that this key held for composers and other musicians as a harbinger of musical greatness. By publishing his first quartet in this key, he invites comparison with that legacy, an invitation he would extend again in 1877 with the first symphony and other important C-minor works.

The musical style in the quartets underscores this comparison and the change in Brahms's address from the parlor to posterity.[54] The first movements in particular are filled with stormy, restless gestures that have frequently been described as "Beethovenian." In the opening measures of the C-minor quartet, for example (see example 6.7), the tremolos and long crescendo that accompany the violins' rushing upward-sweeping melody create an urgency that also underlies much of Beethoven's music from the "heroic" period. More pertinently, the urgency and lack of resolution create a dramatic opening that allows Brahms to sustain suspense over the course of the exposition, as the listener (and performer) waits for the half cadence in m. 7 to be answered with a cadence onto the tonic. When the following more lyrical theme (mm. 11–21) presents a flat-side exploration that is nearly the opposite of the opening theme, the juxtaposition encapsulates the expressive thrust of the entire movement: arduous striving interrupted by only the briefest instances of repose.

Within this generally demanding musical atmosphere, the C-minor quartet contains several passages that evoke the musical past, alluding to the genre's history and potentially offering a sort of "extramusical" agenda behind the work. Thus, like earlier nineteenth-century string quartets, Brahms's quartet meets the challenge of historical comparisons head-on. These allusions demonstrate Brahms's pedigree and make explicit his claim to the mantle of previous composers, to membership in the same exclusive "club" of musical luminaries. Unlike those earlier nineteenth-century works, though, Brahms's references to the past are often couched in gestures that also suggest a contemporary (i.e., late nineteenth-century) understanding of it. For instance, in the C-minor quartet Brahms utilizes an accompaniment pattern connected to nineteenth-century performances of J. S. Bach's D-minor partita for solo violin, a work that Joachim frequently performed in recitals and appearances.[55] Specifically, Brahms's off-beat broken-octave figure (see mm. 24–28 in example 6.7) is the same figuration used to realize the arpeggiated chordal passage of the partita's chaconne throughout the nineteenth century. Example 6.8a shows the original version notated as chords in the lower staff and the typical nineteenth-century realization first documented in Ferdinand David's 1842 edition in the upper staff. Example 6.8b shows the

EXAMPLE 6.7 Brahms, String Quartet in C Minor, op. 51, no. 1, movt. 1, mm. 1–29.

EXAMPLE 6.8A Bach, Partita for Violin (BWV 1004), chaconne, mm. 199–207.

EXAMPLE 6.8B Brahms, left-hand arrangement of Bach's chaconne.

same passage from Brahms's own left-hand arrangement of the chaconne, made in 1877, a few years after the publication of the op. 51 quartets.

This accompaniment pattern simultaneously alludes to Bach's work and to Joachim's performances of the partita. The allusion could also bring to mind for some listeners Brahms's own connection to this work. Upon hearing the quartet in later performances, Clara Schumann, for instance, might have remembered Brahms's admiration for Bach and Joachim expressed in a June 1877 letter that accompanied a copy of his left-hand arrangement:

> The Chaconne is for me one of the most wonderful, incomprehensible pieces of music. On a single staff, for a small instrument, the man writes a whole world of the deepest thoughts and the most powerful feelings. . . . Now if the greatest violinist is not around, then the best enjoyment is probably to let it sound in one's mind, but the piece provokes one to become involved with it in all possible ways. After all, one doesn't always want to hear music merely ringing in thin air, Joachim is not often here, one tries it this way and that.[56]

Thus, in this small gesture, Brahms enfolds his personal admiration for Bach as a composer along with a recognition that he himself must attempt to follow in the master's footsteps. His recognition of Joachim's role in reviving this particular example of Bach's mastery is inherent in the allusion as well. The accompanimental figure saturates the first movement of the C-minor quartet, but it appears most often in the first violin part, the part Joachim would have played in his quartet's public and private performances of the work.

The C-minor quartet lays claim to a progressive approach to musical organization in its finale as well. Reflecting earlier cyclical gestures by Mendelssohn and others, Brahms's last movement refers the listener/analyst/performer back to the quartet's first movement. After the unstable and stormy first movement, the two inner movements retreat into their own separate worlds. The second movement Romanze suggests a quasi-medieval narrative, while the scherzo-like third movement presents a brooding ternary form. The fourth movement, however, begins with a startling return to the opening motive and style of the first movement (compare example 6.9 with the opening motive shown in example 6.7).[57]

EXAMPLE 6.9 Brahms, String Quartet in C Minor, op. 51, no. 1, movt. 4, mm. 1–7.

This one-and-a-half-bar motive returns again and again in the finale at formal seams, lending the entire movement an extended gesture of reminiscence and development.

Regarding the second quartet, Brahms's use of motto-like devices, his handling of tonal centers, and his affinity for contrapuntal display prompt comparisons to earlier self-consciously "progressive" string quartets and their engagement with Beethoven's op. 132 quartet (see chapter 4). Brahms's first movement begins with a four-note motto (A–F–A–E; see example 6.10) that returns at significant formal junctures in this movement, much like the motto of Beethoven's op. 132 and Burgmüller's op. 14. The motive contains Joachim's doleful motto "Frei aber einsam" (Free but lonely), which was also used in the collaborative "F.A.E." sonata for piano and violin with movements by Schumann, Brahms, and Albert Dietrich. After its initial appearance in the quartet, at the head of the movement, the motto is frequently treated in imitation, demonstrating Brahms's contrapuntal prowess. At the end of the exposition, for instance, Brahms evokes a Renaissance polyphonic style as each of the three lower voices enters with the theme in turn (see example 6.11). The motto reappears at the end of the development section or beginning of the recapitulation, where Brahms elides the two sections, creating a seamless form (example 6.12). In this compositionally virtuosic passage, Brahms combines the theme in the first violin with its inversion in the viola. When the second violin joins the first in parallel thirds in mm. 188–91, this passage's function as recapitulation becomes clear, and the arrival on an A^6 chord at the downbeat of m. 195 provides a definitive close to the development section.[58]

Brahms's use of this four-note motto differs from that of his predecessors. It does not prolong dominant harmony or provide a metrically ambiguous introduction,

EXAMPLE 6.10 Brahms, String Quartet in A Minor, op. 51, no. 2, movt. 1, mm. 1–15.

EXAMPLE 6.11 Brahms, String Quartet in A Minor, op. 51, no. 2, movt. 1, mm. 116–34.

EXAMPLE 6.12 Brahms, String Quartet in A Minor, op. 51, no. 2, movt. 1, mm. 176–95.

as Beethoven's op. 132 motto had, although it is tonally ambiguous, with a strong pull toward D minor (iv). The motto does not announce arrival at new keys and formal sections, as Burgmüller's motto did.[59] Rather, Brahms's motto brings with it a few topical associations that prove important in a consideration of his "progressive" quartet style. The opening motto appears in contrapuntally masterful moments of the quartet. It sets the tone of "serious" composition at the beginning of the work with a carefully manipulated, dramatic theme construction within a *stile antico* topic. In later instances, it appears in imitative passages that allude to the past (e.g., Renaissance imitation, Baroque fugal writing). It also allows Brahms to connect the development and recapitulation sections, demonstrating what we might describe as a "progressive" approach to sonata form. Finally, the motto clearly connects this work to Europe's greatest chamber musician of the later nineteenth century, Joseph Joachim. By incorporating his motto into the work and then using it as the springboard for several compositionally brilliant moments, Brahms connects the renowned violinist (and composer) to his own innovative approaches in the string quartet genre. Thus, although op. 51 is publicly dedicated to Theodor Billroth, Joachim's stealthy presence in both works may have been noticeable (via listening or score study) to those in the Brahms-Joachim inner circle. They would, perhaps, have recognized the Bach figuration used throughout the C-minor quartet and the motto of the A-minor work as allusions to Brahms's friend and colleague and to the musical heritage that they both valued.[60]

Examples of Brahms's mature, serious approach to composition, the string quartets of op. 51 have been dubbed by at least one modern commentator "Music as Logic," and they featured prominently in Arnold Schoenberg's assessment of Brahms as a progressive composer.[61] Certainly the terse, economic style of the sonata form movements promotes a reading as highly intellectual, or logical. Significantly, his next quartet, op. 67 in B♭ major, would be his last.[62] Its neo-Classical, Mozartean style suggests further ruminations on the past and on Brahms's own place in musical history, a topic to which the composer would return in his last works for strings alone, the quintets opp. 88 and 111.

Saying Good-Bye: The Two String Quintets

Despite subtle differences made for specific geographical audiences, the two string sextets both address an audience of amateurs playing or listening to music in spaces that straddled the divide between private and public life. Similarly, the three string quartets all address chamber music connoisseurs at a high intellectual level. In both genres, Brahms engaged the form with intensity, produced multiple works that explored its possibilities in a relatively compact period of time, and then moved on to other musical pursuits. He did not come back to the string sextet or quartet after a hiatus of several years, as he did with the piano trio, piano quartet, and solo sonatas for violin and cello. In the case of the string quintet, however, Brahms wrote two works eight years apart and with different purposes (and audiences) in mind. The F-major quintet, op. 88, composed in 1882, is a product of his middle years, after he settled in Vienna and systematically established himself as the leading German composer of his day, an heir to the great traditions of Haydn, Mozart, Beethoven, and Schubert. It demonstrates Brahms's ongoing engagement with the music-political scene of Vienna at that time. On the other hand, the G-major quintet, op. 111, which he ostensibly intended as his last published work when he sent it to Simrock in 1890, bears several markers of the composer's "late" style, evident in many works composed in his last decade. It shows Brahms summing up his musical career and what he considered to be the musical achievements of his generation.

In 1879, Brahms's only rival in the realm of instrumental music, Anton Bruckner, completed a string quintet in F major. When three of its movements were performed at a meeting of the Academic Wagner Society in Vienna two years later in 1881, the performance was reviewed favorably in a few Viennese newspapers, and musicians about town began to stir themselves for a showdown between the two composers. Bruckner's quintet was performed publicly by the Hellmesberger Quartet in 1885 in the large hall of the Wiener Musikverein to an enthusiastic audience, requiring both supporters and critics of Bruckner and his works to address the challenge it proposed to Brahms's supremacy in the chamber music world. Margaret Notley, a modern-day authority on Brahms's milieu in the last two decades of the nineteenth century, connects Bruckner's quintet most clearly to Brahms's chamber music with piano composed and premiered in 1886, especially to the F-major cello sonata, op. 99, noting that the furor over Bruckner's work "manifestly rankled Brahms."[63] I would suggest, though, that his first string quintet, composed in the wake of the initial unveiling of Bruckner's work in the same key and for the same instrumentation, surely also conveys a response to the challenge—Brahms directed his rejoinder at musical connoisseurs, listeners, and critics.

Bruckner's supporters praised his quintet (like his body of works more broadly) for its emotional immediacy and its ability to move the listener. Detractors noted that the work lacked structural integrity and compositional discipline, or the "musical logic" that critics and enthusiasts hailed in Brahms's music and that he emphasized in his own composition lessons and correspondence.[64] Brahms's three-movement quintet combines learned, traditional elements with singular innovations in a pointed display of musical logic. The opening sonata form movement uses conventional, even conservative, binary repeat signs to divide the exposition from the development and recapitulation. It also employs learned topics with fugato-style thematic working out in the development and transitional sections. But within the straightforward sonata design, Brahms's choice of keys points toward an overarching innovation, tonal movement by thirds. The primary theme in the tonic leads to a light, pastoral secondary theme, introduced by the first viola, in A major (III); the finale also presents important materials in F major and A major, creating an opposition between I and III throughout the work rather than the expected I and V. Furthermore, at the end of the first movement's exposition, the codetta (mm. 62–74) emphasizes D major (VI) with snippets of primary-theme motives in euphonious parallel thirds and sixths. Thus, Brahms explores the musical space a third above and a third below the tonic, much like Beethoven did in his "Serioso" quartet, op. 95, which includes structurally important arrivals in F minor (i), A♭ (III), and D major (♯VI). Brahms's exposition ends in A major (III) without a significant exploration of the dominant, and the recapitulation confirms the importance of D major at m. 173, when the secondary theme is recapitulated in that key (VI) rather than in the tonic.

The second movement of the quintet contains many surprising innovations, and perhaps it was in light of the attention that the Bruckner quintet's Adagio movement received that Brahms chose to concentrate such energy in his own Grave movement. (The middle movement of Brahms's work is self-consciously not deemed an Adagio and therefore does not engage the expectations that term connoted in Brahms's and Bruckner's lifetime.)[65] It combines the traditional slow movement with a light-hearted scherzo in a hybridized form. The main Grave section in C♯ minor is twice interrupted, first by an Allegretto section and then by a Presto, both in A major. The movement's coda presents an alternation between C♯ minor and C♯ major, finally resolving on A major in the last measure (see example 6.13). This particular effect situates Brahms's work firmly in his place and time (fin de siècle Vienna) and demonstrates his ability to convey "a thinking subject seeming to choose a key and the associations it has accumulated in the course of the movement."[66]

In creating such a breathtaking moment, Brahms demonstrates his prowess and the connection between thinking and feeling that many critics claimed Bruckner's works (and, by extension, those of the New Germans or Wagnerians generally) lacked. Much of the perceived "danger" of the New German or "progressive"

EXAMPLE 6.13 Brahms, String Quintet in F Major, op. 88, movt. 2, mm. 196–208.

compositional style, as far as Brahms's supporters were concerned, came from these works' appeal solely to the emotional and sensual experience of the audience, without engaging them intellectually. The tendency of audiences, and the populace at large, to be swept away by an emotional display ran counter to the ideals of nineteenth-century Liberalism, which valued rational thinking and clear judgments.

In a last jab at his concert hall adversary, Brahms created a short, light finale that combines two tradition-laden forms associated with the highest accomplishments of Classical—more importantly, of Austro-German—instrumental music: the fugue, associated above all with Bach, and sonata form, associated with the first Viennese Classicists. Brahms presents these learned, self-consciously serious forms in an accessible, rustic style, directly addressing the claims that "conservative" music was necessarily stuffy or dreary.

The Allegro non troppo ma con brio movement opens with an introductory fugal exposition in $\frac{3}{2}$ meter. The sonata form proper begins at m. 23, where a jaunty tune with an almost hunt-like style is presented as a primary theme in F major. When the secondary theme enters in A major (III) at m. 35, the fugal material returns as accompaniment, with full statements of the subject by the first viola and second violin. The development section features elements of the primary theme and the fugue subject simultaneously before introducing the dominant pedal customary to both sonata form retransitions and fugal endings (mm. 91–95).

Brahms's F-major quintet was first performed, as noted above, at Theodor Billroth's home in October 1882 with a mixture of professional and amateur musicians, among the usual circle of friends and colleagues. Like the string quartets, it addresses a group of intellectually engaged connoisseurs (including performers and listeners or readers) in an intimate style well suited to a domestic music room or parlor. At the same time, the quintet feels very much like a "public" work calculated as a musical response to, even an attack on, Bruckner's foray into the chamber music realm. Today known as the "Spring" quintet, this work features an accessible musical style in its surface elements—in the hunt and pastoral topics, the rounded singing themes, and the prevalence of the major mode throughout. The second movement actively "chooses" the major mode and the light, playful tone of the scherzo interruptions at its end rather than the more somber minor-mode Grave music. Brahms's contemporaries already perceived a change in tone in this work, labeling it, the contemporaneous third symphony, and the later chamber works of 1886 more welcoming and less austere than earlier works.[67] Beneath this enticing surface lies an intricately thought-out and executed plan for tonal and motivic development. Brahms's work addresses an audience of both private and public listeners and performers (as well as posterity as a potential audience) to demonstrate that Bruckner's quintet would not get the last word on chamber music's "progressiveness" in the 1880s. Although he never responded in print to the various criticisms and attacks that Bruckner's claque flung at him, Brahms's musical response lives on in the F-major string quintet.

After his fiftieth birthday in 1883, Brahms began to doubt his own creative powers, writing to friends and confidants of his fears that he would not be capable of creating something new again.[68] As his fame grew throughout Europe, Brahms feared that any new work's reception by the public reflected not the merit of the individual work but a general appreciation for his overall achievement, an anxiety that seems especially prevalent in the case of the fourth symphony. Thus Brahms began to distrust public sentiment, though he still longed for the approval and assurance of listening audiences and critics.

Brahms's worries also reflect his place and time. Viennese artists at the fin de siècle were probably more aware of and anxious about the end of their lifestyle and the coming changes in culture and society than any generation before or since. The same technological innovations and cultural institutions that had brought prosperity and growth to Vienna and its sister cities, London and Paris, now seemed to be bringing about their decline and unrest in the populace. From the point of view of Brahms and many of his contemporaries, the inclusive, progressive, and cosmopolitan culture that they celebrated in everyday affairs and in their art and music had begun to crumble into a dark age of xenophobia and anti-Semitism, political conservativism, and religious myopia. The contemporaneous political situation spilled over into the art and music world via criticism and public concert programming.[69] In this climate, musical genres and styles began to connote particular political worldviews that influenced a work's public reception.[70]

The political-musical allegiances seem oddly counterintuitive today ("conservative" music for progressive political leanings, "progressive" music by and for political conservatives), but at the time political reception of art primarily revolved around access. Compositional approaches such as programmaticism, music drama, and later large-scale symphonic and orchestral works in a "progressive" vein (i.e., Bruckner's symphonies) became aligned with the radical Right. These genres and musical styles were more accessible to audiences of listeners gathered in large concert halls and outdoor venues. The Liberal Party and the upper middle class quickly became associated with a "conservative" treatment of traditional forms such as the symphony and chamber music—in other words, with any music that suggested a strong tie to the "elite" traditions of the eighteenth and early nineteenth centuries and that was performed in smaller, more exclusive venues, which demanded higher ticket prices or a sophisticated education in order to participate.

The institutions of musical life were rapidly evolving as well, and the changes in private and public musical outlets affected Vienna's (indeed, Europe's) chamber music scene. The piano's rise in popularity as the premier domestic instrument has been discussed already, as has the effect of this change on domestic string chamber music performances. The popularity of public concerts also influenced the composition and consumption of chamber music, especially after the 1860s. Musicologist Leon Botstein notes that during this period the public became increasingly dependent on professional performances and written reviews in order to engage music of its own time.[71] Domestic performances of two- and four-hand piano arrangements of symphonies and string quartets became common in the second half of the century, and they appear to have replaced the use of string quartet and other chamber ensemble arrangements of such works by the 1890s. In the 1870s through 1890s these arrangements were used primarily to re-create performances heard in concert halls after the fact rather than to explore a newly published work before its orchestral or quartet performance. Thus, published arrangements became souvenirs of performances remembered by mostly passive concert hall listeners.[72]

Even in Brahms's personal circle of friends and colleagues, private performances of chamber music changed considerably in the 1880s and 1890s as important members of the group grew older, became ill, and died. As biographer Malcolm MacDonald notes,

> For a gregarious man with such a need of friendship, Brahms's latter years were cruelly shadowed by the accumulation of losses within his circle. [Karl] Tausig and [Anselm] Feuerbach were among the first of his friends to die, in 1877 and 1880 respectively. Brahms was at Gustav Nottebohm's bedside when his old friend expired at Graz in 1882.
>
> . . . [Karl Georg Peter] Grädener followed in 1883. His old teacher [Eduard] Marxsen and [Carl Ferdinand] Pohl . . . both died in 1887; in the same year [Theodor] Billroth contracted pneumonia that nearly killed him, and was never his old self afterwards.[73]

Even Clara Schumann, with whom Brahms had often shared happy hours at the keyboard in their younger days, experienced hearing loss and pitch distortion in her last years in addition to various rheumatic ailments that prevented her from practicing and performing.

Already by the 1880s, Brahms was exploring a new circle of friends with new outlets for musical performances, and with these acquaintances, Brahms entered into a role and mode of participation different from his earlier (mostly male) friendships and interactions. These later years saw Brahms embracing the ministrations of a variety of women devoted to his art and his person. The musical gatherings in their homes appear more and more like cozy family gatherings involving men, women, and children. In the early 1880s, he met Richard and Maria Fellinger, who would be staunch advocates of his music and his legacy throughout their lives and vicariously through the activities of their children and grandchildren into the late twentieth century.[74] Brahms also frequented the homes of other affluent Viennese friends such as industrialists Victor von Miller zu Aichholz and his wife, Olga, and Arthur Faber, who married former Hamburg

Frauenchor member Bertha Porubszky. In each of these three households, a matriarchal figure presided and took on the role of looking after Brahms as an honorary member of her family. Maria Fellinger helped him refurbish his apartment after the death of his longtime landlady in 1886, and her husband, Richard, had electric wiring added to the apartment as a gift in 1892. Olga von Miller and Bertha Faber cared for Brahms in his final days.

Performances of his chamber music were a regular feature of Brahms's visits to the von Miller, Faber, and Fellinger households, where his later works with piano were performed in both private and semiprivate soirées. Richard Fellinger, Jr., describes many family gatherings in which Brahms performed with other amateur or professional musicians. Some of these performances were quite casual, for the immediate family and mutual friends, while others took on a more formal tone; Fellinger recalls an "Abend-soirée" in April 1886, for instance, that included thirty-five to forty people gathered to hear Brahms's newest compositions. String chamber music played a smaller role in these get-togethers than works with piano and voice, perhaps because Brahms and his hostesses could interact musically in these genres, with the composer at the piano and a family member or visiting friend singing or playing along. For instance, when cellist Robert Hausmann came to Vienna from Berlin to play recitals and concerts, he called on the Fellingers (and stayed in their home, in some instances). There he and other musicians would play Brahms's works, including newly composed pieces, as in the autumn of 1886, when he and Brahms played through the F-major cello sonata and, with violinist Marie Soldat, the C-minor piano trio. Brahms played often at the Fellinger home with Marie Soldat (Soldat-Roeger, after her marriage), who had been a pupil of Joachim. Brahms enjoyed her playing style and remarked, "The little soldier [a pun on her name, "die kleine Soldat"] is a real guy, no?" after her rendition of his violin concerto in 1885.[75] Soldat founded an all-woman string quartet in 1895, and with this and ad hoc groups she played chamber works in public subscription concerts like those hosted by the contemporary Rosé Quartet and its predecessors the Hellmesberger Quartet in Vienna and the Joachim Quartet in Berlin. Although these groups played Brahms's music in domestic settings, these performances became more and more often construed as private rehearsals for a public performance rather than performances for their own sake.

As "his" Vienna with its familiar inhabitants disappeared before his eyes, Brahms memorialized it in the op. 111 string quintet, and he intended to retire at that point, allowing this work to be his last testament to a life well lived. In a letter to his publisher Nicholas Simrock dated 11 December 1890, Brahms wrote, "With that scrap of paper you can take your farewell from my music—because quite generally, it is time to stop," and in an earlier conversation, during the composition of the quintet, Brahms apparently told musicologist Eusebius Mandyczewski, "I'm just not going to do any more. My whole life I've been a hard worker; now for once I'm going to be good and lazy!"[76] The quintet brings together all of the elements of music making that were dear to Brahms, combining his complete mastery of compositional details and sophisticated formal and harmonic language with luscious themes in a seemingly populist style. Kalbeck heard the lush, lyrical opening as particularly Viennese; he ruefully commented to Brahms at the premiere of this work, "Brahms at the Prater?" referring to the amusement park area just east of the city center.[77] In some ways, this passage suggests his songwriting and the domestic style represented in the string sextets—the shimmering accompaniment sets the stage for excitement with its loud tremolos, and the cello's leaping triadic line emphasizes the sunny major mode. The quick ascent to the instrument's highest range gives the theme a youthful vigor (see example 6.14a). Unlike the early sextets, though (or even the op. 88 string quintet), this work places nearly unreasonable demands on the performers. These same cheerful opening measures present a special challenge, as the cello's wide-ranging tune (it traverses nearly three octaves in the first fourteen measures) must be heard in its lowest and highest registers under the *forte* accompaniment in the four upper strings (see example 6.14b).[78] Brahms, Joachim, and the members of the Rosé Quartet, which performed the premiere in 1891, exchanged many comments and suggestions to make this opening passage more playable. Brahms sketched a few different ideas but, in the end, abandoned all attempts to compromise, leaving the nerve-racking section exactly as he had first composed it. The string style throughout the work is uncomfortable for the players, with double-stops, tremolos, and rapid shifts in direction, in addition to unusually wide ranges for all five instruments. In short, the quintet requires a nearly virtuosic technique from all five participants. Whereas the sextets and the op. 88 quintet had been played in private read-throughs and informal performances among Brahms's music-loving friends and acquaintances, this work caused even professionals to seek out alternative playing options.

That refusal to compromise results in a "dissonance" that characterizes Brahms's later chamber music style: the apparent simplicity and gaiety of the musical surface belies the rigorous working out of the structure that supports it, and the virtuosic feat of making an intensely difficult passage sound natural and easy likewise mimics the contradictions that lie at the heart of fin de siècle culture.

EXAMPLE 6.14A Brahms, String Quintet in G Major, op. 111, movt. 1, primary theme.

EXAMPLE 6.14B Brahms, String Quintet in G Major, op. 111, movt. 1, mm. 1–10.

Even Brahms's breezy explanation of his retirement despite his obvious need to continue working indicates the tensions between public façade and private sentiment.

The quintet contains many moments that point to its self-conscious "lateness," signaled by disruptions and meditations, interpolated explorations of motives, and harmonic progressions within a driven formal style. Op. 111 continually establishes rhythmic and harmonic momentum for the express purpose of derailing it with these interruptions. As though he cannot bear to let one developmental opportunity be wasted, Brahms forces the listener and performer to pause in contemplation. For example, the first movement's development section introduces learned-style sequences on D major (V) at m. 69, and these lead to a unison G on the downbeat of m. 79 (see example 6.15). The reintroduction of motive 1 from the primary theme creates a strong sense of arrival, and the listener may hear this moment as the beginning of the recapitulation. But the cello plays motive 1 of the theme in E♭, then in D♭ (mm. 83–85), followed by a developmental detour

EXAMPLE 6.15 Brahms, String Quintet in G Major, op. 111, movt. 1, mm. 79–109.
(continued on next page)

EXAMPLE 6.15 (continued)

EXAMPLE 6.15 (continued)

based on the three-note motive from the head of the main theme. The primary theme picks up again at m. 100, with motive 2 in the first violin and the return of a familiar shimmering accompaniment in the other four voices. This statement, too, is interrupted with stuttering staccatos in mm. 101–2. The music refuses to close but stops and starts over and over again in the forty-nine measures between the end of the exposition (mm. 56–57) and the return of G major that begins the true recapitulation (m. 106).

William Caplin's theory of "formal functions" and their government of musical time helps to explain Brahms's technique and its effect on listeners here.[79] In the development section of the work—a "loose," "in-the-middle" section—Brahms uses gestures of continuation (formal and harmonic sequences, modulation, thematic fragmentation) that lead to gestures that suggest a beginning function (half cadence and tonal stability, larger thematic groupings). The tension that Brahms creates in the subsequent passages by alternating compositional continuation with beginning features runs counter to the Classical style that Caplin's theory codifies. Thus, Brahms utilizes Classical means to new ends, creating disruption and confusion with techniques traditionally associated with order and clarity.

Another aspect of the quintet's "late" style is its artful combination of the most modern string playing and compositional techniques of Brahms's generation with reverent gestures to the past—a combination of "old" and "new" typical of other fin de siècle works as well. The balanced, well-articulated forms of the two outer movements refer back to the clear formal style of Mozart and Mendelssohn rather than to Brahms's own seamless, flowing sonata forms of the 1870s and early 1880s. The apparent clarity and concision of these movements, though, is deceptive, even misleading. The finale, labeled Vivace ma non troppo presto, contains a succession of melodies, motives, and styles one after the other in a breathless (or breathtaking) rush. We can group these melodies into three separate thematic groups in the first eighty measures; they chart a basic three-key harmonic trajectory from an "off-tonic" introduction in B minor (iii) to a main theme in G major and subordinate materials in A major (V of V) and D major (V). When the components of those groups begin to return in their original ordering in m. 81, the formal plan becomes murky—a rondo structure would require earlier returns of the opening refrain; a sonata without development (sonatina) form is possible but highly unorthodox. No other formal paradigm would seem to fit the finale of a four-movement work by a "conservative" composer. In fact, Brahms employs a Schumannesque "parallel form" here, presenting a series of contrasting materials in related keys, then presenting that material again immediately with developmental variations to the original scoring and harmonic underpinnings.[80] The familiarity of the square four- and eight-bar phrase structures and rustic or dance-related topics combined with the full, ringing tones of the open strings available in G major, A major, and D major give this movement a light and accessible feel, despite its formal ambiguity.

Whereas the finale offers a "Classical" surface over an ambiguous or "Romantic" structure, the third movement employs a conservative Classical form to organize more obviously "Romantic" melodic and harmonic features. Unlike Brahms's earlier labeled scherzos, with their often fiery, bravura performance demands and fast tempi, this moderate-tempo movement belongs with his other "intermezzo-like" third movements (such as the scherzo of the string sextet, op. 36).[81] The movement uses the ternary form typical of a scherzo and trio movement; Brahms does not label the two sections to indicate the Classical model as such, choosing instead to let the tempo designation, *Un poco Allegretto*, stand alone. The opening binary section in G minor (mm. 1–60, the scherzo) gives way to a nearly self-sufficient rounded binary section in the parallel major (mm. 61–110, the trio) before an exact recall of the opening "scherzo" without its repetitions (mm. 111–70). Here as elsewhere in the string quintet, though, Brahms includes harmonic or melodic surprises meant to draw the listener's or performer's attention to the composer's active manipulation of time and our perception of it. The "trio" section, for instance, ends with a witty, Haydnesque gesture. The trio's main theme is recalled in the dominant (D major), so that when the music arrives at an F dominant seventh chord over a G pedal in m. 107, we might expect the chord to "resolve" as it did earlier in the movement by collapsing onto a G-minor chord. Instead, the first violinist's arpeggio stops on an A that continues to ring in our ears while the lower four voices hold their dissonant cluster (C, E♭, F, G) through the downbeat of the next measure. The two beats of silence that follow allow the complacent listener a moment to glance up and try to assess what has happened just in time to see and hear the ensemble continue the movement with the return of the scherzo in G minor.

In this quintet, Brahms mixes his own modern compositional approach with gestures that refer to the past and to the variety of influences from which he had benefited. This mixture presents the listener/analyst with an intriguing album of memories and souvenirs from the composer's career, much as his earlier sextets present a sort of memorial to the earlier domestic practice. Much of Brahms's later output serves this purpose, collecting smaller works from earlier episodes of his life and recasting them in light of his more recent achievements. The op. 8 piano trio that he recomposed for a second edition brought out by Simrock in 1891 is one example; others are the late collections of songs and piano pieces and the organ preludes. In these works, Brahms consciously brought his career full circle, summing up musical life in his time with works that continue to speak to musicians today.

* * *

Because he spent most of his performance career as a pianist and conductor, Brahms had few practical reasons to write string chamber works. The six works considered here (along with the third string quartet) are exceptional in his output because they are the only works he composed with no foreseeable opportunities to participate personally in their performance other than as a listener. Yet, Brahms engaged with these genres at important points in his compositional career because he deemed them necessary to his development as a professional musician and composer. We might also interpret them as opportunities for the pianist/conductor/composer to achieve some distance from the act of performance and to enter into a mode of composition that necessitated some detachment from the work's presentation. The string quartet's association in the second half of the nineteenth century with "pure" music and with the highest levels of achievement and compositional rigor, for instance, surely required Brahms to assume a position of confidence and ability that he found difficult to affect, as evidenced by his comment later in life that he had destroyed over twenty quartets before finally publishing op. 51. The string sextets of his early maturity required him to engage in a respectable, middle-class pastime that had previously been unavailable to him, having grown up in a low-income household where he and his family lacked the leisure and resources to pursue such recreations.[82] These works, and the environment that produced them, allowed Brahms to "try on" a compositional career writing such domestic pieces for the sheet music–buying public represented by his then current position as music director at a small court. In the 1860s, this lifestyle was still an option for a young composer who wanted to support a family by writing popular music and leading musical activities in this sort of environment. The quintets likewise gave Brahms a final opportunity to address audiences that he had not yet reached in his earlier works—first the Wagnerians and New German supporters of Bruckner in the op. 88 quintet, then the audience of posterity or of history he embraced in op. 111. Like the other composers considered in this study, Brahms used the string chamber genres to create or commune with diverse groups of consumers and fellow musicians. That several different audiences continued to thrive in his lifetime is evident in his conscious decisions to address them with appropriate musical styles that he seems to have associated with distinct genres. We shall see in the next and final chapter how a slightly younger composer achieved the same diversity of audiences and musical styles within the single genre of the string quartet during the same forty-year period in which Brahms was active.

CHAPTER 7

The Diversity of Dvořák's String Quartet Audiences

As one of the nineteenth century's most prolific composers of string quartets and the composer of one of the century's most popular works in that genre (the "American" quartet, op. 96), Antonín Dvořák ought to get more than a passing mention in any study of the genre. Dvořák's fourteen string quartets outnumber those of Mendelssohn, Schumann, and Brahms combined. But as a perpetual "outsider" to dominant musical hierarchies of his day and of later musicological establishments, Dvořák has rarely been treated as a significant contributor to the ongoing development of chamber music in the last quarter of the nineteenth century.[1] In his own lifetime, Dvořák became an icon for Czech national styles in 1878 with the Slavonic Dances, and this reputation as a composer of works that have been interpreted either as exotic "trifles" or as politically charged nationalist statements caused him much professional angst in the 1880s and 1890s.[2] In those volatile decades, his Czech heritage placed him at the periphery of Austro-German traditions centered in Vienna, and in later decades, his devotion to "conservative" genres (symphony, string quartet, choral music) alienated him from Smetana's legacy and caused early twentieth-century Czech music scholars to exclude him from their assessments of a national school after his death in 1904.[3] In the later twentieth century, though, the public perception of Dvořák and his music tended to rest on works that meet the expectations of listeners and critics who want to hear the Czechness of the composer or the influence of his American encounters in his music's melodic and harmonic surface. His non-"exotic" works have received less attention in scholarship, and they are performed less often than the audibly Czech and American pieces.

The strain of satisfying the disparate expectations of diverse audiences while attempting to establish himself as a composer of "universal" music in the tradition of German Classicism (especially in Vienna) is most evident in Dvořák's string quartets. These works demonstrate his shrewdness in reading the musical climate and responding to it with appropriate stylistic choices that address not only the desire for exotic signifiers or their absence (depending on the listener) but also the types of engagement that listeners and performers would enjoy in different performance settings.

The image of a savvy Dvořák negotiating the conflicting priorities and tastes of listeners in fin de siècle New York, Vienna, Prague, and London conflicts with the simplified profile of the composer promoted in many studies of his life and works. Directly connected to Dvořák's perceived Otherness, the portrayal of a simple, shy "man of the people" who preferred his rural home outside of Prague to the big cities where his music was performed reinforces the differences between him and his (canonic, centrally located) contemporaries.[4] Beethoven, Brahms, Mahler, and Debussy also famously found inspiration and the quiet necessary for composition in idyllic outdoor settings, but only Dvořák is consistently stereotyped as "unspoiled," with a "peasant's love of simple pleasures" or "unassuming and simple."[5] John Clapham, whose English-language scholarship of the 1960s and 1970s single-handedly paved the way for later Anglo-American work, continually notes the composer's lower-class rural background, as well as his supposed innocence and naïveté. This language (unintentionally) reinforces a xenophobic perception of Slavic cultures and their people, held over from the nineteenth century. Eastern European people were considered primitive or underdeveloped in comparison to their cosmopolitan counterparts in Vienna, Berlin, London, and Paris, despite the lively musical and artistic communities in Prague and Pest or Budapest. The documents and evidence of Dvořák's life, however, contradict that image of a country bumpkin astounded at his own success. Dvořák actively sought out opportunities to see and hear his works performed abroad. He traveled widely, despite his apparent agoraphobia, to the major capitals of Europe, including several channel crossings to attend performances in England in the 1880s and his much-discussed sojourn in the United States during the 1890s.[6] He spoke English passably well, in addition to German and Czech. He was, all in all, more worldly than Brahms, who spoke no language proficiently other than German and who never ventured any farther from home than Italy.

Dvořák's ability to address many of the performance scenarios or audiences identified in earlier chapters makes discussion of these works a fitting way to close this study of nineteenth-century string chamber music culture. Dvořák completed six string quartets before writing his A-minor quartet, which he labeled op. 16, in 1875 (see table 7.1). This work reflects a stark change in approach and a conscious decision to follow a "Beethovenian" path, despite his predilection for opera and his dedication to "Wagnerian" ideas associated with the New German School in earlier works. Notably, this change of direction occurred well before his encounters with Brahms or with the Viennese establishment—contrary to popular and textbook portrayals of the composer, which suggest or imply that Dvořák turned to "absolute" music to emulate Brahms. After his international success with the Slavonic Dances three years later, Dvořák received two important commissions from string quartet leaders who hoped to bring his music to larger

TABLE 7.1 Listing of Dvořák's string quartets (publication dates provided for works printed in Dvořák's lifetime)

Opus	Title	Key	Composition	Publication
2	Quartet no. 1	A	1862	—
—	Quartet no. 2	B♭	1868–70	—
—	Quartet no. 3	D	1869–70	—
—	Quartet no. 4	E minor	1870	—
9	Quartet no. 5	F minor	1870	—
12	Quartet no. 6	A minor	1873	—
16	Quartet no. 7	A minor	1874	1875 (Prague)
80	Quartet no. 8	E	1876	1888 (Berlin)
34	Quartet no. 9	D minor	1877	1880 (Berlin)
51	Quartet no. 10	E♭	1878–79	1879 (Berlin)
61	Quartet no. 11	C	1881	1882 (Berlin)
—	*Cypresses* arranged for quartet		1887	—
96	Quartet no. 12, "American"	F	1893	1894 (Berlin)
106	Quartet no. 13	G	1895	1896 (Berlin)
105	Quartet no. 14	A♭	1895	1896 (Berlin)

audiences beyond Prague, and the contrast between these works demonstrates his careful negotiation of concert hall expectations in diverse settings during the 1880s. Finally, the American works, especially the op. 96 string quartet in F major, demonstrate Dvořák's absorption of the domestic style of the first half of the nineteenth century and his ability to transform the traits of that style to create a new accessibility for listeners in the last decade of the century. Dvořák's creation of a public-private style accessible to concert audiences has probably been his greatest legacy in the twentieth century. This chapter aims, among other things, to illuminate the features of Dvořák's earlier string quartets that indicate the composer's engagement with pervasive nineteenth-century string quartet traditions and his successful navigation of the rapidly changing chamber music culture in the last quarter of the nineteenth century.

Works for Readers: Dvořák's Early Efforts and the A-Minor Quartet, Op. 16

In the only book-length treatment of Dvořák's quartets to date, scholar Hartmut Schick notes that the composer followed a defunct eighteenth-century practice in composing chamber music as his first works intended for the public. (Dvořák designated his 1862 string quintet "op. 1" in his catalog and the string quartet he composed in 1868–70 "op. 2." Neither of these works was published until the twentieth century.) Dvořák used these genres as self-directed exercises in the Classical sonata style and to supplement the strictly church-music-oriented training he received at the Prague Organ School. The op. 1 quintet borrows from Classical models (Haydn, Mozart, and early Beethoven), and the op. 2 quartet relies on Romantic ones (later Beethoven, Mendelssohn, and Schumann). The four quartets he composed in 1870 and 1873, on the other hand, contain a variety of more "modern" resonances laden with Wagnerian and Lisztian devices, such as surprising harmonic progressions, unconventional single-movement forms, and themes borrowed from sections of Wagner's *Rienzi* or from Czech revolutionary songs.[7] Taken as a group, these six works almost form a catalog of available compositional models for a young composer in the 1860s and 1870s in Prague. Wagner had visited the city to conduct concerts of his own works in 1863, and Liszt had been an important model and supporter for Smetana and for other nationally minded composers in eastern Europe. As Dvořák searched for compositional models, however, he was also experimenting with the limits of Prague's audiences, their tastes and tolerances for new ideas or for reinterpretations of familiar styles. This point is often overlooked in assessments of the composer's experimentation with "Wagnerian" language in these early quartets and his first attempts at opera—especially the disastrous first version of his *King and Charcoal Burner*.

Although none of these early quartets was published in Dvořák's lifetime, their survival in copied parts suggests that they were performed and discussed at least among his friends and supporters during his early years as a professional musician in Prague. Dvořák's songs and some of the chamber works were performed at the regular soirées held at the home of lawyer and musical amateur Dr. Ludevít Procházka, who edited Prague's musical paper, *Hudební listy*. He was a strong supporter of avant-garde trends in musical life, including a national Czech style based on Lisztian or Wagnerian models. Procházka also edited the journal *Dalibor*, and in 1873 he wrote glowing editorial reviews of Dvořák's large-scale works and published the composer's first song as a supplement to the journal.[8] Smetana had conducted the overture to *King and Charcoal Burner* in a Prague Philharmonic concert in 1872, and the piano quintet was performed in a high-profile concert that same year. Tellingly, the string quartets remained behind closed doors, performed at private concerts among fellow artists and aristocrats. The F-minor quartet Dvořák designated as op. 9 was played at an event organized by a Baron Portheim, and the Young Musicians Circle (Kruh mladých hudebníků) performed the A-minor quartet in the summer of 1875 in a "private" gathering that was, nonetheless, written up in that week's edition of *Dalibor*.[9] These private and semiprivate performances paved the way for his later chamber music success, much like the gatherings of friends playing music together allowed Mendelssohn and Burgmüller, Robert Schumann, and Niels Gade to experiment with new ideas in a safe space and to benefit from honest assessments by like-minded artists.

These first five string quartets document Dvořák's search for a combination of style and audience that would be appropriate for his expressive purposes. Dvořák clearly had no intention of retreading the familiar ground of the Biedermeier composers writing for private domestic consumption; he had an apt model in this style close to home in the works of Václav Veit, whose quartets and quintets (mentioned in chapter 1) were wildly popular in Dvořák's lifetime in Prague and abroad. Like the Budapest-centered German composer Robert Volkmann (1815–83), Dvořák struggled to balance his New German or progressive musical leanings with the tastes of his day and in genres coded as "conservative."[10] In other words, none of the Slavic models available to Dvořák and his generation offered him a way to combine his musical and personal interests with his need for international recognition and acceptance. Dvořák, more than his predecessors and contemporaries, sought to reconcile these apparently oppositional impulses, and his early works in the chamber genres, especially the surviving string quartets, allow us to observe the young composer's progress toward that goal.

The turn in Dvořák's early works from the New German avant-garde to a Classically defined "progressive" style based on the innovations of Beethoven and the earlier Romantic generation has important historiographical and nationalist ramifications. As with Mendelssohn, whose early string quartets engage Beethoven's late style but whose mature works embrace a Mozartean Classicism, modern scholars have treated this turn as a retreat to the conventional and deemed it either a loss of nerve or a correction, depending on their own musical or historiographical priorities. In fact, Dvořák's change of style reflects an astute practical move on his part. He recognized in 1873 that in Prague and elsewhere, the audience for chamber music consisted primarily of domestic amateurs or elite neo-Classicist composers and performers. Meanwhile, the New German supporters had, by and large, rejected chamber music as an appropriate outlet for their ideology. Smetana, who counted himself among the avant-garde Lisztians of the Weimar school, felt he must explain the motivations for his chamber music lest he be interpreted as a closet conservative aping the rules of an outdated style.[11] After experimenting with several available options in the 1860s and 1870s, Dvořák seems to have concluded that if he wanted to write quartets for a modern concert audience, they must be avant-garde in the right way—which is to say that they must be perceived as belonging to a core group of works that shared a common set of values and goals related to chamber music's history and its place in musical life. Beginning with op. 16, Dvořák's string quartets actively engage earlier models from within the chamber music world rather than borrowing techniques from outside of it. Like other ambitious composers before him, he chose the key of A minor and embedded in the work multiple insider references to indicate his membership in the chosen circle of serious music makers in line with Beethoven, Mendelssohn, Schumann, and Brahms. (Simrock had published Brahms's op. 51

string quartets, in C minor and A minor, in 1873, so it is possible that Dvořák had studied them or heard them played informally.)[12]

The most striking connection to that tradition of serious quartet composition—works designed for insiders or for fellow composers—is the reliance on modulations to the submediant, F major (VI). The quartet's sonata form outer movements embrace harmonic and formal ambiguity by incorporating F major as a structural tonal center and by reserving the dominant for brief, codetta-like gestures, as at the end of the first movement's exposition. The first movement begins with a double statement of the opening theme in the tonic, first in a tentative, soft dynamic with clear eight-bar phrasings (mm. 1–16), then in a louder, more agitated style with octave doublings in the two violins and syncopated chords in the accompaniment (mm. 30–36). New thematic material with a new expressive marking at m. 59 (*Un poco piu mosso*) would seem to indicate the secondary theme area, but this passage never actually settles into a key. The waltz-like tune presented in the first violin (see example 7.1) flirts with both C major (by emphasizing G and G^7 chords) and F major (through cadences, though always with C in the bass rather than the root, F).

The theme's seductive, waltz-like sway and four-bar phrasings lend it a comfortable stability, despite the harmonic indecisiveness. In this passage, the music seems to vacillate between the "conventional" option for the secondary key (the relative major) and the "insider's choice" of F major. Dvořák suspends the listener's curiosity or anticipation throughout the second half of the exposition, withholding a strong cadential resolution at several points. First in m. 105, a C dominant seventh chord struck on the downbeat supports a statement of the

EXAMPLE 7.1 Dvořák, String Quartet in A Minor, op. 16, movt. 1, mm. 59–78.

primary theme's head motive in the cello but fails to resolve in F major. Then codetta-like explorations of the primary theme's motives over E-major harmonies hint at a modulation to the dominant, but no independent and fully developed theme appears to confirm it. The rising scale from D to A over ii^7 and V^7 harmonies in mm. 125–26 finally leads to an elegant and definitive cadence on F major at the start of the development section.

The disruption of tonal and formal expectations that F major represents in the first half of the movement continues in the second half, where modal contrast comes into the foreground via a motivic device that recalls Beethoven and Mendelssohn. A brief developmental passage interrupts the recapitulation between the primary and secondary themes, a gesture that extends the moment of indecision that the secondary theme represented in the exposition. Inserted just after reaching the dominant (E major) in m. 269, this short section halts the forward momentum of the recapitulation with a grand pause (the two quarter rests in m. 269) and a three-note question posed by the second violin and viola (see example 7.2). Their E–F♯–G♯ would seem to lead to the tonic (A).

Much like Mendelssohn's "Ist es wahr?" motif in his op. 13 A-minor quartet and Beethoven's "Muß es sein?" motif in his op. 135, Dvorak's "question" draws attention to the composer's continuing presence in the work and invites listeners and performers (or analysts studying the score) to reflect on the decision-making process at play here. The music has reached a formal crossroads: the secondary theme that had been so ambivalent in its initial presentation and notably absent from the development section might transform the tonic to A major and lead to a major-mode ending for the movement, or the music might continue

EXAMPLE 7.2 Dvořák, String Quartet in A Minor, op. 16, movt. 1, mm. 267–83.

in the minor mode, which would require an adjustment of the theme. Dvořák dramatizes this moment of indecision by leaving the leading tone unresolved. The primary theme returns in A♭ major, a respelling of G♯ major that is more comfortable for the players but one that may also be interpreted as a retreat into "flat-side" harmonies—an evasion of the question, as it were. In mm. 275–76, the outer voices insist on a decision, asking again the three-note question posed earlier, here as E♭–F–G♮, which is answered with a more impassioned, *forte* version of the primary motive in F♯ major, VI or ♯VI, depending on one's interpretation of the tonic here as A major or minor. When the secondary theme finally arrives with its *un poco più mosso* indication at m. 296, the new key signature indicates A major, but the theme holds the same ambiguity in this iteration that it did in the exposition, and the primary theme must come to the rescue. Securely seated in A major with drones in the cello and viola and a long-held C♯ in the first violin, the primary theme provides harmonic stability in the major mode for just four measures before Dvořák ends the movement with an A-minor coda (mm. 356–79).

Several aspects of Dvořák's handling of keys and form in this quartet suggest the influence of Robert Schumann's op. 41 string quartets (and, via those works, the influence of Mendelssohn and Beethoven), but the finale provides the most conspicuous points of contact. First, the form of Dvořák's finale bears similarities to the "parallel forms" used by Schumann in his early piano works and in his chamber works—notably, in the finale of the A-major quartet that closes his op. 41 set.[13] Like that model, Dvořák's finale divides into two main sections containing introductory, primary, and secondary thematic materials in distinctive keys; each main section is followed by a shorter developmental interlude, in both cases based on the secondary theme. Second, Dvořák employs an off-tonic introduction procedure that recalls Schumann's first string quartet, op. 41, no. 1, in A minor, whose opening movement is a sonata form in F major preceded by an *introduzione* in A minor.[14] Dvořák's quartet begins with a short introductory section in F major (VI) before presenting the primary and secondary themes in A minor and A major, respectively (see example 7.3). This opening establishes a dichotomy between F major and the tonic (major and minor) that usurps the usual conflict between the primary and secondary themes and keys. By placing that contrast at the beginning of the work, Dvořák is able to maintain contrast of tonal center as an important tension in the form while also introducing (as in the first movement) a contrast of tonic mode.

Some features of Dvořák's finale tone down the radical nature of Schumann's model, whereas others mark Dvořák's movement as a more ambitious and unsettling work. Both suggest Dvořák's aim of entering into a dialogue with his predecessor. Schumann's quartet defies expectations based on sonata form conventions by opening in the tonic, then proceeding with a movement completely outside of that tonal sphere. The first movement goes through the normal series of procedures we expect for a sonata form movement in F major and closes in that key,

EXAMPLE 7.3A Dvořák, String Quartet in A Minor, op. 16, movt. 4, mm. 1–15, introduction, with motives *x* and *y* marked.

EXAMPLE 7.3B Dvořák, String Quartet in A Minor, op. 16, movt. 4, mm. 35–47, primary theme, combination of motives *x* and *y*.

but the rest of the quartet returns to A minor as though ignoring this disruptive opening. Dvořák's quartet, on the other hand, begins off tonic and moves to the expected key, and his introduction comes at the beginning of the last movement, after the tonic has been firmly established by the previous three movements. Yet Dvořák does not mark the opening introduction as such (Schumann's bears the heading "Introduzione" and is separated from the rest of the work by a double barline and change of key signature), and he incorporates the introduction into the rest of the work. Dvořák's opening theme presents two elements that will form the basis of the entire movement: motive *x*, containing a "rolled" triple-stopped chord followed by an accented triplet figure and rests; and motive *y*, a more lyrical homophonic motive marked *dolce* over the continuing triplet tattoo (see example 7.3a, where the motives are marked in the introduction). When the music modulates to A minor for what we might call the "real" exposition, these two motives meld to form the theme that will characterize the tonic, transformed by the removal of rests in the lower parts and the addition of expressive markings (*grandioso* and *fortissimo*) that produce a rousing display of ensemble bravado (see example 7.3b). The *x* motive returns throughout the exposition to mark important departures and arrivals in the movement, for example, at the beginning of transitional passages where the ascending triplet figure pushes the music forward and at the end of these sections where the triple-stopped chords from m. 1 signal a harmonic arrival. Thus, Dvořák closes the quartet by returning to the tonal ambivalence of the first movement and presenting a collaboration between elements presented in the subdominant and those presented in the tonic.

Between these two weighty sonata form movements, Dvořák provides a slow movement in a modified song form and a more conventional scherzo. Like the slow movement of "insider" quartets in A minor by Mendelssohn, Burgmüller, and Schumann, Dvořák's Andante cantabile is set in F major. Previous quartets by Dvořák frequently evoke the *dumka* style, or the Slavic lament style that would become synonymous with slow-tempo Czech nationalist or exotic pieces, much as the polonaise or *hallgató* would musically define Polish or Gypsy musical identities.[15] Dvořák also published several free-standing *dumky* for piano and for other instruments later in his career, and they proved to be popular with publishers and sheet music purchasers because of their national (or exotic) flair. Notably un-dumka-like (i.e., not imbued with specifically Czech or Slavic features), op. 16's slow movement demonstrates Dvořák's ability to write in a "universal" and learned style. The middle section of the ternary form incorporates a new eight-measure theme in C major and four variations. The variations travel through a variety of keys and textures, giving this middle section a development-like quality that allows Dvořák to demonstrate his compositional prowess within a lyrical context in much the same way that Schumann's strophic Adagio movement had in his A-minor quartet. This technique would become characteristic of Dvořák's mature string quartets. Three of the four works considered in this chapter, for instance, include a miniature set of worked-out variations on a theme introduced in the middle section of the movement.

On the one hand, Dvořák's A-minor quartet is somewhat more conservative than similar works by his neo-Classical predecessors, such as Mendelssohn and Schumann or Brahms. The four movements are completely separate from each other; the quartet is not cyclical, and it does not bear overt extramusical cues such as mottos or ciphers. The "Slavonic" elements that colored his earlier string chamber works, with the inclusion of folk songs such as the "Hey, Slavs!" quotation in the E-minor quartet (B. 19, no. 4), and his other works from the 1870s are not evident in this quartet. On the other hand, Dvořák's bid for acceptance into a pan-German association of "serious" composers demonstrates a daring attempt to think beyond the confines of his present situation in Prague. Rather than modeling his career on those of his local heroes or following the path laid out by supporters and patrons in Bohemia, Dvořák set out to present himself to the world as a Czech composer who had absorbed the styles of Viennese and North German Classicists and who was capable of addressing them in a shared language of contemporary innovation and tradition. In this work, Dvořák laid claim to the traditions of Beethoven and of the Leipzig School, separating himself from Weimar's New German ideology and, at least temporarily, from its Czech representatives in Prague. He chose to write for an international audience of musical elites who would recognize and appreciate his engagement with the A-minor tropes of earlier generations.

This work was probably included in the packet of materials that Dvořák sent with his Austrian Stipendium application in 1874, though it is not listed among those works in later reminiscences. The Austrian Empire sponsored this competition to support the work of poor young artists; Dvořák first learned of it in early 1874, and he applied for the fellowship that year, winning four hundred gulden to supplement his income. In the wake of this affirmation of Dvořák's talent, the Prague-based publisher Starý published the op. 16 string quartet.[16] Over the next three years, Dvořák continued to explore the chamber genres with continued stipends. He completed two string quartets between 1875 and 1878 (quartets no. 8 in E major and no. 9 in D minor), as well as a string quintet and a sextet, two piano trios, and a piano quartet. Although they were included in his later Stipendium applications and, therefore, seen and perhaps heard by the jury of the competition, the two quartets were not publicly performed or published until much later, after some revision.[17] Dvořák dedicated the D-minor quartet to Johannes Brahms when it was published in 1880 as op. 34. Brahms was a member of the Stipendium committee, and he was impressed enough by Dvořák's works to strike up a correspondence and friendship with the younger composer. In 1878 Brahms urged his own publisher (and friend) Nicholas Simrock to publish some of Dvořák's more accessible works, first the Moravian Duets for soprano, alto, and piano (op. 38) and then the first set of Slavonic Dances for piano four hands (op. 46). Thanks to a favorable review of the latter work on the day it was released, the dances were a huge financial success, and Dvořák became a household name throughout musical Europe virtually overnight.[18]

Works for Listeners: Style and Audience in the E♭-Major and C-Major Quartets, Opp. 51 and 61

In the 1880s, German publishers clamored for Dvořák's newest works, and soloists and ensembles played the Slavonic Dances on piano and in his orchestrated version in German, Austrian, British, Italian, French, and American cities. At the same time that most audiences and performers could not get enough of Dvořák and his Slavic-spiced music, however, Vienna's political establishment reacted to recent upheavals in the Austrian Empire with increasingly xenophobic, even anti-Slavic sentiments that spilled over into artistic and musical affairs.[19] In these years, Dvořák had difficulty getting his non-Slavic works published or premiered—he made a special plea to Brahms to intercede with Simrock regarding the two string quartets, for instance, but these works were delayed nonetheless.

Despite these setbacks, Dvořák received several important commissions just after the breakthrough of the Slavonic Dances, including requests for new string quartets from two of Europe's leading violinists at that time. The two quartets, though completed under similar circumstances within two years of each other, could not be more different. Dvořák wrote the Quartet No. 10 in E♭ Major, op. 51, for violinist Jean Becker (1833–84), founder and leader of the Florentine Quartet; Dvořák completed the work in early 1879, and Simrock published it immediately.[20] Becker requested Slavonic elements, and Dvořák obliged by including Czech or Slavic themes or dance styles in each movement, as many previous commentators have noted. The Quartet No. 11 in C Major, op. 61, on the other hand, is often described as a more "Classical" piece, meaning without such overt signs of the composer's "exotic" heritage. Joseph Hellmesberger (1828–93) commissioned this work in 1881 after having played Dvořák's string sextet (op. 48) and the op. 51 quartet in a private soirée attended by Brahms. Hellmesberger announced the premiere date of this new work before receiving it from Dvořák, forcing the composer to finish it hurriedly in the last two weeks of October 1881. Noting that Dvořák began a movement in F major but rejected this and started over in C, despite being pressed for time, Clapham speculates: "Dvořák seems to have been at pains to write a work that was sufficiently worthy of being performed for the first time in Vienna, which more than any other city had a right to be regarded as the home of the string quartet, and where comparisons would be made with the quartets of the Viennese masters."[21] Although the presence or absence of Czech national idioms contributes to the audible differences between these works, the more significant factor at play is Dvořák's consideration of the different performance scenarios involved. The contrast in tone of presentation between these quartets surely results from Dvořák's conscious decision to address specific groups of listeners by handling the ensemble differently in the two quartets. At the very least, the musical style of the resulting works reflects the disparate settings for which they were intended.

In addition to its Slavonic features, the E♭ quartet's compositional character exudes an uncommon intimacy and leisureliness, despite its commission for public presentations. In comparison to the more theatrical, almost overbearing style of its later cousin, op. 51 issues a friendly invitation to revel in the melodious sounds of the four string instruments. Jean Becker and his quartet, preparing for a tour of Switzerland and the surrounding areas, would be playing op. 51 in semipublic venues on the road, including large and small concert halls, town halls and gathering places, and salons in private homes, as was typical for traveling performers at this time. The four movements of the quartet reflect those smaller and more intimate spaces via dynamics, texture, and thematic design; the moderation and consistency at play in all of these features give the work a smooth, lyrical effect.

The first movement of op. 51, for instance, opens with two measures of arpeggiated tonic chords in the lower three voices, each of which enters the texture individually (see example 7.4). The staggered entrances serve two purposes. First, they create a static wash of sound that pulls the listener into a rocking rhythm that will dominate the movement. This opening sets a tone of relaxed engagement with its unhurried, repetitive melodic and rhythmic patterns. Second, the individual entrances emphasize the quartet's makeup of four distinct voices and players in dialogue, as opposed to a simultaneously struck chord or unison. Although the four instruments here will work together as a cohesive unit, they retain separate identities throughout the quartet. Indeed, as the primary theme unfolds in mm. 3–12 in the first violin part, the accompanying voices take turns joining it in parallel figurations, as in m. 4 (violins 1 and 2) and m. 7 (violin 2 and viola). The viola takes up the primary theme in m. 13, when the harmony shifts to A♭ major; this thematic exchange further emphasizes the communal character of this movement.

EXAMPLE 7.4 Dvořák, String Quartet in E♭ Major, op. 51, movt. 1, mm. 1–16.

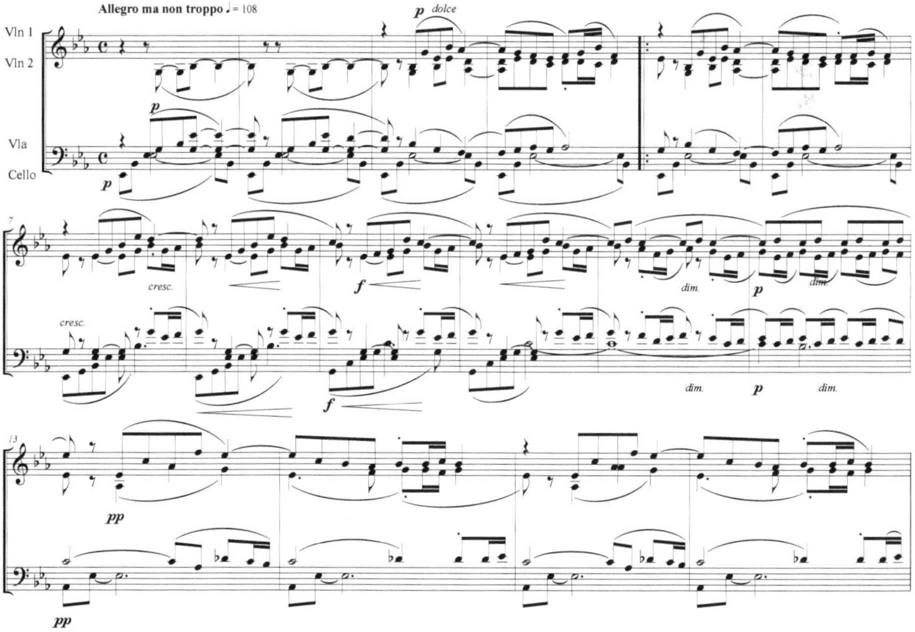

The first movement of the C-major quartet, op. 61, on the other hand, begins with the primary theme in the first measure, played here, too, by the first violin but in a more soloistic fashion (see example 7.5). The accompanying voices strike a tonic chord and hold it for two measures, and the harmony quickly shifts with a ***fp*** accent on the downbeat of m. 3 to an A diminished seventh chord. Here, an ostinato begins in the viola before moving into the bass (cello) voice. Over the next thirty measures, Dvořák continually utilizes harmony and texture to create waves of increasing tension followed by brief moments of resolution, and with each new passage the contrast between tension and relaxation heightens, resulting in a series of plateaus. In the first of these, for example (mm. 1–27), two of the four voices hold long chord tones, creating an atmosphere of expectation and mystery, as the diminished chords of mm. 3–8 and 11–19 continually fail to resolve as expected. The tension increases in m. 20, when a full-textured triplet passage in the upper three voices leads from piano to fortissimo and from the lower range of the instruments up three octaves to a melodic peak on a C-major (tonic) chord that ushers in a variant of the opening motif. The movement as a whole is filled with short passages like this one building to a climactic arrival of one sort or another, keeping the listener ever on the edge of his or her seat, rather than (as in the E♭ quartet, op. 51) settling into a familiar groove and presenting a longer lyrical theme.

The overall character of each quartet's opening movement and its realization of sonata form reinforce the first impressions of these very different openings. The more public C-major work (op. 61) is designed to overwhelm and impress Vienna's concert hall listeners with the power of the ensemble and the virtuosic leadership of the first violinist. Themes and modulatory passages appear in the lead violin part first, and the inner voices' broken-chord figurations provide an active and full backdrop. The sheer variety of textures, timbres, and dynamics, as well as the speed with which the music switches from one to the next, creates a rollicking experience for listener and player alike. See, for example, the brief development section. Beginning with the primary theme, Dvořák provides a soft, contemplative interpretation in A minor passed among the four voices with shimmering thirds in the accompaniment (mm. 118–25), then a bucolic song-like version in F major with an arpeggiated pizzicato bass line (mm. 126–31), before moving on to a learned-style *forte* treatment of the second half of the theme. This last idea takes over the development at m. 135, where it is marked *feroce* (fierce) and presented with *fortissimo* and sforzando markings to emphasize the change of mood. Sequencing through a series of major and minor keys, this section gradually builds to a dense texture by adding double-stopped ostinatos in the inner voices. When the tension of this thick, loud passage resolves in m. 149 (in G♯ minor), the style takes a marked shift again, with a suddenly contrapuntal passage that combines the familiar primary theme with new angular counter-melodies (mm. 149–59). At the end of the development section, increasingly loud

EXAMPLE 7.5 Dvořák, String Quartet in C Major, op. 61, movt. 1, mm. 1–27.

and accented dominant harmonies explode in a boisterous return of the tonic and the primary theme at m. 178, resulting in a triumphant atmosphere.

Although the development section of the C-major quartet is short at just over fifty measures, it explores a variety of styles and topics economically. For this reason, perhaps, earlier commentators have focused on the "Beethovenian" or "Classical" quality of the quartet as a whole, but we should note, too, that this topical variety has a particularly strong effect in the concert hall when performed by a dynamic, personality-led ensemble such as the Hellmesberger or Joachim Quartet.[22] The quick changes of mood and physical exertions of the quartet members playing these passages—the visual spectacle of their bowings, the short rests, the constantly shifting intraensemble pairings, and so on—make this an especially appealing work to hear and see played by a star ensemble in a resonant hall. The extreme dynamics and articulations also ensure that the music is intelligible in a larger space because the motivic fragments stand out from each other more easily.

By contrast, the intimate, leisurely character of the E♭ quartet continues throughout its first movement, as emphasized by the retransition at the end of its development section. The music arrives "home" at the tonic much earlier and with less fanfare than in the C-major quartet described above. The beginning of the E♭ work's recapitulation is marked with the secondary theme in m. 128 (see example 7.6), eschewing the "double return" of the tonic and primary theme. When the primary theme returns in its original form at m. 182, the dominant supports a cadenza-like descent down the chromatic scale in the first violin, marked *dim.* and *poco ritard.* This transition—"relaxing into" the tonic rather than bursting in on it—perfectly exemplifies the differences in tone between this

EXAMPLE 7.6 Dvořák, String Quartet in E♭ Major, op. 51, movt. 1, mm. 176–88.

work and the C-major quartet. It may also demonstrate the different leadership and performance styles of Jean Becker and Joseph Hellmesberger.

The inner movements of the E♭-major quartet reflect Becker and his group's subtle interpretive approach and the cozy, fraternal atmosphere of their performance venues. The work contains two slow movements; both are marked *Andante con moto*. The second movement, a dumka with *Vivace* sections that feature the Czech *furiant* dance style, provides a dance pair to replace the usual scherzo. The slow outer sections feature bardic gestures such as the strummed accompaniment in the cello (evoking a lute or lyre) that assist in creating the tone of ancient folk-rooted storytelling and singing in an exotic land.[23] They evoke the closeness of the hearth and the camaraderie of those gathered to listen and participate in singing. The paired lines and responsorial performance of the themes maintain the "exotic" Czech flavor of the work, but they also emphasize a communal, conversational experience that draws assembled listeners (in the quartet's presentation of the movement) into a vicarious participation in the piece (see example 7.7). The third movement, labeled *Romanze*, also imitates a domestic-style song with bardic or archaic elements, including modal mixture and the use of open-fifth drones. These generic resonances enhance the illusion in the E♭-major quartet of domestic privacy within a public concert performance.

The inner movements of the C-major quartet, op. 61, in contrast, draw the listener's attention more clearly to the composer's craft and the performers' skills. Its third-movement scherzo and trio, in particular, show off Dvořák's familiarity with the stringed instruments, as well as his compositional mettle. The short (eighty-four-measure) scherzo section in A minor is dwarfed by the extended trio, which begins with a simple rounded binary theme in A major. This forty-four-measure

EXAMPLE 7.7 Dvořák, String Quartet in E♭ Major, op. 51, movt. 2, mm. 1–13, "Dumka" (bardic gestures and communal singing reinforce a feigned "privacy" in the public quartet experience).

section sets up the expectation that the trio will parallel the scherzo in length and style. What follows, however, is a colorful set of variations on that opening theme in D major (IV), C♯ major (III), and B♭ major (♭II). As Dvořák presents these variations, he treats the listener to a kaleidoscopic display of accompaniment styles, textures, and timbres, specifically notating open-string usage in the final variation, for instance, to ensure a bright, ringing tone and to provide a rustic variation on the otherwise elegant tune. The variations increase in "busyness" (faster passagework and thicker, more active textures) as the movement proceeds and in range as the violins move into the third octave above middle C and the cello remains in its lowest octave at the bottom of the bass clef (see example 7.8). The movement effectively puts the quartet's abilities on display for Vienna's discerning concert audiences in an unusual, concentrated movement designed to keep the listeners guessing at what might come next.

In contrast to the common image of Dvořák as a simple, patriotic, affectionately rural man from peasant stock, these works demonstrate the composer's quick-witted ability to adjust his musical style appropriately to any audience he needed or wanted to address. His savvy understanding and manipulation of the musical marketplace has been downplayed in much previous scholarship, but the chamber

EXAMPLE 7.8 Dvořák, String Quartet in C Major, op. 61, movt. 3, mm. 259–76.

works prove that Dvořák paid attention to the press and managed his own image better and more actively than did some of his peers. We see this same attention to appearances and to audience needs in his works from the 1890s, during and after his experiences living in the United States.

A Work for Players and Listeners: Op. 96 as a Concert Hall Tribute to Domestic Performance Traditions

Dvořák's most familiar and best-loved works today stem from the three years he resided in the United States between 1892 and 1895. The ninth symphony, "From the New World," the "American" string quartet in F major (op. 96), and the "American" string quintet in E♭ major (op. 97) may be his most frequently performed works in the twentieth century, though the late cello concerto (begun in America and premiered in London in 1896) and the opera *Rusalka* (composed in 1900–1901, using some material from the American sketchbooks) are frequently performed as well.[24] Many commentators have noted that the "American" chamber works, opp. 96 and 97, are more "Czech" than American in style, coming as they do from the composer's vacation days in Spillville, Iowa, where he was delighted to find a community of Czech farmers to alleviate his fierce homesickness. These works evoke or engage many of the features of the domestic string style that had become common in the 1830s and 1840s and that still formed an important part of musical life in the 1890s via reprints and later editions. The popular works of that period, including quartets and quintets by Prague composer Václav Veit, were still circulating in reprints well into the last decades of the century, even though the youngest generation of composers had largely sidestepped the genre in favor of either more lucrative forms, such as easy piano works and parlor songs, or more ambitious ones for larger forces. Previous treatments of Dvořák's American chamber works have focused on their nationalist elements, especially on determining which of the possible North American folk traditions influenced Dvořák's compositional choices (African American spirituals, traveling Indian shows and other exposure to Native American musics, or European immigrants' music).[25]

I will focus here on the domestic elements of these works that connect them to examples by Spohr, Onslow, Kuhlau, and Schubert discussed in chapter 3, using the string quartet as the primary example. Because he was writing at the end of the nineteenth century and with the public concert hall in mind, Dvořák approached this tradition with aims different from those of his predecessors. Dvořák's contract for the National Conservatory in New York required him to give up to six public concerts per year, so his summer sojourn was not merely a vacation but an opportunity to finish compositions for those concerts.[26] Dvořák's quartet reinterprets and reframes the domestic style for fin de siècle concert audiences and provides an idealized, theatrical re-creation of the domestic style for denizens of the fast-paced modern world. The chamber works were influenced by

Dvořák's unsettling experience of modern (i.e., turn-of-the-century) life in New York City, with its crowded tenements and early skyscrapers, its noise and pollution, and a general hustle-bustle of 1.5 million residents living in close, uncomfortable proximity to one another.[27] Although he had lived most of his adult life in the metropolitan capital of Bohemia (Prague) and had made extended trips to Vienna and London, the urban atmosphere of New York City took Dvořák by surprise.[28] According to one source, the population of central Prague in 1880 was just 162,000 people, increasing to just over 201,000 by 1900; including the outer districts brings the total population to around 350,000 in 1880, still only 23 percent of New York City's population at the time.[29] The sharp contrast of that urban lifestyle to the idyllic country existence of Spillville's Czech residents ignited a powerful nostalgia in Dvořák, which he expressed in the F-major string quartet; it captivated audiences then and continues to do so now. In a fast-paced age of technical revolutions that increase demands on one's time and attention (in Dvořák's lifetime: industrialization; in ours: the digital revolution), the pastoral style of these works soothes the fears and concerns of performers and listeners alike. For this reason, the F-major quartet has remained one of the composer's most popular works—not only because it is accessible and requires less rigorous listening, as some have suggested, but because it speaks to the nostalgia that modern audiences feel for an idealized simpler, more "authentic" life on the land among neighbors and friends. Dvořák's "American" chamber works successfully re-create the "private" domestic experience that lies at the heart of idealized portrayals of eighteenth- and nineteenth-century European chamber music for the modern concert stage.

Especially in the two outer movements of this quartet, Dvořák utilizes a surprising economy of thematic material and emphasizes lyrical themes and their repetition to create shared dialogue while maintaining a freshness of materials that makes this work accessible and interesting to listeners and players. Dvořák achieves here a happy middle ground between the sometimes sprawling sonata-allegro forms of earlier domestic works, which repeat long lyrical melodies and melodic sequences almost ad infinitum, and the tightly wound, motivically driven sonata movements of post-Beethovenian "serious" quartets, which present themes and their development with such brevity that the work can feel like a whirlwind. The topical associations that Dvořák draws upon in these movements reinforce the sense of community that lies at the heart of the domestic style and at the heart of the chamber music experience.

The "American" quartet relies on short melodies and direct movement from one theme to the next to create its easygoing atmosphere. The lengthy developmental and transitional procedures more common in his "serious" public works such as opp. 16 and 61 are notably absent here, resulting in an almost medley-like arrangement of themes in diverse keys. The opening sonata form movement takes up only 178 measures, compared to the 327-measure and 379-measure openings of op. 61 (the C-major quartet composed for Hellmesberger in Vienna) and op. 16 (Dvořák's first published quartet). Tellingly, the "rustic" E♭-major quartet Dvořák composed for Becker comes closest to this work's brevity, at just 206 measures. The exposition of the "American" quartet movement moves swiftly from the viola's F-major theme to arrive at E major in m. 26 in preparation for the secondary theme. Although the secondary key is the somewhat unusual mediant (A major), the drone-filled transitional passage in E major prepares it so clearly that the modulation comes as no surprise. Dvořák's pentatonic secondary theme (mm. 44–51) gives way to a closing gesture based on the primary theme's head motive, which leads smoothly back to the primary theme at the repeat of the exposition or to the development. The entire process, trimmed down to the bare necessities of the form with appealing eight-measure melodies and regular, predictable harmonic progressions, takes place in just sixty-three measures. The exposition's leisurely folkloric style and stable, even static harmonic foundation evoke a collegial gathering of friends, mirroring or documenting Dvořák's interactions with amateur musicians in Spillville and, perhaps, New York.

This quartet is described as a technically accessible one, with commentators often citing the fact that Dvořák, a violist, could play the first violin part in casual performances of it. That accessibility is evident in the short development section, where the three accompanying parts are active, even busy, but never strenuous, and the repeated figurations and ostinatos add to the exciting atmosphere without requiring sustained attention to fine details. Like the domestic works of the first half of the century, these parts invite or encourage players and listeners to attend to the main theme being played by another ensemble member and then to join in when the theme is repeated. Its first half, for example, treats individual components of the primary theme and moves to D major via a *fortissimo* section in C♯ major. As in the opening, the viola and first violin take turns exploring motives from the main theme, here accompanied by reiterated tonic and dominant chords, often in syncopated rhythms and double-stopped to increase the volume and intensity of the developmental passagework.

Hartmut Schick describes the brief fugato passage that appears in m. 96 as "small, pointedly simple," and "scantily motivated" because in his analysis, it does not answer a formal or thematic need required by musical logic.[30] However, if we interpret this brief fugato as a culmination of the active exchanges among instruments that precede it, the passage serves a clear purpose. Here at the fulcrum of the movement—the balancing point between the exposition and the recapitulation—Dvořák emphasizes an almost provincial "learnedness" (this is not, after all, a fully worked-out fugue) and the civil cooperation of the ensemble members in polite, orderly dialogue that has emerged from the less structured but collegial interactions of the earlier sections.

The leisurely repetition and carefully balanced ensemble interactions continue in the inner movements of op. 96. The second movement, a dumka-like slow movement in D minor, is filled with antecedent and consequent phrases played by two ensemble members in dialogue. For instance, the first violin introduces the eight-measure primary theme over rocking syncopated accompaniments in the inner voices (mm. 3–10). The theme contains several ornamental gestures that invite a quasi-improvised, rhythmically free interpretation by the player. In m. 11, the cello repeats this melody exactly (it is notated in the same clef and register as the violin part; the player is expected to play the theme an octave lower than written) while the violin takes up the syncopated accompaniment. These exchanges become shorter and more intense as the movement goes on, and three of the four voices have an opportunity to participate in the communal lament. (Dvořák's instrument, the viola, always accompanies in this movement, despite its highlighted role in the previous movement as the first and main presenter of the primary theme.)

In the movement's B section (mm. 31–81), parallel motion in a quasi-improvisational style leads to folk-like heterophonic textures when two instruments—usually the first violin and cello—collaborate to present a melody. For example, in mm. 35–40 (see example 7.9), the outer voices (together in the top staff of the example) begin in straightforward parallel sixths, but they diverge in mm. 36–37 as the second beat in each bar receives some ornamentation. At m. 38, they return to parallel motion in sixths and thirds, but each voice soon adds its own ornamentations, as one might expect in an improvised duet. The placement of this impassioned duet in the highest ranges of the two instruments adds to its emotional immediacy, as do the leaps in the melodic line, which encourage ornamental slides in performance. These personal interactions among the players

EXAMPLE 7.9 Dvořák, String Quartet in F Major, op. 96, movt. 2, mm. 35–42 (heterophonic textures, parallel motion between violin 1 and cello).

certainly contribute to the movement's "exotic" Czech style, and some listeners may hear them as reminiscent of African American spirituals when listening for "American" signifiers. These two cultural points of reference share the musical features of lament singing practiced worldwide, and both traditions are rooted in the communal sharing of grief or hardship. As Dvořák enjoyed the opportunity to feel as though he belonged to the tight-knit Czech American community in Iowa, he celebrated not just the features that made it different from the central tradition of Austro-German and European musical conventions but also the features that transcended those differences and that make for satisfying chamber music performance experiences.

The third movement's scherzo likewise emphasizes communal dialogue, and it does so in more obvious ways by passing thematic material around the ensemble equitably and predictably, giving all the members a chance to play the important themes. The scherzo contains two trio sections, resulting in a binary AB A'B' structure that lends itself to reinterpretations of familiar melodies. The varied return of the A material, for instance, allows the viola to pair with the cello in the main theme, which was originally presented by the second violin and cello (compare mm. 1–8 with mm. 97–104). The two trio sections, though, provide the greatest opportunity for shuffling instrument pairs. Trio 1 (mm. 49–96) introduces a new theme in F minor with an 8 + 8 + 8 phrase structure. The first violin's countermelody moves into the viola in m. 73 when the theme is repeated; each eight-measure component of the theme's first presentation is repeated with a new voicing so that each ensemble member takes a turn with the melody or countermelody.

Dvořák's constant shifting of orchestration in these trios provides an opportunity for each of the players to take on a starring role in the movement, however briefly. It also adds interest for listeners, as the changing textures and timbres give the scherzo a vibrant, lively quality despite the repetition of the same simple eight-measure phrase twelve times over the course of the movement. Thus, while aspects of the compositional style hark back to the domestic entertainment music of the earlier nineteenth century represented by Onslow, Spohr, and portions of Schubert's string chamber music, those same elements in the new context of the concert hall create a laid-back concert style for listeners who may never have played an instrument before. Here as elsewhere, we see Dvořák's attention to the differing needs of multiple audiences within the same work.

The rondo finale evokes pioneer communities and the friendly dialogue idealized in the rough-hewn counterpoint of the first movement within the framework of an accessible domestic quartet. Here the communal experience is signified by topical references rather than instrumentation. The three main thematic sections (A, B, and C) of the seven-part rondo feature music related to lively dancing, to singing, and to worshiping—all activities that accentuate idealized portrayals of life in a tight-knit community such as Spillville or another small town or neighborhood with a shared group identity. The work opens with a thirty-two-measure introduction, followed by the A theme in F major (see example 7.10). After the theme's repetition (mm. 51–68), the first violin immediately begins the B theme in A♭ major.[31] The first violin's lyrical line, marked *dolce*, floats above the syncopated accompanying ostinatos in the inner voices, while the cello's pizzicato accompaniment gives the whole passage the flavor of a dance band's lively rendition of a favorite folksong (example 7.11).

EXAMPLE 7.10 Dvořák, String Quartet in F Major, op. 96, movt. 4, mm. 33–48 (rondo's A theme).

EXAMPLE 7.11 Dvořák, String Quartet in F Major, op. 96, movt. 4, mm. 69–87 (rondo's B theme).

The C theme that enters in m. 155 in D♭ evokes a hymn-like or chorale-like texture with four-measure phrases in half-notes (see example 7.12). The *pianissimo* marking and sudden absence of rhythmic ostinatos gives this passage a reverent quality. The hymn is interrupted by the dance tune in mm. 171–78 but returns in a more forcefully religious guise in mm. 179–98. In A minor here, the tune appears in four-part homophony instead of with its earlier imitative entrances. The repetition of the theme by the cello in mm. 199–214 introduces ornamentation in the first violin's accompaniment that ushers in the characteristic dotted rhythm of the A section's ostinato.

As he did in the first movement, here Dvořák uses the central episode of the finale's form, the extended C section, to present a combination of elements that encapsulate the community identity of Spillville and its citizens and perhaps of idealized portrayals of pioneer or provincial towns like it that serve as important

EXAMPLE 7.12 Dvořák, String Quartet in F Major, op. 96, movt. 4, mm. 155–96 (rondo's C theme).

touchstones for national identities among both American and European cultures. The rustic dance style of the A section embodies a general liveliness and celebratory atmosphere associated with, for instance, barn raisings and harvest festivals. It also depicts here the specifically Czech identity of the gatherings in Spillville and Bohemian settlements like it throughout the Midwest or in smaller towns and cities throughout the mother country in Europe, reminding listeners and performers of the personal and cultural connections between the New and Old Worlds. For Dvořák personally, the opportunity to play the organ in Spillville's community church allowed him to return to the roots of his musical training and early professional experiences at the Prague Organ School.[32]

Whether it expresses an image of "American" culture, Czech culture, or simply domestic entertainment, Dvořák's op. 96 quartet reminds listeners and performers that the essence of a community's identity rests in its members' sociable meetings and interactions with each other, and the quartet itself, with its accessible domestic style, offers an opportunity to have those interactions in a musical gathering, whether as a listener or as a performer. By manipulating the domestic style that had long been integral to chamber music composition, Dvořák conveys the importance of casual recreational music making for a community's well-being.

* * *

Much more than an innocent, unassuming peasant who wrote crowd-pleasing folkish works, Dvořák was a consummate professional who operated within a dizzying array of musical niches during his lifetime. In terms of geographical locales, economic and social resources, and linguistic or musical sophistication, Dvořák's "serious" works, his compositions for the string quartet in particular, embrace an astounding diversity of audiences. Although it would be easy to equate Dvořák's manipulations of musical style as manifestations of greed or a pragmatic need to please musicians and audiences who could offer him pay or future work, that would be the least charitable and most arrogant assessment of the composer's activities. Dvořák did not simply compose music to order in exchange for money; instead, he paid close attention to the needs of his fellow musicians and music lovers, as many of the composers considered in this book did. By doing so, Dvořák was able to carefully craft music that would communicate with a particular audience in a language that they would understand. Dvořák and his contemporaries operating at the end of the period had a more difficult job of this than many of their artistic forebears, as the needs of the musical public were shifting rapidly in response to political, economic, and social pressures. In the course of his lifetime, Dvořák engaged each of the audiences considered here in some way: he addressed some works to the professional musical elite (op. 16 in A minor), some to concert hall listeners in a "semiprivate" mode (op. 51 in

E♭ major), and some to more rigorous and high-profile concert attendees (op. 61 in C major). He resituated the domestic style in such a way that it could address concert hall listeners of a more casual type (op. 96 in F major). He even created arrangements for string quartet of some of his less accessible works (the string quartet arrangements of his song cycle *The Cypresses*, which I did not discuss here). Thus, at the end of the century, Dvořák summed up the dominant trends of the string chamber music of his generation.

APPENDIX 1

J. Strunz, string quartet transcription of no. 18, "Prière" (Prayer), from Meyerbeer's *Robert le Diable*

Robert le Diable (arrangement for string quartet)

18. Prière

Meyerbeer

Jacques Strunz

B
Choral response
Priest's intonation
très marqué
Vln. I
Vln. II
Vla.
Vc.
(transition to B flat Major)
cresc.
pp
ff
p

C
Chorale tune in B flat
Vln. I
Vln. II
Vla.
Vc.
très doux
pp
Chorale tune in F (tonic)
Priest's intonation
très marqué
ff
p
dim.

"Coda"
Vln. I
Vln. II
Vla.
Vc.
pp
dim.
ppp
tremolo
ff
perdendosi

APPENDIX 2

C. W. Henning, string quartet transcription of no. 8, "Leise, leise, fromme Weise" (Gently, gently, pious words), from Weber's *Der Freischütz*

Der Freischütz (arrangement for string quartet)

No. 8, "Leise, leise, fromme Weise"

C. M. von Weber
C. W. Henning

21
30
Recit.
Recit.
Recit.
Recit.
38
Adagio
pp
pp
pp
pp
47

58
pp
65
68
71

Section 3: Transition

Section 4: Fast Aria
Vivace con fuoco.
Orch. Violins
cresc.
Agathe

Orch. Violin
Agathe
Flutes
Agathe
p

Winds
Agathe

182
cresc.
mf
mf
190
cresc.
ff
f
ff
f
ff
ff
196

APPENDIX 3

M. Kässmayer, string quartet arrangement of "Mein Herz ist im Hochland" (My heart is in the Highlands) from *Deutsche Lieder*, op. 14, no. 4

Mein Herz ist im Hochland (Op. 14, no. 4)

M. Kässmayer

3. Tune in Cello

4. Tune in Violin 2

54
Vln. I
Vln. II
Vla.
Vc.
cresc.
p
61
rit.
a tempo
pp
5. "Finale"
flute-like effects via harmonics
69
Flagolet.
Più lento
sul ponticello

6. "Finale" cont'd with pizzicato variation

NOTES

Introduction. String Chamber Music and Its Audiences in the Nineteenth Century

1. For information and reproductions of paintings, see Davidson, *The World of Mary Ellen Best.*

2. Dahlhaus, *Nineteenth-Century Music*, 78, emphasis added. Dahlhaus attributes the break in development to the rise of the public chamber music concert and a sort of pandemic Beethoven anxiety, noting that, "however supreme Beethoven's symphonies and string quartets may have reigned in the concert repertoire, the later development of these eminently Beethovenian genres was, from the standpoint of composition, checkered and disjoint" (ibid., 78).

3. The aims of this project are much indebted to the philosophy put forth by Locke in "Nineteenth-Century Music."

4. For examples of this bifurcation of the nineteenth century according to musical style developments, on the one hand, and social ones, on the other, see Dahlhaus, *Nineteenth-Century Music*; and Plantinga, *Romantic Music*. Resources such as Samson's *Cambridge History of Nineteenth-Century Music* demonstrate a similar bipartite approach by including chapters on specific composers or genres (often treated as autonomous works) separate from chapters considering musical practices of the period. James Parakilas's work on the piano and its history, most notably in *Piano Roles*, has been crucial in reorienting nineteenth-century music scholarship toward the social life of music in this period.

5. Assessing the winner of a string quartet competition sponsored by the Mannheim Musikverein in 1842, Schumann noted, "The idea of offering a prize for a quartet was a good one. For one thing, because the category is such a noble one, a high degree of cultivation among the contestants is presupposed; furthermore, the quartet has come to a standstill. Who does not know the quartets of Haydn, Mozart, and Beethoven, and who would wish to say anything against them? . . . [B]ut it is no good sign that the later generation, after all this time, has not been able to produce anything comparable. Onslow alone met with success, and later Mendelssohn, whose aristocratic-poetic nature is particularly amenable to this genre" (*Neue Zeitschrift für Musik* 16 [1842]: 142–43, as quoted in Plantinga, *Schumann as Critic*, 187). I will discuss Schumann's musical response to this situation in the form of his three string quartets, op. 41 (composed and published in the same year as this review), in chapter 4.

6. Christina Bashford has worked extensively with the "ephemera" produced by concert life in the nineteenth century. See "Writing (British) Concert History" and "Historiography and Invisible Musics."

7. Anderson, *Imagined Communities*. For application to nineteenth-century musical life, see Celenza, "Imagined Communities Made Real."

8. Scott, *Sounds of the Metropolis.*

9. The classic text on the formation and impact of the public sphere remains Jürgen Habermas, *Strukturwandel der Öffentlichkeit* (1962), translated as *The Structural Transformation of the Public Sphere.*

10. An early example that demonstrates the difficulty of defining who does and does not belong to the middle classes is Weber's "The Muddle of the Middle Classes." Weber expanded his discussion of the middle classes in his subsequent book, *Music and the Middle Classes*; the revised 2003 edition published by Ashgate includes an extensive new preface summarizing developments in the field between 1980 and 2000. In the 1990s, social scientists and cultural historians began to revise their collective understanding of the middle classes, which had focused mainly on the working class or laborers through the 1980s. Following the fall of the Berlin Wall in 1989, research on the bourgeoisie expanded considerably. Germanist Jonathan Sperber noted at the time that "the workers are out; the Bürger are in" ("Burger, Bürgertum, Bürgerlichkeit, Bürgerliche Gesellschaft," 271). Scholars of French, Italian, Russian, and other European societies have also embraced the bourgeoisie in the past twenty years. See Pilbeam, *The Middle Classes*; Kocka and Mitchell, *Bourgeois Society*; and Kaelble, *The European Way.*

11. German-language scholarship divides the middle-class professions into two categories: the *Wirtschaftsbürgertum*, or economic middle class, and the *Bildungsbürgertum*, or educational and service-oriented middle class. The word *Bürgertum* does not translate simply as "middle class" in the English sense but connotes citizenship and responsibility, privilege associated with achievement, and cultural sophistication. This concept of *Bürgertum* is important for understanding artistic culture and cultural values in the German states and in central European Jewish culture.

12. See Roussellier, "Liberalism."

13. Kaelble, *European Way*, 17.

14. See Kocka, "The European Pattern"; and Blackbourn and Eley, *The Peculiarities of German History.* On music and the cultivated bourgeoisie, see Gramit, *Cultivating Music.*

15. Hence, most famously, Karl Marx's critique of the bourgeoisie in works such as *Capital* (1867) and *The Communist Manifesto* (with Friedrich Engels, 1848).

16. On the rise of leisure and entertainment in early nineteenth-century Germany, see Wurst, *Fabricating Pleasure*, esp. chap. 2, "The Differentiation of the Middle Class," 23–40. On men's leisure time in nineteenth-century France, see Harrison, *The Bourgeois Citizen.* An entertaining and insightful portrait of a single gentleman collector and amateur scientist at this time is Ewing, *The Lost World of James Smithson.*

17. This period also saw the recognition and celebration of childhood as a separate stage of human development between infancy and adulthood. See also the development of the *Bildungsroman* as explored by Moretti, *The Way of the World.*

18. For an overview, see Wolff, "The Culture of Separate Spheres." The *Journal of Women's History* published an issue devoted to this question in the spring of 2003 that included Davidoff, "Gender and the 'Great Divide.'" Davidoff and Catherine Hall coauthored *Family Fortunes*; as Davidoff notes in the 2003 *JWH* essay, this book provided one of the focuses for the critique of separate spheres that followed. For more information and discussion of the critique, see the introduction to Harrison, *The Bourgeois Citizen.* Information on this phenomenon in German lands is less readily available.

19. See Hoffmann, "Civility."

20. Harrison also discusses music-centered *cercles* and associations; see *The Bourgeois Citizen*, 100–106.

21. Wilma Neruda (1839–1911), also known as Lady Hallé, stands out in the history of female professional musicians. She made her London debut as a violinist in 1849, studied with Leopold Jansa in Vienna, and later had a career as a touring soloist before marrying. She performed in many public chamber concerts, famously leading string quartets in the Monday Popular Concerts in London in 1872.

22. Bashford, "Historiography and Invisible Musics."

23. Leppert, *Music and Image*, see esp. chap. 6, "The Male at Music," 107–46.

24. Bashford, "Historiography and Invisible Musics." See especially the appendix (pp. 335–46), which includes sixty-six quotations from primary sources related to amateur chamber music performances. Further evidence of semiprivate music making comes from the notebooks of Liverpool musician Henry Rensburg, who hosted chamber music soirées in his home from at least 1880 to 1927. See Bell, "Chamber Music in the Home."

25. Harrison, *The Bourgeois Citizen*, 104.

26. David Gramit has explored the various ways in which music was discussed in the letters between university student Adolph Müller in Halle and his family and friends at home in Bremen during the first decade of the nineteenth century ("Everyday Extraordinary").

27. November, "Theater Piece and Cabinetstück."

28. Quoted from Ellis, *Richard Wagner's Prose Works*, 86. Later Wagner concludes that instrumental music "has issued from the heart of German family-life; that it is an art which can neither be understood nor estimated by the mass of a crowded audience, but solely by the home-like circle of the few" (ibid., 92). See also discussion by Ruth Solie in *Music in Other Words*, esp. chap. 4, "Biedermeier Domesticity and the Schubert Circle."

29. Another binary set of descriptors pertinent to the present study and noted by Solie is Biedermeier/Romantic. See also Hunter, "Haydn's London Piano Trios."

30. Benedict Anderson's discussion in *Imagined Communities* of nationalism's reliance on print media and other forms of mass communication in the nineteenth and twentieth centuries, though controversial in some ways, forms an excellent launching pad for the discussion of printed material and its role in cultural life. Franco Moretti has also explored the role of the printed word (and other visual media) in nineteenth-century, middle-class culture; see his *The Way of the World* and *Graphs, Maps, Trees*. In *The Bourgeois*, Moretti deals specifically with several of the ideas explored in this study as they impact the novel.

31. See Celenza, "Imagined Communities Made Real."

32. Fauquet, *Les sociétés de musique*; and Cooper, *The Rise of Instrumental Music*.

33. See Weber, *The Great Transformation of Musical Taste*, esp. chap. 4, "The Rise of the Chamber Music Concert."

34. Levy, "Thomas Massa Alsager, Esq."; Bashford, *The Pursuit of High Culture*; and Potter, "From Chamber to Concert Hall." Documentation of chamber music concerts in nineteenth-century Vienna or other German-speaking lands is less centralized. William Weber discusses Viennese chamber concerts in his *Music and the Middle Classes*, and Viennese examples appear in Tully Potter's work, but no full-length study similar to those of Cooper and Fauquet on Paris or that of Bashford on London exists on German cities.

Chapter 1. Publishing Chamber Music: Archival Evidence for Chamber Music Production and Consumption

1. On the history of the miniature score, see Hopkinson, "The Earliest Miniature Scores"; Benton, "Pleyel's *Bibliothèque Musicale*"; and Lenneberg, "Revising the History of the Miniature Score." We will return to George Onslow in chapter 3.

2. Elvers and Hopkinson, "A Survey of the Music Catalogues of Whistling and Hofmeister."

3. In 2004 a research team based at Royal Holloway of the University of London began an international cooperative project (funded by the United Kingdom's Arts and Humanities Research Council) dedicated to creating a searchable database of the complete run of Hofmeister-Whistling catalogs; it can now be accessed free of charge from anywhere in the world at http://www.hofmeister.rhul.ac.uk/2008/index.html.

4. Lawford-Hinrichsen, *Music Publishing and Patronage, C. F. Peters.*

5. These three firms' complete correspondence records are also preserved in their respective archives. This enormous collection of information presents many avenues for future research. The firms regularly exchanged letters with music sellers and bookstores, with composers and performers, and with agents for the same.

6. For a discussion of alternate approaches to the piano quintet and its role in nineteenth-century musical life, see Sumner Lott, "Negotiation Tactics in Louise Farrenc's Piano Quintets, opp. 30 and 31."

7. Stapleton, "Veit, Václav."

8. Wurst, *Fabricating Pleasure*, 96.

9. Le Guin, *Boccherini's Body.*

10. On technical advances in music distribution, see Lenneberg *On the Publishing and Dissemination of Music, 1500–1850*; and Devriès-Lésure, "Technological Aspects." On German publishing in the first third of the nineteenth century, see Beer, *Musik zwischen Komponist, Verlag und Publikum.*

11. This work is one of seven piano trios by Marschner (1795–1861), who remains better known today for his fantastic operas, such as *Der Vampyre* (1827) and *Hans Heiling* (1833). He also composed two piano quartets and three duos for violin and piano, as well as a set of scherzos for piano trio and a set of impromptus for violin and piano.

12. This entry is unusually detailed; many of the chamber music entries in the *Calculationsbuch* show no credits, despite the logical conclusion that reprints indicated sales. The discrepancy in bookkeeping may reflect simple sloppiness, or it may have been due to differences in the contracts between more and less savvy composers; if a composer insisted on receiving royalties from later reprints or a percentage of profits, it follows that the press would go to a greater effort to document the reprints and the company's monetary results. If the composer received a flat fee for the work, the publisher might have no incentive to document the reprintings.

13. The presence of circulating libraries might explain the typically small print-run sizes for works by, for instance, Robert Schumann. See Lenneburg, "Early Circulating Libraries." On circulating libraries in Britain, see King, "Music Circulating Libraries in Britain."

14. Widmaier, *Der deutsche Musikalienleihhandel.*

15. Ibid., 154.

16. Lithography is a chemical printing process developed in the 1790s and refined for commercial use in the 1830s. The printer or engraver draws the image onto a smooth stone or metal plate with a waxy crayon and then applies a layer of gum arabic to create hydrophobic (water-repellent) and hydrophilic (water-loving) regions. The oily ink adheres only to the hydrophobic areas, and the hydrophilic areas remain clean, repelling the ink and ensuring crisp, clean prints. This process also allowed color printing and was used to produce posters, book illustrations, maps, playing cards and novelty items, and other paper ephemera.

17. On *Bildung* and its importance in German middle-class culture, see vol. 3, *1800–1870: From the Reorganization of Germany to the Foundation of the German Empire* (1987) and vol. 4, *1870–1918: From the Foundation of the Empire to the End of the First World War* (1991), of Jeismann and Lundgreen, *Handbuch der deutschen Bildungsgeschichte*. For a study of the topic in English, see Bruford, *The German Tradition of Self-Cultivation*.

18. Previous studies of transcriptions and arrangements have tended to focus on the piano because it played a central role in domestic music and in the reception of works for larger forces. See Christensen, "Four-Hand Piano Transcription and Geographies of Nineteenth-Century Musical Reception" and "Public Music in Private Spaces." See also Parakilas, "The Power of Domestication in the Lives of Musical Canons." On arrangements for chamber ensemble, see Jokiharju, "Reflections of Instrumental Chamber-Music Making in Sheet Music Related to the Gluck-Calzabigi Operatic 'Reform.'"

19. The *Auflagebücher* for Schlesinger, now housed in Frankfurt am Main at the headquarters of the Robert Lienau Verlag, include information about print runs for some early editions only. They indicate plate numbers, from which publication dates can be derived, and the year in which the plates were melted down for reuse. Thus, we have information about what was published but not what was reprinted.

20. In the last decade of the nineteenth century, Lienau published the works of Eduard Franck (1817–93) after the composer's death—presumably at the request of his son Richard, also a composer. This collection included several chamber pieces, and these works account for five of the twenty-one original works the firm printed after 1871.

21. Kässmayer also composed original string quartets and quintets. His first works in these genres were published in Vienna by Glöggl and by Spina and in Berlin by Bote und Bock. He appears to have signed on with Lienau-Schlesinger in 1870 for the folk song arrangements, and Lienau published his later quartets and other original works in addition to more novelty-like works, such as his *Musical Miscellanies*, a work that combines themes from multiple preexisting works to humorous effect in a series of short movements.

22. Gelbart, *The Invention of "Folk Music and "Art Music."*

Chapter 2. "Domesticating" the Foreign in Arrangements of Operas, Folk Songs, and Other Works for Chamber Ensembles

1. Jonathan Kregor has shown that Liszt's transcriptions and arrangements—which he created throughout his long career, not just during his years as a touring virtuoso—served a variety of purposes and played a significant role in his development as a composer. See Kregor, *Liszt as Transcriber*.

2. Some of the arrangements discussed here, as well as those distributed by other firms, are also available today in online databases such as the Petrucci Music Library (better known as the International Music Score Library Project, or IMSLP, available at www.imslp.org) and the Classical String Quartet digital archive hosted by Duke University (http://library.duke.edu/digitalcollections/quartets/).

3. This work was also published in a string quartet arrangement by the Viennese firm Chemische Druckerei. It excerpts the same numbers as Starke's arrangement and may in fact be a pirated edition.

4. *Jean de Paris* treats a medieval courtly love scenario in which the dauphin, who is betrothed to a princess from the countryside, disguises himself as a bourgeois gentleman

and offers his services as escort to his bride-to-be on her voyage to court; this allows him to get to know her before the wedding and tests her virtue when she falls in love with "Jean" during the journey.

5. On the history of the opera and a discussion of the work and its aesthetic, see Brzoska, "Meyerbeer: *Robert le Diable* and *Les Huguenots*."

6. Some of the omissions may in fact represent changes made in the Berlin version of the opera. Further research utilizing archival evidence from the Berlin performances would show how this version reflects German tastes and to what extent they differed from French ones.

7. Parakilas, "The Power of Domestication in the Lives of Musical Canons."

8. Marie Taglioni (1804–84) was taught by her father, who also created the ballet *La sylphide* (1832) to showcase her dancing *en pointe*. Taglioni scandalized Paris when she began to habitually shorten her costume skirts in order to display her footwork for audiences. On Meyerbeer's use of ballet and Taglioni's influence in particular, see Jürgenson, "The 'Ballet of the Nuns' from *Robert le Diable* and Its Revival."

9. *La juive* takes place in Konstanz, a German town on the border with Switzerland, during the 1454 Council of Constance, which ended the Great Schism and restored order to the Catholic Church. This event and the contemporaneous defeat of the religious reformers the Hussites form the backdrop to the two central stories: (1) forbidden love between the Jewess, Rachel, and the (married) Christian prince, Leopold, disguised as a commoner named Samuel; and (2) the violent reunion of Rachel's adoptive father, Eleazar, and his archenemy, Cardinal Brogni, who killed Eleazar's sons many years earlier. At the end of the opera, Rachel is revealed to be the long-lost daughter of Brogni. He thought she had died at the hands of brigands while he was in Rome burning heretics (including Eleazar's family). The middle of the opera concerns the revelation that "Samuel" is Christian, to which Rachel responds that she will give up everything to be with him; then that he is Leopold, at which point Rachel denounces him publicly, and they are both condemned to die.

10. French composers used Italianate forms borrowed from conventions in *opera seria* and *bel canto* traditions. See Huebner, "Italianate Duets in Meyerbeer's Grand Operas."

11. Beginning in the late 1870s, the André firm, based in Offenbach am Main, published a similar collection for string quartet titled *Das Liebhaberquartett: Eine Sammlung der beliebtesten Opern in Form von Potpourris leicht bearbeitet für 2 Violinen, Alt[o], & Violoncell[o] von Georg Banger* (The amateur quartet: A collection of the most beloved operas in the form of potpourris easily worked out [implying light technical demands] for string quartet by Georg Banger). The title page for nos. 1–17 in the set lists a variety of older and newer works for the stage by French and German composers.

12. The Litolff collection includes Bellini's *Norma* and *Somnambule*, Donizetti's *L'elisir d'amore*, Méhul's *Joseph*, and Rossini's *Barbier de Séville* in addition to works by Weber and Mozart.

13. Hopfe, about whom further information is not available, also published a collection of programmatic works titled *Leichte Trios für Pianoforte, Violine, und Violoncello* with the Mahlo firm in Berlin. At least three works were published: *Frühlingssehnsucht*, *Türkischer Marsch*, and *Der Carneval von Venedig*.

14. Renaud de Vilbac and Augustin Lefort, *Les trios dramatiques pour piano, violon (ou flûte), et violoncelle, sur les opéras célèbres*, 2 vols. (Braunschweig: H. Litolff, 1870). Volume 2 is available online through the Sibley Music Library's score digitization project, http://imslp.org/wiki/Trios_dramatiques_(Vilbac,_Renaud_de), accessed 25 September

2013. Volume 2 includes works by Mozart (*Die Zauberflöte* and *Le nozze di Figaro*), Rossini (*Il barbiere di Siviglia*), and Weber (*Der Freischütz* and *Oberon*).

15. If we adopt a gender-coded interpretation of sonata form, as some commentators in the late nineteenth and twentieth centuries did, it may be worth noting that Hopfe places Ottavio's aria tune in the traditional "masculine theme" role and introduces the material associated with Anna in the subordinate "feminine theme" position. Ottavio's aria text "Go and console my dearest treasure / and attempt to dry her tears" characterizes his resolve to fulfill his duty as fiancé, despite his own misgivings.

16. Wilhelmj also made a string quartet version of Schubert's Introduction, Theme, and Variations for flute and piano, which Schubert based on his song "Trockne Blumen" from *Die schöne Müllerin*.

17. On the intersections of folk music, nationalism, and emerging conceptions of "art" music, see Gramit, *Cultivating Music*, esp. chapter 3, "The Dilemma of the Popular"; and Gelbart, *The Invention of "Folk Music" and "Art Music."*

18. See Leon Botstein's widely cited article charting a decline in literacy throughout the nineteenth century, "Listening through Reading."

19. Kässmayer's stock in trade was his musical humor, which he was not afraid to use on himself. See his 1872 work for string quartet with orchestra titled *Musikalische Mesalliancen* (Musical misalliances); it combines themes from the high learned tradition with those of a lighter nature. The four movements are "Beethoven—Strauss," "Haydn—Offenbach," "Schubert—Kässmayer," and "Bach—O du lieber Augustin."

20. Music publisher Silvertrust Editions released new editions of these collections in 2013. See http://www.editionsilvertrust.com/kassmayer-complete.htm, accessed 21 November 2014.

21. Robert Burns (1759–96) contributed over 350 songs in Scots and Scots-inflected English to musical collections by James Johnson and George Thomson in addition to publishing other poems independently. He borrowed heavily from the Scottish folk or traditional repertory for his songs and lyrics.

22. Kässmayer does not use the Scottish tune "Failte na miosg" as indicated in James Johnson's *Scots Musical Museum*, vol. 3, in which Burns's lyric was published in 1790.

23. Gelbart traces the influence of Scottish folk song and investigations of it in *Invention of "Folk Music."* Sarah Clemmens Waltz explored the topic of the Scottish Highlands as inspiration for German Romantic music in her dissertation and subsequent articles. See also Daverio, "Schumann's Ossianic Manner." On Herder's conception of folk song and his study of Ossian, see Wienker-Piepho, "Herder and the Development of His Volkslied Concept."

24. Parakilas, "The Power of Domestication," 7.

Chapter 3. Music for Men of Leisure: An Examination of the Domestic String Style

1. Onslow's father, Edward (son of the 1st Earl of Onslow), left his native England in 1781 in the wake of some sort of homosexual scandal; he married a rich Frenchwoman and lived the rest of his life in peace outside of Paris. George Onslow, therefore, did not inherit a noble title, but the extent of his wealth places him at the upper echelon of the "middle class" of his day.

2. For Onslow's biography, see Jam, *George Onslow*. Viviane Niaux, in *George Onslow*, delves more deeply into matters of musical style. For analysis of the chamber music, see Nobach, *Untersuchungen zu George Onslows Kammermusik*.

3. For Kuhlau's biography, the only available English source is Mehring, *Friedrich Kuhlau in the Mirror of His Flute Works*. Carl Thrane's 1886 biography (in German), titled *Friedrich Kuhlau*, was reissued in 1979 by Frits Knuf in the Netherlands.

4. See Bohlman, "On the Unremarkable in Music." See also Gramit, "Unremarkable Musical Lives."

5. Mehring, *Friedrich Kuhlau*, 51–55.

6. I thank Jennifer Ronyak for sharing information regarding a manuscript copy of Schumann's personal library catalog. A number of more widely read critics also reviewed Onslow's music favorably in journals such as the *Allgemeine musikalische Zeitung*, the *Allgemeine Wiener Musikzeitung*, and the *Revue et gazette musicale*.

7. See Brown, *Louis Spohr*.

8. Spohr, *Louis Spohr's Autobiography*, 150.

9. Ibid., 151.

10. Ibid., 186.

11. "Wenn ich nun einmahl wieder nach Leipzig komme, so bringe ich Ihnen meine ersten 3 Quartets für Streichinstrumente mit, welche wir dann auf Ihrer hübschen Landstelle probiren können" (Kuhlau to C. F. Peters [C. G. S. Böhme], 4 August 1829, in Busk, *Kuhlau Breve*, 137). All translations from this source are mine.

12. Gorm Busk posits that the op. 122 quartet belongs to this group of works, but I believe that Kuhlau was referring to as-yet unwritten works. Op. 122 clearly belongs to the later set of quartets commissioned from Kuhlau by a Copenhagen businessman.

13. "Dann muss ich aber eine Composition grösserer Art schreiben, worüber mir wohl der ganze nächste Winter vergehen wird, nämlich: ein hiesiger reicher Kaufmann u. grosser Musikfreund, hat mich aufgefordert für ihn 6 Quartetten für Bogeninstrumente zu componiren. Er honorirt mir diese Arbeit sehr generös, und will die Herausgabe selbst besorgen. Da ich nun schon lange wünschte mich auch in dieser Gattung von Composition zu versuchen, so habe ich diesen Auftrag mit Vergnügen angenommen. So bald ich dieses Werk vollendet habe, werde ich Ihnen schreiben wie es mir gelungen ist, und dann wieder fleissig für Sie . . . componiren" (Kuhlau to Aristide Farrenc, 18 July 1831, no. 164, in Busk, *Kuhlau Breve*, 176).

14. Busk suggests that the patron was Christian Waagepetersen (1787–1840), whom he describes as a wine merchant (*Vinhandler*) and *Hofagent*. He gives no indication of musical abilities or other credentials.

15. Katrin Bartels argues in *Das Streichquintett im 19. Jahrhundert* that Onslow developed the quintet into a recognizable genre with its own style.

16. Czerny, *School of Practical Composition*, 2:6, emphasis mine.

17. Ibid., 17.

18. See Levy, "The Quatuor Concertant in Paris in the Latter Half of the Eighteenth Century"; and Hickman, "The Flowering of the Viennese String Quartet in the Late Eighteenth Century."

19. For more information on late eighteenth-century quartet styles, see Parker, *The String Quartet, 1750–1797*.

20. For an analysis of Spohr's sextet and connections between it and Brahms's two string sextets, see Sumner Lott, "Domesticity in Brahms's String Sextets."

21. See Bartels, *Das Streichquintett*.

22. Although she mentions briefly the differences between Onslow's quartets and quintets, Christiana Nobach does not comment on the social setting of domestic chamber

music. She treats the quartets and quintets as a homogeneous group (*Untersuchungen zu George Onslows Kammermusik*, 83–85).

23. The Onslow quintet, op. 39, is available online in the Sibley Music Library's digital scores repository at http://hdl.handle.net/1802/5869.

24. Leonard G. Ratner introduced the analytical tool he called "topical analysis" in his *Classic Music*. Others have extended his list of topics and styles significantly. See, for example, Allanbrook, *Rhythmic Gesture in Mozart*; Agawu, *Playing with Signs*; Bellman, *The* Style hongrois *in the Music of Western Europe* and "Aus alten Märchen"; Dickensheets, "Nineteenth-Century Topical Analysis" and *The Nineteenth-Century Sonata Cycle as Novel*; and Monelle, *The Musical Topic*.

25. Cellists read this clef an octave below the written pitch. This nineteenth-century usage may be to avoid the tenor clef, which cellists at that time may not have been comfortable reading at sight; the clef resembles a choral tenor clef, often used for the same reason.

26. "The Bullet" quintet is discussed in detail in chapter 5 as an example of autobiographical programmatic chamber music.

27. For further discussion of ways in which composers might "script" social interactions in piano chamber genres such as the piano trio, see Sumner Lott, "Dussek's Chamber Music."

28. Schubert's repetition of secondary themes has been discussed by Scott Burnham in "Landscape as Music, Landscape as Truth." Burnham analyzes the G-major string quartet (also discussed below) and addresses Adorno's 1928 essay on Schubert, translated in its entirety in the same issue of *19th-Century Music* by Jonathan Dunsby and Beate Perrey.

29. Schubert's quartet was completed in 1826, just five years before Kuhlau's op. 122 and Onslow's op. 38. Although Schubert's music precedes the others discussed here, Spohr's, Kuhlau's, and Onslow's earlier publications were available to Schubert and known throughout the musical world of his time. It is unlikely that the later composers knew Schubert's "late" works, though, as they were not available in print until 1870 in the case of the Quartettsatz and 1851 in the case of the G-major quartet (op. post. 161). The string quintet in C major, discussed below, was similarly only available after the midcentury.

30. Thomas A. Denny has addressed the critical "problem" of repetition in relation to Schubert's finales. See his dissertation, "The Finale in the Instrumental Works of Schubert," and "Too Long? Too Loose? And Too Light? Critical Thoughts about Schubert's Mature Finales." See also Levy, "Covert and Casual Values in Recent Writings about Music," on the implicit valuing of motivic over lyrical melodic styles.

31. Solie, "Biedermeier Domesticity and the Schubert Circle."

32. Otto Deutsch collected, transcribed, and edited the enormous quantity of biographical evidence on Schubert throughout the twentieth century. He first published it as *Franz Schubert: Die Dokumente seines Lebens und Schaffens* in 1914, then revised and enlarged it with newly discovered documents in 1964 as part of the complete works edition published by Bärenreiter. An English edition produced between these two publications contains documents not included in Deutsch's earlier work that were incorporated in the later one. See Deutsch, *Schubert: A Documentary Biography* (simultaneously published as *The Schubert Reader*). Deutsch continued his work with *Schubert: Memoirs by His Friends*. All quotations from Deutsch's collected sources come from the English editions of his work unless otherwise stated.

33. Sonnleithner, "Musikalischen Skizzen." Sonnleithner published his account of the Schubert family gatherings as the fourth of a six-part series titled Musikalischen Skizzen

aus Alt-Wien, which documents Viennese domestic music making in the early decades of the nineteenth century. Otto Deutsch's *Schubert Reader* reproduces excerpts from parts 4 and 5.

34. As quoted in Deutsch, *Schubert: Memoirs by His Friends*, 341.

35. Ibid., 340.

36. Sonnleithner supplied information about these gatherings to his friend Wilhelm Böcking (another amateur musician who played in these gatherings), who wrote the report for inclusion in the series. It would have been considered unseemly for Sonnleithner to write the account of his own family's private entertainments.

37. Deutsch, *The Schubert Reader*, 441.

38. About the performance, Schwind wrote: "Schubert's Quartet has been performed, rather slowly in his opinion, but very purely and tenderly. It is on the whole very smooth, but written in such a way that the tune remains in one's mind, as with the songs, all feeling and thoroughly expressive. It got much applause, especially the minuet, which is extraordinarily tender and natural. A mandarin next to me thought it affected! A single hearing, what can that mean to the likes of us, let alone to such a gobbler-up of notes?" (ibid., 333).

39. Barth, an amateur singer, lived at the Schwarzenberg palace near the city center because he was employed as an accountant in the household of the powerful noble family. He frequently performed Schubert's vocal quartets and other choral works in both formal and informal settings. He was a regular participant in the Sonnleithner musical evenings and an early member of the Gesellschaft der Musikfreunde.

40. A surviving note from Schubert to Lachner requests the parts and score be returned to violinist Joseph Slawjk, who would play the work in a later rehearsal (ibid., 613).

41. This event was Schubert's only benefit concert and the only public concert that showcased his works alone during his lifetime. Unfortunately, its scheduling collided with two separate events that threatened to completely overshadow the composer's achievement in the press: violin virtuoso Nicolo Paganini was in Vienna giving concerts at this time, and the anniversary of Beethoven's death was commemorated with a "private musical entertainment" at the Gesellschaft der Musikfreunde's main performance space. The Beethoven concert featured the F-major quartet, op. 135, performed by the same group of string players who presented Schubert's string quartet movement in his concert (Böhm, Holz, Weiss, and Linke).

42. On the concept of Schubert's *Mädchencharakter*, see Messing, *Schubert in the European Imagination*.

43. The initially controversial debate over Schubert's sexuality—the "Steblin/Solomon debate," as it has been dubbed—seems to have subsided somewhat in recent years, though scholars continue to revisit it occasionally, bringing new evidence and interpretations to light. To revisit the arguments, see Solomon, "Franz Schubert and the Peacocks of Benvenuto Cellini"; and the several articles published in a special issue of *19th-Century Music* four years later: "Schubert: Music, Sexuality, Culture," *19th-Century Music* 17, no. 1 (1993).

44. On the expression of this exclusion and Schubert's "late" style, see Bellman, *The* Style hongrois *in the Music of Western Europe*, esp. chap. 7, "Schubert."

45. As quoted in Deutsch, *The Schubert Reader*, 339.

46. Ibid.

47. DeLong, "The Conventions of Musical Biedermeier"; and Dickensheets, "Nineteenth-Century Topical Analysis."

Chapter 4. Redefining the "Progressive" Style in Responses to Beethoven's Late Quartets

1. On allusion in musical works, see Burkholder, "The Uses of Existing Music"; Reynolds, *Motives for Allusion*; and Straus, *Remaking the Past*. Regarding Harold Bloom's theory of the "anxiety of influence" and its application to musical works like those discussed here, see Knapp, "Brahms and the Anxiety of Allusion" and *Brahms and the Challenge of the Symphony*. See also Hull, "Brahms the Allusive."

2. For symphonic examples of this critique, see Bonds, *After Beethoven*.

3. Brendel was particularly disappointed with Schumann's symphonic and chamber works of the early 1840s. In 1845 he noted that "just as Schumann was . . . less successful with older forms (e.g., the sonatas) than with the free outpourings of his inner self, so it appears that his expression is also not entirely successful in some of these later works" ("Robert Schumann with Reference to Mendelssohn-Bartholdy," 335). See also Stevenson, "The Music Criticism of Franz Brendel," esp. chap. 2, "Brendel's Application of Hegelian Thought to Music History and Aesthetics."

4. Bent, *Music Analysis in the Nineteenth Century*; and Marx, *Musical Form in the Age of Beethoven*.

5. Hepokoski and Darcy, *Elements of Sonata Theory*. I do not use the categories and labels employed by Hepokoski and Darcy, though I have found their analyses of individual works and their concept of sonata "deformations" (variations on the standard model) very useful. For an overview of sonata theory and other formal analysis types, see Bergé, *Musical Form, Forms, and Formenlehre*, which contains essays on analytical techniques by William Caplin, James Hepokoski, and James Webster.

6. See Knittel, "From Chaos to History: The Reception of Beethoven's Late Quartets," "'Late,' Last, and Least: On Being Beethoven's Quartet in F Major, Op. 135," and "Wagner, Deafness, and the Reception of Beethoven's Late Style."

7. *Allgemeiner Musikzeitung zur Beförderung der theoretischen und praktischen Tonkunst, für Musiker und Freunde der Musik überhaupt* (Frankfurt am Main, 1827–28), translation quoted from Knittel, "From Chaos to History," 72.

8. Schindler, *Beethoven as I Knew Him*.

9. Schmidt, "'In vierfach geschlungener Bruderumarmung aufschweben': Beethoven und das Streichquartett als ästhetische politische und soziale Idee."

10. A. B. Marx, *Berliner Allgemeine musikalische Zeitung* 5 (1828), quoted in ibid., 357, my translation.

11. For a discussion of the changing understanding of performance and the performer's relationship to the work and the composer during the early nineteenth century, see Hunter, "'To Play as if from the Soul of the Composer': The Idea of the Performer in Early Romantic Aesthetics."

12. As we shall see in chapter 7, Antonín Dvořák composed his seventh string quartet in A minor just at the moment in his career when he chose to follow in the footsteps of previous Classical and neo-Classical composers, as opposed to the programmatic and operatic models of the New German School; this became his first published chamber work. Brahms's A-minor string quartet, op. 51, no. 2, and its engagement with these tropes is discussed in chapter 6.

13. Michael Tusa has discussed Beethoven's obsession with this key in his early period and has posited that it held special meaning extending even to the composer's structural

conception of C-minor works; for Beethoven, this key seems to have been specifically linked to Mozart and his works. See Tusa, "Beethoven's 'C-Minor Mood.'"

14. The quartet genre's close association with personal tragedy and confession in the later nineteenth century (as displayed in Smetana's "From My Life" quartet, discussed in chapter 5) may be traced to this movement. See Sullivan, "Conversing in Public: Chamber Music in Vienna, 1890–1910."

15. See Senner, Wallace, and Meredith, *The Critical Reception of Beethoven's Compositions by His German Contemporaries*. For modern commentary and analysis, see Ratner, *The Beethoven String Quartets*; Kerman, *The Beethoven Quartets*; Wallace, "Background and Expression in the First Movement of Beethoven's Op. 132."

16. Hepokoski and Darcy define a rotation as "a referential thematic pattern established as an ordered succession at the piece's outset" (*Elements of Sonata Theory*, 611). Their sonata theory focuses on a cyclical interpretation of musical form based on large-scale recurrences. Thus, the primary goal of a work (whether strophic, theme-and-variations form, rondo, ostinato grounded, or sonata form) is to return, at the end of a rotation, to the beginning of the thematic pattern; each rotation through the pattern may be varied or altered to produce a different effect, and the recyclings often "build cumulatively toward a longer-range goal" (ibid.).

17. Chua, *The "Galitzin" Quartets*.

18. A miscommunication between Mendelssohn and his publishers combined with delays in the engraving process to cause the reversed opus numbers and near-simultaneous release of the two quartets. See Todd, "Chamber Music of Mendelssohn."

19. Lindblåd (1801–78) traveled to Germany and Paris during 1825–27; he studied for a brief period with Carl Friedrich Zelter in Berlin, where he met and befriended Mendelssohn. Their correspondence spans from 1825 to Mendelssohn's death in 1847. See *Bref till Adolf Fredrik Lindblad*.

20. Mendelssohn to Adolf Fredrik Lindblåd, February 1828, in ibid., 19–20.

21. Todd, "Chamber Music of Mendelssohn," 185. Todd interprets Mendelssohn's interest in intermovement linkage as an "organic relationship of the parts and the whole," employing a biological metaphor that would become prevalent in discussions of music later in the century and remain important (and problematic) throughout the early twentieth century. See Solie, "The Living Work: Organicism and Musical Analysis"; and Levy, "Covert and Casual Values in Recent Writings about Music."

22. Rosen, *The Romantic Generation*, 581. Also see Schmidt-Beste, "Mendelssohn's Chamber Music"; and Bitercik, *The Early Works of Felix Mendelssohn*, 227–91.

23. Quoted in Todd, "Chamber Music of Mendelssohn," 185.

24. The questioning motto also bears a striking resemblance to the "Muß es sein? Es muß sein!" (Must it be? It must be!) motto associated with Beethoven's op. 135 quartet in F major.

25. This cyclical approach would have far-reaching implications in the works of later composers, including Robert Schumann, whose piano quintet, op. 44, also recalls its first-movement theme in the finale.

26. Rosen, *The Romantic Generation*, 578–80.

27. Anderson, *Imagined Communities*.

28. Kopitz, *Der Düsseldorfer Komponist Norbert Burgmüller*; and Jensen, "Norbert Burgmüller and Robert Schumann."

29. Porter, "The Reign of the *Dilettanti*" and "The New Public and the Reordering of the Musical Establishment."

30. "Und so verbanden uns bald Haydns, Mozarts und Beethovens Quartette, bald andere Bestrebungen fortan zu manchem schönen und vergnügten Abend" (Kopitz, *Der Düsseldorfer Komponist*, 189).

31. Burgmüller traveled to Aachen to take the waters with friends and died there. Though reports circulated at the time suggested that it may have been suicide, he probably drowned during (or after) an epileptic seizure, as Müller describes in his writings. See ibid., 276–89.

32. The third movement (Tempo di Menuetto) returns to A minor and presents a fairly straightforward minuet and trio; the trio is in A major with a rustic topic, as is typical of minuets from the late eighteenth century.

33. Schumann, "Erster Quartett-Morgen," *Neue Zeitschrift für Musik* 8, no. 46 (8 June 1838): 181. The remaining Quartett-Morgen reports appeared in *NZfM* 8, no. 49 (19 June 1838), 9, no. 10 (3 August 1838), 9, no. 13 (14 August 1838), and 9, no. 20 (7 September 1838). My translation.

34. Schumann wrote positively about Hirschbach's works and encouraged him as a music critic and composer—perhaps Schumann saw a bit of himself in this contemporary. Hirschbach's string quartets are remarkably experimental, employing literary mottos and songs that create quasi-programmatic works. Several of the quartets are grouped together as a cycle titled "Lebensbilder" (Pictures from life). Unfortunately, the works have not yet been reprinted.

35. "Es ist ein Quartett zur Unterhaltung guter Dilettanten, die noch vollauf zu thun haben, wo der Künstler vom Fach mit einem Ueberblick schon die ganze Seite herunter gelesen; ein Quartett bei hellem Kerzenglanz unter schönen Frauen anzuhören, während wirkliche Beethovener die Thüre verschließen und in jedem einzelnen Tact schwelgen und saugen" (Schumann, "Zweiter Quartett-Morgen," 194, my translation).

36. Leon Plantinga discusses this review (and the Quartett-Morgen reports generally) in a brief section on the string quartet in *Schumann as Critic*, 183–88.

37. See Brown, "Study, Copy, and Conquer." Brown also gives an excellent account of the conception, completion, and publication of Schumann's quartets in her dissertation, "'A Higher Echo of the Past.'"

38. Roesner, "The Chamber Music," discusses the works' interrelationships and suggests that Schumann approached Classical formal and tonal principles "as gesture and rhetoric . . . or as subterfuge" (123). Roesner focuses on the ways that these works demonstrate Schumann's respect for the genre and the "unique conception of musical form" that they evince.

39. Roesner, "Schumann's Parallel Forms," introduced the notion of a "parallel form" in Schumann's works that engages sonata form but deviates significantly from earlier (now considered "standard") iterations of that form. Roesner suggests that these deviations present a critique of Classical formal approaches and demonstrate Schumann modifying those forms to better suit his own Romantic expressive language.

40. Brown provides an insightful analysis of the A-minor finale in "Study, Copy, and Conquer," 407–22.

41. *Neue Zeitschrift für Musik* 11, no. 18 (30 August 1839): 70–71, reprinted in *Gesammelte Schriften*, 186, and translated in Schumann, *Music and Musicians: Essays and Criticisms by Robert Schumann* (1877), 172–76 (quote from 172). Notably, this contribution was not included in Rosenfeld and Wolff's selections in their 1946 edition of *On Music and Musicians*.

42. John Daverio discusses Schumann's insistence about publishing the full score in terms of the difficulty of performing these works, particularly in comparison with contemporary works (such as Mendelssohn's op. 44 quartets). See *Robert Schumann*, 254–55.

43. Schumann's famous 1835 review of Berlioz's *Symphonie fantastique* was based on Franz Liszt's arrangement for piano. He had not yet heard the work played by an orchestra, and the full score would not be published until 1845.

44. Berwald's correspondence indicates that at least two earlier quartets were completed, though only one survives—a quartet in G minor from 1818. See the commentary in Berwald, *Sämtliche Werke*, Band 11 (*Streichquartette*).

45. The scant literature on Franz Berwald and his works remains mostly in Swedish, although a few English and German sources are available. The following biographical information is drawn from the article by Layton and Grimley, "Berwald"; Pergament, "Franz Berwald"; Layton, "Berwald's Chamber Music"; and Thoor, "The Private Life of Mr. Franz Berwald."

46. A few smaller-scale works date from the 1810s: a due-concertante, a string quartet, and a quartet and septet for piano and winds.

47. After his chamber works were well received abroad by such luminaries as Liszt and Hans von Bülow, Berwald began to receive public support and encouragement in Sweden; in the 1860s he became a member of the Stockholm Concert Society, and his opera *Estrella de Soria* was performed at the Royal Opera. During the last eight years of his life, he composed or revised several large choral works and completed a second opera.

48. Berwald may well have met Liszt or at least encountered his music during his travels throughout Continental Europe in the 1830s and 1840s. A documented connection, though, does not exist before 1856.

49. Beethoven's op. 131 string quartet also explores several keys in its opening fugue and then uses those tonalities to anchor subsequent movements. See Kerman, *The Beethoven Quartets*, 327–30.

50. Krummacher, "Gattung und Werk Zu Streichquartetten von Gade und Berwald."

Chapter 5. Creating "Progressive" Communities through Programmatic Chamber Music

1. On eighteenth-century predecessors to programmaticism, see Will, *The Characteristic Symphony in the Age of Haydn and Beethoven*. Roger Scruton's entry for "programme music" in *The New Grove Dictionary of Music and Musicians* defines the term rather narrowly, with a focus on Liszt's conception of program music and its development in the later nineteenth century. Ralph P. Locke's entry in *The Harvard Dictionary of Music*, on the other hand, makes no distinction between characteristic and programmatic works but embraces all music with an extramusical component from the Middle Ages forward ("Program Music," 680–83).

2. Scruton emphasizes the presence in programmatic music of distinct subject and object, which he ascribes to Berlioz, particularly to the use of the solo viola in *Harold en Italie* "to create a sharp division between the individual protagonist . . . and the external circumstances of his experience" ("Programme Music," Oxford Music Online, Grove Music Dictionary).

3. James Hepokoski's work on Strauss's tone poems provides an excellent model for this type of analysis. See his "Fiery-Pulsed Libertine or Domestic Hero? Strauss's *Don Juan* Revisited" and "Structure and Program in *Macbeth*."

4. Halévy, "Notice historique sur la vie et les travaux de George Onslow." Halévy's obituary was translated into German and published in the *Niederrheinische Musik-Zeitung* in

the same year (1855), demonstrating Onslow's continuing popularity in German-speaking lands and in France.

5. Gottfried Wilhelm Fink writes, "In August 1829 in fact, he was struck by a musket-ball on a boar hunt; it went through his cheek and lodged itself in the back of his throat. Only after a long return journey was it removed. He suffered badly; people said that he was already dead.—It was this incident that he sought to portray in tones [in Tönen zu schildern] with this work" (*Allgemeine musikalische Zeitung* 8 [23 February 1831]: 8, my translation). The *Gazette musicale de Paris* published a similar account by François Stoepel in 1834; Stoepel's "Biographical Study" of Onslow gave a list of his publications up to that point, a biographical sketch including the infamous hunting accident, and an assessment of Onslow's musical style that likens it to the more sublime moments in the works of Beethoven. (Stoepel and Onslow collaborated on an article about Beethoven's later works the following year; see note 9.) Stoepel, "George Onslow, esquisse biographique," *Gazette musicale de Paris* 1, no. 19 (11 May 1834): 1–3.

6. See, for example, Marx, *Musical Form in the Age of Beethoven.*

7. For more information on the hunt topos in nineteenth-century music, see Monelle, *The Musical Topic.*

8. Onslow wrote in 1832: "I have received [Beethoven's last quartets] in score from Germany, and I am more than ever convinced that an author cannot be more extravagant. If one likes such music, how can mine ever be tolerated?" (quoted in Hayes, "Onslow and Beethoven's Late Quartets," 277). Despite this assessment, Hayes points out several concordances between Onslow's later string quartets—especially those of op. 46 (published in 1834)—and the late works of Beethoven.

9. The article was coauthored with Onslow's friend François Stoepel, "Beethoven et ses derniers quatuors," *Gazette musicale de Paris* 2, no. 25 (21 June 1835): 205–7.

10. Celenza, "Imagined Communities Made Real."

11. For a list of the Copenhagen Davidsbund members and descriptions of their activities, see Celenza, *The Early Works of Niels W. Gade*, 15–18.

12. The two complete movements and the incomplete third movement of this work are published in series 2, vol. 2 of the complete works edition published by the Copenhagen Foundation for the Publication of the Works of Niels Gade and distributed by Bärenreiter. The string quartets were edited by Finn Egeland Hansen.

13. Pages from Gade's composition diary, including the entry for the F-major quartet, are reproduced in Celenza, *The Early Works of Niels W. Gade*, 43–46.

14. 1827 version, from *Goethe's Werke: Vollstandige Ausgabe letzter Hand*, 1:75–76.

15. Celenza, *The Early Works of Niels W. Gade*, 82.

16. Gade planned or began composing at least five quartets that he never completed, and two completed works remained unprinted in his lifetime. The Quartet in D Major, op. 63, of 1887 was his only published string quartet.

17. Ibid., 82.

18. Celenza notes that the final coda section "appears to be a hybrid of the primary and secondary themes," lending the secondary theme added weight and importance throughout the movement (ibid., 76).

19. Curtis, *Music Makes the Nation.*

20. Elizabeth Way Sullivan explores this legacy in some detail in her dissertation "Conversing in Public: Chamber Music in Vienna, 1890–1910"; see especially her chap. 5, "'Histories of the Heart Translated into Notes': Chamber Music and the Extramusical Dimension."

21. "Meine Kompositionen gehören nicht in das Gebiet der *absoluten Musik*, in der man schließlich mit musikalischen Zeichen und dem Metronom gut auslangt" (Smetana to Adolf Cech, quoted in Wiese, *Tschechische Kammermusik*, 32).

22. In the mid-1850s, Smetana lost three daughters within two years: two-year-old Gabriela in June 1854; four-year-old Bedřiska in September 1855; and the infant Katerina in May 1856. The death of his oldest daughter, though, affected him most deeply. His diary entry notes, "Nothing can replace Fritzi [Bedřiska's nickname] the angel whom death has stolen from us" (Large, *Smetana*, 63).

23. Smetana, *Letters and Reminiscences*, 191.

24. Large, *Smetana*, 318.

25. Ibid.

26. Smetana's own comments suggest this connection between fate and the falling fifth; contemporaneous and recent readings consider it an allusion to Beethoven's fifth symphony. See Large, *Smetana*, 318; and Wiese, *Tschechische Kammermusik*, 51–52.

27. Smetana, *Letters and Reminiscences*, 190.

28. Of the Largo sostenuto, a sonatina form in A♭ major, Smetana says simply that it "recalls to me the happiness of my first love for the girl who later became my wife" (Large, *Smetana*, 318). This portion of the work receives the least emphasis in both programs, and it does not clearly connect to the nationalist ideology of the later program at all.

29. As one might expect, this portion of the work has drawn the most commentary from scholars and performers. For a sampling, see Large, *Smetana*, 317–21; Wiese, *Tschechische Kammermusik*, 60–61; and Krummacher, *Geschichte des Streichquartetts*, 2:298–306.

30. Smetana's "private" program communicated to Srb-Debronov is translated in Large, *Smetana*, 318; the "public" program is reproduced in full in *Tschechische Kammermusik*, 53. My translation.

31. For an excellent discussion of these events related to the emergence of a Czech art in Dvořák's (slightly later) works, see Brodbeck, "Dvořák's Reception in Liberal Vienna." Brodbeck also includes a summary of the pro- and anti-Czech legislation from the midcentury forward by way of introduction to the issue.

32. Smetana performed the piano part in Onslow's piano sextet op. 30 as a young man. See Wiese, *Tschechische Kammermusik*, 34.

Chapter 6. Audience and Style in Brahms's String Chamber Music

1. For discussions of the three genres considered in this chapter and their relationship to Brahms's compositional development, see Webster, "Schubert's Sonata Forms and Brahms's First Maturity"; and Notley, "Discourse and Allusion: The Chamber Music of Brahms."

2. The primary composers of new works for the domestic string chamber music market—the musical style discussed in chapter 3—died or retired around the midcentury, and they were (in general) not replaced by younger composers writing for this market. (Kuhlau died young in 1832, Onslow died in 1853, Spohr in 1859, Veit in 1864, and Kalliwoda in 1866.) Reprinted music from the first half of the century and from the Classical period, which had been significant even when it occurred alongside new works, became the main representative of string chamber music in the sheet music marketplace in the last decades of the century.

3. An earlier version of this discussion was published as Sumner Lott, "Domesticity in Brahms's String Sextets." For previous treatments of Brahms's sextets, see Kube, "Brahms' Streichsextette"; Ruf, "Die Zwei Sextette von Brahms"; and Ruf, "Kammermusik."

4. Neither Kube nor Ruf mentions Louis Spohr's string sextet. Only Niels Gade published a sextet for the same instrumentation between the publication of Brahms's op. 18 in 1862 and his op. 36 in 1866; the other sixteen works follow Brahms's op. 36. Gade's E♭ sextet, op. 44, was published by Kistner of Leipzig in May 1865.

5. Schubert's style looms large in Brahms's sextets, as Webster and others have discussed, and Brahms did not fully evade the two-cello quintet, as the materials that eventually became his piano quintet, op. 34, started life as a (two-cello) quintet for strings.

6. As discussed in chapter 1 and in previous chapters, chamber music concerts were rare outside the major capitals of Paris and London; Vienna did not boast a regular series until Hellmesberger established his concerts in 1849. Chamber music was a private-sphere entertainment or activity until the last quarter of the century, or about the time that Brahms published his string quartets.

7. Webster, "Schubert's Sonata Forms and Brahms's First Maturity," 60.

8. After Robert Schumann's funeral in 1856, Brahms had taken on some of Clara's piano students, including Laura von Meysenburg, whose family then invited him to visit the small principality. During the weeklong visit, Brahms played for the court nearly nonstop and impressed the music-loving prince and his compatriots enough to earn a position as musician to the court, beginning in late 1857. See Avins and Eisinger, *Life and Letters*, 145; and MacDonald, *Brahms*, 48–49. For information on Brahms's life in Detmold, see Schramm, *Johannes Brahms in Detmold.*

9. The most comprehensive source on Brahms's Frauenchor activities, the chorus's membership, its repertoire, and individual members' recollections remains Drinker, *Brahms and His Women's Choruses.*

10. When Brahms dedicated the op. 39 set of waltzes to his close friend the Viennese music critic Eduard Hanslick in 1867, the composer wrote: "I was thinking of Vienna, of the pretty girls with whom you play duets, of you yourself, who like such things, and what not" (quoted in MacDonald, *Brahms*, 191). Thus these domestic-style pieces for public consumption may well have evoked for Brahms his idyllic days as a young man surrounded by beautiful women in Hamburg and Detmold.

11. This theme has also been described as a *Ländler*; see Webster, "Schubert's Sonata Forms and Brahms's First Maturity," 61; and Ruf, "Kammermusik zwischen Exklusivität und Öffentlichkeit," 432. If so, the rough, countrified manner of the dance has been smoothed out with slurs that deemphasize the downbeat and a soft dynamic that suggests an indoor rather than an outdoor style.

12. See Littlewood, *The Variations of Johannes Brahms*, on the variations movements of opp. 18 and 36 (135–68). At the end of his treatment, Littlewood offers a "poetic interpretation" of the sextets based on similarities between these variations and other variation forms in Brahms's song output. He connects the sextets and their similar songs to themes of love, death, and transformation without discussing the funeral-march style or topos as realized in op. 18.

13. Letter dated 15 October 1859, in Avins and Eisinger, *Life and Letters*, 203–4.

14. For an analysis of Spohr's op. 140 and its relationship to Brahms's string sextets, see Sumner Lott, "Domesticity in Brahms's String Sextets."

15. See McCorkle, *Thematisch-bibliographisches Werkverzeichnis*, 62–66, on the first performance of op. 18. For a discussion of Joachim's string quartet concerts in Berlin, see Eshbach, "The Joachim Quartet Concerts at the Berlin Singakademie."

16. Quoted in Altmann, preface, iv. My translation.

17. Rockstro, *A History of Music*, 79. Rockstro (1823–95) studied composition and piano with Mendelssohn at the Leipzig Conservatory in 1845–46.

18. Hermann Härtel acquired the rights to Brahms's early works but chose not to publish this and some other mature works based on the assessment of an in-house critic. See Bozarth, "Brahms and the Breitkopf & Härtel Affair."

19. Swafford, *Johannes Brahms*, 117.

20. I thank Jennifer Ronyak for sharing information about this privately owned document. Brahms's own library, which was donated to the Gesellschaft der Musikfreunde in Vienna at the time of his death, apparently did not contain works by Onslow. See Hofmann, *Die Bibliothek*.

21. For Hellmesberger's biography, see Strasser, "Joseph Hellmesberger (1828–1893): Eine philharmonische Vaterfigur."

22. Over the next few years, Brahms would move away briefly to help his family members or consider taking a position in another locale. He longed for a permanent position in Hamburg, though his hometown took an embarrassingly long time to recognize his talent. Only in 1871 did Brahms move to Vienna on a permanent basis, and from then on he considered himself at home there. MacDonald, *Brahms*, 123–42.

23. Altmann notes that the sextet met with success in other locations immediately, suggesting that Viennese tastes differed from those of other cities. Both sextets were wildly popular in London, for example, and apparently in North America as well: "The sextet very soon experienced great success in other places, most of all Hamburg, [although this success] strangely enough failed to appear at the first Viennese performance by the Hellmesberger [quartet] in autumn 1862" (Das Sextett hatte aber sehr bald auch an anderen Orten, vor allem in Hamburg, großen Erfolg, der merkwürdigerweise bei der ersten Wiener Aufführung durch Hellmesberger im Herbst 1862 ausblieb) (Altmann, preface, iv, my translation).

24. Later incarnations of the *style hongrois* in Adagio movements and their meaning in Brahms's expressive language have been discussed by Jonathan Bellman, "Brahms," in Bellman, *The* Style hongrois *in the Music of Western Europe*; and Margaret Notley, "Adagios in Brahms's Late Chamber Music: Genre Aesthetics and Cultural Critique," in Notley, *Lateness and Brahms*; see esp. 195–203, subtitled "Brahms's Renewal: The Adagios in Gypsy Style."

25. On salon music and domestic pianists' predilections, see Widmaier and Ballstaedt, *Salonmusik*. Another example of "Oriental" influence on parlor piano genres is Robert Schumann's "Bilder aus Osten," a set of impromptus for piano four hands composed in 1848, during the period that Schumann seems to have turned to a *Hausmusik* aesthetic in his new compositions for piano and his revisions of earlier piano works. See Newcomb, "Schumann and the Marketplace."

26. One of these parlor piano pieces was commissioned by a visiting dignitary from Russia and published by Cranz as "Souvenir de la Russie."

27. Pascall, *Brahms beyond Mastery: His Sarabande and Gavotte, and Its Recompositions*.

28. For a firsthand account of the club and its history, see Ryan, *Recollections*.

29. Ibid., 96.

30. Letter dated 4 May 1866, quoted in Barkan, *Johannes Brahms and Theodor Billroth: Letters from a Musical Friendship*, 5. Barkan's collection includes all the letters originally published by Otto Gottlieb-Billroth in *Billroth und Brahms im Briefwechsel* (Berlin: Urban & Schwartzenberg, 1935), with additional letters not available to Gottlieb-Billroth at the time of his publication. Some of these letters are presented in new translations in Avins and Eisinger, *Life and Letters*.

31. Barkan, *Johannes Brahms and Theodor Billroth*, 6.

32. Brahms had been working on symphonic movements and sketches that would become the first symphony since at least 1862, and he reworked some materials into various nonsymphonic compositions throughout the late 1850s and 1860s. See David Brodbeck, *Brahms, Symphony No. 1, Op. 67*, esp. chap. 1, "Frustrated Efforts."

33. For an expanded discussion of the op. 51 string quartets, including analysis of the inner movements not included here, see Sumner Lott, "At the Intersection of Public and Private Musical Life."

34. Botstein, "Brahms and His Audience."

35. See Schubring, "Five Early Works by Brahms." Frisch interpreted Schubring's 1862 critique in light of contemporaneous musical politics in Frisch, "Brahms and Schubring: Musical Politics at Mid-Century."

36. On the reception of *Ein Deutsches Requiem*, see Beller-McKenna, *Brahms and the German Spirit*, esp. chap. 3, and "Brahms's Choral Music."

37. Biographer Jan Swafford discusses the work's success immediately following the April 1868 premiere in Bremen: "Reinthaler [music director for the Bremen cathedral and a strong advocate of Brahms's music] repeated the work in Bremen a few weeks later, and during the next year it was done twenty times across Germany. From there it spread to Russia, England, and Paris and to choral groups around the West, in an age when there were able and enthusiastic amateur groups everywhere" (*Johannes Brahms*, 331).

38. McCorkle, *Thematisch-Bibliographisches Werkverzeichnis*, 171, my translation.

39. The so-called "War of the Romantics" (Alan Walker's term) pitted self-styled "progressives," who supported Liszt and Wagner early in the century and/or Bruckner later in the century, against composers and performers they deemed "conservative," musicians like Brahms and Joachim, backed by critics such as Eduard Hanslick. In 1870s Vienna, the younger generation of Bruckner supporters (e.g., Hugo Wolf and Gustav Mahler) saw Brahms and his circle as a roadblock to the musical progress they hoped to foster.

40. The first quote comes from a letter to Theodor Billroth, announcing Brahms's intention to dedicate the quartets to him, and will be discussed below. The image of a giant Beethoven tramping ominously behind nineteenth-century composers comes from Kalbeck's biography. Kalbeck writes that Brahms remarked to Hermann Levi: "You have no idea how it feels for the likes of us, to always hear a giant like that marching behind us" (Du hast keinen Begriff davon, wie es unser einem zu Mute ist, wenn er immer so einen Riesen hinter sich marschieren hört), and Levi later communicated it to Kalbeck (*Johannes Brahms*, 1:165).

41. As translated in Avins and Eisinger, *Life and Letters*, 458.

42. Letter from Brahms to Billroth, dated by Billroth July 1873, quoted here as translated in ibid., 455–56. As Avins notes, Brahms's "droll little ulterior motive" and use of quotation marks around the words "sextet-player" make a playful joke at Billroth's expense. Early in their friendship, Billroth planned to perform the second viola part in a private reading of Brahms's G-major string sextet in the presence of the composer. He became so nervous

that he required a replacement, which amused Brahms greatly. Barkan quotes Billroth's letter to his friend Prof. Lübke (*Johannes Brahms and Theodor Billroth*, 6).

43. A handy English-language source for Billroth and other of Brahms's friends is Clive, *Brahms and His World: A Biographical Dictionary*. For a detailed account of Billroth's life, see Absolon, *The Surgeon's Surgeon: Theodor Billroth, 1829–1894*.

44. Barkan, *Johannes Brahms and Theodor Billroth*, 35.

45. He asked Brahms to choose the program but suggested that he play a duet with pianist Ignaz Brüll and his cello sonata with Hausmann.

46. Barkan, *Johannes Brahms and Theodor Billroth*, 191.

47. Ibid., 192.

48. Ibid., 40, 129, 130.

49. Ibid., 41.

50. Ibid., 75.

51. Ibid., 83.

52. Avins and Eisinger, *Life and Letters*, 456.

53. Beethoven's only C-minor string quartet (op. 18, no. 4) is not usually included in this grouping of intense works, though it certainly stands out from its fellow quartets in that opus; it is the only minor-mode work of the set, and it finishes with a Gypsy rondo finale. For a study of Beethoven's compositional approach in this key, see Tusa, "Beethoven's 'C-Minor Mood.'"

54. Walter Frisch has described the new tone of the quartets in similar terms: "The luxuriance of opp. 25, 26, and 34 and the spaciousness of their thematic-harmonic-formal processes become reduced to a style of extreme concentration" (*Brahms and the Principle of Developing Variation*, 111).

55. Beatrix Borchard notes that the chaconne was the most frequently performed work in Joachim's repertory (*Stimme und Geige: Amalie und Joseph Joachim*, 500–502). Joachim also turned to the D-minor partita when giving impromptu performances, such as the jubilee celebration of his fiftieth year of active concertizing in March 1889, when his biographer and student Andreas Moser reports: "As the applause was unceasing, Joachim at last took the fiddle from [Hugo] Olk's hands, as a sign that he would play his thanks to them, and with the words, 'Let's return to Bach,' he put the fiddle under his chin and gave the Bach Chaconne in a way that he could hardly have surpassed in his earlier years" (*Joseph Joachim*, 277).

56. Avins and Eisinger, *Life and Letters*, 515–16.

57. Previous commentators have noted this return and discussed it in terms of thematic transformation or developing variation. See especially Frisch, *Brahms and the Principle of Developing Variation*, 109–20.

58. A final instance of the motto occurs in the closing fourteen measures of the movement, as the learned style returns to end the work in a solemn manner.

59. There is no evidence to suggest that Brahms knew Burgmüller's and Berwald's A-minor string quartets, but he did own a copy of Burgmüller's F-minor piano sonata, and that composer's op. 14 string quartet was published in 1844, so it would have been available to Brahms. Both Schumann and Mendelssohn championed the composer's second symphony as well, making it more likely that Brahms might have sought out the late composer's works.

60. The third movements of these quartets likewise contain pointed references to earlier works from the musical traditions that Brahms and his circle valued. See Sumner Lott, "At the Intersection of Public and Private Musical Life."

61. Notley, "Discourse and Allusion," 255. On musical logic, see also her *Lateness and Brahms*, chap. 1, "Brahms as Liberal, Bruckner as Other." For Schoenberg's analysis of the quartets, see his essay "Brahms the Progressive."

62. Like the second symphony (in D major, op. 73, composed in 1877), the third quartet explores a pastoral, relaxed style, creating a counterbalance to the weightier op. 51 quartets. See Frisch, "The Snake Bites Its Tail: Cyclic Processes in Brahms's Third String Quartet"; and Krummacher, "Von 'allerlei Delikatessen': Überlegungen zum Streichquartett Op. 67."

63. Notley has published extensively on Brahms and his milieu at the end of the century. Her 2007 book, *Lateness and Brahms*, draws together and extends many threads of scholarly inquiry explored in earlier articles and book chapters.

64. Ibid., 22–26. Brahms's term was "thinking logically in music."

65. See Notley, "Late Nineteenth-Century Chamber Music and the Cult of the Classical Adagio."

66. Notley, *Lateness and Brahms*, 3.

67. For example, see Louis Köhler's book *Johannes Brahms und seine Stellung in der Musikgeschichte* (1880) and statements in contemporaneous criticism by Hugo Wolf, Wilhelm Tappert, and biographer and critic Kalbeck. Notley notes that some critics cited this new style as a flaw, "suggest[ing] that Brahms had compromised his integrity with the style change" (*Lateness and Brahms*, 48).

68. Swafford, *Johannes Brahms*, 510–34.

69. See McColl, *Music Criticism in Vienna*.

70. In addition to McColl, see Notley, "Volksconcerte in Vienna and Late Nineteenth-Century Ideology of the Symphony."

71. Botstein, "Listening through Reading: Musical Literacy and the Concert Hall."

72. James Deaville discusses an earlier instance of this phenomenon related to Liszt's performances of his own virtuosic piano works and the effect his performances had on sales of the printed sheet music in "Publishing Paraphrases and Creating Collectors: Friedrich Hofmeister, Franz Liszt, and the Technology of Popularity."

73. MacDonald, *Brahms*, 295.

74. Brahms scholarship is indebted to the Fellingers' accounts of Brahms's later years and Maria Fellinger's affecting photographs of the composer with her family. Musicologist Imogen Fellinger, a great-granddaughter of Maria Fellinger, made many significant contributions to our understanding of Brahms and his music as well. On the Fellingers and their relationship to Brahms, see Fellinger, *Klänge um Brahms: Erinnerungen von Richard Fellinger*.

75. Soldat's gendered reception in the press and among her friends and fellow musicians lies outside the scope of the present study, but contemporaneous perceptions of her or of the music she played as masculine or manly deserve further attention. Suffice it to say here that her entry into the world of string chamber music (along with dozens of women like her) does not negate the association of genres like the string quartet with manly intellectual activity, but it does problematize it significantly; these associations began to shift in the final two decades of the period, and they deserve their own book-length study. Two previous studies merely scratch the surface of this provocative subject: Musgrave, "Marie Soldat 1863–1955: An English Perspective"; and Kühnen, "Ist die kleine Soldat nicht ein ganzer Kerl? Die Geigerin Maria Soldat-Roeger." Several essays in Cornelia Bartsch, Beatrix Borchard, and Rainer Cadenbach, eds., *Der "männliche" und der "weibliche" Beethoven* (Bonn: Beethoven-Haus, 2003) also touch on this subject.

76. For the letter to Simrock, see Avins and Eisinger, *Life and Letters*, 674; Mandyczewski quoted in Swafford, *Johannes Brahms*, 566. Brahms's retirement lasted less than a year, as

he was reinvigorated by the clarinet playing of Richard Mühlfeld, which prompted him to compose the four late clarinet works (a trio with violin and cello, op. 114, the quintet with string quartet, op. 115, and two sonatas for clarinet and piano, op. 120). The late intermezzi and *Fantasiestücke* and *Vier ernste Gesänge* are also due to this late flourishing of inspiration.

77. Quoted in Notley, "Quintet No. 2," 137.

78. See Avins and Eisinger, *Life and Letters*, 675–78.

79. Caplin, *Classical Form*.

80. On parallel forms in Schumann, see Roesner, "Schumann's Parallel Forms"; and Brown, "Higher Echoes of the Past in the Finale of Schumann's 1842 Piano Quartet."

81. For examples of Brahms's normative scherzo style, see the piano quintet, op. 34; the Alla Zingarese movement of the piano quartet, op. 25; the op. 4 scherzo for piano; Brahms's scherzo in C minor for the F.A.E. sonata; and the scherzo of the "Werther" piano quartet, op. 60.

82. Whether or not Brahms performed in "sailor bars" among prostitutes or in family-friendly pubs during his youth (a matter much discussed by Styra Avins, Charles Rosen, and Jan Swafford), the fact remains that his family was not well off, that he helped to support them from a young age through professional performances, and that they lacked the necessary resources to support a recreational music life approximating the much more comfortable circumstances the composer achieved as an adult.

Chapter 7. The Diversity of Dvořák's String Quartet Audiences

1. A noteworthy exception is Schick, *Studien zu Dvořáks Streichquartetten*.

2. David Brodbeck, in "Dvořák's Reception," has chronicled reactions to Dvořák, his music, and his fame in the Viennese press and among musicians based in Vienna during this period, as well as the impact of political considerations on the reception of works such as the seventh symphony.

3. In the first decade of the twentieth century, journalists, critics, and scholars contrasted the "conservative" and internationally successful Dvořák to the suffering, "progressive" Smetana and deemed Dvořák's success a betrayal of the Czech national tradition (Ottlová, "The Controversy over the Place of Antonín Dvořák in the History of Czech National Music").

4. An exception to this image may be David Hurwitz's music guide for general readership *Dvořák: Romantic Music's Most Versatile Genius*.

5. Clapham, *Antonín Dvořák*, 9, 47, 66. One of the more frequently reproduced images of the composer illustrates this stereotype: a late photograph of Dvořák depicts him sitting in the courtyard of his home in Vysoka surrounded by the pigeons he raised there.

6. Dvořák's three years in North America have generated more scholarship about the composer than any other aspect of or period in his long career. See Beckerman, *New Worlds of Dvořák: Searching in America for the Composer's Inner Life*; Tibbetts, *Dvořák in America*; and selected essays in Beckerman, *Dvořák and His World*.

7. In addition to Schick, *Studien zu Dvořáks Streichquartetten*, see Katz and Beckerman, "The Chamber Music of Smetana and Dvořák"; Gabrielova, "Dvořák und Beethoven: Nochmals zu Dvořáks frühen Streichquartetten"; and Gabrielova, "Antonín Dvořák and Richard Wagner."

8. Clapham, *Antonín Dvořák*, 25–26.

9. Burghauser, *Antonín Dvořák*, 136. The quartet was publicly premiered three years later in the Prague Kammermusikverein concerts.

10. Schick mentions Volkmann alongside Smetana as a significant model for Dvořák, though he notes that Dvořák's aims clearly extended beyond the provincial fame of such figures. Notably, Smetana's few chamber works serve primarily to demonstrate his lack of interest in the field—he composed his first string quartet and piano trio in response to personal tragedy and trauma, not out of an inherent interest in the form.

11. About the E-minor quartet "From My Life," Smetana explained in a letter to his friend Josef Srb-Debronov, "I did not set out to write a quartet according to recipe or custom in the usual forms" (Large, *Smetana*, 318). He later revised this disclaimer for public distribution to "my quartet is no formal game with tones and with motives, that proves what the tone-poet is able [to do]" (Wiese, *Tschechische Kammermusik*, 53). See chapter 5 for a full discussion of this work.

12. Violinist Antonín Bennewitz (1833–1926) may have introduced Dvořák to string quartets by these composers; he had held positions in Salzburg and Stuttgart between his studies at the Prague Conservatory and his appointment as violin instructor there in 1866. Bennewitz was an avid promoter of chamber music; he directed the Kammermusikverein (Chamber Music Society) concerts and led a professional quartet that bore his name beginning in 1876, in addition to playing in other ad hoc ensembles. He served as director of the conservatory from 1882 to 1901, when Dvořák took over that position.

13. On "parallel form," see Roesner, "Schumann's Parallel Forms"; and Brown, "Higher Echoes of the Past."

14. See chapter 4 for an analysis and discussion of Schumann's op. 41 in the context of the A-minor quartet tradition.

15. The *dumka* would often be paired with its up-tempo cousin the *furiant*, as a Gypsy lament might accompany a *czardas* or the polonaise might lead to a mazurka. (I differentiate here between Gypsy and Hungarian styles, though in the nineteenth century these were thought to be one and the same.)

16. Prior to this, Dvořák had published two collections of themes from *King and Charcoal Burner*, arranged for piano (B. 22 and B. 43, published in 1873 and 1875—neither with an opus number) and a set of six "Songs from the Dvůr Králové Manuscript" (B. 30, published in 1873 as his op. 7).

17. The sextet was published in 1879, but the other works listed here were delayed until 1880 or 1888.

18. The review by Louis Ehlhert appeared in the Berlin *National-Zeitung* on 15 November 1878.

19. Note that this is the same decade in which Bruckner's F-major string quintet was introduced to the Viennese public, prompting Brahms's response with his op. 88 quintet in the same key. The difficult political situation in Vienna affected individual musicians differently, but it is appropriate to point out that this period prompted reappraisals of priorities for all artists connected to the Viennese establishment.

20. John Clapham reports that Simrock's edition came out too late for the Florentine Quartet to include it in the quartet's programs during the Swiss tour for which the work was intended. If this is true, it is not clear why the quartet would not play the work from the manuscript or from hand-copied parts, as many ensembles did when performing new, proprietary music. Otakar Sourek (*The Chamber Music of Antonín Dvořák*, 83) reports that the first public performance of the work was in July 1879 by the Joachim Quartet in

Berlin and gives no explanation as to why the Florentine did not play it earlier. Jarmil Burghauser (*Thmatický Katalog*, 200) indicates a performance by the Florentine in either November (notated with a question mark) or December (in parentheses) of 1879.

21. Clapham, *Antonín Dvorák*, 175. Clapham's speculation reaffirms Sourek's earlier assessment, which notes "a distinctly noticeable bias towards Beethoven[ian] Classicism" (*The Chamber Music*, 90). Clapham does not address Dvořák's by-then-difficult relationship to Viennese audiences or the dominant anti-Czech sentiment in the Viennese press. In their chapter on the chamber music of Smetana and Dvořák, Derek Katz and Michael Beckerman note that "Dvořák probably suspected that a less obviously ethnic work would stand a better chance in conservative Vienna" ("Chamber Music of Smetana and Dvořák," 336).

22. The Prague Quartet's performance on its 1989 Deutsche Grammophon collection emphasizes the stylistic variety I have described here by adhering to Dvořák's markings and drawing a distinct difference between legato and staccato playing. The performers attend carefully to indicated note lengths and dynamics, rendering a performance with lightning-fast changes of mood. The Guarneri Quartet, on the other hand, smoothed out some of those differences by shortening double-dotted notes and making more subtle dynamic and articulation changes. The 1972 performance, rereleased on RCA's Red Seal label in 2009, demonstrates how "Classical" this work can sound and how easily it can be fitted into a "Beethovenian" conception of the Viennese quartet tradition.

23. In a different context, we might interpret these as "Ossianic" gestures, borrowing some of the Highlands exoticism and archaism that was common in works by Schubert, Schumann, and Mendelssohn in the first half of the nineteenth century. See Clemmens Waltz, "The Highland Muse in Romantic German Music."

24. Significantly, the concerto and *Rusalka* both postdate the American sojourn, reinforcing the importance of that period for the composer's international and lasting success. The dozens of works composed, published, and performed in the twenty years leading to that brief period have received considerably less attention from performers and scholars, with the exceptions of the *Stabat Mater* and the fourth song, "Songs My Mother Taught Me," from his *Gypsy Songs*, both works from 1880.

25. On American and European composers' interest in Native American music, see Pisani, *Imagining Native America in Music*. On Dvořák's American period, see the works cited in note 6.

26. Dvořák's employment contract, initiated by Jeannette Thurber, was purchased in 2013 from the Thurber family by the Dvořák American Heritage Association based in New York. See Michael Cooper, "The Deal That Brought Dvořák to New York," *New York Times*, 23 August 2013, online edition.

27. Social activist and reporter Jacob Riis (1849–1914) reported that the population density of New York in 1890 was 60 per acre, or 38,451 people per square mile, based on that year's census records. In Manhattan alone, the crowding was much worse, with 114 persons per acre, or 73,299 per square mile. Riis documented the conditions of tenement dwellers and other impoverished New York City residents in his photojournalistic masterwork *How the Other Half Lives* (New York: Scribner, 1891), which shocked upper-class readers who apparently had no prior knowledge of their neighbors' plight.

28. Beckerman chronicles Dvořák's difficulty with the crowdedness of the city and with his recurrent agoraphobia, which seems to have worsened during his stay there. See *New Worlds of Dvořák*, 177–91.

29. According to Richard Burton in *Prague*, the population density of Prague's Old Town in 1890 was approximately 644 per hectare, though the Jewish ghetto (Josefov) alone was nearly three times that before the district was razed in the early 1890s.

30. Schick, "What's American about Dvořák's 'American' Quartet and Quintet?," 76.

31. Dvořák deftly employs a Schubertian direct modulation familiar from the C-major string quintet, D. 956. The A theme ends on C (V), as though anticipating a return to F major, but the bass line leaps down to A♮ on the downbeat, instantly shifting the harmony from V to ♮III.

32. Schick describes Dvořák's "reminiscences of his organ playing in the church at Spillville" as a "lapse in matters of style," as evidence of the work's "uncivilized" character bucking the trends of Germanic compositional practice ("What's American," 76).

BIBLIOGRAPHY

Absolon, Karel. *The Surgeon's Surgeon: Theodor Billroth, 1829–1894*. 4 vols. Lawrence, KS: Coronado Press, 1979–89.

Agawu, Kofi. *Playing with Signs: A Semiotic Interpretation of Classic Music*. Princeton, NJ: Princeton University Press, 1991.

Allanbrook, Wye Jamison. *Rhythmic Gesture in Mozart: "Le nozze di Figaro" and "Don Giovanni."* Chicago: University of Chicago Press, 1984.

Altmann, Wilhelm. Preface to Johannes Brahms, Sextet for 2 Violins, 2 Violas, and 2 Violoncellos in B♭ Major, op. 18, score, iii–v. London: E. Eulenburg, 1950.

Anderson, Benedict. *Imagined Communities: Reflections on the Origin and Spread of Nationalism*. 2nd ed. London: Verso, 1991.

Applegate, Cecilia, and Pamela Potter, eds. *Music and German National Identity*. Chicago: University of Chicago Press, 2002.

Avins, Styra, and Josef Eisinger, eds. and trans. *Johannes Brahms: Life and Letters*. Oxford: Oxford University Press, 1997.

Baldassarre, Antonio. "Der klarste Träger musikalischer Ideen, der je geschaffen wurde: Untersuchungen zur Gattungsgeschichte des Streichquartetts zwischen 1830 und 1870." Ph.D. diss., Universität Zürich, 2005.

Barkan, Hans, ed. and trans. *Johannes Brahms and Theodor Billroth: Letters from a Musical Friendship*. Norman: University of Oklahoma Press, 1957.

Bartels, Katrin. *Das Streichquintett im 19. Jahrhundert*. Göttingen: Vandenhoech und Ruprecht, 1996.

Bartsch, Cornelia, Beatrix Borchard, and Rainer Cadenbach, eds. *Der "männliche" und der "weibliche" Beethoven*. Bonn: Beethoven-Haus, 2003.

Bashford, Christina. "Historiography and Invisible Musics: Domestic Chamber Music in Nineteenth-Century Britain." *Journal of the American Musicological Society* (*JAMS*) 63, no. 2 (2010): 291–360.

———. "Learning to Listen: Audiences for Chamber Music in Early Victorian London." *Journal of Victorian Culture* 4, no. 1 (1991): 25–51.

———. *The Pursuit of High Culture: John Ella and Chamber Music in Victorian London*. Woodbridge, UK: Boydell and Brewer Press, 2007.

———. "Writing (British) Concert History: The Blessing and Curse of Ephemera." *Notes* 64, no. 3 (March 2008): 458–73.

Bayreuther, Rainer. "Gibt es eine neudeutsche Kammermusik? Versuch einer theoretischen Annäherung und Exemplifizierung an Raffs Streichquartett op. 192/2." In *Aspekte historischer und systematischer Musikforschung: Zur Symphonie im 19. Jahrhundert, zu Fragen der Musiktheorie, der Wahrnehmung von Musik und Anderes*, edited by Christoph-Hellmut Mahling and Kristina Pfarr, 265–86. Mainz: Are, 2002.

Beckerman, Michael, ed. *Dvořák and His World*. Princeton, NJ: Princeton University Press, 1993.

———. *New Worlds of Dvořák: Searching in America for the Composer's Inner Life*. New York: Norton, 2003.

Beer, Axel, ed. *Musik zwischen Komponist, Verlag und Publikum: Die Rahmenbedingungen des Musikschaffens in Deutschland im ersten Drittel des 19. Jahrhunderts*. Tutzing: Schneider, 2000.

———. "Überlegungen zum Begriff Kammermusik im 18. und 19. Jahrhundert." In *Aspekte der Kammermusik vom 18. Jahrhundert bis zur Gegenwart*, edited by Christoph-Hellmut Mahling, Kristina Pfarr, and Karl Bohmer, 1–8. Mainz: Villa Musica, 1998.

Behr, Johannes. *Johannes Brahms—vom Ratgeber zum Kompositionslehrer: Eine Untersuchung in Fallstudien*. Kassel: Bärenreiter, 2007.

Bell, Nicolas. "Chamber Music in the Home: Henry Rensburg's Concerts in Liverpool." *Brio* 45, no. 1 (2008): 43–52.

Beller-McKenna, Daniel. *Brahms and the German Spirit*. Cambridge, MA: Harvard University Press, 2004.

———. "Brahms's Choral Music." In *The Cambridge Companion to Brahms*, edited by Michael Musgrave, 171–94. Cambridge: Cambridge University Press, 1999.

Bellman, Jonathan. "Aus alten Märchen: The Chivalric Style of Schumann and Brahms." *Journal of Musicology* 13, no. 1 (1995): 117–35.

———. *The* Style hongrois *in the Music of Western Europe*. Boston: Northeastern University Press, 1993.

Bent, Ian D. *Music Analysis in the Nineteenth Century*. Cambridge: Cambridge University Press, 1994.

Benton, Rita. "Pleyel's *Bibliothèque musicale*." *Music Review* 35 (1975): 1–4.

Bergé, Pieter, ed. *Musical Forms, Form, & Formenlehre: Three Methodological Reflections*. Leuven: Leuven University Press, 2009.

Berwald, Franz. *Streichquartette*. In *Sämtliche Werke*, vol. 11, edited by Nils Castegren, Lars Frydén, and Erling Lomnäs. Kassel: Bärenreiter, 1965.

Biddle, Ian, and Kirsten Gibson. *Masculinity and Western Musical Practice*. Aldershot: Ashgate, 2009.

Bitercik, Greg. *The Early Works of Felix Mendelssohn: A Study in the Romantic Sonata Style*. Philadelphia: Gordon & Breach, 1992.

Blackbourn, David, and Geoff Eley. *The Peculiarities of German History: Bourgeois Society and Politics in Nineteenth-Century Germany*. Oxford: Oxford University Press, 1984.

Bohlman, Philip. "On the Unremarkable in Music." *19th-Century Music* 16, no. 2 (1992): 203–16.

Bonds, Mark Evan. *After Beethoven: Imperatives of Originality in the Symphony*. Cambridge, MA: Harvard University Press, 1996.

———. "Replacing Haydn: Mozart's 'Pleyel' Quartets." *Music & Letters* 88 (2007): 201–25.

———. "The Sincerest Form of Flattery? Mozart's 'Haydn' Quartets and the Question of Influence." *Studi musicali* 22 (1993): 365–409.

Borchard, Beatrix. *Stimme und Geige: Amalie und Joseph Joachim, Biographie und Interpretationsgeschichte*. Vienna: Böhlau, 2005.

Botstein, Leon. "Brahms and His Audience: The Later Viennese Years." In *The Cambridge Companion to Brahms*, edited by Michael Musgrave, 51–76. Cambridge: Cambridge University Press, 1999.

———, ed. *The Compleat Brahms*. New York: W. W. Norton, 1999.
———. "Listening through Reading: Musical Literacy and the Concert Audience." *19th-Century Music* 16, no. 2 (1992): 129–45.
Bozarth, George. "Brahms and the Breitkopf & Härtel Affair." *Music Review* 55, no. 3 (1994): 202–13.
Bref till Adolf Fredrik Lindblad fran Mendelssohn, dohrn, . . . och andra. Stockholm: Albert Bonniers, 1913.
Brendel, Karl Franz. "Robert Schumann with Reference to Mendelssohn-Bartholdy and the Development of Modern Music in General." Translated by Jürgen Thym. In *Schumann and His World*, edited by R. Larry Todd, 317–37. Princeton, NJ: Princeton University Press, 1994.
Brodbeck, David. *Brahms, Symphony No. 1, Op. 67*. Cambridge: Cambridge University Press, 1997.
———. "Dvořák's Reception in Liberal Vienna: Language Ordinances, National Property, and the Rhetoric of Deutschtum." *Journal of the American Musicological Society* 60, no. 1 (2007): 71–131.
———. "Hanslick's Smetana and Hanslick's Prague." *Journal of the Royal Musical Association* 134, no. 1 (2009): 1–36.
———. "Medium and Meaning: New Aspects of the Chamber Music." In *The Cambridge Companion to Brahms*, edited by Michael Musgrave, 98–132. Cambridge: Cambridge University Press, 1999.
Brown, Clive. *Louis Spohr: A Critical Biography*. Cambridge: Cambridge University Press, 1984.
Brown, Julie Hedges. "Higher Echoes of the Past in the Finale of Schumann's 1842 Piano Quartet." *JAMS* 57, no. 3 (2004): 511–564.
———. "'A Higher Echo of the Past': Schumann's 1842 Chamber Music and the Rethinking of Classical Form." Ph.D. diss., Yale University, 2000.
———. "Study, Copy, and Conquer: Schumann's 1842 Chamber Music and the Recasting of Classical Sonata Form." *Journal of Musicology* 30, no. 3 (2013): 369–423.
Bruford, Walter H. *The German Tradition of Self-Cultivation: Bildung from Humboldt to Thomas Mann*. Cambridge: Cambridge University Press, 1975.
Brzoska, Matthias. "Meyerbeer: *Robert le Diable* and *Les Huguenots*." In *The Cambridge Companion to Grand Opera*, edited by David Charlton, 189–207. Cambridge: Cambridge University Press, 2003.
Burghauser, Jarmil. *Antonín Dvořák: Thmatický Katalog*. Prague: Státní Nakladatelství Krásné Literatury, 1960.
Burkholder, J. Peter. "The Uses of Existing Music: Musical Borrowing as a Field." *Notes* 50, no. 3 (1994): 851–70.
Burnham, Scott. "Landscape as Music, Landscape as Truth: Schubert and the Burden of Repetition." *19th-Century Music* 29, no. 1 (2005): 31–41.
Burton, Richard. *Prague: A Cultural and Literary History*. New York: Interlink, 2003.
Busk, Gorm. *Kuhlau Breve: Udgive og med kommentarer af Gorm Busk*. Copenhagen: Engstrøm og Sødring Musikforlag, 1990.
Caplin, William. *Classical Form: A Theory of Formal Functions for the Instrumental Music of Haydn, Mozart, and Beethoven*. Oxford: Oxford University Press, 1998.
Celenza, Anna Harwell. "Imagined Communities Made Real: The Impact of Robert Schumann's *Neue Zeitschrift für Musik* on the Formation of Music Communities

in the Mid-Nineteenth Century." *Journal of Musicological Research* 24, no. 1 (2005): 1–26.

———. *The Early Works of Niels W. Gade: In Search of the Poetic.* Aldershot: Ashgate, 2001.

Christensen, Thomas. "Four-Hand Piano Transcription and Geographies of Nineteenth-Century Musical Reception." *JAMS* 52, no. 2 (1999): 255–98.

———. "Public Music in Private Spaces: Piano-Vocal Scores and the Domestication of Opera." In *Music and the Cultures of Print*, edited by Kate van Orden, 67–93. New York: Garland, 2000.

Chua, Daniel K. L. *The "Galitzin" Quartets of Beethoven: Opp. 127, 132, and 130.* Princeton, NJ: Princeton University Press, 1995.

Clapham, John. *Antonín Dvořák: Musician and Craftsman.* New York: St. Martin's, 1966.

Clive, Peter. *Brahms and His World: A Biographical Dictionary.* Lanham, MD: Scarecrow, 2006.

Colclough, Stephen. *Consuming Texts: Readers and Reading Communities, 1695–1870.* Basingstoke: Palgrave Macmillan, 2007.

Cooper, Jeffrey. *The Rise of Instrumental Music and Concert Series in Paris, 1828–1871.* Ann Arbor: UMI Research Press, 1983.

Curtis, Benjamin. *Music Makes the Nation: Nationalist Composers and Nation Building in Nineteenth-Century Europe.* Amherst, NY: Cambria Press, 2008.

Curtis, Robert Lee. *Ludwig Bischoff: A Mid-Nineteenth-Century Music Critic.* Cologne: Arno Volk, 1979.

Czerny, Carl. *School of Practical Composition.* Translated by John Bishop. London: R. Cocks & Co., 1848.

Dahlhaus, Carl. *Musik des 19. Jahrhunderts.* Translated as *Nineteenth-Century Music* by J. Bradford Robinson. Berkeley: University of California Press, 1989.

———, ed. *Studien zur Trivialmusik des 19. Jahrhunderts.* Regensburg: Bosse, 1967.

Daverio, John. *Crossing Paths: Schubert, Schumann, and Brahms.* Oxford: Oxford University Press, 2002.

———. *Robert Schumann: Herald of a "New Poetic Age."* Oxford: Oxford University Press, 1997.

———. "Schumann's Ossianic Manner." *19th-Century Music* 21, no. 3 (1998): 247–73.

Davidoff, Leonore. "Gender and the 'Great Divide': Public and Private in British Gender History." *Journal of Women's History* 15, no. 1 (Spring 2003): 11–27.

Davidoff, Leonore, and Catherine Hall. *Family Fortunes: Men and Women of the English Middle Class, 1780–1850.* 1994; London: Routledge, 2002.

Davidson, Caroline. *The World of Mary Ellen Best.* London: Chatto & Windus, 1985.

Deaville, James. "The Controversy Surrounding Liszt's Conception of Programme Music." In *Nineteenth-Century Music: Selected Proceedings of the Tenth International Conference*, edited by Jim Samson and Bennett Zon, 98–124. Burlington, VT: Ashgate, 2002.

———. "Publishing Paraphrases and Creating Collectors: Friedrich Hofmeister, Franz Liszt, and the Technology of Popularity." In *Franz Liszt and His World*, edited by Christopher H. Gibbs and Dana Gooley, 255–88. Princeton, NJ: Princeton University Press, 2006.

DeLong, Kenneth. "The Conventions of Musical Biedermeier." In *Convention in Eighteenth- and Nineteenth-Century Music: Essays in Honor of Leonard G. Ratner*, edited by Wye Jamison Allanbrook, Janet M. Levy, and William P. Mahrt, 195–223. Stuyvesant, NY: Pendragon, 1992.

Denny, Thomas A. "The Finale in the Instrumental Works of Schubert." Ph.D. diss., University of Rochester, 1981.

———. "Too Long? Too Loose? And Too Light? Critical Thoughts about Schubert's Mature Finales." *Studies in Music Australia* 23 (1989): 25–52.

DeNora, Tia. *Beethoven and the Construction of Genius: Musical Politics in Vienna, 1792–1803*. Berkeley: University of California Press, 1995.

Deutsch, Otto E. *Schubert: A Documentary Biography.* Translated by Eric Blom. London: Dent and Sons, 1947.

———. *Schubert: Memoirs by His Friends.* Translated by Rosamond Ley and John Nowell. New York: Macmillan, 1958.

———. *The Schubert Reader: A Life of Franz Schubert in Letters and Documents.* New York: W. W. Norton, 1947.

Devriès-Lésure, Anik. "Technological Aspects." In *Music Publishing in Europe 1600–1900: Concepts and Issues, Bibliography*, edited by Rudolf Rasch, 63–88. Berlin: Berliner Wissenschafts-Verlag, 2005.

Dickensheets, Janice. "The Nineteenth-Century Sonata Cycle as Novel: A Topical and Literary Analysis of the Second Piano Sonata of Johannes Brahms." D.A. thesis, University of Northern Colorado, 2004.

———. "Nineteenth-Century Topical Analysis: A Lexicon of Romantic Topoi. I." *Pendragon Review: A Journal of Musical Romanticism* 2, no. 1 (2003): 5–19.

Drinker, Sophie. *Brahms and His Women's Choruses.* Merion, PA: Sophie Drinker, 1952.

Ellis, William Ashton, trans. *Richard Wagner's Prose Works.* Vol. 7. London: Kegan Paul, Trench, Trübner, 1898.

Elvers, Rudolf, and Cecil Hopkinson. "A Survey of the Music Catalogues of Whistling and Hofmeister." *Fontes Artis Musicae* 19 (1972): 1–7.

Eshbach, Robert. "The Joachim Quartet Concerts at the Berlin Singakademie: Mendelssohnian Geselligkeit in Wilhelmine Germany." In *Brahms in the Home and the Concert Hall: Between Private and Public Performance*, edited by Katy Hamilton and Natasha Loges, 22–42. Cambridge: Cambridge University Press, 2014.

Ewing, Heather. *The Lost World of James Smithson: Science, Revolution, and the Birth of the Smithsonian.* New York: Bloomsbury, 2007.

Fauquet, Joël-Marie. *Les sociétés de musique de chambre à Paris de la Restauration à 1870.* Paris: Amateurs de Livres, 1986.

Fellinger, Richard. *Klänge um Brahms: Erinnerungen von Richard Fellinger.* Mürzuzschlag: Österreichische Johannes Brahms-Geselschaft, 1997.

Ferris, David. "Public Performance and Private Understanding: Clara Wieck's Concerts in Berlin." *JAMS* 56, no. 2 (2003): 351–408.

Frisch, Walter. "Brahms and Schubring: Musical Criticism and Politics at Mid-Century." *19th-Century Music* 7, no. 3 (1984): 271–81.

———. *Brahms and the Principle of Developing Variation.* Berkeley: University of California Press, 1984.

———. "The Snake Bites Its Tail: Cyclic Processes in Brahms's Third String Quartet, Op. 67." *Journal of Musicology* 22, no. 1 (2005): 154–72.

Fryden, Lars, and Erling Lomnäs. Preface to *Streichquartette. Sämtliche Werke*, vol. 11, edited by Nils Castegren, Lars Frydén, and Erling Lomnäs. Kassel: Bärenreiter, 1965.

Gabrielova, Jarmila. "Antonín Dvořák and Richard Wagner." *Musicology* 6 (2006): 305–15.

———. "Dvořák und Beethoven: Nochmals zu Dvořáks frühen Streichquartetten." In *The Work of Antonín Dvořák (1841–1904): Aspects of Composition, Problems of Editing, Reception*, edited by Jarmila Gabrielová and Jan Kachlík, 52–64. Prague: Institute of Ethnology, Academy of Sciences of the Czech Republic, 2007.
Garratt, James. *Music, Culture, and Social Reform in the Age of Wagner*. Cambridge: Cambridge University Press, 2010.
Gelbart, Matthew. *The Invention of "Folk Music" and "Art Music": Emerging Categories from Ossian to Wagner*. Cambridge: Cambridge University Press, 2007.
Gibbs, Christopher. *The Life of Schubert*. Cambridge: Cambridge University Press, 2000.
Goehr, Lydia. *The Imaginary Museum of Musical Works: An Essay in the Philosophy of Music*. 2nd ed. Oxford: Oxford University Press, 2007.
Goethe, Johann Wolfgang von. *Goethe's Werke: Vollständige Ausgabe letzter Hand*. 40 vols. Stuttgart: J. G. Cotta, 1827–30.
Gramit, David, ed. *Beyond the Art of Finger Dexterity: Reassessing Carl Czerny*. Rochester, NY: Rochester University Press, 2008.
———. *Cultivating Music: The Aspirations, Interests, and Limits of German Musical Culture, 1770–1848*. Berkeley: University of California Press, 2002.
———. "Everyday Extraordinary: Music in the Letters of a German Amateur, 1803–08." *19th-Century Music* 34, no. 2 (2010): 109–40.
———. "'The Passion for Friendship': Music, Cultivation, and Identity in Schubert's Circle." In *The Cambridge Companion to Schubert*, edited by Christopher Gibbs, 56–71. Cambridge: Cambridge University Press, 1997.
———. "Selling the Serious: The Commodification of Music and Resistance to It in Germany, circa 1800." In *The Musician as Entrepreneur, 1700–1914: Managers, Charlatans, and Idealists*, edited by William Weber, 81–101. Bloomington: Indiana University Press, 2004.
———. "Unremarkable Musical Lives: Autobiographical Narratives, Music, and the Shaping of the Self." In *Musical Biography: Towards New Paradigms*, edited by Jolanta Pekacz, 159–78. Aldershot: Ashgate, 2006.
Graybill, Roger. "Brahms's Integration of Traditional and Progressive Tendencies: A Look at Three Sonata Expositions." *Journal of Musicological Research* 8, no. 2 (1988): 141–68.
Habermas, Jürgen. *The Structural Transformation of the Public Sphere: An Inquiry into a Category of Bourgeois Society*. Translated by Thomas Berger with Frederick Lawrence. Boston: MIT Press, 1989.
Halévy, Fromental. "Notice historique sur la vie et les travaux de George Onslow." *Revue et gazette musicale de Paris* 22, no. 40 (1855): 307–12.
Hanslick, Eduard. *On the Musically Beautiful: A Contribution towards the Revision of the Aesthetics of Music*. Translated by Geoffrey Payzant. Indianapolis, IN: Hackett, 1986.
Harrison, Carol E. *The Bourgeois Citizen in Nineteenth-Century France: Gender, Sociability, and the Uses of Emulation*. Oxford: Oxford University Press, 1999.
Hayes, Robert. "Onslow and Beethoven's Late Quartets." *Journal of Musicological Research* 5, no. 4 (1985): 273–96.
Hepokoski, James. "Fiery-Pulsed Libertine or Domestic Hero? Strauss's *Don Juan* Reinvestigated." In *Richard Strauss: New Perspectives on the Composer and His Work*, edited by Bryan Gilliam, 135–75. Durham, NC: Duke University Press, 1992.
———. "Structure and Program in *Macbeth*: A Proposed Reading of Strauss's First Symphonic Poem." In *Richard Strauss and His World*, edited by Bryan Gilliam, 67–89. Princeton, NJ: Princeton University Press, 1992.

Hepokoski, James, and Warren Darcy. *Elements of Sonata Theory: Norms, Types, and Deformations in the Late Eighteenth-Century Sonata*. Oxford: Oxford University Press, 2006.

Hickman, Roger. "The Flowering of the Viennese String Quartet in the Late Eighteenth Century." *Music Review* 1 (1989): 157–80.

Hoffmann, Stefan-Ludwig. "Civility, Male Friendship, and Masonic Sociability in Nineteenth-Century Germany." *Gender & History* 13, no. 2 (2001): 224–48.

Hofmann, Kurt. *Die Bibliothek von Johannes Brahms Bücher- und Musikalienverzeichnis*. Hamburg: Karl Dieter Wagner, 1974.

Hopkinson, Cecil. "The Earliest Miniature Scores." *Music Review* 32 (1972): 138–44.

Horstmann, Angelika. *Untersuchungen zur Brahms-Rezeption der Jahre 1860–1880*. Hamburg: K. D. Wagner, 1986.

Huebner, Steven. "Italianate Duets in Meyerbeer's Grand Operas." *Journal of Musicological Research* 8, nos. 3–4 (1989): 203–58.

Hull, Kenneth. "Brahms the Allusive: Extra-compositional Reference in the Instrumental Music of Johannes Brahms." Ph.D. diss., Princeton University, 1989.

Hunter, Mary. "Haydn's London Piano Trios and His Salomon String Quartets: Private vs. Public?" In *Haydn and His World*, edited by Elaine Sisman, 103–30. Princeton, NJ: Princeton University Press, 1997.

———. "'To Play as if from the Soul of the Composer': The Idea of the Performer in Early Romantic Aesthetics." *JAMS* 58, no. 2 (2005): 357–98.

Hurwitz, David. *Dvořák: Romantic Music's Most Versatile Genius*. Pompton Plains, NJ: Amadeus, 2005.

Illiano, Roberto, and Luca Sala, eds. *Instrumental Music and the Industrial Revolution: Proceedings of the International Conference, Cremona, 1–3 July 2006*. Bologna: Ut Orpheus, 2010.

Jam, Baudime. *George Onslow*. Clermont-Ferrand: Les Éditions du Mélophile, 2003.

Jeismann, Karl-Ernst, and Peter Lundgreen, eds. *Handbuch der deutschen Bildungsgeschichte*. 6 vols. Munich: C. H. Beck, 1996–98.

Jensen, Eric Frederick. "Norbert Burgmüller and Robert Schumann." *Musical Quarterly* 74, no. 4 (1990): 550–65.

Jokiharju, Ouiti. "Reflections of Instrumental Chamber-Music Making in Sheet Music Related to the Gluck-Calzabigi Operatic 'Reform.'" In *Instrumental Music and the Industrial Revolution: Proceedings of the International Conference, Cremona, 1–3 July 2006*, edited by Roberto Illiano and Luca Sala, 391–408. Bologna: Ut Orpheus, 2010.

Jürgenson, Knud. "The 'Ballet of the Nuns' from Robert le Diable and Its Revival." In *Meyerbeer und das europäische Musiktheater*, edited by Arnold Jacobshagen and Sieghart Döhring, 73–86. Laaber, Germany: Laaber, 1998.

Kaelble, Hartmut, ed. *The European Way: European Societies during the Nineteenth and Twentieth Centuries*. New York: Berghahn, 2004.

Kalbeck, Max. *Johannes Brahms*. 4 vols. Tutzing, Germany: H. Schneider, 1976.

Kallberg, Jeffrey. *Chopin at the Boundaries: Sex, History, and Musical Genre*. Cambridge, MA: Harvard University Press, 1996.

Katz, Derek, and Michael Beckerman. "The Chamber Music of Smetana and Dvořák." In *Nineteenth-Century Chamber Music*, edited by Stephen Hefling, 315–47. New York: Routledge, 2004.

Kerman, Joseph. *The Beethoven Quartets*. New York: W. W. Norton, 1966.

King, Alexander Hyatt. "Music Circulating Libraries in Britain." *Musical Times* 119 (1978): 134–38.

Knapp, Raymond. "Brahms and the Anxiety of Allusion." *Journal of Musicological Research* 18, no. 1 (1998): 1–30.

———. *Brahms and the Challenge of the Symphony.* Stuyvesant, NY: Pendragon, 1997.

Knittel, K. M. "From Chaos to History: The Reception of Beethoven's Late Quartets" Ph.D. diss., Princeton University, 1992.

———. "'Late,' Last, and Least: On Being Beethoven's Quartet in F Major, Op. 135." *Music & Letters* 87, no. 1 (2006): 16–51.

———. "Wagner, Deafness, and the Reception of Beethoven's Late Style." *Journal of the American Musicological Society* 51, no. 1 (Spring 1998): 49–82.

Kocka, Jürgen. "The European Pattern and the German Case." In *Bourgeois Society in Nineteenth-Century Europe*, edited by Jürgen Kocka and Allan Mitchell, 3–39. Oxford: Berg, 1993.

Kocka, Jürgen, and Allan Mitchell, eds. *Bourgeois Society in Nineteenth-Century Europe.* Oxford: Berg, 1993.

Kopitz, Klaus. *Der Düsseldorfer Komponist Norbert Burgmüller: Ein Leben zwischen Beethoven, Spohr, Mendelssohn.* Kleve, Germany: B.o.s.s., 1998.

Kregor, Jonathan. *Liszt as Transcriber.* Cambridge: Cambridge University Press, 2010.

Krummacher, Friedhelm. "Gattung und Werk—zu Streichquartetten von Gade und Berwald." In *Gattung und Werk in der Musikgeschichte Norddeutschlands und Skandinaviens*, edited by Friedhelm Krummacher and Heinrich W. Schwab, 154–75. Kassel: Barenreiter, 1982.

———. *Geschichte des Streichquartetts.* Vol. 2, *Romantik und Moderne.* Laaber, Germany: Laaber-Verlag, 2005.

———. "Von 'allerlei Delikatessen': Überlegungen zum Streichquartett op. 67." In *Johannes Brahms: Quellen—Text—Rezeption—Interpretation: Internationaler Brahms-Kongress, Hamburg 1997*, edited by Friedhelm Krummacher and Michael Struck, 127–41. Munich: Henle, 1999.

Kube, Michael. "Brahms' Streichsextette und ihr gattungsgeschichtlicher Kontext." In *Die Kammermusik von Johannes Brahms: Tradition und Innovation*, edited by Gernot Gruber, 149–74. Regensburg: Laaber-Verlag, 2001.

Kühnen, Barbara. "Ist die kleine Soldat nicht ein ganzer Kerl? Die Geigerin Maria Soldat-Roeger (1863–1955)." In *Ich fahre in mein liebes Wien: Clara Schumann—Fakten, Bilder, Projektionen*, edited by Elena Ostleitner and Ursula Simek, 137–50. Vienna: Löcker, 1996.

Large, Brian. *Smetana.* New York: Praeger, 1970.

Lawford-Hinrichsen, Irene. *Music Publishing and Patronage, C. F. Peters: 1800 to the Holocaust.* Kenton: Edition Press, 2000.

Layton, Robert. "Berwald's Chamber Music." *Musical Times* 109, no. 1,502 (1968): 319–21.

Layton, Robert, and Daniel M. Grimley, "Franz (Adolf) Berwald." In *The New Grove Dictionary of Music and Musicians*, 2nd ed., edited by Stanley Sadie. Oxford: Oxford University Press, 2001.

Leguin, Elisabeth. *Boccherini's Body: An Essay in Carnal Musicology.* Berkeley: University of California Press, 2005.

———. "'One Says That One Weeps, but One Does Not Weep': *Sensible*, Grotesque, and Mechanical Embodiments in Boccherini's Chamber Music." *JAMS* 55, no. 2 (2002): 207–54.

Lenneberg, Hans, trans. *Breitkopf und Härtel in Paris: The Letters of Their Agent Heinrich Probst between 1833 and 1840*. La vie musicale en France au XIXe siècle. Stuyvesant, NY: Pendragon, 1990.
———. "Early Circulating Libraries and the Dissemination of Music." *Library Quarterly* 52, no. 2 (1982): 122–30.
———. "Music Publishing and Dissemination in the Early 19th Century: Some Vignettes." *Journal of Musicology* 2, no. 2 (1983): 174–83.
———. *On the Publishing and Dissemination of Music, 1500–1850*. Hillsdale, NY: Pendragon, 2003.
———. "Revising the History of the Miniature Score." *Notes* 45 (1988–89): 258–61.
Leppert, Richard. *Music and Image: Domesticity, Ideology, and Socio-cultural Formation in Eighteenth-Century England*. Cambridge: Cambridge University Press, 1988.
Levy, David. "Thomas Massa Alsager, Esq.: A Beethoven Advocate in London." *19th-Century Music* 9, no. 2 (Fall 1985): 119–27.
Levy, Janet. "Covert and Casual Values in Recent Writings about Music." *Journal of Musicology* 5, no. 1 (1987): 3–27.
———. "The Quatuor Concertant in Paris in the Latter Half of the Eighteenth Century." Ph.D. diss., Stanford University, 1971.
Littlewood, Julian. *The Variations of Johannes Brahms*. London: Plumbago Books, 2004.
Locke, Ralph P. "Nineteenth-Century Music: Quantity, Quality, Qualities." *Nineteenth-Century Music Review* 1, no. 1 (2004): 3–41.
———. "Paris: Centre of Intellectual Ferment." In *The Early Romantic Era: Between Revolutions, 1789 and 1848*, edited by Alexander L. Ringer, 32–83. Music and Society. Englewood Cliffs, NJ: Prentice Hall, 1991.
———. "Program Music." In *The Harvard Dictionary of Music*, 4th ed., edited by Don M. Randel, 680–83. Cambridge, MA: Belknap Press, 2003.
———. Review of *Les Sociétés de Musique de Chambre à Paris de la Restauration à 1870*. *JAMS* 43, no. 3 (1990): 504–12.
Loesser, Arthur. *Men, Women, and Pianos: A Social History*. New York: Simon and Schuster, 1954.
Loges, Natasha, and Katy Hamilton, eds. *Brahms in the Home and the Concert Hall: Between Public and Private Lives*. Cambridge: Cambridge University Press, 2014.
MacDonald, Malcolm. *Brahms*. London: Dent, 1990.
Marx, A. B. *Musical Form in the Age of Beethoven: Selected Writings on Theory and Method*. Edited and translated by Scott Burnham. Cambridge: Cambridge University Press, 1997.
McColl, Sandra. *Music Criticism in Vienna, 1896–1897: Critically Moving Forms*. New York: Clarendon, 1996.
McCorkle, Margit. *Johannes Brahms: Thematisch-bibliographisches Werkverzeichnis*. Munich: Henle, 1984.
McKay, Elizabeth Norman. *Franz Schubert: A Biography*. Oxford: Clarendon Press, 1996.
Mehring, Arndt. *Friedrich Kuhlau in the Mirror of His Flute Works*. Edited by Jane Rausch, translated by Laszlo and Doris Tikos. Warren, MI: Harmonie Park Press, 2000.
Messing, Scott. *Schubert in the European Imagination*. Rochester, NY: University of Rochester Press, 2006.
Monelle, Raymond. *The Musical Topic: Hunt, Military, and Pastoral*. Bloomington: Indiana University Press, 2006.
Moretti, Franco. *Atlas of the European Novel, 1800–1900*. New York: Verso, 1998.

———. *The Bourgeois: Between History and Literature.* New York: Verso, 2013.
———. *Graphs, Maps, Trees: Abstract Models for a Literary History.* New York: Verso, 2005.
———. *The Way of the World: The* Bildungsroman *in European Culture.* New York: Verso, 1987.
Moser, Andreas. *Joseph Joachim: A Biography (1831–1899).* Translated by Lilla Durham. London, 1901.
Musgrave, Michael. "Marie Soldat 1863–1955: An English Perspective." In *Beiträge zur Geschichte des Konzerts: Festschrift Siegfried Kross*, edited by Reinmar Emans and Matthias Wendt, 319–30. Leipzig: Gudrun Schröder, 1990.
Newcomb, Anthony. "Once More between Program Music and Absolute: Schumann's Second Symphony." *19th-Century Music* 7, no. 3 (1984): 233–50.
———. "Schumann and Late-Eighteenth-Century Narrative Strategies." *19th-Century Music* 11, no. 2 (1987): 164–74.
———. "Schumann and the Marketplace: From Butterflies to *Hausmusik.*" In *Nineteenth-Century Piano Music*, 2nd ed., edited by R. Larry Todd, 258–315. New York: Routledge, 2004.
Niaux, Viviane. *George Onslow: Gentleman Compositeur.* Clermont-Ferrand: Presses Universitaires Blaise-Pascal, 2003.
Nobach, Christiana. *Untersuchungen zu George Onslows Kammermusik.* Kassel: Bärenreiter, 1985.
Notley, Margaret A. "Brahms as Liberal: Genre, Style, and Politics in Late Nineteenth-Century Vienna." *19th-Century Music* 17, no. 2 (1993): 107–23.
———. "Discourse and Allusion: The Chamber Music of Brahms." In *Nineteenth-Century Chamber Music*, edited by Stephen Hefling, 242–86. New York: Schirmer, 1998.
———. *Lateness and Brahms: Music and Culture in the Twilight of Viennese Liberalism.* Oxford: Oxford University Press, 2007.
———. "Late Nineteenth-Century Chamber Music and the Cult of the Classical Adagio." *19th-Century Music* 23, no. 1 (1999): 33–61.
———. "Quintet No. 2 for Two Violins, Two Violas, and Cello in G Major, Op. 111." In *The Compleat Brahms*, edited by Leon Botstein, 137–39. New York: Norton, 1999.
———. "Volksconcerte in Vienna and Late Nineteenth-Century Ideology of the Symphony." *JAMS* 50, nos. 2–3 (1997): 421–53.
November, Nancy. "Theater Piece and Cabinetstück: Nineteenth-Century Visual Ideologies of the String Quartet." *Music in Art: International Journal for Music Iconography* 29, nos. 1–2 (2004): 134–50.
Ottlová, Marta. "The Controversy over the Place of Antonín Dvořák in the History of Czech National Music." *Czech Music* 1 (2008): 39–43.
Parakilas, James. *Piano Roles: Three Hundred Years of Life with the Piano.* New Haven, CT: Yale University Press, 1999.
———. "The Power of Domestication in the Lives of Musical Canons." *repercussions* 4, no. 1 (1995): 5–25.
Parker, Mara. *The String Quartet, 1750–1797: Four Types of Musical Conversation.* Burlington, VT: Ashgate, 2002.
Pascall, Robert. *Brahms beyond Mastery: His Sarabande and Gavotte, and Its Recompositions.* Royal Musical Association Monographs 21. Aldershot: Ashgate, 2013.
Pergament, Moses. "Franz Berwald: 1796–1868." *Monthly Musical Record*, October 1946, 176–82.

Pierreuse, Bernard. *Catalogue général de l'édition musicale en France: Livres, méthodes et partitions de musique sérieuse en vente*. Paris: Éditions Jobert, 1984.

Pilbeam, Pamela. *The Middle Classes in Europe, 1789–1914: France, Germany, Italy, and Russia*. London: Macmillan, 1990.

Pisani, Michael. *Imagining Native America in Music*. New Haven, CT: Yale University Press, 2006.

Plantinga, Leon. *Romantic Music: A History of Musical Style in Nineteenth-Century Europe*. New York: W. W. Norton, 1984.

———. *Schumann as Critic*. New Haven, CT: Yale University Press, 1967.

Porter, Cecelia Hopkins. "The New Public and the Reordering of the Musical Establishment: The Lower Rhine Music Festivals, 1818–67." *19th-Century Music* 3, no. 3 (1980): 211–24.

———. "The Reign of the *Dilettanti*: Düsseldorf from Mendelssohn to Schumann." *Musical Quarterly* 73, no. 4 (1989): 476–512.

Potter, Tully. "From Chamber to Concert Hall." In *The Cambridge Companion to the String Quartet*, edited by Robin Stowell, 41–59. Cambridge: Cambridge University Press, 2003.

Rasch, Rudolf, ed. *Music Publishing in Europe 1600–1900: Concepts and Issues, Bibliography*. Berlin: BWV, 2005.

Ratner, Leonard G. *The Beethoven String Quartets: Compositional Strategies and Rhetoric*. Stanford, CA: Stanford Bookstore, 1995.

———. *Classic Music: Expression, Form, and Style*. New York: Schirmer, 1980.

Reynolds, Christopher. *Motives for Allusion: Context and Content in Nineteenth-Century Music*. Cambridge, MA: Harvard University Press, 2003.

Riemann, Erika. *Schumann's Piano Cycles and the Novels of Jean Paul*. Rochester, NY: University of Rochester Press, 2004.

Rockstro, William Smyth. *A History of Music for the Use of Young Students*. 3rd ed. London: Robert Cocks, 1879.

Roesner, Linda Correll. "The Chamber Music." In *The Cambridge Companion to Schumann*, edited by Beate Perrey, 123–47. Cambridge: Cambridge University Press, 2007.

———. "Schumann's Parallel Forms." *19th-Century Music* 14, no. 3 (1991): 265–78.

———. "Studies in Schumann Manuscripts." Ph.D. diss., New York University, 1973.

Rosen, Charles. *The Romantic Generation*. Cambridge, MA: Harvard University Press, 1995.

Roussellier, Nicolas. "Liberalism." In *Europe 1789–1914: Encyclopedia of the Age of Industry and Empire*, edited by John Merriman and Jay Winter, 3:1341–50. Detroit: Charles Scribner's Sons, 2006.

Ruf, Wolfgang. "Die zwei Sextette von Brahms: Eine analytische Studie." In *Brahms-Analysen, Referate der kieler Tagung 1983*, edited by Friedhelm Krummacher and Wolfram Steinbeck, 121–33. Kassel: Bärenreiter, 1984.

———. "Kammermusik zwischen Exklusivität und Öffentlichkeit: Zum Sextett op. 18 von Johannes Brahms." In *Leitmotive: Kulturgeschichtliche Studien zur Traditionsbildung*, edited by Marianne Sammer et al., 427–34. Kallmunz, Germany: Lassleben, 1999.

Ryan, Thomas. *Recollections of an Old Musician*. New York: E. P. Dutton, 1899. https://archive.org/stream/recollectionsofo00ryan.

Samson, Jim, ed. *The Cambridge History of Nineteenth-Century Music*. Cambridge: Cambridge University Press, 2002.

Scherer, Frederic. "The Evolution of Free-Lance Music Composition, 1650–1900." *Journal of Cultural Economics* 25, no. 4 (2001): 307–19.

———. *Quarter Notes and Bank Notes: The Economics of Music Composition in the Eighteenth and Nineteenth Centuries*. Princeton, NJ: Princeton University Press, 2004.

Schick, Hartmut. *Studien zu Dvořáks Streichquartetten*. Laaber, Germany: Laaber, 1990.

———. "What's American about Dvořák's 'American' Quartet and Quintet?" *Czech Music* 18, no. 2 (1994): 72–83.

Schindler, Anton. *Beethoven as I Knew Him: A Biography* (1860). Edited by Donald MacArdle, translated by Constance S. Jolly. London: Faber & Faber, 1966.

Schmidt, Dörte. "'In vierfach geschlungener Bruderumarmung aufschweben': Beethoven und das Streichquartett als ästhetische, politische und soziale Idee in der zeitgenössischen Publizistik." In *Der "männliche" und der "weibliche" Beethoven, edited by* Cornelia Bartsch, Beatrix Borchard, and Rainer Cadenbach, 351–68. Bonn: Verlag Beethoven-Haus, 2003.

Schmidt-Beste, Thomas. "Mendelssohn's Chamber Music." In *The Cambridge Companion to Mendelssohn*, edited by Peter Mercer-Taylor, 130–48. Cambridge: Cambridge University Press, 2004.

Schoenberg, Arnold. "Brahms the Progressive." In *Style and Idea*, translated by Leo Black, 398–441. Berkeley: University of California Press, 1984.

Schramm, Willi. *Johannes Brahms in Detmold*. Leipzig: F. Kistner & C. F. W. Siegel, 1933. Reprint, Hagen, Germany: Lineppe, 1983.

Schubring, Adolf. "Five Early Works by Brahms." Translated by Walter Frisch. In *Brahms and His World*, 2nd ed., edited by Walter Frisch and Kevin Karnes, 165–215. Princeton, NJ: Princeton University Press, 2009.

———. "Schumanniana No. 4: The Present Musical Epoch and Robert Schumann's Position in Music History." Translated by John Michael Cooper. In *Schumann and His World*, edited by R. Larry Todd, 362–74. Princeton, NJ: Princeton University Press, 1994.

Schumann, Robert. "Erster Quartett-Morgen." *Neue Zeitschrift für Musik* 8, no. 46 (8 June 1838): 181–82. The remaining Quartett-Morgen reports appeared in *NZfM* 8, no. 49 (19 June 1838): 193–95; 9, no. 10 (3 August 1838): 42–43; 9, no. 13 (14 August 1838): 51–52; and 9, no. 20 (7 September 1838): 79–80.

———. *Music and Musicians: Essays and Criticisms by Robert Schumann*. Edited and translated by Fanny Raymond Ritter. London: William Reeves, 1877.

Scott, Derek. *Sounds of the Metropolis: The Nineteenth-Century Popular Music Revolution in London, New York, Paris, and Vienna*. Oxford: Oxford University Press, 2008.

Scruton, Roger. "Programme Music." In *The New Grove Dictionary of Music and Musicians*, 2nd ed., edited by Stanley Sadie. Oxford: Oxford University Press, 2001.

Senner, Wayne M., Robin Wallace, and William Meredith, eds. *The Critical Reception of Beethoven's Compositions by His German Contemporaries*. Lincoln: University of Nebraska Press, 1999.

Slowik, Kenneth. Notes to *George Onslow, String Quintets Opp. 38, 39, & 40*. L'Archibudelli and Smithsonian Chamber Players, Sony Classical SK 64308 (1995).

Smetana, Bedřich. *Letters and Reminiscences*. Edited by František Bartoš, translated by Daphne Rusbridge. Prague: Artia, 1955.

Solie, Ruth. "Biedermeier Domesticity and the Schubert Circle, a Rereading." In *Music in Other Words: Victorian Conversations*, 118–52. Berkeley: University of California Press, 2004.

———. "The Living Work: Organicism and Musical Analysis." *19th-Century Music* 4, no. 2 (1980): 147–56.
———. *Music in Other Words: Victorian Conversations*. Berkeley: University of California Press, 2004.
Solomon, Maynard. "Franz Schubert and the Peacocks of Benvenuto Cellini." *19th-Century Music* 12, no. 3 (1989): 193–206.
Sonnleithner, Leopold. "Musikalischen Skizzen aus Alt-Wien IV." *Monatschrift für Theater und Musik* 8 (1862): 177–80.
Sourek, Otakar. *The Chamber Music of Antonín Dvořák*. Translated by R. F. Samsour. Westport, CT: Greenwood, 1977.
Sperber, Jonathan. "Burger, Bürgertum, Bürgerlichkeit, Bürgerliche Gesellschaft: Studies of the German (Upper) Middle Class and Its Sociocultural World." *Journal of Modern History* 69, no. 2 (1997): 271–97.
Spohr, Louis. *Louis Spohr's Autobiography, Translated from the German*. London: Longman, Green, Longman, Roberts & Green, 1865. Reprint, New York: Da Capo Press, 1969.
Stapleton, Karl. "Veit, Václav." In *Oxford Music Online*, http//:www.oxfordmusiconline.com.
Stevenson, Karen. "The Music Criticism of Franz Brendel." Ph.D. diss., Northwestern University, 1994.
Strasser, Otto. "Joseph Hellmesberger (1828–1893): Eine philharmonische Vaterfigur." *Musikblatter der Wiener Philharmoniker* 48, no. 4 (1993): 117–24.
Straus, Joseph N. *Remaking the Past: Musical Modernism and the Influence of the Tonal Tradition*. Cambridge, MA: Harvard University Press, 1990.
Sullivan, Elizabeth Way. "Conversing in Public: Chamber Music in Vienna, 1890–1910." Ph.D. diss., University of Pittsburgh, 2001.
Sumner Lott, Marie. "At the Intersection of Public and Private Musical Life: Brahms's Op. 51 String Quartets." *Journal of the Royal Musical Association* 137, no. 2 (2012): 243–305.
———. "Domesticity in Brahms's String Sextets, Opp. 18 and 36." In *Brahms in the Home and the Concert Hall: Between Private and Public Performance*, edited by Natasha Loges and Katherine Hamilton, 43–94. Cambridge: Cambridge University Press, 2014.
———. "Dussek's Chamber Music: Blurring the Boundaries between Private and Public Musical Life." In *Jan Ladislav Dussek: A Bohemian Composer En Route through Europe*, edited by Roberto Illiano and Rohan H. Stewart-MacDonald, 281–328. Bologna: Ut Orpheus, 2012.
———. "Iron Hand with a Velvet Glove? String Quartet Performance in the Late-Nineteenth and Early-Twentieth Centuries." *Journal of Musicological Research* 25, nos. 3–4 (2006): 263–89.
———. "Negotiation Tactics in Louise Farrenc's Piano Quintets, Opp. 30 and 31 (1839–40)." *Ad Parnassum: A Journal of 18th- and 19th-Century Instrumental Music* 8, no. 15 (2010): 7–66.
Swafford, Jan. *Johannes Brahms, a Biography*. New York: Random House, 1997.
Thoor, Alf. "The Private Life of Mr. Franz Berwald." *Artes* 3 (1996): 133–45.
Thrane, Carl. *Friedrich Kuhlau*. Leipzig: Breitkopf und Härtel, 1886. Reprint, Amsterdam: Frits Knuf, 1979.
Thym, Jürgen. "Schumann in Brendel's *Neue Zeitschrift für Musik* from 1845 to 1856." In *Mendelssohn and Schumann: Essays on Their Music and Its Context*, edited by Jon W. Finson and R. Larry Todd, 21–36. Durham, NC: Duke University Press, 1984.

Tibbetts, John, ed. *Dvořák in America: 1892–95*. Portland, OR: Amadeus, 1993.
Todd, R. Larry. "The Chamber Music of Mendelssohn." In *Nineteenth-Century Chamber Music*, edited by Stephen E. Hefling, 170–207. New York: Schirmer, 1998.
Tusa, Michael. "Beethoven's 'C-Minor Mood': Some Thoughts on the Structural Implications of Key Choice." In *Beethoven Forum 2*, edited by Christopher Reynolds, Lewis Lockwood, and James Webster, 1–27. Lincoln: University of Nebraska Press, 1993.
Walker, Alan. *Franz Liszt*. Vol. 2, *The Weimar Years*. Ithaca, NY: Cornell University Press, 1987.
Wallace, Robin. "Background and Expression in the First Movement of Beethoven's Op. 132." *Journal of Musicology* 7, no. 1 (1989): 3–20.
Waltz, Sarah J. Clemmens. "The Highland Muse in Romantic German Music." Ph.D. diss., Yale University, 2007.
Weber, William. *The Great Transformation of Musical Taste: Concert Programming from Haydn to Brahms*. Cambridge: Cambridge University Press, 2008.
———. "The Muddle of the Middle Classes." *19th-Century Music* 3, no. 2 (1979): 175–85.
———. *Music and the Middle Classes: The Social Structure of Concert Life in London, Paris, and Vienna between 1830 and 1848*. 2nd ed. Burlington, VT: Ashgate, 2002.
———, ed. *The Musician as Entrepreneur, 1700–1914: Managers, Charlatans, and Idealists*. Bloomington: Indiana University Press, 2004.
Webster, James. "Schubert's Sonata Forms and Brahms's First Maturity." *19th-Century Music* 2, no. 1 (1978): 18–35; and 3, no. 1 (1979): 52–71.
Wheelock, Gretchen A. "Engaging Strategies in Haydn's Op. 33 String Quartets." *Eighteenth-Century Studies* 25, no. 1 (1991): 1–30.
———. *Haydn's Ingenious Jesting with Art: Contexts of Musical Wit and Humor*. New York: Schirmer, 1992.
Widmaier, Tobias. *Der deutsche Musikalienleihhandel. Funktion, Bedeutung und Topographie einer Form gewerblicher Musikaliendistribution vom späten 18. bis zum frühen 20. Jahrhundert*. Saarbrücken, Germany: Pfau, 1998.
Widmaier, Tobias, and Andreas Ballstaedt. *Salonmusik: Zur Geschichte und Funktion einer bürgerlichen Musikpraxis*. Stuttgart: Steiner, 1989.
Wienker-Piepho, Sabine. "Herder and the Development of His Volkslied Concept during His Time in Riga." In *Singing the Nations: Herder's Legacy*, edited by Dace Bula and Sigrid Rieuwerts, 30–39. Trier: Wissenschaftlicher Verlag Trier, 2008.
Wiese, Walter. *Tschechische Kammermusik: Smetana—Dvořák—Janáček*. Winterthur, Switzerland: Amadeus, 2004.
Will, Richard. *The Characteristic Symphony in the Age of Haydn and Beethoven*. Cambridge: Cambridge University Press, 2002.
Wolff, Janet. "The Culture of Separate Spheres: The Role of Culture in Nineteenth-Century Public and Private Life." In *The Culture of Capital: Art, Power, and the Nineteenth-Century Middle Class*, edited by Janet Wolff and John Seed, 117–34. New York: St. Martin's, 1988.
Wolff, Janet, and John Seed, eds. *The Culture of Capital: Art, Power, and the Nineteenth-Century Middle Class*. New York: St. Martin's, 1988.
Wurst, Karin. *Fabricating Pleasure: Fashion, Entertainment, and Cultural Consumption in Germany, 1780–1830*. Detroit: Wayne State University Press, 2005.
Zeydel, Edwin H. *Goethe the Lyricist*. University of North Carolina Studies in the Germanic Languages and Literatures 16. Chapel Hill: University of North Carolina Press, 1955.

INDEX

MARIE SUMNER LOTT is an assistant professor of music history at Georgia State University and winner of a 2013 ASCAP-Deems Taylor award.

The University of Illinois Press
is a founding member of the
Association of American University Presses.

University of Illinois Press
1325 South Oak Street
Champaign, IL 61820-6903
www.press.uillinois.edu